REPUBLIC *of* WORDS

Republic of Words

The Atlantic Monthly and Its Writers *1857–1925*

SUSAN GOODMAN

University Press of New England

Hanover & London

UNIVERSITY PRESS OF NEW ENGLAND
www.upne.com

Manufactured in the United States of America
Designed by Eric M. Brooks
Typeset in Miller Text by Passumpsic Publishing

University Press of New England is a member of the Green Press Initiative. The paper used in this book meets their minimum requirement for recycled paper.

Library of Congress Cataloging-in-Publication Data
Goodman, Susan, 1951–
Republic of words: The Atlantic monthly and its writers, 1857-1925 / Susan Goodman.
p. cm.
Includes bibliographical references and index.
ISBN 978-1-58465-985-3 (cloth : alk. paper)—
ISBN 978-1-61168-196-3 (e-book)
1. Atlantic monthly (Boston, Mass.: 1857) I. Title.
PN4900.A7G77 2011
051—dc23 2011022396

5 4 3 2 1

To my father,

RALPH RUDNICK

CONTENTS

PREFACE

The Atlantic is an ocean; the *Atlantic* a *notion*.

OLIVER WENDELL HOLMES

THE STORY OF THE *Atlantic Monthly* reflects the story of a nation and its aspirations. With roots firmly grounded in the antislavery movement, its founders made a pledge to the American people to work for the nation's greater good, or what they endorsed as "the American idea," which amounted to a national conscience. Their goal was great, but so were the people dedicated to its achievement. In bringing together the likes of Ralph Waldo Emerson, Harriet Beecher Stowe, and Nathaniel Hawthorne, the *Atlantic* played its appointed role in its appointed city. Perhaps only Boston could have given rise to a magazine whose cornerstones rested on the principles of public service, intellectual honesty, and democracy.

Founded in 1857, as the United States staggered toward civil war, the *Atlantic* served the cause of freedom through literature. Its readers and contributors saw it as the voice of the nation and, through the years of war, the voice of the Union. Abraham Lincoln knew that the magazine could persuade the public "to stand firm."[1] Worried about Great Britain's ties to the Confederacy, he encouraged Harriet Beecher Stowe to galvanize members of England's antislavery community. The *Atlantic* published her appeal, addressed to the women of Great Britain and Ireland, in the same month that Lincoln issued the Emancipation Proclamation (January 1863). When the Confederacy made sovereignty a condition of peace later that year,

Lincoln turned again to the *Atlantic*. Not only did he want Jefferson Davis's exact words published—"We are not fighting for slavery; we are fighting for independence"—he wanted to read the proof. Lincoln believed that this statement in this magazine could save the Union "half a dozen battles."[2]

Wielding influence far beyond its immediate readership, the *Atlantic Monthly* successfully cast itself as the conscience of the American public. Contributors spoke to the nation's status, character, and warring ambitions. They agreed to disagree on a vast range of issues, from the complexities of economics and religion to the hazards of war and peace. In the 1880s, for example, the *Atlantic Monthly* ran pieces on America's minorities, Western water rights, anti-Semitism, and the mill-girls of Lowell, Massachusetts. During World War I, it published reports from Belgium and the front. Along with essays for and against American intervention, it drew contributors from France, England, and the United States, including Woodrow Wilson, Maurice Barrès, John Dewey, and H. G. Wells. Wars, social reforms, artistic movements, and national politics mark the *Atlantic*'s epic journey.

Fully aware of the magazine's status, American writers believed it difficult to make a reputation except by publishing there. Mark Twain insisted that an *Atlantic* review of *Innocents Abroad* made his career. Henry James bullied the magazine to take his first novel, *Watch and Ward*. And Edith Wharton, fresh from the success of *The Valley of Decision* (1902), wondered why she had not yet been asked for a story. Even Twain seems a model of decorum in comparison to a rebuffed Kentucky poet who challenged the editor in chief to a backwoods duel, or a war to the knife. A record of *Atlantic Monthly* authors reads like a *Who's Who* in American literature. Its initial stable of contributors, among them Ralph Waldo Emerson and Henry Wadsworth Longfellow, expanded over the next half century to include Frederick Douglass, Louisa May Alcott, Sarah Orne Jewett, Kate Chopin, Henry Adams, Frank Norris, Jack London, Owen Wister, and Robert Frost.

The long and exceptional history of the *Atlantic*'s fortunes has been addressed by Mark de Wolfe Howe and by Ellery Sedgwick, whose invaluable study—subtitled *Yankee Humanism at High Tide and Ebb*—focuses on its editors, its internal workings, and its relation to a cluster of magazines such as *Scribner's* and *Harper's*, with which the *Atlantic* competed. My approach to the magazine has a different emphasis. Although alerting readers to the "Promethean" role this monthly messenger of culture and its disparate editors played, my story—or, rather, collection of stories—offers another perspective. I approach the chronicle of the magazine through the people who wrote for it.

From the beginnings, the *Atlantic*'s authority rested on its contributors: the poets, novelists, essayists, political figures, scientists, geologists, explorers, social scientists, and their fellow writers in multiple fields, new or old. To think about the magazine's contributors as men and women with lives beyond the *Atlantic Monthly* is to come to the magazine in fresh ways. Most of this book's thirty short chapters feature an episode or phase in a writer's lifetime. Each is connected to the magazine but adds a personal context. If history itself is innately piecemeal, this book is consciously so. Yet each chapter speaks in its way about the magazine's self-made responsibilities and the writer's sense of an underlying national consciousness.

In the *Atlantic*'s pages Clarence King brings the American West to eastern readers in stories about the Sierra peaks and the scams of gold-mining thieves; the Harvard botanist Asa Gray defends and the Swiss geologist Louis Agassiz rebuts Charles Darwin's theories of evolution; John Muir makes his argument for preserving the nation's virgin lands; W. E. B. Du Bois challenges Booker T. Washington for leadership of the African American community; Jane Addams analyzes the pros and cons of charity; and Jacob Riis, in company with President Theodore Roosevelt, walks the slums of New York and lobbies for their transformation.

In its mix of lives and literature, *Republic of Words* focuses on men and women who appear to embody forces greater than themselves. Thomas Wentworth Higginson, leader of the first regiment of freed black soldiers, is a case in point, as is Percival Lowell, the scientist who traveled imaginatively between the Far East and Martian civilization. If asked how a magazine that at its peak in the nineteenth century counted only fifty thousand subscribers made such a profound difference in the way Americans thought, I would say this: the distinguishing character of the *Atlantic Monthly* lay in the people who wrote for it, America's foremost writers, who saw themselves as cultural trailblazers and whose voices could be heard well into the twentieth century. I like to think that the overlapping voices of the *Atlantic*, individually and collectively, add to the cultural history of the United States from the Civil War's prologue to World War I's aftermath.

While the *Atlantic* still flourishes, *Republic of Words* stops at what might seem an arbitrary point, the year 1925. In that year—which saw the Harlem Renaissance at its height and the first issue of the *New Yorker*—the *Atlantic Monthly* struggled to respond to the demands of post–World War I readers. "Culture," with a capital "C," had always been the *Atlantic Monthly*'s trademark, though writers schooled by H. L. Mencken and Ezra Pound began to mock the magazine's brand of culture as "Kulchur" and saw the magazine as stuffy or commercial. If its tables of contents previously outlined a literary history of the United States, they now contained glaring omissions. These omissions also belong to my story, which takes into account a world of publishing circumstances, literary friendships and influences, political alliances, and social upheavals. Needless to say, the *Atlantic Monthly* survived its crises to become the magazine contemporary readers know simply as the *Atlantic*, an abbreviation frequently used by its founders. For reasons of tradition and convenience, this book follows their example.

I

I Beginnings

If there is one thing in American literature that is almost like a patent of nobility, it is being one of the original "*Atlantic* group."

HELEN J. WINSLOW, *Literary Boston of To-Day*, 1902

ON A SPRING DAY in 1857, a group of men met for dinner at Boston's elegant Parker House hotel. They were the founders of the *Atlantic Monthly*, and what they achieved that day would shape not only the nation's ways of reading and thinking but also, at times, its course of history. Their host, the publisher Moses Phillips, believed the collective genius in the room would have been hard to match. "Each one," he proudly told his niece, "is known alike on both sides of the Atlantic, and is read beyond the limits of the English language."[1]

Ralph Waldo Emerson, outspoken opponent of slavery and father of American Transcendentalism, took the seat of honor to Phillips's right. Henry Wadsworth Longfellow, unofficial poet laureate of the United States, sat opposite Emerson. Oliver Wendell Holmes, a leading scientist and the wittiest man in Boston, faced the celebrated historian of the Dutch Republic, John Lothrop Motley, whose handsome looks reminded Lady Byron of her straying husband. James Russell Lowell, patrician author of fiery antislavery verse, looked directly at Emerson's future biographer, James Elliott Cabot, while Francis Underwood, an assistant editor at Phillips, Sampson and Company, took his place at the end of the table. When the company rose from dinner five hours later, the *Atlantic Monthly* had become a reality. It was the proudest day of Moses Phillips's life, and though no bells rang from Boston's churches, those who looked back on this day recognized it as a new chapter in American culture.

When in the nineteenth century so many other magazines failed, it seems astonishing that the *Atlantic* survived beyond a few issues. The competition with Philadelphia's *Graham's*, *Godey's*, and *Sartain's*, and New York's *Putnam's*, *Harper's New Monthly*, and *Knickerbocker* was fierce. America sprouted so many magazines that one commentator compared them to mushrooms doomed by a killing frost "in the form of debts due and bills unpaid."[2] Emerson and the feminist Margaret Fuller had struggled through four shaky years with the *Dial*, a magazine devoted to literature, philosophy, and religion. Lowell grimly closed shop after three issues of his antislavery *Pioneer*. Apart from the general pitfalls of starting a magazine, and the warnings of businessmen that no time was the right time, the *Atlantic* seemed doomed at the outset. The Panic of 1857 began in August, a month after the Parker House dinner, when the New York branch of the Ohio Life Insurance and Trust Company failed, triggering a worldwide depression. Foreign investors questioned the strength of American banks, and markets for manufactured goods disappeared. Boston's waterfront, once the raucous hub of international commerce, fell eerily quiet.

Yet if the time was wrong, the place was right. To many, a Boston-based literary magazine seemed overdue. Readers associated the new magazine with the attributes of its mother city, the imaginative center of the nation's literary life. Home to beans, bluestockings, and Harvard University in nearby Cambridge, the city had the reputation of a latter-day Athens. In 1630, John Winthrop, governor of the Massachusetts Bay Colony, whose image appeared on the title page of the *Atlantic*'s first issue, had proclaimed: "We shall be as a city upon a hill. The eyes of all people are upon us."[3] Oliver Wendell Holmes swore that "a man can see further . . . from the top of the Boston State House, and see more that is worth seeing, than from all the pyramids and turrets and steeples in all the places in the world."[4] Boston owed much of its cultural authority to its role in American history. Today visitors to the Massachusetts capital follow the Freedom Trail past Paul Revere's house and the Granary Burying Ground, where Revere rests not far from victims of the Boston Massacre and three signers of the Constitution. In the winter of 1773, on nearby Washington Street, more than five thousand people had gathered at the Old South Meeting House to protest the British tax on tea. Opposite the Meeting House, the Old Corner Bookstore sheltered the Puritan heretic Anne Hutchinson before her banishment. It was here, at a time when America faced the prospect of dissolution, that the *Atlantic* made its headquarters.

Long a center of the antislavery movement, Boston claimed leading abolitionists such as William Lloyd Garrison, editor of the *Liberator*, and Charles Sumner, founder of the Free Soil Party. Shortly before the founding of the *Atlantic*, Sumner nearly died on the floor of the U.S. Senate when Preston Brooks, a South Carolina congressman, beat him with a cane. Sumner survived because his assailant's cane fortuitously broke. After the incident, Brooks received dozens of new canes from approving constituents willing to sacrifice the republic for slavery or the principle of states' rights. The contest over slavery came to a head in 1857, when the U.S. Supreme Court issued its ruling in the *Dred Scott* case, which not only denied slaves the right to sue but also overturned the Missouri Compromise outlawing slavery north of the Mason-Dixon Line. "So now the lists are open," James Russell Lowell wrote a friend, "and we shall soon find where the tougher lance-shafts are grown, North or South."[5]

Those invited to the Parker House dinner had been chosen partly for their antislavery sympathies. When Francis Underwood, a staunch abolitionist and former state senator, determined to found the magazine, he approached people thought to be "friends of freedom." Lowell, for example, vigorously opposed the expansion of slavery into the territories. Emerson vowed never to uphold the Fugitive Slave Act, which returned escaped slaves to their owners: "If you put a chain around the neck of a slave," he warned, "the other end fastens itself around your own."[6] Harriet Beecher Stowe had made more than a million readers aware of slavery's human toll and found herself lionized in the North and demonized in the South. The best-selling novel of its day, *Uncle Tom's Cabin* proved that literature and politics could go profitably hand in hand. Afraid of alienating Southern readers, however, the publisher, Moses Phillips, had rejected the novel, making the worst mistake of his career. He did not intend to make a second. Phillips reckoned that his firm's large list of readers and experience with distribution would give him an edge over competitors. With the support of Stowe—the most famous woman in America—and authors like Emerson, the magazine promised to transform his firm, known until then as a jobbing house for cheap editions, into a premier publishing house.

The "united states" that called themselves a nation in the mid-nineteenth century evolved in the consciousness of writers, most of them with ties to the *Atlantic*. In Lowell's popular *Biglow Papers*, for instance, characters debate the great issues of the day: what might be called American ideas in American speech. Later Lowell claimed to be the first poet to have expressed the American idea, by which he meant principles of democracy in a nation without slavery.[7] His *Biglow Papers*, which helped shape readers' understanding of their vast, raw country and its people, also anticipated a trend toward a new literary realism, which became the defining hallmark of the *Atlantic*.

As the magazine's first editor, Lowell assumed that art and politics served complementary ends. He assured readers that though he would not hesitate to draw on "foreign sources," he would feature American writers. Someone chary of the magazine's assertions might have seen its muscle-flexing title as a challenge to those across the Atlantic, especially the British, whose critics continued to set standards for American writers. The *Atlantic*'s first issue, with its dun-colored covers and black lettering, looked tasteful if unimposing. It made, however, a Promethean announcement:

> In politics, *The Atlantic Monthly* will be the organ of no party or clique, but will honestly endeavor to be the exponent of what its conductors believe to be the American idea. It will deal frankly with persons and with parties, endeavoring always to keep in view that moral element which transcends all persons and parties, and which alone makes the basis of a true and lasting prosperity. It will not rank itself with any sect of anties [naysayers]: but with that body of men which is in favor of Freedom, National Progress, and Honor, whether public or private.

Below this statement, readers found a list "of persons interested in the enterprise"; along with the founders and Stowe, they included Herman Melville, Nathaniel Hawthorne, John Greenleaf Whittier, William H. Prescott, William C. Bryant, and Lydia Maria Child, joined by England's Wilkie Collins and Elizabeth Gaskell. Heralding "a new era in the history of civilization," the editors pledged to be "fearless and outspoken."[8]

Twenty years before, Emerson had attended a ceremony for the new monument, commemorating the Battle of Lexington and Concord, with the dramatic lines of "Concord Hymn" (1837): "Here once the embattled farmers stood, / And fired the shot heard round the world."[9] Those associated with the *Atlantic* might have substituted "writer-warriors" for "farmers," but Emerson captures their ambitions. If not "unacknowledged legislators," they provided a moral compass for a still raw country. In keeping with the magazine's mission to spread knowledge, Lowell sent copies to postmasters, clergy, and teachers who could subscribe at two-thirds the subscription price, and, recognizing the magazine's need for customers, he made a more general promotion, promising wit and humor in every issue.

The official history of the *Atlantic* is full of contradictions. While the founders saw themselves issuing a cultural declaration of independence from the "muses of Europe," they also served—and borrowed from—a broader international community.[10] Henry Adams recalled how the literary world of his youth "agreed that truth survived in Germany alone, and Carlyle, Matthew Arnold, Renan, Emerson, with scores of popular followers, taught the German faith." Adams wanted nothing more than to escape the intellectual fetters of Boston. "The first door of escape that seemed to offer a hope led to Germany," he wrote, "and James Russell Lowell opened it."[11] Lowell and life taught Adams that no one remains untouched by time. The same might be said of the *Atlantic*, which predictably grew from and responded to national crises. After touting the magazine's nationalism, Lowell opened the inaugural issue with a British writer's essay on the playwright and founder of the comic magazine *Punch*, Douglas Jerrold.

The *Atlantic*'s assertion of an "American idea" came at a time when the United States teetered on the verge of civil war. To a Southerner like Edgar Allan Poe, who had urged a boycott of Lowell's antislavery writings, its Republican roots were clear: "no Southerner who does not wish to be insulted, and . . . revolted by a bigotry the most obstinately blind and deaf, should ever touch a volume by this author."[12] For its announced role in the war of public opinion, many Southerners felt the same about the *Atlantic*.

2

Forging Traditions

JAMES RUSSELL LOWELL

> Lowell spoke for the better nature . . . of his people . . . his influence more than that of any other save Lincoln . . . redeemed America for freedom.
>
> ELIHU ROOT, commemoration of Lowell's centenary, 1919

EXCEPTING HIS SPEECH, many Americans might have taken James Russell Lowell for a stereotypical Englishman. A handsome, "compact little man" at five foot five he had an *haute-en-bas* manner. Annie Fields—whose husband James never got Lowell's full respect as the *Atlantic*'s second editor—thought him "deeply pervaded with fine discontents."[1] William Dean Howells, a young contributor from the Midwest, remembered how gauche he felt meeting Lowell: "At the first encounter with people, he always was apt to have a certain frosty shyness, a smiling cold, as from the long, high-sunned winters of his Puritan race. . . . No one could be sweeter, tenderer, warmer than he; but you must be his captive before he could do that."[2] People read Lowell's confidence in his crisp enunciation and "elect diction." To the starstruck Howells, he seemed to glitter when he spoke. And no wonder: as editor of the *Atlantic*, Lowell became the country's first man of letters, holding the future of Howells and other supplicants in his hands.

The British novelist John Galsworthy once said that though Lowell could not match Emerson as a thinker, Thoreau as a philosopher, or Holmes as a wit, he "ran the gamut of those qualities . . . and as critic and analyst of literature surpassed them all."[3] Lowell's great gifts were offset by a temperament that led to flights of romantic reverie and, at other times, toward self-destruction. His behavior gave rise to the nonce word "suavagery," a combination of the suave and the savage, which seemed, to those who knew his family, a tragic legacy.[4] Lowell ascribed his "dark" moods to "the drop of black blood" he inherited from his mother.[5] His bouts of depression dated from early manhood and coincided with inexplicable periods of blindness. One biographer attributed Lowell's testiness and volubility to excessive drinking, for which he purportedly received treatment in a Staten Island sanatorium.[6]

Whatever the biological basis of Lowell's swings in mood, they were not improved by his brother's ruinous mismanagement of the family's assets. Nineteenth-century Americans viewed bankruptcy as a criminal, if not moral offense. The shame of her son's insolvency nearly killed Lowell's mother, whose eccentricities worsened at this time, resulting in her institutionalization. Crossed in love and thinking his future stolen, Lowell remembered holding a gun to his head and fingering the trigger. He and his contemporaries were well versed in the symptoms of nervous prostration. The pioneering neurologist George M. Beard argued that the pace and stress of American life had a deleterious effect on the nation's health. Noting the incidence of breakdown among her peers, Henry Adams's wife, Clover, joked that "the insane asylum seems to be the goal of every good and conscientious Bostonian."[7]

Lowell had found his calling when he met the poet and antislavery activist Maria White, whom he married in 1844. Each contributed to the *Anti-Slavery Standard*, for which he served as corresponding editor. Needing more income and disinclined to use his training as a lawyer, Lowell tried his hand at lecturing. He delivered his first lecture extemporaneously to three thousand temperancers. Soon he joined the ranks of antislavery speakers who proselytized, as his biographer said, like Peter the Hermit during the First Crusade.[8] The same year that Lowell published *The Biglow Papers* (1848), he also published his satiric *Fable for Critics*. In 1855 he delivered a series of twelve lectures on British literature at the Lowell Institute. Endowed by one relative (John Lowell Jr.) and overseen by another (John Amory Lowell), the Institute sought to provide free education to the public. The response to his lectures paved the way for him the next year to succeed Henry Wadsworth Longfellow as Harvard's Smith Professor of Modern Languages.[9] It must have seemed unbearably ironic to Lowell that his career soared at a time when his personal life fell apart. In February 1850, his infant daughter Rose died, with his mother following in March. Two years later, his baby son, Walter, died in Rome. When the family returned to Cambridge, Maria Lowell's health deteriorated. After her death in October 1853, he wrote about the change her passing made at Elmwood, the family's "old-fashioned mansion" near Harvard Square:[10]

> For it died that autumn morning
> When she, its soul, was borne
> To lie all dark on the hillside
> That looks over woodland and corn.[11]

With the security of his family at stake, Lowell had lobbied vigorously for the editorship of the *Atlantic*, and its annual salary of twenty-five hundred dollars. Only a handful of editors earned half that much.[12] Lowell would have preferred solely to write, as he told a friend, but the magazine had its compensations: it freed him from debt and compelled him to walk to the printing office alongside the Charles River.[13] Friends agreed that Lowell had little aptitude for the details of putting out a magazine, which fell on his assistant, Francis Underwood. Notoriously absentminded, Lowell was known to stuff his hat with manuscripts as if it were a satchel. It took one stiff wind rising from the Charles to drown a writer's hope. Notwithstanding occasional lost manuscripts, he won contributors' hearts by offering fifty dollars for a poem and six dollars a page for prose—ten to those "whose names were worth the other four dollars."[14] He himself took six. Although subsequent critics denigrated Lowell as a "schoolroom poet"—for the ease with which children could memorize his rhyming verses—he won Emerson's sincerest praise. After reading "The Washers of the Shroud" in the *Atlantic*, Emerson marveled: "What a certificate of good elements in the soil, climate, and institutions is Lowell, whose admirable verses I have just read!"[15]

Lowell envisioned his editorship of the *Atlantic* as an extension of his unforgettable if eccentric teaching. The critic Barrett Wendell described him leaning back in a chair, his hands thrust in the pockets of his shabby sack-coat, talking "away across country until he felt like stopping." Sometimes he paced the room in his "heavy laced boots," looking "at nothing in particular," before beginning: "Here before us . . . [is] a great poem—a lasting expression of what human life had meant to a human being, dead and gone these five centuries. . . . Let us read, as sympathetically as we make ourselves read, the words of one who was as much a man as we; only vastly greater in his knowledge of wisdom and of beauty."[16]

Lowell's practice of sympathetic reading became the hallmark of *Atlantic* reviews. A review of George Eliot's *Scenes of Clerical Life* began with one of the magazine's central premises: that fiction represents and influences its age.[17] As Horace Scudder, a future editor of the *Atlantic*, would write, "Though he held the editorship but a little more than two years he stamped the magazine with the impress of his high ideals in literature and criticism . . . and he was most generous in his critical aid to contributors."[18] Wanting to unite "all available talent of all shades of opinion," Lowell aimed to make the magazine "free without being fanatical." At the same time, he believed that a magazine should "have opinions . . . and not be afraid to speak them," though names of authors were withheld until July 1862, and then listed only in the contents. Half of the pleasure of reading was guessing who wrote what—if, that is, Moses Phillips hadn't already leaked the author's name to the press.

From the beginning, Lowell provided a template for the *Atlantic* by reserving about half of its pages for essays. In the first issue, for example, he published Oliver Wendell Holmes's funny, urbane treatment of serious issues in "The Autocrat of the Breakfast-Table," along with Rose Terry Cooke's local-color story "Sally Parson's Duty," set in rural Massachusetts. Behind his choices, his rejections and acceptances, his passion for the magazine, Lowell sought to improve the quality of American culture, which, for all its differences, he saw emanating from European traditions. The *Atlantic* acknowledged the cross-cultural exchange with a section called "Literary Notices" and articles on the Manchester Exhibition of paintings and Florentine mosaics.

Heavy on poetry, the first issue of the *Atlantic* offered verses from Lowell, John Greenleaf Whittier, Henry Wadsworth Longfellow, and Ralph Waldo Emerson, whose sixteen-line poem "Brahma" almost single-handedly guaranteed the success of the magazine. "What does it mean?" people asked:

> If the red slayer think he slays,
> Or if the slain think he is slain,
> They know not well the subtle ways
> I keep, and pass, and turn again.[19]

The novelist J. R. Trowbridge recalled how he suddenly found himself wrenched off the street and asked to explain the poem by an assailant who produced a much-crumpled paper from the "recesses of a waistcoat pocket."[20] Oliver Wendell Holmes thought he knew what the poem was about: he described "Brahma" as "the nearest approach to a Torricellian vacuum of intelligibility that language can pump out of itself."[21] However cryptic, "Brahma" provoked a craze of parodies, and orders for the second number doubled those of the first. On the back cover of the second issue (December 1857), the publishers announced that "a magazine of the first class—earnest, able, scholarly, and yet attentive to popular wants—has become a necessity to the American public."

As editor, Lowell lived up to his advice for would-be poets to "put all your beauty in your rhymes / Your morals in your living."[22] If not morals, he applied ethical principles to his editorship. The *Atlantic* reflected his wish to educate the populace about historical traditions that had bearing on the present. Defining his role in terms of civic uplift, he aimed to produce critical, independent thinkers who would take their rightful place on the world stage. Lowell did not shy away from controversy. He advocated education for women, poked fun at religious orthodoxy, and stood firm against slavery—all the while trying to make the magazine "interesting to as many classes of people" as possible.[23]

Never doubting the magazine's power to direct public thought, Lowell considered it every citizen's duty to participate in the process of democracy, even if that meant criticizing national traits and policies. Apart from an essay analyzing the Indian Mutiny, the November issue contained Parke Godwin's assessment of American materialism. "One cries," Godwin wrote, "that we Americans are an unconscionably greedy people, ever hastening to get rich, not satisfied with our gains, and, in the frantic eagerness of accumulation, disregarding alike justice, truth, probity, and moderation."[24] Though Godwin shared Lowell's sense of righteous indignation, the men parted ways over Lowell's editorial practice of making additions and deletions to an author's work without consultation. Outraged that Lowell added a six-page appendage to his essay on the Buchanan administration (April 1858), Godwin severed his ties with the magazine. "If the Deity should consult New England about making a new world," he wrote Lowell, "they would advise that it should be made the size of Massachusetts, have no city but Boston and insist in making an occasional donation to a charitable institution and uttering shallow antislavery sentiments."[25] After Godwin stopped contributing, Lowell wrote most of the magazine's antislavery essays himself. His argument echoed that of Frederick Douglass, who saw slavery corrupting whites as well as blacks. Returning to the rhetoric of his days working for the *Anti-Slavery Standard*, Lowell supported Lincoln's candidacy in 1860, claiming that the election of a Democrat would prove "that there is no higher law than human interest and cupidity."[26] In January 1861, tired of the government's policy of appeasement, Lowell wrote that "a dissolution of the Union would be a terrible thing, but not so terrible as an acquiescence in the theory that Property is the only interest that binds men together in society, and that its protection is the highest object of human government."[27]

Despite its auspicious start, the *Atlantic* might have folded in 1859 after the death of its founder and publisher, Moses Phillips. James T. Fields arrived home from Europe to learn that his partner George Ticknor had offered ten thousand dollars for the magazine on a whim and had it promptly accepted. Lowell, with no illusions about his tenure, understood that the new owners could save his salary by installing Fields as editor. He duly offered his resignation in May 1861.

Ticknor and Fields felt it necessary to assure foreign contributors that, as they took control of the *Atlantic Monthly*, everything would be done "to increase the magazine's interests, to enlarge its circle of attraction, and to raise its standard of ability in all departments." They planned no changes "in the general character of the magazine" and would preserve relations "with authors on both sides of the Atlantic." Apart from underscoring the international base of the magazine, the owners promised that the *Atlantic* would "never be a sectional journal" or hampered by censorship.[28] That promise would be broken with the commencement of the Civil War.

Five months before Lowell resigned, South Carolina seceded from the Union, and Mississippi, Florida, Alabama, Georgia, Louisiana, and Texas soon followed. In February, when Jefferson Davis swore to serve the Confederacy, Lowell told *Atlantic* readers that "we shall need something like a Fugitive Slave Act for runaway republics."[29] At 4:30 a.m. on 12 April 1861, fifty Confederate cannons fired on Fort Sumter. The day the country dreaded had arrived. The war, which further radicalized Unionists like

Lowell, gave a new urgency to the founders' original questions as to what was the United States, and who were its peoples? The *Atlantic*'s relationship with Great Britain, which had commercial interests in a Southern victory, also became complicated. Although the magazine continued to draw on British writers, it grew impatient with assertions in the British press that Americans "were a mere mob accidentally aggregated by a loose bond of contiguity, moved by no nobler motive than dollar-worship, and governed, on the whole, by blackguards."[30] The magazine responded by criticizing England's greed for American cotton when it had colonies to plunder.[31]

Despite its quarrel with British foreign policy, the *Atlantic* retained a loose web of transatlantic relationships. Until international copyright law went into effect in 1891, British and American publishers routinely stole from one another. The *Atlantic* traditionally built its author pool and reputation through transatlantic friendships, like that of Lowell's with the British critic, historian, and mountaineer Leslie Stephen. Coming from traditions of public service, Stephen and Lowell grew up in insular communities where, for reasons of either religion or economics, they felt like outsiders. What Stephen's biographer Noel Anan said of English society applied to Boston's community of "Brahmins," who prided themselves on their cultural and hereditary ties to England: "The same blood can be seen appearing among the headmasters of the public schools and the Fellows of Oxford and Cambridge colleges; the same tone of voice can be heard criticizing, teaching, and leading middle class opinion in the periodicals; and the same families fill the vacancies among the senior permanent officials in a Civil Service open to talent."[32] The iconoclastic streak in the Stephen family, which fed Leslie Stephen's agnosticism, stretched back to his grandfather, a friend of the British emancipator William Wilberforce, and forward to his daughter, Virginia Woolf.

Lowell's friendship with Leslie Stephen began in 1863, shortly after the battle at Gettysburg, when Stephen called at Elmwood.[33] In those days, he fancied himself a radical for wanting to learn about a country as insignificant as the United States. To Stephen, looking at cows tethered outside Elmwood's dining room window, Lowell seemed a second cousin: "No stay-at-home Englishman of an older generation, buried in some country corner, in an ancestral manor, and steeped to the lips in old-world creeds, could have been more thoroughly racy of the soil" or "proud of belonging to a genuine national stock."[34] Lowell nevertheless had to answer doubts about his identity as an American when compatriots looked askance at his foreign travels and an honorary degree from Cambridge. Lowell responded: "If I am not an American, who ever was?"[35]

However advanced, Lowell's thinking grew out of his time, and while his attitude toward African Americans remained forward-thinking, his attitude toward Jews adds a disturbing dimension to his portrait. Leslie Stephen described him in the 1870s ranting through the soup course and into his second brandy: "To begin with nomenclature: all persons named for countries or towns are Jews; all with fantastic compound names, such as Lilienthal, Morgenroth; all with names derived from colors, trades, animals, vegetables, minerals; . . . In short, it appeared that this insidious race had penetrated and permeated the human family more universally than any other influence except original sin." When asked what would happen once the Jews had got "absolute control of finance, the army and navy, the press, diplomacy, society, titles, the government, and the earth's surface," Lowell whispered, "That is the question which will eventually drive me mad."[36] Yet he "was quite sure . . . that he had a line of Jewish blood himself."[37]

Nearly twenty years after Lowell's editorship of the *Atlantic* (1857–1861), Stephen had the pleasure of welcoming Lowell, the godfather of his daughter Virginia, to London as U.S. Minister to the Court of St. James. The usually critical press welcomed Lowell as a native son, and when he died in 1892, Stephen led a movement to have him memorialized at Westminster Abbey. On a late November day in 1893, lords and ladies, diplomats, and literati gathered in the vestibule of the Chapter-house to honor the American poet. The ceremony marked the unveiling of a bust of Lowell placed to catch the light from a stained glass window depicting the protagonist of Lowell's poem "Sir Launfal"; the patron saint of Boston, Lincolnshire, and Boston, Massachusetts, Saint Botolph; and—honoring his commitment to the antislavery cause—figures meant to represent emancipated slaves.[38]

3

John Brown's War

Was dying
all they had the
skill to do?

JAMES RUSSELL
LOWELL,
"Ode Recited
at the Harvard
Commemoration,"
21 July 1865

READERS OF THE July 1861 *Atlantic* noted a significant change on the title page: an American flag replaced the image of Governor Winthrop. Lest there be any mistake about the *Atlantic*'s loyalty to the Union, its new editor, James T. Fields, ordered company stationery edged in red, white, and blue. The magazine's prospectus for 1861 was, in essence, propaganda before its time: "The life of the Republic, the best interests of the nation, demand of literature a manly and generous action, and the conductors of this journal will remit no efforts in enlisting the best talent of the country to support with vigor and eloquence those opinions and principles which brace the great public heart to stand firm on the side of Freedom and Right. An elevated national American spirit will always be found illustrated in these pages."[1] Fields seemed determined, as William Lloyd Garrison had said in his inaugural issue of the *Liberator*, "to lift up the standard of emancipation in the eyes of the nation, within sight of Bunker Hill and in the birthplace of liberty."[2] In 1862, Fields accepted a few verses from Julia Ward Howe, which cost the magazine a mere four dollars. Her "Battle-Hymn of the Republic" appeared in February, the month Jefferson Davis was inaugurated president of the Confederate States of America. It would become the Union anthem.

From the outset of the Civil War, the *Atlantic* dropped any pretense of even-handed coverage, though it continued to present a smattering of opposing views.[3] Lowell's essay titled "The Pickens-and-Stealin's Rebellion" (June 1861) celebrated the Fall of Fort Sumter for galvanizing the North. The attack swayed public opinion more in a day, he argued, than all the antislavery rhetoric of the last thirty years. Viewing the present crisis within the short history of the United States, he focused on two points: that the Civil War completed the work of the War for Independence; and that it gave Americans, through their experience of shared suffering and a recommitment to democratic principles, a greater sense of "nationality."[4]

Not all *Atlantic* contributors suffered from war fever. Abolitionists, intent on ending slavery, had different aims from unionists and the so-called "Conscience Whigs," whom they criticized for seeking political solutions to moral problems. Nor did those who wanted to abolish slavery necessarily believe in the equality of blacks. Oliver Wendell Holmes became an ardent proponent for war, yet he was also a unionist who wrote to Theodore Parker, an abolitionist Unitarian minister, that the white race must continue to keep the upper hand.[5] In 1850, Holmes had admitted three African American students to Harvard's medical school. After their admittance sparked a protest and counterprotest by white students, he told the black students they would have to leave at the end of the term.[6]

Friends like James Russell Lowell would have preferred both Holmes and Hawthorne to be more outspoken against slavery. "I don't quite understand what we are fighting for, or what definite result can be expected," Hawthorne told a friend: "Whatever happens next, I must say that I rejoice that the old Union is smashed. We never were one people, and never really had a country since the constitution was formed."[7] In July 1862, the *Atlantic* published a satire from Hawthorne titled "Chiefly about War-Matters," "By a Peaceable Man" (July 1862), in which Hawthorne recounted his trip to Washington, D.C., to interview political leaders. He arrived the day sixty thousand men crossed the Potomac toward Manassas. Friends as they were, Fields objected to passages in Hawthorne's spoof that struck him as unpatriotic, notably Hawthorne's description of Lincoln's discomfort with questions about "the conduct of the war." Hawthorne had written that "the President's Yankee aptness and not-to-be-caughtness stood him in good stead, and he jerked or wiggled himself out of the dilemma with an uncouth dexterity that was entirely in character."[8] Though agreeing to Fields's deletion of the passage, along with references to Lincoln as "Uncle Abe," Hawthorne included in his essay a series of footnotes written ostensibly by his pro-Union editor. "We are compelled to omit two or three pages," the editor concedes, "in which the author describes the interview, and gives his idea of the personal appearance and deportment of the President."[9]

Hawthorne extended his jest with a letter to the editor from the Peaceable Man in the October 1862 issue, which puns on Fields's name: "You can hardly have expected to hear from me again, (unless by invitation to the field of honor,) after those cruel and terrible notes upon my harmless article in the July Number. . . . Not that I should care a fig for any amount of vituperation, if you had only let my article come before the public as I wrote it, instead of suppressing precisely the passages with which I had taken most pains, and which I flattered myself were most cleverly done."[10] Claiming that he approved the war "as much as any man," Hawthorne may have meant his essay to modify the *Atlantic*'s Republican bias.[11]

Political rifts among the *Atlantic*'s inner circle did not escape the sharp eye of Rebecca Harding (soon to be Rebecca Harding Davis), who saw the escalating war from two sides. Davis lived in the factory town of Wheeling, Virginia (later West Virginia, after the two states separated during the Civil War), the setting of her gritty novella *Life in the Iron-Mills* (April 1861). Davis's connection to the *Atlantic* made her welcome in Concord, "the biggest little place in America."[12] An astute observer, she left a record of her 1862 visit in her autobiography *Bits of Gossip*. She believed that every person should write "not the story of his own life, but of the time in which he lived,—as he saw it,—its creed, its purpose, its queer habits, and the work which it did or left undone in the world."[13] The years leading up to the Civil War had given Davis a double perspective: "When you crossed into Pennsylvania," she recalled, "you had to defend your slave-holding friends against the Abolitionists . . . and when you came home you quarreled with your kindly neighbors for calling the Abolitionists 'emissaries of hell.'"[14] To her, the luminaries of the *Atlantic* had a surprising innocence—not entirely benign. "While they thought they were guiding the real world, they stood quite outside of it, and never would see it as it was."[15]

Davis's New England acquaintances seemed to care more about ideas than about people. It disturbed her that they referred to soldiers, who were sons and brothers, lovers and husbands, as "the army."[16] The ascetic-looking poet John Greenleaf Whittier stretched her patience to its limit when he expounded on slavery and the South "with a gentle, unwearied obstinacy" of his Quaker faith.[17] But of all the *Atlantic* circle, she most disliked Amos Bronson Alcott: a windbag chanting paeans to war while he warmed himself before the Hawthornes' fireplace. She had met his daughter, Louisa, at a reception in Boston, where Alcott stood out among the complacent crowd. Davis's new acquaintance introduced herself by noting: "These people may say pleasant things to you, but not one of them would have gone to Concord and back to see you, as I did to-day." She had made the journey to get the only decent dress she owned, a much mended, claret-colored wool. "My name," she volunteered, "is Louisa Alcott," and added that she had once worked as a second maid.[18] A few months after their conversation, Alcott left Concord to nurse Union soldiers in a Georgetown hospital and gather material for *Hospital Sketches* (1863). Typhus transformed the nurse into a patient, whose cure—doses of calomel or mercurous chloride—slowly killed her over the next decades. Alcott returned home to write her most famous novel, *Little Women*. Following its success, her father advertised himself as "The Concord Sage and Gifted Sire of Louisa M. Alcott!"[19]

Davis's skeptical, and at times condescending, memories of her time in Concord anticipated a new dispensation. To those whose youth preceded the Civil War, to be "Emersonian" signaled intellectual daring. But something happened in the five years between the *Atlantic*'s founding and Davis's visit to Concord that made people no longer see "everything as Mr. Emerson had seen it for us."[20] Perhaps they never had. Three years before Lowell accepted the editorship of the *Atlantic Monthly*, his nephew Charles had stunned the audience at Harvard's commencement by announcing in his best Uncle-James fashion that "the old men, the men of the last generation, can not teach us of the present what should be, for we know as well as they, or better; they should not tell us what can be, for the world always advances by impossibilities achieved. . . . Though men are never too old to learn, they are often too young to be taught."[21] He titled his address, which anticipated postwar sentiment, "The Reverence Due from Old Age to Youth."

In a sense the beginnings of the Civil War might be seen less as the bombardment of Fort Sumter than as John Brown's attack on the arsenal at Harpers Ferry. An hour before midnight on the night of 16 October 1859,

Brown and his band of twenty-one men had overpowered the watchmen at the Baltimore & Ohio Railroad bridge, cut the telegraph wires linking Harpers Ferry to the outside world and, realizing a year's planning, easily captured the armory, arsenal, and rifle works. Brown's guerrillas rounded up prominent citizens on the assumption that their slaves would begin a revolution leading to the national abolition of slavery. Instead he and his men soon found themselves trapped by armed citizens. A number of the impromptu militia camped out in the town's saloons or took potshots at the body of one of Brown's Raiders killed in his attempt to swim to safety. Brown made a tactical error when he allowed a train to pass through Harpers Ferry. The baggage master, a freedman, was killed by a stray bullet as the train journeyed past Harpers Ferry, and at the train's final destination his body served as a silent announcement of the attack.

Around sunset on 17 October, Lt. Col. Robert E. Lee and his company of U.S. marines secured the armory yard. The young lieutenant J. E. B. Stuart waved a white flag to bring Brown a proposal: surrender immediately and his men would be held in protective custody awaiting orders of the president. Brown refused. One of his sons, sent to talk with townspeople under the protection of a similar white flag, had been executed on the spot. Troops overran the engine house Brown used as a bunker and took him prisoner. A third of his men had already died. Suffering from a bayonet wound received in the attack, Brown was removed to Charles Town for trial on charges of treason, rebellion, and murder.

Two weeks after Brown's capture, Henry David Thoreau delivered his stirring speech "A Plea for Captain John Brown," whom he described as a "transcendentalist above all, a man of ideas and principles."[22] Brown's trial lasted nearly a month. It took the jury forty-five minutes to reach their verdict of "guilty on all counts." Emerson predicted that having discouraged any attempts to rescue him, Brown would "make the gallows glorious like the cross."[23] On 2 December, the condemned man stepped into the open cart, drawn by white horses, which took him to a large cornfield on the outskirts of Charles Town. Stonewall Jackson commanded the cadets who formed a ring around a just-completed scaffold. Five days later John Brown's body went home to North Elba, New York. His wife told the *Atlantic*'s Thomas Wentworth Higginson, who had funneled money to Brown, that if she had to see "the ruin" of her house, she hoped that it would benefit "the poor slaves." She little divined how, within two years, Union soldiers would march to her husband's name.[24] Higginson had hoped to rescue Brown until he realized it meant almost certain failure. In the aftermath of the raid, the press referred to Higginson as one of the "Secret Six" who had helped to finance Brown's attack. They included Julia Ward Howe's husband, Samuel Gridley Howe; the Transcendentalist minister Theodore Parker; and the philanthropist Gerrit Smith. Of them all, only Higginson supported Brown to the end. After Howe fled to Canada and Smith committed himself to a lunatic asylum, Higginson asked: "Is there no such thing as honor among confederates?"[25]

Three months after Brown's execution, an anonymous reviewer tried to come to terms with the man and his legacy in an *Atlantic* review of James Redpath's book *The Public Life of John Brown*. Redpath, an émigré from England, reported from Kansas for Horace Greeley's *New York Tribune*, which also published Higginson. In 1856, Redpath found his calling as John Brown's propagandist. By pure chance, he had come upon Brown's encampment as U.S. soldiers and the Missouri militia hunted him and his band of Free State volunteers for the murder of five proslavery men along Pottawatomie Creek. To Redpath, Brown was not only innocent of these crimes but also a holy warrior, who lost a son defending the free-soil town of Osawatomie from proslavery guerrillas. Redpath's articles helped to transform Brown into a national figure. The reviewer for the *Atlantic* felt that Redpath's hagiography of Brown—too violent, too extravagant—only hurt the cause he died for. "He has shown himself incompetent to appreciate the character of the man whom he admires, and he has, consequently, done great wrong to his memory." In short, the book should never have been written.[26] Nevertheless, it quickly sold over forty thousand copies. In 1856, a drama called "Ossawattomie Brown" opened on Broadway.

As if to unfinished business, the *Atlantic* would return repeatedly to the story of John Brown, publishing, in July 1871, R. H. Dana's essay "How We Met John Brown." Dana, an abolitionist and author of the popular *Two Years before the Mast*, recalls how his party got lost in the Adirondacks and stumbled upon Brown's homestead. In retrospect, Dana cannot quite reconcile the upright farmer with the revolutionary. Was Brown a madman or a martyr? At last he concludes that whatever judgment history "may pronounce upon his expedition into Virginia, old John Brown . . . [had] a grasp on the moral world."[27] *Atlantic* writers found Brown less troubling with the passing of time. In 1861, a contributor noted that Americans applauded democratic uprisings in Poland but not on their own soil.[28] In 1872, an anonymous writer stated that those who helped Brown—or more likely marched to war singing verses of "John Brown's Body" lying "a-mold'ring in the grave"—need not regret their actions or blush for . . . a hero as undaunted, as patient, and as completely under Divine guidance as any whom history or romance describes. Those who are dead did not; those who are still living need not."[29]

Atlantic contributors approached the war from a number of perspectives. In September 1861, five months after his son's enlistment, Oliver Wendell Holmes wrote that the war "has taught us, as nothing else could, what we can be and are. . . . It is at this very moment doing more to melt away the petty social distinctions which keep generous souls apart from each other, than the preaching of the Beloved Disciple himself would do. We are finding out not only that 'patriotism is eloquence,' but that 'heroism is gentility.'"[30] Other *Atlantic* writers saw the war in equally inflated terms, hoping that it would fulfill the utopian promises of the Constitution. A number of contributors concentrated their efforts on sympathetic accounts of the history and accomplishments of American blacks. The abolitionist Moncure Conway wrote about the astronomer Benjamin Banneker (January 1863), and Harriet Beecher Stowe sketched a portrait of the traveling preacher and "Libyan sibyl" Sojourner Truth (April 1863), perhaps best known for her speech at the Ohio women's rights convention, "Ain't I a Woman?" With the exception of Theodore Winthrop's "Life in the Open Air" (August 1862) and Thomas Wentworth Higginson's accounts of leading a black regiment, there were few reports of battles or the terrible toll on civilians. Instead writers tended to focus on the political consequences of war.

Though the *Atlantic*'s support for carrying out of the war never faltered, Fields may have thought its actual reportage unpatriotic or outside the responsibility of the magazine. His attitude shifted in the years following the war as contributors recovered or reassessed events of historical importance. In 1866, for example, the *Atlantic* published an account of the first northern challenge to the Fugitive Slave Law by former slaves, written by its leader, William Parker.[31] Parker had received help constructing his narrative of the "Christiana Rebellion" from a number of people, including Osborn Perry Anderson, a participant in the raid on

Harpers Ferry, and James Gilmore, a popular writer and former owner of *Knickerbocker Magazine* whom readers knew as Edmund Kirke. During the Civil War, President Lincoln had sent Kirke on a secret mission to meet with Southern leaders. He was the one who reported Jefferson Davis's statement that the war would continue until the federal government acknowledged the South's right to self-government.[32] The *Atlantic* published Kirke's account of his "visit to Richmond" in September 1864. Subscribers received their issues late that month because Fields had waited for Lincoln to approve the wording.

Published four years before the passage of the Fifteenth Amendment to the U.S. Constitution, "The Freedman's Story" made an argument for black enfranchisement based on its author's literacy and, perhaps more radically, on his manhood. In his introduction, Kirke, identified only by the initials *E. K.*, explained that he had revised the manuscript for publication by weaving "its facts into a story which would show the qualifications of the Southern black for the exercise of the right of suffrage." The reader should know, however, that "the author of this narrative—of every line in it—is William Parker." Describing Parker as the "principal actor in the Christiana riot," which "more than any other event, except the raid of John Brown, helped to precipitate the two sections into the mighty conflict," he submitted this document "to that impartial grand-jury, the American people."[33]

The Christiana Rebellion began in Christiana, Pennsylvania, on 11 September 1851, when William Parker woke to someone hollering, "Kidnappers! Kidnappers!" Parker's house sheltered fugitives from a Maryland plantation owned by Edward Gorsuch. Gorsuch's slaves had a chance to flee the day before, but Parker, working with antislavery organizers, convinced them to hold their ground. Gorsuch died trying to reclaim his "property," and Parker fled to Frederick Douglass's house in Rochester, New York, before settling with his family in Buxton, Ontario."[34] His history—along with Higginson's histories of Nat Turner and Denmark Vesey, leaders of aborted slave rebellions in Virginia and South Carolina, respectively—formed part of the magazine's larger campaign to combat stereotypes about slaves.

In 1872, William Parker returned to his old home and site of the rebellion before attending commencement at Lincoln University, the nation's oldest historically black institution of higher education. His presence was particularly fitting, since the Christiana Rebellion had prompted the Reverend John Miller Dickey and his wife to found the school in 1854. To those who commemorated the hundredth anniversary of the Christiana Rebellion in 1951, the story of William Parker epitomized "the tragedy of mankind everywhere who would be free, but must resort to violence to obtain their freedom." The keynote speaker, Horace Mann Bond, looked forward to a day when every person had equal protection under the law, and there would be "no Christiana Riots nor its multiplication in war's violence."[35] Those who wrote for the *Atlantic* supported a similar message of progress that would fulfill the promise of the republic. Like Higginson, they believed that a new era of American civilization would produce a new American literature and that the *Atlantic* would lead the way.

4

The Battle of the Hundred Pines

THOMAS WENTWORTH HIGGINSON

The whole drama of the war seemed to reverse itself in an instant.

THOMAS W. HIGGINSON, "Up the St. Mary's," *Atlantic*, April 1865

IF THE CIVIL WAR, as Holmes Sr. noted, asked sacrifices of everyone, few were willing to sacrifice as much as Thomas Wentworth Higginson, a Unitarian minister, militant abolitionist, and commander of the first regiment of black soldiers. Higginson had come to national attention for his opposition to the Fugitive Slave Act (1850), which made it a crime for federal officials not to return escaped slaves to their owners. Anyone helping an escaped slave was subject to six months' imprisonment and a fine of one thousand dollars. Four years after the act became the law of the land, Higginson had stood with two thousand other protestors outside Boston's federal courthouse protesting the arrest of an escaped slave, Anthony Burns. Higginson, who came prepared to break down the courthouse door rather than let Burns be returned to slavery, led an impromptu squad of black men armed with a battering ram. Marshalls beat them back, and in the chaos, a deputy died. Undeterred, Higginson went back to his pulpit in Worcester, where he exhorted his parishioners to plant themselves "on the simple truth that God never made a Slave, and that man shall neither make nor take one here! . . . No longer conceal Fugitives and help them on, but show them and defend them. Let the Underground Railroad stop here!"[1]

Higginson's preaching could not save Burns. On 2 June 1854, a guard of 120 armed men escorted him past houses draped with black flags. Hissing demonstrators lined the way to the Boston pier, and people in nearby apartments tossed homemade cayenne pepper bombs from upper-story windows. At State Street the crowd confronted two cannons prepared to fire. By the time the Custom House came in sight, many of the troops and protesters were drunk. Someone smashed a bottle of sulfuric acid, and mob and military, including both lancers on horseback and footmen with fixed bayonets, charged. The ensuing melee failed to halt the march toward the wharf, where, at 3:20, Burns boarded the steamer that took him back to slavery.[2] Indicted for his part in Burns's aborted rescue, but not for the murder of a federal marshal, Higginson never stood trial. The prosecutor dropped the case for lack of evidence.

Higginson's enemies liked to say that this fighting parson could never be accused of underestimating his own importance; his friends, that he simply stated the obvious. Whatever people thought of Higginson himself, he paid with his person for what he believed, and he believed that the first man to command a successful regiment of black troops would "perform the most important service in the history of the war."[3] Resigning from the white regiment of the Fifty-First Massachusetts Volunteers in 1862, he agreed to command the First South Carolina Volunteers of escaped slaves from South Carolina and Florida. Soon after, Robert Shaw organized the Fifty-Fourth Massachusetts Volunteer Infantry, composed of Northern blacks and commemorated in the movie *Glory*. Higginson was convinced that the destiny of American blacks rested on the shoulders of his troops. Should they desert or fail in comprehension or courage there would be no more efforts to arm freed slaves, whose service to the Union argued their right to liberty and full citizenship. Higginson trusted that their performance under fire would demoralize the South and shame "the nation into recognizing them as men."[4] Who else, he reasoned, had more incentive to fight than those fighting for [their] dignity, "homes and families"?[5]

Before Robert E. Lee and Ulysses S. Grant met at Appomattox, nearly two hundred thousand black Americans joined the Union army, over half of them in Confederate territory.[6] Higginson's own recruiting benefited from news of the Emancipation Proclamation, despite orders from Southern generals like Kirby Smith that black soldiers should receive no mercy and that their commanders were to be hanged on the spot. Eager to test his men, Higginson proposed a week-long expedition to gather supplies after white troops brought news of stockpiled lumber—badly needed for tent flooring—along the banks of St. Marys River.

Rising in the Okefenokee Swamp or the Seminoles' "Land of Trembling Earth," the St. Marys River forms part of the border between Georgia and Florida. Higginson's expedition up the St. Marys began on 23 January 1863, when 462 officers and men boarded the steamers *John Adams*, *Planter*, and *Ben De Ford* at Beaufort, South Carolina, with plans to meet at St. Simon's Island. After confiscating stores of Rebel railroad iron at the island, the regiment edged along to Township Landing on the Florida coast. Higginson wanted his men tested by fire as soon as possible so that they could apply what "they had learned in camp."[7] The plan was simple: surround the house and cabins at the landing, follow the path one of his corporals had carved as a slave, and surprise the enemy in his own backyard.

Shortly after midnight, Higginson led a detachment of a hundred soldiers, dressed in the unit's red pants, which looked black in the dark woods. He would carry the smell of crushed pine in his memory for the rest of his life. Hearing nothing as he marched except the croaking of frogs and the bark of an occasional dog, Higginson caught himself imagining the grave courtesy with which he would accept his enemy's tendered sword. His reverie broke with the sudden clatter of galloping horses, the clashing of metal, and the groans of men wounded in the melee. Afterward no one could say for certain what had happened. One second there was nothing more than moist darkness; the next a towering Pegasus of a horse reared in the path, with its ghostlike rider shouting, "Charge!" The recruit standing next to Higginson fell to the ground, dead. Word rippled through the ranks that the colonel had fallen. Fearing that his men would scatter and knowing that their greatest danger lay in confusion, Higginson ordered them to fix their bayonets. A number who misheard his order quixotically charged the cavalry. The battle lasted anywhere between ten minutes and an hour before their attackers vanished as mysteriously as they appeared. Higginson later learned that the Confederate troops had lost their commander.

The volunteers of the First South Carolina, who continued their nine-day mission and brought back large supplies of iron, brick, and lumber, six prisoners, and twenty-five sheep, won more than the Battle of the Hundred Pines that day. Higginson, having dodged "flying bullets with a notebook and pencil in hand," continued to fight for the rights of his soldiers in the pages of the *Atlantic*.[8] In "Up the St. Mary's" (April 1865), he testified publicly to the loyalty and bravery of his troops:

> Braver men never lived. One man with two bullet-holes through the large muscles of the shoulders and neck brought off from the scene of action, two miles distant, two muskets; and not a murmur has escaped his lips. Another, Robert Sutton, with three wounds, one of which, being on the skull, may cost him his life, would not report himself till compelled to do so by his officers. . . . He is perfectly quiet and cool, but takes this whole affair with the religious bearing of a man who realizes that freedom is sweeter than life. . . . And one of those who were carried to the vessel a man wounded through the lungs asked only if I were safe, the contrary having been reported. An officer may be pardoned some enthusiasm for such men as these.[9]

After the war, Higginson worked to have the government pay black soldiers, as they did white soldiers, from the date of their enlistment. The bill that passed on 1 August 1864 gave black soldiers full pay provided they were free by 19 April 1861. It excluded men, like many of Higginson's troops, who had previously escaped from slavery. Higginson added an appendix titled "The Struggle for Pay" to *Army Life in a Black Regiment*, which charts his efforts to have the bill apply to all black Americans who served the cause.

A month after William Tecumseh Sherman ordered the evacuation of Atlanta, Higginson published a chapter from *Army Life in a Black Regiment* in the *Atlantic*, titled "A Night on the Water" (October 1864). Nine months had passed since his regiment took and gave its first fire at the Battle of the Hundred Pines. "A Night on the Water" might be read as an allegory of the years leading up to the war, when death invaded Arcadia. The title's "night" began a little before midnight and "lasted precisely one hour."[10] Handing his watch to his lieutenant for safekeeping and removing his clothes, Higginson swam from the shore toward enemy lines. He considered and dismissed thoughts of fever, rheumatism, alligators, and rebel sentries as he floated "past one marshy islet after another," encased in "some concave globe, some magic crystal," with himself at its "enchanted center."[11] Time evaporated, and the material world shrank to whatever sat at eye level. "At one of these moments," he wrote, "it suddenly occurred to my perception . . . that I was in a powerful current, set the wrong way." Higginson remembered the awful half minute when "the whole vast universe appeared to swim in the same watery uncertainty in which" he floated and his compass had failed.[12] Uncertainty in the face of human insignificance became a constant theme for post–Civil War writers, who struggled to come to terms with recent history and new hypotheses about concepts such as time, self, memory, and their broken country.

"The stern logic of events," Frederick Douglass would write in December 1866, "has determined the interests of the country as identical with and inseparable from those of the negro."[13] Over the next years, the *Atlantic* pushed for educational reform as a kind of immunization against racial prejudice. The policy foreshadows W. E. B. Du Bois's dream of an unbiased Talented Tenth, the intellectual elite of all races. Only "when the freedmen are lost in the mass of freemen, the work [and sacrifice of the war] will be complete."[14] More hopefully, *Atlantic* writers argued that the contributions of educated blacks to local economies and culture would eventually ease racial tensions.

In 1878, Higginson revisited the scenes of war. He found Jacksonville, Florida, which he had last seen in flames, a summer watering place for tourists. Beaufort, South Carolina, glimmered with new paint. He rarely met one of his ex-soldiers who did not own his own house and land. Sergeant Hodges had become a master carpenter; Corporal Hicks, a preacher; and Sergeant Shemeltella, an entrepreneur who sold game to markets in Charleston and Savannah. The war had resulted, he wrote, in a more equitable distribution of wealth between capitalist and laborer, which should lead to a lasting peace benefiting both whites and blacks.[15] His hopes for a more equitable distribution would turn to ash in the reconstructed South, which, fearing competence and integrity as harbingers of social equality, systematically destroyed the dreams of citizens like Sergeant Hodges.

The country's failure to lay John Brown to rest suggests that Rebecca Harding Davis's reservations about the Concord seers had the sting of truth. Who could, in retrospect, exalt a war in which one of every four

Union soldiers died, though more from disease than a ball or bayonet?[16] Then, too, cities such as Atlanta, Charleston, Vicksburg, and Richmond lay in ruins. With barns and bridges burned, and vigilantes terrorizing the population, the countryside fared no better. Blood had "poured out on the battle-fields—for what?" asked the diarist Mary Boykin Chesnut, who had watched regiments of ragtag soldiers pass through the Confederate capital with tin pans tied to their waists and bread or bacon on the end of their bayonets.[17] She and others could not repress the thought of wasted lives. "Where be now these silent hosts?" John Greenleaf Whittier asked *Atlantic* readers in May 1865: "Where the camping-ground of ghosts?"[18]

Atlantic writers mourning the human cost of the war did not forget the rights of freed men and women. In June 1865, C. C. Coffin observed that people had been willing for black men to carry guns and fire bullets at the enemy, but not to "march up to the ballot-box, and fire a peaceful ballot against the same enemy." He challenged America to teach the world. "Make the freedman a voter, a land-owner, a tax-payer, permit him to sue and be sued, give him in every respect free franchise, and the recompense will be security, peace, and prosperity." Anything less, he warned, would "bring trouble in its train."[19]

Thomas Wentworth Higginson would have agreed with these words; few people did more than he to lift the fortunes of black Americans. But all Americans owe him another debt. This soldier, clergyman, and a stalwart of the *Atlantic Monthly* was also a man of letters who believed in woman's equality. Seven months before he received the letter asking him to command the First Regiment of South Carolina Volunteers, he published an *Atlantic* essay titled "Letter to a Young Contributor" (April 1862), in which he encouraged submissions particularly from women authors. His essay prompted many responses, including one from an unknown poet named Emily Dickinson, who included four poems unlike any he had read. The two corresponded until Dickinson's death in 1886, and the *Atlantic* published part of that correspondence in an essay titled "Emily Dickinson's Letters" (October 1891). Throughout the correspondence, Dickinson addressed Higginson as her mentor. Responding to his criticism, she wrote:

> Thank you for the surgery; it was not so painful as I supposed. I bring you others, as you ask, though they might not differ. While

my thought is undressed, I can make the distinction; but when I put them in the gown, they look alike and numb.

You asked how old I was? I made no verse, but one or two, until this winter, sir.... I could not weigh myself, myself. My size felt small to me. I read your chapters in The Atlantic, and experienced honor for you. I was sure you would not reject a confiding question.

Is this, sir, what you asked me to tell you? Your friend,

E. DICKINSON.[20]

After Dickinson's death, Higginson observed that her "wholly new and original poetic genius" presented a "problem never yet solved." "What place," he wondered, "ought to be assigned in literature to what is so remarkable, yet so elusive of criticism."[21] In 1890, he and Mabel Loomis Todd edited the first volume of Dickinson's poetry, regularizing her capitalization and punctuation. Higginson's introduction states that "the verses of Emily Dickinson belong emphatically to what Emerson long since called "the Poetry of the Portfolio,"—something produced absolutely without the thought of publication, and solely by way of expression of the writer's own mind."[22] Though his explanation seems self-serving, his and Todd's edition probably saved Dickinson from obscurity. Both Dickinson and Higginson have suffered from popular perceptions of their characters. She has come down to many present readers as "the belle of Amherst" (Higginson called her "my partially cracked poetess at Amherst"); he is largely remembered, by those who ignore his support of civil rights and women's suffrage, as the lout who changed her verse.[23]

When Higginson died in May 1911, the *New York Times* described him as the last of a breed: "His views, his aims, his methods of public action were those of the radical democrat—the type of democrat that in our country has pretty well disappeared—inspired by abstract ideas and sustained by the most rigorously a priori reasoning from those ideas."[24] A stubborn and generous man, self-righteous and fearless, Higginson believed that "the human soul, like any other noble vessel, was not built to be anchored, but to sail."[25]

5

Dueling Visions

LOUIS AGASSIZ AND ASA GRAY

Darwin was convulsing society.

HENRY ADAMS, *The Education of Henry Adams*, 1918

THE DEBATE ABOUT EMANCIPATION had as its backdrop nineteenth-century debates about evolution, which was arguably the debate of the century. But "debate" seems a word too gentle for the intellectual battles waged by the opponents and proponents of Charles Darwin's theory across Europe and the United States, where issues of religion and race hinged on the arguments splitting international scientific communities. The most important American arguments took place in the laboratories of Harvard University, where Asa Gray, the country's leading botanist, defended Darwin's theory, and his popular adversary, the Swiss naturalist Louis Agassiz, opposed it. As the two men's essays appeared in the pages of the *Atlantic*, contributors wondered whether those of African descent belonged to the same species as those of European descent. Could a "degraded and degenerate race," as Agassiz, the magazine's chief science writer, wrote, accept the responsibilities of citizenship, let alone freedom? He admitted that even raising the question flew in the face of "all our ideas of the brotherhood of man and unique origin of our species."[1]

A world-renowned scientist and a father of modern scientific methods in the United States, Agassiz was known to many general readers for his beautifully illustrated volumes titled *Recherches sur les poissons fossils*, published between 1833 and 1843. The son of a Protestant minister, he received his training in Switzerland and Germany, where he met his first wife, Cécile Braun, before studying comparative anatomy in France with Georges Cuvier, the founding father of vertebrate paleontology. Agassiz accepted a university professorship at the Lyceum of Neuchatel, which allowed him to marry Cécile and pursue his interests in ichthyology and geology. At Neuchatel, and later in the British Isles, he noticed signs of glaciers in unlikely places. His theory that sheets of ice had once covered the earth stunned the scientific community in 1837.

Not only a brilliant scientist, Agassiz had an uncanny knack for making friends and allies. He had long wanted to study the geology of the United States, and an unusual number of people made that possible for him in 1846. Jean de Charpentier, whose glacial theories influenced Agassiz's own, convinced Charles Lucien Bonaparte to underwrite Agassiz's travel expenses. Agassiz then approached the dean of German science, Alexander von Humboldt, in the hope that the King of Prussia might support a long stay at Harvard. He followed this request with a similar one to the great English geologist Charles Lyell, wondering whether Lyell might use his Boston connections to arrange a series of lectures. Everything happened according to plan: the King of Prussia granted him a stipend; Lyell enlisted his old friend and trustee of the Lowell Institute, John Amory Lowell, to offer fifteen hundred dollars for a course of lectures; and Agassiz began practicing his English. Word of "this big geologico-everything-French-Swiss gun," whom the great Cuvier had mentored, spread quickly in Cambridge's small scientific community.[2] Those who lined up to attend his lectures, titled "Plan of Creation in the Animal Kingdom," were charmed by Agassiz's accented English and his combining of science and theology, which not only clarified irregularities in the natural world as "God's leetle joke," but assured Bostonians that they were, indeed, the chosen species.[3]

The success of his lectures astounded Agassiz, who determined to remain in the United States when his appointment expired. Even scandal could not stop Boston's embrace of its distinguished guest. Agassiz's colleagues and wife, Cécile, had warned him about his trusted assistant, Edward Desor. Their predictions proved true when, after a falling-out, Desor sought to discredit Agassiz by attacking his character. The most serious accusations concerned Cécile, who, having chosen to remain in Europe with their three children, died from influenza during Agassiz's absence. Desor attributed her death to Agassiz's "desertion." Both Desor and Agassiz agreed to have a panel of Boston's leading citizens investigate all accusations of misconduct, including Desor's claim that Agassiz had an affair with an Irish servant named Jane, who worked in his rooming house. Testimony took a step toward the salacious when a witness recalled having seen Jane sew a button on the fly of Agassiz's trousers—as he wore them. The panel found this and every one of Desor's charges—including his claim that Agassiz had plagiarized his findings—to be untrue. Instead the panel found that Desor had plagiarized Agassiz, and Desor returned to Europe a ruined man. As for Jane, she married a man of property in Roxbury.

The Desor affair damaged neither Agassiz's reputation nor his prospects with Elizabeth Cary, an intellectual woman who became the first president of Radcliffe College in 1894. Their marriage at Boston's King Chapel in April 1850 completed the Americanization of Louis Agassiz by making him, and eventually his children with Cécile, part of Lizzie's extended Brahmin family of Carys, Cabots, and Gardners. His home became a gathering place for Cambridge scientists, such as Charles Sanders Peirce and Cornelius Felton, who had a hand in his friend's courting.

A large part of Agassiz's success came from his identification with the *Atlantic*, which under its new editor James T. Fields added the word "science" to the list of fields the magazine covered: literature, art, and politics. Fields promoted Agassiz as the people's scientist, and few could deny his charisma. The Saturday Club, whose members included Emerson, Hawthorne, Holmes, and Longfellow, began to be known as Agassiz's Club. Fish vendors on Boston's wharf proudly showed the country's leading ichthyologist their wares. Strangers asked him where he kept his shop, or was it a restaurant? As one admirer described Agassiz's effect on people, "To know him was to willingly promise service to science for all time, and to feel amply repaid in fulfilling that promise."[4]

In an era when science became more professionalized, Agassiz gave an insecure nation a vision of its future leadership in scientific endeavor. "Naturalist as I am," he wrote, "I cannot but put the people first. . . . What a people! . . . I should in vain try to give . . . an idea of this great nation. . . . Their look is wholly turned toward the future."[5] Agassiz insisted that any scientific discoveries he made belonged solely to the United States.

One of Agassiz's earliest admirers was Asa Gray, the Fisher Professor of

Natural History at Harvard, who accompanied Agassiz on part of his initial tour of America's foremost centers of science. Of Scotch-Irish descent, Gray was Agassiz's temperamental opposite, an introspective, cautious man who believed, above all, in scientific sharing. He could have become a farmer in upstate New York, except that his early enthusiasm for collecting plants and minerals made him seem, in his father's eyes, better fitted for a doctor's life. The man who lent his name to Harvard's Gray Herbarium had little interest in doctoring, though, as chance had it, his medical studies brought him to the attention of John Torrey, a professor of chemistry and botany with whom he worked on *Flora of North America.* Not even Gray's admirers could call him a fluent lecturer, yet his handsome looks and sincerity made him a popular teacher. A different man in the classroom, Gray would fly into class at a half run. Darting and jumping around the room until exhausted, he often plunked himself down cross-legged on the floor to think. According to his students, he hated shams and false displays of learning: "nothing pleased him more than to prick the bubble of pomposity or, by some well-timed remark, to check the stream of those who talked for the sake of talking."[6] Agassiz might have taken note. Gray did for botany what Agassiz did for science generally: he formulized the field for a nation of amateur botanists at a time when people understood that a yellow rose signified jealousy and a camellia stood for perfection. Readers of Gray's most popular book—*Manual of the Botany of the Northern United States, from New England to Wisconsin and South to Ohio and Pennsylvania Inclusive*—knew it simply as Gray's *Manual.*

Unlike Gray, Agassiz loved an audience and devoted little time to self-reflection. One colleague described him as "incomparable in the discovery of facts—but I am becoming continually more dissatisfied with him as a generalizer."[7] This criticism encompassed the religious assumptions informing Agassiz's scientific explanations. Though religious himself, Gray agreed with Charles Darwin that science had thrown "no light on the far higher problem of the essence or origin of life." The scientist's first duty was to deal with evidence, all the time knowing that "speculations run beyond the bounds of true science with as many flaw[s] & holes as sound parts."[8] Agassiz, who counted Aristotle among his favorite authors and reread him every few years, began by assuming that God had a master plan. He explained that glaciers had once covered the earth's surface; as they melted, he said, they scoured the planet clean of every living thing in their path. He called these massive sheets of ice "God's plough" and argued that nothing could have survived a catastrophe second only to Noah's flood. In other words, for the earth to be populated with plants and animals, new species would have had to appear simultaneously in different regions. This reasoning led Agassiz to disbelieve Darwin's hypothesis about evolution in *Origin of the Species*.

Darwin himself feared the effect of his conclusions on contemporaries who believed that the universe had a fixed hierarchy of life. When the Bishop of Oxford, Samuel Wilberforce, famously asked Thomas Huxley whether he claimed descent from a monkey through his grandfather or his grandmother, Huxley had stunned the bishop and the audience by saying that he would not be ashamed to have a monkey for an ancestor, "but he would be ashamed to be connected with a man who used great gifts to obscure the truth."[9] He might well have been Gray responding to Agassiz's denial of troublesome evidence. The consequences of Darwin's theory worried the general public as much as those who attended the debate. Huxley's answer challenged the literal accuracy of the Bible as well as common assumptions about the ordering of species and their assumed counterpart in racial pecking orders. Unmoved, Agassiz stood with Wilberforce—and with most *Atlantic* readers—on the side of polygenesis or the separate origin of species and races.

Gray knew Huxley as "Darwin's bulldog," but also as a brilliant classifier of invertebrates, who would conclude that birds evolved from small carnivorous dinosaurs. Huxley, however, left the recruiting of Gray to one of Darwin's closest friends, Joseph Dalton Hooker. As England's preeminent botanist, Hooker received gifts of specimens from people around the globe, which he shared with his American colleague. By way of Hooker, Gray promised Darwin that his theories would get a fair hearing in the United States. Gray's thoughtful review of *Origin of Species* for the *American Journal of Science* pleased Darwin enough for him to include it as the preface to the book's second American edition. As a token of his appreciation and esteem, he sent Gray a sand dollar from his youthful voyage on the *Beagle*.

To Gray, any unexamined rejection of evidence threatened the integrity of science. Agassiz knew a rival when he saw him, and Gray was a rival for national preeminence and, more practically, for donors needed to build his herbarium at Harvard. Thanks to Agassiz's phenomenal talent for extracting money from the state legislature and private patrons, the Museum of Comparative Zoology had become a reality in November 1859.[10] His success owed much to the way he framed his argument; the museum was, in the language of one report, "a scientific treasury, from which the teacher and divine may draw illustrations of beauty and power, illustrating the word by the work of God."[11] However comforting the public found Agassiz's pronouncements about correspondences between nature and God's divine plan, Gray objected to those unempirical assertions.

Once Gray decided to challenge Agassiz, he wanted to make him growl "like a cudgeled dog."[12] Gray approached his *Atlantic* readers by conceding the difficulty of accepting change, whether in the form of a new pair of breeches or a theory about the origin of life. In "Darwin on the Origin of Species," he used an everyday illustration to make his case, allowing that *The Atlantic* affected "the older type of nether garment. . . . We still hoped, with some repairs and make-shifts, the old views might last out our days. *Après nous le déluge*." Gray explained that variation and natural selection need not exclude the idea of specific creation, since some things are beyond knowing. The remainder of his essay answered a series of questions about the origin of species that undercut Agassiz's assertions. Gray affected a measured voice that was itself reassuring. He mentioned Agassiz only once and then to use his findings in support of Darwin's theory of evolution. Finally, he concluded, it is not the theory that causes opposition, but its logical extensions, which "makes the whole world kin."[13] He hoped that evolution would continue to work for the good of humankind and encouraged his readers to decide for themselves by recommending Appleton's latest edition of Darwin's book.

Gray's second *Atlantic* essay, also titled "Darwin on the Origin of Species," addressed criticism of Darwin's book. For those doubters like Agassiz who insisted on separate species while noting similarities within and among species, he posed a rhetorical question: "What amount of difference is compatible with community of origin"? Those who believe in the cataclysmic destruction of all life and repopulation of species do not allow, Gray wrote, for geographical and other physical explanations that would explain the "material connection between successive species."

> Who would have thought that the peach and the nectarine came from one stock? But, this being proved, is it now very improbable

> that both were derived from the almond, or from some common amygdaline progenitor? Who would have thought that the cabbage, cauliflower, broccoli, kale, and kohlrabi are derivatives of one species, and rape or colza, turnip, and probably rutabaga, of another species? And who that is convinced of this can long undoubtingly hold the original distinctness of turnips from cabbages as an article of faith? On scientific grounds may not a primordial cabbage or rape be assumed as the ancestor of all the cabbage races, on much the same ground that we assume a common ancestry for the diversified human races?[14]

Gray was left at the end of this essay with the same fears plaguing his first: What were the greater implications of Darwin's hypothesis? Did he and others have the courage to meet them?

His last essay, titled "Darwin and His Reviewers," attacked Agassiz most directly by presenting him as a philosopher rather than a scientist. According to Gray, Agassiz wrongheadedly insisted that because "species are ideas . . . the objects from which the idea is derived cannot vary or blend" or have "a genealogical connection." This thinking went against the common view of species that though they were "generalizations," they had an objective basis in Nature. Gray explained this point by comparing different sorts of chairs, each of which "has its varieties" shading "off by gradations into another. And—note it well—these numerous and successively slight variations and gradations, far from suggesting an accidental origin to chairs and to their forms, are very proofs of design." Gray concluded with the assurance that Darwin's theory "leaves the argument for design, and therefore for a Designer, as valid as it ever was":

> to do any work by an instrument must require, and therefore presuppose the exertion rather of more than of less power than to do it directly;—that whoever would be a consistent theist should believe that Design in the natural world is coextensive with Providence, and hold fully to the one as he does to the other [variation], in spite of the wholly similar and apparently insuperable difficulties which the mind encounters whenever it endeavors to develop the idea into a complete system, either in the material and organic, or in the moral world.[15]

Darwin could not have been more pleased with Gray's defense, which turned Agassiz's findings against himself. Paying half the publishing costs for printing the essays in pamphlet form, Darwin had 250 copies shipped to England. Apart from advertising it in periodicals, he sent copies to colleagues, including Huxley's opponent, the Bishop of Oxford, Samuel Wilberforce.[16] One of his readers, who said he'd never consider becoming a Darwinist, quipped that he might actually be a Grayite.[17]

Unlike Darwin, who seldom left his study or ventured even as far as London, Agassiz needed no emissaries for his theories. While Gray and certainly Thomas Huxley may have spoken for Darwin better than Darwin could speak for himself, no one matched Agassiz at his best. Although Agassiz did not have the final word on evolution, he had the words many ordinary citizens wanted. In 1862, the *Atlantic* ran one of its few serials containing illustrations and charts, Agassiz's *Methods of Study in Natural History*. Oliver Wendell Holmes spoke for many readers when he sent his congratulations: "I look with ever increasing admiration on the work you are performing for our civilization. It very rarely happens that the same person can take at once the largest and deepest scientific views and come down without apparent effort to the level of popular intelligence. . . . I did not think it necessary to say these . . . words, but I wanted the privilege, because I feel them sincerely."[18]An exasperated Gray joked with Darwin about Agassiz's popularity. He could make the public believe that hairy elephants and bears had sunbathed in the tropics until "all of a sudden it changed to bitter winter—so suddenly that they could not run away, nor even rot, but were frozen up before there was time for either!"[19] Gray was right about the public's respect for Agassiz. His *Methods of Study in Natural History* went into nineteen editions its first twenty years. In the preface, Agassiz states that he finds "a repulsive poverty" in "material explanations" of the world, which are

> contradicted by the intellectual grandeur of the universe; the resources of the Deity cannot be so meagre, that, in order to create a human being endowed with reason, he must change a monkey into a man. This is, however, merely a personal opinion, and has no weight as an argument; nor am I so uncandid as to assume that another may not hold an opinion diametrically opposed to mine in a spirit quite as reverential as my own. But I nevertheless insist, that

this theory is opposed to the processes of Nature, as far as we have been able to apprehend them.[20]

The antagonism between Gray and Agassiz passed into Cambridge lore. Gossip had Agassiz challenging Gray to a duel. There was no calling on seconds, no pistols drawn at dawn, but there were words on a train returning from New Haven, after both men attended a meeting of the Scientific Club. According to Gray's wife, their disagreement began at the meeting and continued on the train. It ended with Agassiz asserting that Gray was no gentleman.

Although Agassiz's findings should have led him toward accepting the basic premises of evolution, he repeatedly pulled back at the last minute. Whether a failure of courage, a bow to convention, or an implacable belief, his refusal to see a difference between God's creation of variable species and laws by which species vary made him, in the eyes of his peers, a lesser scientist than the 1850s had promised. The larger political context reflected in the debate over Darwin's *Origin of Species* did not escape Agassiz and Gray's contemporaries who heard Darwin speaking directly about what it meant to be human. While centered on evolution, the Agassiz-Gray conflict fed issues at the core of the Civil War and American society itself. Southerners, for example, cited Agassiz to argue a "scientific" basis for racial inequality. "With Agassiz in the war," one Southerner exulted, "the battle is ours."[21]

Days before General Lee surrendered in April 1865, Agassiz headed an expedition to Brazil. Leaving from the port city of Manaos, Brazil, the expedition snaked its way to the Lake of Hyanuary on the western side of the Rio Negro, a tributary of the seemingly endless Amazon. The American secretary of the navy, the American minister to Brazil, and officials of the Pacific Mail Steamship Company put themselves at Agassiz's disposal. The crewmates formed a distinguished lot; the Brazilian contingent was led by the president of the province, His Excellency Dr. Epaminondas. Louis Agassiz headed the American expedition, accompanied by his wife and the twenty-three-year-old medical student William James, who wavered between thinking him a mesmerist or a charlatan. James told his mother that "offering your services to Agassiz is as absurd as it would [be] for a S. Carolinian to invite Gen. Sherman's soldiers to partake of some refreshment when they called at his home."[22] Agassiz had his own doubts about James, whom he considered pitiably uneducated. If nothing else, the voyage, which imaginatively paralleled that of Darwin's *Beagle*, convinced James that he was "cut out for a speculative rather than an active life."[23] Readers of the *Atlantic* followed the expedition in *A Journey in Brazil*, Elizabeth and Louis Agassiz's joint account of their travels compiled from her notes. They parted from Brazil with "a deep-seated faith in her future progress and prosperity."[24] Agassiz believed that goodwill generated by his and the Brazilian government's endeavor brought about the opening of the Amazon River to international trade.

Instrumental in the founding of the American Association for the Advancement of Science and the National Academy of Sciences, Agassiz saw his efforts lead to explanations of a world that eventually left him—the father of glaciology and paleoichthyology—behind. His rival, Asa Gray, fared better, for he was spared the bitterness of seeing part of his work set aside. Though both died more than a century ago, their thrusts and counterthrusts still echo across the world as scientists and creationists debate the origins of the human life.

6

Reconstructions

OLIVER WENDELL HOLMES SR. & JR.

Every society
that amounts . . .
to anything has
it own annals.

HENRY JAMES,
"Mr. and Mrs. Fields,"
1915

TO OLIVER WENDELL HOLMES and other Bostonians who had sons fighting in "the Harvard Regiment," the day of 17 September 1862 passed in an anxious muddle of rumors about the Battle of Antietam.[1] That night Holmes awoke to the sound of someone pounding on his door. The telegram he received read: CAPTAIN HOLMES WOUNDED SHOT THROUGH THE NECK THOUGHT NOT MORTAL AT KEEDYSVILLE. A professor of anatomy, Holmes fastened on the word "through," as he instinctively cataloged the possible damage: "Windpipe, foodpipe, carotid, jugular, half a dozen smaller, but still formidable vessels, a great braid of nerves, each as big as a lamp-wick, spinal cord,—ought to kill at once, if at all."[2] He knew his anatomy, and the odds of surviving such wound, yet at that moment, the younger Holmes, his wound stuffed with lint and his gullet with opium, lay in a farmer's best featherbed. His father had no idea that the crisis had passed.

The next afternoon, Holmes set off to retrieve his son. His journey took over a week, with stops in New York, Philadelphia, Baltimore, Frederick, and Middletown, before the final leg by wagon to the little town of Keedysville, Maryland, whose every building now served as a makeshift ward. Holmes arrived a day too late. The previous morning, his son had begun wending his way back home by hitching a ride in a milk cart to Hagerstown, where a couple named

Kennedy spotted the dazed young officer stumbling about, and took him home. While Holmes Jr. recuperated, Holmes Sr. frantically traveled from Frederick through Baltimore and Philadelphia, then on to Harrisburg, haunted by images of his son's life "ebbing away in some lonely cottage, nay, in some cold barn or shed, or at the wayside, unknown, uncared for." Meanwhile his son reclined in the parlor of his hostess, Mrs. Kennedy, surfeited with delicacies and flirting with another houseguest—a very pretty Miss Jones who had been instructed to soothe her patient with song.[3] "All this," the father recounted for *Atlantic* readers, "after the swamps of the Chickahominy, the mud and flies of Harrison Landing, the dragging marches, the desperate battles, the fretting wound, the jolting ambulance, the log-house, and the rickety milk-cart!"[4] Father and son finally stumbled across one another at the Harrisburg train station. "How are you, Boy?" the doctor asked. To which "the boy," looking down a full foot at his five-foot-three-inch father, responded, "How are you, Dad?"[5] The story has a postscript. Four decades after Antietam, Wendell Holmes and his wife dined with the woman he had met at the Kennedys and had not seen since. To Mrs. Holmes's satisfaction, the former Miss Jones had gained more pounds than years. At the evening's end, Mrs. Holmes found the chief justice of the U.S. Supreme Court brooding in his study, aware, for the first time, he said, how many years had passed since the massacre at Antietam.

In the aftermath of Antietam, Holmes Sr.'s shaggy-dog narrative of his ordeal, published in the *Atlantic* as "My Hunt after 'the Captain'" (December 1862), incensed his son by seeming to profit from the war. Wendell Holmes had heard his father criticized as a Johnny-come-lately to the cause, a conceited little mannequin, blathering about "our boys" and "men who quarrel with the captain when the ship is in trouble."[6]And, to some degree, he shared this view of his father and those other fireside patriots who had no firsthand experience of the enemy's determination or the North's strategic and tactical blunders. "I don't think you realized the unity or determination of the South," he scolded his father three months after Antietam. "I think you are hopeful because (excuse me) you are ignorant."[7] Twenty-three thousand soldiers died or were wounded at Antietam. As one soldier wrote home, no description could convey the carnage: "The dead lay where they fell in hundreds, the bodies horribly disfigured by 36 hours exposure to the sun & rain, coal black, most of them & swollen, to 3 times their natural size."[8] Wendell Holmes had been shot while retreating: "We have stood side by side in a line," he grimly reminisced: "—we have charged and swept the enemy—and we have run away like rabbits—all together."[9] When wounded in the heel at Fredericksburg, he would have preferred to lose his foot than return to battle, where the chances of survival were slim. "Within forty eight hours, there are funeral services for four of your friends," a Harvard undergraduate wrote, "followed by others as battle after battle takes place."[10] Holmes Jr. counted among his fallen friends and cousins the nephews of James Russell Lowell and Paul Revere's grandson. He had little patience with civilians like his father, who to his dismay gathered souvenirs at battle sites. In "My Hunt after 'the Captain,'" he lists items found on the "bloody cornfield of Antietam": a "bullet or two, a button, a brass plate from a soldier's belt," and a letter from James Wright of Cleveland County, North Carolina, which he wanted his widow to have.[11]

The war deepened Wendell Holmes's dissatisfaction with a father who not only embarrassed but also baffled him. Weighing his father's failings, he wrote that had he "the patience to concentrate all his energy on a single subject, which is perhaps saying if he had been a different man, he would have been less popular, but he might have produced a great work. I often am struck by his insight in things that he lightly touched. But, as I say, it is the last 5% that makes the difference between the great and the clever."[12] Yet well in advance of Louis Pasteur's work on germs and infectious diseases, Holmes Sr. had urged physicians to wash their hands before dealing with patients; he understood that they carried puerperal fever from one childbed to another. "In my own family," he wrote, "I had rather that those I esteemed the most should be delivered, unaided, in a stable, by the mangerside, than that they should receive the best help, in the fairest apartment, but exposed to the vapors of this pitiless disease. Gossiping friends, wet-nurses, monthly nurses, the practitioner himself, these are the channels by which, as I suspect, the infection is principally conveyed."[13] The butt of jokes by physicians who thought gentlemen never had dirty hands, Holmes stood his ground. Ignaz Semmelweis, who came to the same conclusion a few years later, found that the death rate decreased when physicians and assistants washed their hands in a chlorine solution before assisting at births. Throughout his career, Holmes advocated the humane treatment of patients and the use of the latest technology, including stethoscopes. The medical school he started in Boston later became part of the Harvard Medical School. Titles of his lectures included "Medical Delusions of the Past" and "Homoeopathy and Its Kindred Delusions." In addition to naming the *Atlantic*, he coined the term "anaesthesia," from the Greek word *anaisthesia*, meaning "lack of sensation."

On the eve of the Civil War, the defining moment in his country's history, the senior Holmes had speculated, brilliantly, about the ways science and technology would change human beings' understanding of themselves and their world. He could address the issue of technology as both a consumer and the developer of the Holmes Stereo Viewer, an instrument that revolutionized photography by creating three-dimensional images. For fifty years, it remained, until the wide accessibility of movies in the 1930s, the stereoscope of choice. In "The Stereoscope and the Stereograph," Holmes wrote that he was almost afraid to guess "what is to come of the stereoscope and the photograph." Visible objects, he said, will lose their importance except as they provide a template or mold for forms themselves. His observation raised several "frightening" specters, including doubts about the authenticity of objects and reality itself. "Matter in large masses must be fixed and dear," he hypothesized, while "form is cheap and transportable. We have got the fruit of creation now, and need not trouble ourselves with the core." In other words, we have separated form from matter by substituting an illusion, which seems more real, its meaning more precise, than the original. Over time, he reasoned, a photograph threatens to modify or subsume memory itself by its rendering of nature's complexity. More disquieting, the gap between form and substance promises to desensitize people to experience as "every conceivable object of Nature and Art" scales "off its surface from us," and those realities once assumed to be true become relative.[14] By this logic, aesthetic properties might seem expressions of nature, but are in fact sleights of hand.

Holmes anticipated stereographs ushering the next European war into the homes of average Americans through stereographic images of bursting shells, which

> shall preserve the very instant of the shock of contact of the mighty armies that are even now gathering. . . . We are looking into stereoscopes as pretty toys [he warned], and wondering over the photograph as a charming novelty; but before another generation has

> passed away, it will be recognized that a new epoch in the history of human progress dates from the time when He who . . . took a pencil of fire from the hand of the 'angel standing in the sun,' and placed it in the hands of a mortal.[15]

World War I would be etched in people's imaginations by photographs of gassed soldiers and demolished buildings.

Holmes's talents may have stretched too far, but however much Wendell Holmes thought his scientific and literary production less than perfect, he was in fact a brilliant man. Though Wendell called his father's poetry frivolous and provincial, "Old Ironsides" (1830)—written when Holmes Sr. was twenty-one—has been credited with saving the USS *Constitution* ("the eagle of the sea") from the scrap heap. Abraham Lincoln liked to recite "The Last Leaf," a poem that Edgar Allan Poe ranked among the finest in the language and whose last stanza reads:

> And if I should live to be
> The last leaf upon the tree
> In the spring,
> Let them smile, as I do now,
> At the old forsaken bough
> Where I cling.[16]

James Russell Lowell credited Holmes's revival of his popular series "The Autocrat of the Breakfast-Table" with keeping the first issues of the *Atlantic* afloat. Holmes followed that series with two others, "The Professor at the Breakfast-Table" and "The Poet at the Breakfast-Table." William Dean Howells thought that Holmes's mix of anecdote, aphorisms, poetry, science, philosophy, and narrative constituted a new form he called the "dramatized essay."[17] In Holmes's hands, the dramatized essay gathers a group of people around a table for conversation, while also continuing their individual storylines. The format allows each to pontificate, like the professor himself, on a topic close to the speaker's heart.

While some might think that Holmes Sr. and Jr. shared little else than a name, their ambitions simply took different forms. "The more I live in the world," William James told his younger brother, Henry, four years after Appomattox, "the more cold-blooded, conscious egotism and conceit of people afflict me. . . . All the noble qualities of Wendell Holmes, for instance, are poisoned by them."[18] The same had long been said of the senior Holmes. Whatever Wendell Holmes's quarrels with his father, he respected him enough not to drop the Jr. from his name during Holmes Sr.'s lifetime.

Apart from the notable exception of his son, "My Hunt after 'the Captain'" won broad praise from *Atlantic* readers. Over time, Holmes Jr. amended his father's account. When asked "How are you, Boy?" he claimed to have answered, "Boy, nothing."[19] Apocryphal or true, his reconstruction of the family history differs markedly from his father's version in both detail and tone. His would always be a generation set apart by war: "The soldiers of the war need no explanations," he said in one of his most memorable speeches, "In Our Youth Our Hearts Were Touched on Fire": "They can join in commemorating a soldier's death with feelings not different in kind, whether he fell toward them or by their side."[20] To honor those who died in battle, he drank a ceremonial glass of wine on the anniversary of Antietam each year until his death at ninety-three.

Though he wrote largely about the law for students of the law, Wendell Holmes Jr. captured the country's mood when he observed that the "life of the law" grew from experience rather than logic. Experience and logic each presented a set of choices with any number of consequences and results, and each proved to be more random and morally relative than assumed. One of the founders of what has been called "sociological jurisprudence" and later "legal realism," Holmes discovered through systematic study that judges trying to apportion damages in a liability case tended to rationalize their decisions by citing other cases. He recognized, in other words, the unacknowledged judicial practice of precedence. Contrary to the thinking of his time, he saw the law as a living, subjective entity. "The felt necessities of the time," as he explained in *The Common Law* (1881), "the prevalent moral and political theories, intuitions of public policy, avowed or unconscious, even the prejudices which judges share with their fellow-men, have had a good deal more to do than the syllogism in determining the rules by which men should be governed."[21] Put another way, the law is not fixed or innate, since it responds to social, political, and economic pressures.[22] This belief led Holmes to the far-reaching conclusion that the law "embodies the story of a nation's development through many centuries."[23]

In their own ways, Oliver Wendell Holmes Sr. and Jr. address the postwar dispensation in which reality became more idiosyncratic. Holmes Sr.'s protagonist of "The Professor at the Breakfast-Table" argued that every individual holds religious beliefs peculiar to themselves, that one person's "truth must always differ from" another's.[24] The solution to differing beliefs lies in an individual's having the freedom to choose an ethical course of behavior. The father's and son's differing accounts of their reunion underscore a larger problem about the fallibility and manipulation of memory. As the nation grappled with the legal status of renegade states and newly freed men and women, it also faced the extraordinary challenge of inventing a new national story. One smaller story concerns Oliver Wendell Holmes Jr., who, seeing President Lincoln in his trademark stovepipe hat exposed on a parapet at Fort Stevens, shouted, "Get down, you damn fool, before you get shot." According to Holmes, Lincoln responded, "I am glad you know how to talk to a civilian."[25] The repeated telling of this or any story may have less to do with its accuracy than its being a good contribution to the historical record.

When Oliver Holmes Sr. helped to found the *Atlantic*, he had a humanist's belief in the lessons of history and the power of words. Before the end of the Civil War, he saw a new breed of photojournalists like Mathew Brady challenging these assumptions. In "Doings of the Sunbeam" (July 1863), Holmes contemplated the constructed nature of narrative through the field of photography:

> Let him who wishes to know what war is look at this series of illustrations. These wrecks of manhood thrown together in careless heaps or ranged in ghastly rows for burial were alive but yesterday. How dear to their little circles far away most of them—how little cared for hereby the tired party whose office it is to consign them to the earth! . . . Many, having seen it and dreamed of its horrors, would lock it up in some secret drawer, that it might not thrill or revolt those whose soul sickens at such sights. It was so nearly like visiting the battlefield to look over these views, that all the emotions excited by the actual sight of the stained and sordid scene, strewed with rags and wrecks, came back to us, and we buried them in the recesses of our cabinet as we would have buried the mutilated remains of the dead they too vividly represented. Yet war and battles should have truth for their delineator.[26]

As so often in his life, Holmes was decades ahead of his contemporaries and foresaw, perhaps more than his fellow scientists, the social and moral implications of technology. He suggests, for example, that the very power of images might ensure their being set aside or buried in drawers—as many were, or used for the glass in greenhouses. He knew that the manipulation of photographs pointed toward the manipulation of any kind of spoken or edited account. Brady's haunting battlefield photographs illustrate Holmes's point. Designed to document the war, they were actually compositions whose various elements had been arranged for heightened effect, including the corpses of soldiers slaughtered at Antietam. Viewing Brady's photographs of Antietam, however, Holmes did not question their truth. He had gone there looking for his son, and the "sight of these pictures," he wrote in the *Atlantic,* is a commentary on civilization such as a savage might well triumph to show its missionaries."[27]

Holmes Sr. knew that not only the war but technology had changed ways of seeing. The front page of *Harper's Weekly* 2 August 1862 issue carried, for example, a stunning, full-page wood engraving of black workers cutting the canal opposite Vicksburg. Laborers move in concert as they dig their way through overarching trees and thick vegetation toward the promise of victory. Except in accounts like that of Holmes Sr. and the next generation of realists, the *Atlantic*'s commitment to realism did not extend to the inclusion of costly illustrations. *Harper's Weekly*, by contrast, employed artists like Winslow Homer and sent them to the battlefields. Many began their painting careers apprenticing for commercial lithographers. Their drawings went to a team of carvers, each working on a two-inch square of what would become a larger mosaic. Individual blocks were then screwed together to form a master stamp. Because they gave a sense of immediacy, illustrations conveyed an entirely different sense of authority than the printed word. Their appeal might be gauged by their subscription figures: *Harper's Weekly* had two hundred thousand subscribers to the *Atlantic*'s thirty thousand.

Holmes, father and son, shared the consequences of family misunderstandings just as they shared with war-shaken contemporaries the multiple and contested realities of the war's legacies. The word "reconstruction" describes the period immediately following the war (1865–1877), in which the government tried to legislate, with the Fourteenth and Fifteenth Amendments, a more equitable society—one that gave blacks citizenship and ensured the right of males to vote. For those associated with the *Atlantic*, "reconstruction" took on a broader definition as it applied to the process of re-creating a national narrative out of competing stories.

7

James and Annie Fields

THE BUSINESS OF HOSPITALITY

> She was so intrinsically a charming link with the past and abounded so in the pleasure of reference and the grace of fidelity. . . . He had a conception of possibilities of relation with his authors and contributors that I judge no other member of his body in all the land to have had.
>
> HENRY JAMES, "Mr. and Mrs. Fields," 1915

JAMES T. FIELDS (1817–1881) brought to his editorship of the *Atlantic Monthly* (1861–1871) both a more elastic notion of culture than that of James Russell Lowell and, perhaps most important, the resources of his young wife, Annie West Adams (1834–1915). Fields had an infectious exuberance that made people feel better and brighter in his presence. His Byronic collars and wildly swirling hair dated from the time he hoped to be a poet. Other duties compelled this son of a poor widow from Portsmouth, New Hampshire, to apprentice himself in his early teens to Carter and Hendee, Boston booksellers located on the corner of Washington and School Streets. He remained with the successive owners of the firm, until he became, at twenty-six (1843), a junior partner in the newly christened publishing house of Ticknor, Reed and Fields. The year he married Annie (1854), the firm bore just two names, Ticknor and Fields. Five years later, Fields owned a stake in the *Atlantic Monthly*. In years to come, the name of the firm changed again as it lost and acquired partners: Ticknor and Fields became Fields, Osgood and Company in 1868. It then next merged with Hurd and Houghton (1878), which after buying the *Atlantic* for twenty thousand dollars in 1873, became Houghton, Osgood & Company. In 1880, it combined with the Riverside Press to form a new partnership, Houghton Mifflin & Company. Despite the many changes of fortune, one thing remained constant: the firm's support of its flagship publication, the *Atlantic Monthly.*

As editor, Fields had three related goals. He intended to broaden the magazine's appeal, increase its circulation, and bring to maturity a new crop of authors, many of them women, who studied ordinary people and also the regions which gave rise to their particular, if not peculiar points of view. As the novelist Elizabeth Stuart Phelps testified: "He advocated the political advancement of our sex, coeducation, and kindred movements without any of the apologetic murmur so common among the half-hearted or the timid. His fastidious and cultivated literary taste was sensitive to the position of women in letters. He was incapable of that literary snobbishness, which undervalues a woman's work because it is a woman's."[1]

With the possible exception of Harriet Prescott Spofford's Gothic romance, *Sir Rohan's Ghost* (1860), the *Atlantic*'s collection of women writers concentrated on explicit, largely New England locales; they spotlighted the lonely realities of daily life and introduced a range of unlikely female protagonists, from hired girls to elderly spinsters, whose lives they infused with a quiet heroism. In "Miss Lucinda" (August 1861), Rose Terry Cooke wrote: "I have a reverence for poor old maids as great as for the nine muses. Commonplace people are only commonplace from character. . . . So forgive me once more, patient reader, if I offer you no tragedy in high life, no sentimental history of fashion and wealth, but only a little story about a woman who could not be a heroine."[2] Stories like Cooke's which played with stereotypes of gender and region provided a bridge from more sentimental fiction to realism. Not only did they announce the magazine's New England roots while broadening its appeal; they also portrayed the human consequences of social and economic inequities.

Regional writers set the course for greater realism in American fiction and social criticism. Phelps broke into the *Atlantic* with "The Tenth of January" (1868), a fictional account of the fire that killed scores of mostly immigrant women workers at the Pemberton Mills in Lawrence, Massachusetts. A feminist, Phelps lectured on dress reform in a bathing dress and supported temperance and antivivisectionist efforts with such *Atlantic* works as *A Singular Life* (serialized 1895) and "Loveliness" (August 1899). An equally strong partisan for women's rights, Mary Abigail Dodge wrote under the name Gail Hamilton. She debunked myths about motherhood ("A Spasm of Sense," April 1863) and answered the Rev. John Todd's antifeminist polemic *Woman's Rights* with a book titled *Woman's Wrongs: A Counter-Irritant* (1868).

Fields's championship of literary realism and women writers, who comprised a third of the magazine's contributors, reflected a post-Darwinian, post–Civil War reality, and also the reality of the marketplace, which brought changes in the production, distribution, and readership of American fiction. Book prices had tripled between 1860 and 1865, with inflation showing no signs of lessening. Apart from rising manufacturing costs, the *Atlantic* had to compete for readers not only with *Harper's* and *Putnam's* but also with another seven hundred American magazines. By 1870 that figure had risen more than threefold.[3] Difficult as the situation was for businessmen, it suited authors, who typically had more wares than one source could handle.

By the 1890s, unknown writers could command five to six dollars for a thousand words, while the most popular authors earned as much as $150. "The best literature," an author-editor explained, "now first sees the light in the magazines, and most of the second-best appears first in book form. The old-fashioned people who flatter themselves upon their distinction in not reading magazine fiction or magazine poetry make a great mistake and simply class themselves with the public whose taste is so crude that they cannot enjoy the best."[4] The growing status of magazines had significant consequences for the publishing industry. First, authors could build reputations and support themselves through serial publication. Second, magazines began to be perceived as trendsetters, and magazine editors the new judges of literary standards.

Lowell had envisioned the *Atlantic* as a standard bearer of democracy, without addressing the practical consequences of democratization. For example, he and his friend Charles Eliot Norton never tired of bemoaning the magazine's sloppy grammar and lowering of intellectual content after Lowell's departure. Conveniently forgetting that Norton had criticized Lowell for publishing the "second rate love stories" of women writers, neither considered the alternative: that the magazine would not have survived had it or its parent company continued a policy of holding the "barbarians" at the gate.[5]

Editors like Lowell and Fields who believed in the equalizing powers of literature balanced their knowledge of what books sold against their sense of which were "the best." Trusting that literature should be first and foremost readable, Fields sold the notion of high culture, hoping "to open a market . . . among the unbuying crowd hidden away in the dust holes of our country."[6] The firm brought out a Diamond Edition aimed at feeding the public's addiction to cheap pocketbooks. It was a far cry from their premier Blue-and-Gold Editions, with rich blue covers, gold-page edges, and gold-stamped spines that inspired one poet to write:

> And thanks to you, who put this precious wine,
> Red from the poet's case, in flasks so fine.
> The hand may clasp it, and the pocket hold;—
> A casket small, but filled with perfect gold.[7]

Fields's concessions supported luxuries like the *North American Review*, an earnest, highbrow quarterly that the company bought in 1864 and Lowell and Norton edited at a loss. It was an old joke in publishing that the content of a book deteriorated in proportion to its ornamentation; and Fields, having prided himself on publishing books that bibliophiles praised for the quality of their bindings and the weight of their paper, introduced a second-tier "Red Line Edition" with color-tinted pages. He drew the line at "dime" novels, named after their price, which captivated readers—including President Lincoln—from all age groups and classes. Blaming the often lurid content of dime novels for a general decline in taste and morals, Fields interviewed Jesse Pomeroy, a fourteen-year-old serial killer held in the Charlestown State Prison, about his reading habits. He wanted to know if books about "'killing and scalping injuns' and 'running away with women'" had excited Pomeroy to murder. To his inquisitor's satisfaction, Pomeroy responded, "Yes, sir . . . it seems to me they did."[8]

Fields brought his understanding of middle-class tastes and aspirations to his editorship of the *Atlantic*. He muted the magazine's scholarly tone and reserved more space for serialized novels. Under his leadership, circulation rose to fifty thousand, though it still fell far behind that of *Harper's*. Fields's triumph lay in his genius for combining business and friendship. On his wedding trip to England, he introduced Annie to Alfred, Lord Tennyson, and to the talented but irascible Walter Savage Landor. In Italy, they called on Elizabeth and Robert Browning. As their itinerary suggests, Fields sought out and engaged a string of famous writers. He trumped his competitors by arranging Charles Dickens's 1867–1868 lecture tour of the United States. For Dickens's Boston lectures, the company received a 5 percent commission, and Fields the pleasure of hosting a legend. According to local lore, at parting the men wept in one another's arms.

Fields had made his fortune backing English authors, but with fellow publishers stocking their lists with cheap English reprints, he staked his future and the future of his house on native talent. He had convinced Nathaniel Hawthorne to make a novel out of the short story that became *The Scarlet Letter*, and he stole Henry Wadsworth Longfellow away from Cary & Hart, Longfellow's primary publisher. Between 1857 and 1880, Longfellow published seventy-two poems in the *Atlantic*. Writers like Longfellow, who could afford to, sometimes turned down better-paying magazines and immediate book publication for what one writer called "the company" this periodical kept.[9] Rebecca Harding Davis agreed, crediting the success of *Atlantic* authors to Fields, "the shrewdest of publishers and kindest of men."[10] Like many, she considered "being read by the *Atlantic* audience part of the pay."[11]

Nor did it not hurt that Fields paid *Atlantic* contributors on the acceptance rather than publication of their work. He managed not to lose Richard Stoddard as a contributor, though Stoddard had a reputation for demanding every penny. It was said that Stoddard would have gone to Hades to collect the price of a poem. Fields also won the loyalty of contributors by advancing royalties and reimbursing English authors before international copyright law demanded it. He employed the best printers and bookbinders, publicized the firm and its authors by hosting lavish banquets, and extolled books as if they were patent medicines. Seeing no division between the house and the magazine, he treated *Atlantic* reviews as free advertisements. Authors reviewing for the *Atlantic* followed Fields's policy of quid pro quo. As one writer shamelessly told the publisher, "I puff your books without any regard to their quality."[12] Despite the fine words and apparent gratitude of Fields's authors, they understood the bottom line as well as he.

Fields ran both his business and his house as if they were private clubs. He kept an autograph album, filled with humorous impromptu verses and commendations, on display at the Old Corner Bookstore, where—rumor had it—a stranger could make the acquaintance of all Boston. The gambrel-roofed brick storefront functioned as a club in a city of clubs. One writer quipped, "A man no sooner finds that he is having a good time in Boston than he forms himself into a club."[13] There was the Wednesday Club, not to be confused with the Thursday Club, the Town and Country Club, the Round Table, the Papyrus Club, and the Tavern Club, which along with wine, song, and general high jinks, provided a system of mentoring and ascension not available to women. Spoofing the plethora of clubs, Mark Twain proposed the Stomach Club and the Modest Club, whose qualifications for membership—"aggravated modesty, unobtrusiveness, native humility, learning, talent, intelligence; and unassailable character"—doomed its realization.[14] The men who belonged to Boston's clubs typically had ties to Harvard. Often they lived in neighborhood compounds, insulated by immediate family and cousinships of various kinds. These families tended to intermarry, pooling family resources in trusts and business ventures. Every editor of the *Atlantic*, for example, reviewed, published, and employed friends and fellow club members, who returned the favor by talking up the magazine.

Atlantic contributors, both famous and up-and-coming, stopped by the bookstore to chat with Fields, who did not need much persuading to desert the little green-curtained corner that served as his office—or to perform his famed parlor trick of accurately predicting which customer would purchase what book. His house on Charles Street was more exclusive but no less full of guests. Technically it belonged to the firm, which rented it to Fields for eleven hundred dollars a year and offset his entertaining expenses by taking a hundred dollars off the charge.

If Boston was the hub of the universe, then Fields's house was the hub of the hub. Generations of writers came knocking, from William Makepeace Thackeray to Henry James and Willa Cather. James called the house, the gardens of which sloped down to the Charles River, a "waterside museum." Every corner had its treasure: an autographed copy of Byron's poems, a locket of Keats's hair, a portrait of Alexander Pope by Sir Joshua Reynolds, or a volume of Pope once owned by Abraham Lincoln. When one friend first stepped into the moss-green library, which ran the whole length of the house with alcoves like bookends on either side, she felt surrounded by an "enchanted wood" belonging to "a rarer race of beings."[15] Cather too remembered "the long, green-carpeted, softly lighted drawing room and the dining-table where Learning and Talent met, enjoying good food and good wit and rare vintages, looking confidently forward to the growth of their country in the finer amenities of life."[16] With "relics and tokens so thick on its walls as to make it positively, in all the town, the votive temple to memory," 148 Charles Street offered a haven from contemporary life.[17] These sepia-colored memories do not, however, do justice to the hosts or their house, which brimmed with "jollitude" after the doors closed and guests like Harriet Beecher Stowe felt free to be themselves.[18]

Friends conceded that there were "doubtlessly other homes as interesting, as enviable," but no other had Annie Fields, whose youth and shy beauty made her popular among her husband's client-friends. One enthusiast described her hair as dark, breaking waves "full of glancing golden lights." Most noted the rich, soothing sway of her voice as she read for their entertainment.[19] Because she filled every room of her house with fresh blossoms, intimates nicknamed her "Mrs. Meadows" and "Flower." Annie played both a practical and a symbolic role for the *Atlantic*. Apart from advising her husband, she created an oasis of civility and fellowship. Her veneration of the arts and artists lent an air of glamour and higher purpose to the commercial aspects of authorship.

Ann West, who had known James T. Fields almost as long as she could remember, had received the perfect training for her job as Mrs. Fields. She attended George B. Emerson's School for Young Ladies (run by the Concord philosopher's brother), where she studied Latin, French, and Italian, science, practical mathematics, and the classics. "Rich in reference and quotation," she harbored secret writing aspirations of her own.[20] Willa Cather recognized a quality in Annie that few others did. "No woman could have been so great a hostess," she writes, "could have blended so many strongly specialized and keenly sensitive people in her drawing-room, without having a great power to control and organize."[21] In 1902, the critic Helen Winslow would declare that there was "no power in Boston today like that of Mrs. Fields."[22]

James and Annie Fields built their relationship on a common devotion to literature. In her diary, Annie describes a perfect July day she and her husband passed at their Cape Ann summer home in Manchester, Massachusetts. Annie invited her "dear boy" to a shaded "nook in the pasture" where they could hear and glimpse the ocean and plunge their feet "into the cool delicious grass." With the Atlantic before them, Annie read him Henry James's "Compagnons de Voyage." At its conclusion, she felt a strange impulse to weep, "not from the sweet, low pathos of the tale," she said, "but from the knowledge of the writer's success. It is so difficult to do anything well in this mysterious world."[23] Fields accepted the story that so moved his wife. Personally he thought its young author "precociously dismal."[24] "Compagnons de Voyage" appeared in the *Atlantic* under its American title, "Traveling Companions" (November and December 1870).

More than one writer thought that the *Atlantic* came into full being under Fields's fostering. As the anecdote about Henry James suggests, however, Fields and his wife worked in concert, with little separating their personal from their professional lives. Annie Fields had the power to open or close the door to her husband's publishing house as well as the house on Charles Street. At a time when women had become more prominent as writers and consumers of literature, her husband particularly counted on her for the "woman's point of view." She supplied that and more by soothing chaffed egos, providing assistance with research and proofs, and keeping a perpetually open house, which people like Sophia Hawthorne and her children took as their private hotel for otherwise unaffordable visits to Boston. Those who tried to use Annie as a conduit to her husband underestimated her shrewdness but not often her patience. She was known to murmur, "With a great gift . . . we must be willing to bear greatly."[25] The Fieldses seldom had a night or even a morning to themselves once they began providing breakfasts. Annie served William Dean Howells his first blueberry pancakes. The Fieldses' schedule, not to mention their lack of privacy, would have daunted less hardy souls. "It was Clara Kellogg or Christine Nilsson or Celia Thaxter or Rebecca Harding or Mrs. Stowe, that you found your vis-à-vis at breakfast or at dinner."[26] Yet for many years the combination of business and pleasure made business all the easier. It is one thing to argue with one's publisher about royalty percentages and advertising budgets, and another to abuse the hospitality of a generous host.

Under Fields, the *Atlantic* consolidated a canon of literature based squarely in New England. He balanced competing tastes, expanded circulation, increased advertising, and helped to make authorship a profession as well as a vocation. His greatest gift was perhaps not to the magazine itself but to a younger generation of men and women who in the aftermath of the Civil War would transform American literature.

8

Harriet Beecher Stowe Tests the Magazine

She always spoke and behaved as if she recognized herself to be an instrument breathed upon by the Divine Spirit.

ANNIE FIELDS,
Life and Letters of Harriet Beecher Stowe,
1897

"HER NAME," Annie Fields wrote in her life and letters of Harriet Beecher Stowe, "was a kind of sacred talisman, especially in New and Old England."[1] Even Annie's hyperbole does not quite capture the degree of admiration Stowe excited as the titular head of a global antislavery movement. Visiting England in 1853, she accepted an antislavery petition signed by more than half a million women. The Duchess of Sutherland expressed her admiration with the gift of a gold bracelet fashioned in the form of a slave's manacle. The bracelet consisted of three links, one inscribed with the date marking the end of the slave trade in England, and another with the end of slavery in all English territories. The third link awaited the day the United States would adopt a constitutional amendment abolishing slavery.[2] When Stowe died in 1896, the *New York Times* announced the closing of a chapter in American history in which slavery if not servitude had come to an end.

The friendship between Stowe and Annie Fields began like one of Henry James's novels —in Florence the year before America found itself at war. Annie had attended a reception at a palace on the Arno. "There were music and dancing," she remembered, "and there were lively groups of ladies and gentlemen strolling from room to room, contrasting somewhat strangely in their gayety with the solemn pictures hanging on the walls, and a sense of shadowy presence which seems to haunt those dusky interiors." And there, too, was Mrs. Stowe. Before Annie could gather her wits to say something, Stowe and her entourage of companions had sailed on to the next group: According to Annie, Stowe "was a small woman, with pretty curling hair," "far-away dreaming eyes," and a tendency to become so absorbed in whatever interested her at hand that the rest of the world might not have existed.[3]

Stowe soon repaired her neglect of Mrs. Fields with a call. "Apart from the pleasure," she had "particular *business* to arrange" with Annie's husband: "I have begun a story for the *Atlantic* & want to talk with him about it."[4] After that the families saw each other almost daily at expatriate dinners and readings. Their voyage home on the *Europa*—along with the Hawthornes—took two weeks, long enough to cement a lifelong intimacy between Annie and Stowe, and for Stowe to make final arrangements with the firm for *Agnes of Sorrento*, her historical novel about a young virgin swept up in the political upheavals of fifteenth-century Italy. Fields supported contemporaneous printing of the novel in England's *Cornhill Magazine* and arranged for Stowe to receive half the profits of all book sales. He agreed to pay two hundred dollars for each installment—a rate that doubled her usual *Atlantic* reimbursement and quadrupled the fifty dollars she received for pieces in the company's children's magazine, *Our Young Folks*.

Stowe had every right to expect special consideration at the *Atlantic*, which Moses Phillips might not have supported without her promise to contribute. He hoped that her name would attract some of the 300,000 English-speaking readers who bought *Uncle Tom's Cabin* its first year. Stowe had appeared in the initial issue of the magazine with a story titled "The Mourning Veil," and in the third issue with an article called "New England's Ministers." Ticknor and Fields bought the *Atlantic* as *The Minister's Wooing* reached its penultimate installment in November 1859. Often compared to Nathaniel Hawthorne's *The Scarlet Letter*, *The Minister's Wooing* was a brave book, full of inconvenient truths. Set in the eighteenth century and focusing on New England's participation in the slave trade, it asked, "What shall a man do with a sublime tier of moral faculties, when the most profitable business out of his port is the slave-trade," when "gold made in it was distilled from human blood, from mothers' tears, from the agonies and dying groans of gasping, suffocating men and women"? Stowe pointed out the humbug of missionaries who brought "heathens" to the United States "to enjoy the light of the gospel" and showed how the solace of another woman can give more comfort than a minister's abstractions. "These hard old New England divines," she wrote, "were the poets of metaphysical philosophy, who built systems in an artistic fervor, and felt self exhale from beneath them as they rose into the higher regions of thought. But where theorists and philosophers tread with sublime assurance, woman often follows with bleeding footsteps;—women are always turning from the abstract to the individual, and feeling where the philosopher only thinks."[5] Though Stowe masked her criticism through the mediums of romance and humor, she assailed hierarchies of social, religious, and political power that kept women and blacks in their place. Her novel exemplified the spirit of the *Atlantic*'s founding promises.

However much the male editors of the *Atlantic* commiserated about Stowe's creative spellings of common words, they benefited from her uncanny understanding of popular taste and moral standing. The summer of 1859, they reached out to women contributors by hosting a dinner in Stowe's honor at the Revere House. Conceived as a *bon voyage* before the Stowes sailed again for Europe, the dinner proved to be unusually awkward. After much negotiation, Stowe attended dressed in a Quakerish silk, her hair adorned—as Thomas Wentworth Higginson described it—by "a peculiar sort of artificial grape-leaf garland." Rose Terry Cooke and Julia Ward Howe had sent regrets, leaving Stowe and a very shy, almost speechless Harriet Prescott the lone women. Stowe's request that no alcohol be served "caused some wry faces among the gentlemen, not used to such abstinence at 'Atlantic' dinners," or for that matter at their clubs, which functioned like upscale bars. Despite its being said that those present rivaled the wit of Samuel Johnson's circle, this was not an event when, as Oliver Wendell Holmes wrote, "the atmosphere of intellect and sentiment is so much more stimulating than alcohol that if I thought fit to take wine, it would be to keep me sober."[6] Conversation improved when one of the diners handed his glass to the waiter, who returned it with an amber-colored liquid. For the remainder of the evening the men "*nipped*" at their water.[7] The failure of the evening meant that women would continue to be excluded from all-male dinners where the future of the magazine was discussed and careers assured. As one guest would say of the

Atlantic's experiments with mixed gatherings, adding women was like "adding water to a cup of tea."[8]

Despite the ill-conceived celebration, Stowe needed the *Atlantic* as much as it needed her. Assured of Fields's goodwill, she tended to put his projects behind those of less amicable editors. She reserved the right to sell elsewhere, giving her Maine novel, *The Pearl of Orr's Island*, to the *Independent*, for example, though it had been promised to the *Atlantic*, which had to make do with the less popular *Agnes of Sorrento*. Fields extended the same courtesies to her that he extended to Nathaniel Hawthorne, including access to monies not yet earned. When her son enlisted as a second lieutenant in the Massachusetts Heavy Artillery in 1862, the firm advanced the cost of his uniform and equipment ($250) against his mother's account. Annie grumbled in her diary about what she perceived to be her friend's cavalier behavior about finishing *Oldtown Folks*, for which she received a ten-thousand-dollar advance. Though Stowe maintained a fiction with Fields of accepting whatever he deemed fair payment, she dictated the financial terms of their transactions and even acted as an agent for her "old Rabbi" of a husband, Calvin Stowe. Yet Fields lost Calvin's best-selling book, titled *Origin and History of the Books of the Bible*, to the Hartford Publishing Company, which sold twenty-five thousand copies in six months. The *Atlantic* settled for a chapter on the Talmud (June 1868).

In the 1860s, the *Atlantic* carried Stowe's *House and Home Papers* (1864), followed by the *Chimney-Corner* series (1865–1866), which sold ten thousand copies by 1868. Stowe thought of the *Chimney-Corner* pieces as sermons that preached a doctrine of altruism to the armies of women mourning their Civil War dead. She advised them to devote themselves to nursing hospitalized veterans and schooling former slaves.

These dramatized essays about domestic tensions, and more practically about the buying of carpets and stoves and middle-class accoutrements for the parlor, might be seen in the same light as Oliver Wendell Holmes's *Autocrat* series. For the *House and Home Papers*, Stowe settled on a male narrator named Christopher Crowfield. The first essay, titled "Ravages of the Carpet" (January 1864), shows how material additions to a home can make it just a house. One purchase requires another until the Crowfields' comfortable parlor becomes too "nice" for the family. Of his redecorated parlor, Crowfield says:

> It was as proper and orderly a parlor as those of our most fashionable neighbors; and when our friends called, we took them stumbling into its darkened solitude, and opened a faint crack in one of the window-shades, and came down in our best clothes, and talked with them there. Our old friends rebelled at this, and asked what they had done to be treated so, and complained so bitterly that gradually we let them into the secret that there was a great south-room which I had taken for my study, where we all sat, where the old carpet was down, where the sun shone in at the great window . . . and the wood-fire crackled, in short, a room to which all the household fairies had emigrated.[9]

Stowe's *House and Home Papers* spoke to an increased emphasis on consumerism, which she managed at once to make both alluring and displeasing. Edith Wharton would repeat her warnings in *The Decoration of Houses* (1897) when she remarked that a man found more comfort at his club than in his wife's drawing room. "Hang it," a new husband says on his way to Delmonico's in Stowe's second installment, "a fellow wants a home somewhere!"[10] Stowe's preaching did not stop her from building a mansion at Nook Farm any more than Wharton's halted her construction of The Mount in Lenox, Massachusetts. The success of her *House and Home Papers* (1864) led Stowe to propose working exclusively for the magazine. "I had rather write for the Atlantic sole & only," she told Fields, who accepted her offer, "than to write for several if I can do as well by it." Apart from royalties, Stowe received twenty-four hundred dollars a year.[11]

Stowe's friendship with Annie, which spanned thirty-four years, predictably centered on the *Atlantic*. Stowe counted on Annie to read proof, provide descriptions and recipes, run an occasional errand, and intercede with Fields when she needed more time or an advance on royalties. For one of the *House and Home Papers* (July 1864), Stowe wrote Fields: "Please let Annie look it over & if she and you think I have said too much of the Waltham watches [Stowe urged her readers to buy American products] make it right—also—insert what I had to leave blank the number of *The Atlantic* in which the article appears. . . . If Annie thinks of any other thing that ought to be mentioned & will put it in for me she will serve both the cause & me."[12]

The public could not sustain the pitch of its antebellum admiration for

Stowe, who came to symbolize a past many wanted to ignore or forget. Time, as always, contributed to her eclipse. Annie would recall her friend reading *Uncle Tom's Cabin* to an audience that could barely remember the Civil War. But apart from the vagaries of time, Stowe contributed to the diminishment of her own reputation by delivering "a story which would have suited and delighted the taste of a Borgia family circle . . . into every household in the United States."[13] Her botched attempt to defend the widow of Lord Byron against the slanders of a former mistress brought drastic repercussions for the *Atlantic Monthly*.

The magazine had weathered other public relations blunders. Reviewers called Charles Reade's novel *Griffith Gaunt: or, Jealousy* (December 1865–November 1866) "an unpardonable insult to morality" for its acknowledgment of female sexuality.[14] That English critics took the novel in stride says much about America's lingering Puritanism. *Atlantic* readers frequently objected to the elder Holmes's dismissal of incompetent clergy and even to his interest in psychology. *The Guardian Angel* (January–December 1867), whose orphaned heroine revolts against the tyranny of Calvinism, inspired a spate of cancelled subscriptions. One reviewer explained that Holmes had "succeeded in irritating and repelling from the magazine many who had formerly read it with pleasure."[15]Amelia Holmes wished that her husband—who dedicated the novel to his publisher, James T. Fields, "a wise, faithful, and generous friend"—would stop writing entirely because he created such an uproar. But nothing Holmes did to drive away subscribers came close to Stowe's blunder.

Stowe's infatuation with the wife of Lord Byron, whose magnificent poems were offset by his reputation for libertinism, began in 1853. "She is of slight figure," Stowe wrote, "formed with exceeding delicacy. . . . No words addressed to me in any conversation hitherto have made their way to my inner soul with such force as a few remarks dropped by her on the present religious aspect of England—remarks of such quality as one seldom hears." When Stowe returned to England four years later, Lady Byron confided the sensational story of her husband's affair with his half-sister, Augusta Leigh. The confession profoundly affected Stowe, who left "with a strange sort of yearning, throbbing feeling": "You make me feel quite as I did years ago, a sort of girlishness quite odd for me."[16] Lady Byron had extracted a promise from Stowe to defend her reputation should the occasion arise.

Lady Byron died in the spring of 1860. Nine years later, with Fields abroad and after much discussion among the *Atlantic*'s inner circle, Stowe honored her promise by publishing "The True Story of Lady Byron's Life" (September 1869). She felt compelled to act after reading a review of a book by Byron's last mistress, the Countess Guiccioli, which blamed Lady Byron for her husband's straying. Stowe's rebuttal of Guiccioli's portrait might not have excited attention without this sentence about Byron's incestuous relationship with Augusta: "He fell into the depths of a secret adulterous intrigue with a blood relation, so near in consanguinity that discovery must have been utter and expulsion from civilized society."[17] Stowe told William Dean Howells, Fields's assistant editor since 1867, that she trembled at what she was doing, but she felt compelled—as she wrote in her essay—to save "the youth of America" from "that brilliant, seductive genius" whose "better feelings [were] choked and overgrown by the thorns of base, unworthy passions."[18] Others suspected her of more material motives. Yet knowing that the entire support of her family fell on her for the next few years, Stowe decided "that justice demands it of me, & I *must* not fail."[19]

No one at the *Atlantic* anticipated the backlash, though someone might have remembered the British public's reaction to the Byrons' separation years earlier. When Byron departed from Piccadilly for Dover, people had lined up to get a glimpse of the reprobate. With Fields abroad, Howells sought the advice of James Russell Lowell and Oliver Wendell Holmes. As fate or temperament would have it, Lowell voted against publication, Holmes for. (Lowell believed that incest occurred in "lonely farmhouses and not in cities swarming with public women.")[20] The responsibility for the decision lay immediately with Howells, who after wrestling with his conscience, went forward with the publication.

Holmes speculated that Howells lacked the courage to tell Stowe no. Howells told his father that "always supposing that she has producible evidence in support of her story, I don't see why it shouldn't have been told." His decision turned out to be the greatest miscalculation in an otherwise brilliant career. Since Stowe had nearly every fact in her essay wrong, including the length of Lady Byron's marriage, the vague allegation of incest lost power. Her violation had to do with "taste," rather than morals, and made her appear to be a scurrilous libeler. Echoing Stowe, Howells defended his decision to his father, saying that "the world needed to know just how base, filthy and mean Byron was, in order that all glamour should be forever removed from his literature, and the taint of it should be communicated only to those who love sensual things."[21] Howells reported to Fields that "Mrs. Stowe's sensation of course benumbs the public to everything else in it. So far her story has been received with howls of rejection from almost every side where a critical dog is kept." Rather wistfully, he assured his employer that "I haven't got into difficulty with any one, made you enemies or changed the general policy of the magazine."[22]

Shortly after Howells wrote to Fields, Stowe and her publisher came under attack in the religious press. A notice in the *Independent*, which counted Stowe among its contributors, accused her of gross opportunism:

> An authoress of her reputation gets hold of a disgusting story about Byron—a story which, true or false, is revolting and obscene. She sells it to a publisher; and for weeks before its appearance the press is inundated with little preliminary puffs, whetting and goading on the meanest curiosity on the part of the public. The coming disclosures are advertised, announced, heralded, and trumpeted everywhere; and, of course, the result is a tremendous success . . . and the circulation of the magazine is thereby made enormous.[23]

Elizabeth Cady Stanton, the women's rights activist and editor of *Revolution*, rose to Stowe's defense. Stanton saw both the response to Lady Byron and to Stowe as part of the public's general degradation of women. To her and other feminists, Stowe had exposed abuses in marriage that needed to be addressed.

Fields's plan to have the British magazine *Macmillan's* simultaneously publish Stowe's article exacerbated the controversy. As if undesirable publicity were not enough, the executors of Lady Byron's estate accused Stowe of publishing unauthorized materials and irredeemably damaging their client's memory. Meanwhile, British critics took her censure of Byron as a condemnation of their nation, while American critics blamed Stowe's lapse of taste on her adoration of royalty. The transatlantic potshots at Stowe were gathered in a book titled *The Stowe-Byron Controversy: A Complete Résumé of Public Opinion, with an Impartial Review of the Merits of the Case*. Needless to say, Ticknor and Fields did not publish it. Although Charles Dickens declined to contribute, he allowed himself a blast to Fields: "Wish Mrs. Stowe was in the pillory."[24]

One of the *Independent*'s predictions did not come true. The "story which would have suited and delighted the taste of a Borgia family-circle" failed to swell the *Atlantic*'s circulation figures. On the contrary, Fields learned when the smoke cleared that the magazine had lost fifteen thousand, or nearly a third, of its fifty thousand subscribers. A lesser man than Fields might have fired Howells, who never came to terms with his own folly and, in retrospect, blamed Stowe. "She was quite the person to take *au grand serieux* the monstrous imaginations of Lady Byron's jealousy and to feel it on her conscience to make public report of them when she conceived that the time had come to do so."[25]

With "The True Story of Lady Byron's Life," the *Atlantic* squandered some of the moral high ground that marked its founding. Taking Oliver Wendell Holmes's advice that the battle needed to be fought in England, not in the United States, Stowe published through Sampson Low & Son, of London, an explanation for English readers called *Lady Byron Vindicated: A History of the Byron Controversy, from Its Beginning in 1816 to the Present Time* (1870). "This is war to the knife," she wrote James Osgood, "—& the enemy are perfectly unscrupulous."[26] On 30 December 1869, the *New York Times* published her introduction to the book, in which Stowe asked whether any man would refuse to clear his mother's name or any woman her sister's. Dismissing her plea, reviewers could not accept the idea that Lady Byron would remain with her husband for three years trying to save his soul after she discovered the nature of his relationship with Augusta.

In 1882, friends of Stowe and the magazine gathered at The Old Elms, the Newtonville home of William Claflin, Massachusetts's former governor and a recently retired U.S. congressman, to celebrate the anniversary of her seventieth birthday. The party followed the usual format of *Atlantic* dinners hosted by Henry Houghton. John Greenleaf Whittier, Rebecca Harding Davis, and Oliver Wendell Holmes, Stowe's supporter during the Byron scandal, recited poems in her honor. The tributes inevitably focused on the personal as well as historical importance of *Uncle Tom's Cabin*. Joel Chandler Harris, who claimed to have read *Uncle Tom's Cabin* "on the plantation where Uncle Remus held forth," acknowledged Stowe's influence on Southern writers like himself. Frederick Douglass sent his regrets and a letter praising her vision: "Hers was the word for the hour, and it was given with skill, force, and effect. Let us honor her birthday, and hold up her example of great talents devoted to a great cause to the appreciation and edification of present and future generations."[27] When the time came for Stowe to thank friends, she made a point of noting, as if with Douglass in mind, the extraordinary progress of freed slaves since the Civil War.

In 1889, Stowe's family objected to Florine Thayer McCray's biography of Stowe, which mentions her interest in spiritualism and competed with her son Charles's own biography. In the introduction to *Harriet Beecher Stowe, the Story of Her Life*, Charles Stowe explains that his is not an ordinary biography, for it tells less what his mother did than what she was. Not shying away from the firestorm that jeopardized his mother's reputation, he wrote that both he and his father had tried to persuade her from "dragging out into the light of day a scandal so reeking with moral rottenness as to befoul each and every mind that should come in contact with it. . . . A colder and more cautious nature might have acted very differently under the circumstances," but she could not stand by and see a friend outraged.[28]

The *Atlantic*'s publication of "The True Story of Lady Byron's Life" brings into relief changing social mores and literary tastes. Readers did not respond to the image of Lady Byron, bereft of all guidance but God's, battling with the "fiends of darkness" for "her husband's soul."[29] To her contemporaries, Stowe had committed an unpardonable violation of manners; to a younger generation, including the controversial poet Algernon Charles Swinburne, she was a "filthy female moralist" who had defamed the defenseless dead.[30] In the face of unwavering criticism, Holmes comforted Stowe by noting that "Guiccioli fanciers" would naturally resent good women, such as Lady Byron and herself, who elevated "the standard of humanity at large, and of womanhood in particular." "The scum," as Holmes called the supporters of Byron and his mistress, were rising to the surface.[31] Stowe's error of judgment became part of *Atlantic* lore, but disastrous as it was, the magazine eventually recovered. By 1922, the year that Katherine Fullerton Gerould published "Men, Women, and the Byron-Complex," the furor over Stowe's article seemed quaint. Gerould joked that no past or present woman, whether friend or foe, has yet managed to keep her head about Byron—Mrs. Stowe certainly included.

9

Battle of the Books

We found Gail Hamilton a most comfortable and desirous guest to have in the house. . . . I had no idea there was such a sensible woman of letters in the world. She is just as healthy-minded as if she had never touched a pen.

NATHANIEL HAWTHORNE to James T. Fields, 1 July 1862

MARY ABIGAIL DODGE, who wrote under the pen name Gail Hamilton, thought herself lucky in her publisher. Ticknor and Fields was the country's premier press, and the *Atlantic*, which carried more than two dozen of her essays, its best monthly. To James T. Fields, Hamilton, with "a thought, an opinion, an epigram for everything," appeared an obvious successor to Oliver Wendell Holmes.[1] Yet someone who was intimidated, to quote one of Hamilton's admirers, by neither "the spectacle of the judge, nor the surplice of the priest" made him wary.[2] For once he and his wife disagreed, with Annie delighting in Hamilton's iconoclastic high jinks. When Annie had visited Hamilton at her country home, she saw her rescue two chicks in a sudden storm. Yellow hair whipping about her face, the chicks nestling in fists against her chest, and the wind pinning her in place, Hamilton threw back her head and laughed. Annie knew on the spot that they would be friends.

Asked to describe herself for a book on eminent women of the day, Hamilton poached a few lines from Edgar Allan Poe's poem "The Bells." "I am," she wrote:

> Neither man nor woman
> I am neither brute nor human,
> I am a ghoul!

Hamilton thought herself marred after a childhood accident left her blind in one eye. She half-seriously told a friend: "Thee says thee cannot look in Annie Fields' face and blame her for anything, but thee makes up for it the moment thee looks in my face."[3] Contemporaries attributed Hamilton's "ghoulishness" solely to her tongue. "Was she suckled, like Romulus and Remus, by a she-wolf in her infancy?" her biographer asks. "Were vipers her cherished toys in childhood?"[4] Fields and even Annie would have to answer with a resounding yes.

Hamilton took her pen name from her hometown of Hamilton, Massachusetts, where she grew up on a farm and attended school in Ipswich. She began writing poetry and sketches when teaching and edited *Wood's Magazine*. A cousin of Senator Blaine's wife, she passed several seasons in Washington, D.C., writing editorials and leading a Bible class, open to people of all faiths. According to friends, Hamilton's one foible, apart from excessive frankness, was a love of fancy dress. Hamilton may have been more honest. "The trouble with me," she said, "is that I like" every living thing, even flies. "I think a fly is real good company. . . . How do you suppose life presents itself to a fly? When they get too numerous for comfort, we just buy a little poison paper, and death comes to them with no dread or fright, only as a fragrant and luring feast—a sweet intoxication. Oh, I wouldn't give up the flies for anything!"[5] When the Fieldses' friendship with Hamilton ended abruptly in February 1868, they felt rather like the flies she describes.

The quarrel—or "battle," as it came to be known—began with an article in the *Congregationalist* called "Pay of Authors," which stated that the average author received a full 10 percent return on a book's retail price. After mulling the figure over, Hamilton wrote Fields asking for an explanation of her royalties. The facts, as she understood them, were these: after the first run, Fields had paid her a 10 percent royalty (amounting to two thousand dollars) on all volumes of the collection *Country Living and Country Thinking*. For her next three books, because of the war and uncertainties in the trade, she had agreed to accept fifteen cents per copy. At the time, fifteen cents equaled the 10 percent royalty, but as the price of her books rose, the percentage of her overall royalty had dropped. When the market improved, neither she nor Fields renegotiated their oral agreement, and the house continued to pay her at the lower rate.

Fields made the mistake of ignoring Hamilton's query about royalties for weeks. He dismissed its threat that perhaps she should consult a friend who was also a judge; and when he did answer, his explanation—that the firm spent more on publishing and advertising her books than that of an "average" author—put her on the defensive. Hamilton might have stewed in silence if she hadn't heard that Hawthorne's widow, Sophia, felt cheated too. Sophia's case was different but no less unpleasant or damaging to Fields's reputation and morale. He prided himself on his friendship with her husband and had vigorously promoted his books and reputation with the publication of *The Scarlet Letter*. "You smote the rock of public opinion on my behalf" is how Hawthorne phrased the efforts of the man who almost single-handedly made his career.[6] Fields allowed Sophia's sister Elizabeth Peabody access to his records, in which she found no irregularities. As Elizabeth Peabody wrote Fields, she would be "*happy*" to give her testimony that his business dealings with the Hawthornes had been "legally righteous," if, as she seems to imply, not entirely honorable.[7] The Hawthornes dropped their demands after consulting a lawyer. Gail Hamilton did not, though James R. Osgood, Fields's new partner after the retirement of George Ticknor, offered olive branches in the form of dollars. She insisted on taking the dispute to a board of arbitration.

In the intervening months, the fracas grew nasty, potentially scaring authors away from Ticknor and Fields, as well as the *Atlantic*, which relied on its contributors' willingness to accept modest rates of compensation for greater glory. Fields could not afford for them to feel that they'd been duped. William Ticknor's son, Howard, fired Hamilton as one of the editors of *Our Young Folks*. Fields and others in his firm grumbled about her behavior as they lobbied the public with strategically placed newspaper articles about the unrealistic demands of authors. She, in turn, sent letters to other Ticknor and Fields authors, including Longfellow, Stowe, and Whittier, casting doubt on whether they, too, had received fair compensation. They declined to be involved, which did not stop Hamilton from complaining about "Boston infidelity."[8] From arbitration, Hamilton had hoped to receive all back royalties with interest and three thousand dollars, the cost of preparing her case. The judges played Solomon by granting her $1,250 for the volumes not included in the written contract, which covered *Country Living and Country Thinking*, and a 10 percent royalty thereafter. More important, they absolved Fields of any intention to defraud and scolded both parties for sloppy business practices.

The board's decision further incensed Hamilton, who reiterated her case in *A Battle of the Books*, a scathing history of her "Holy War" against her publisher, which mocks the *Atlantic* for claiming that "there are no business men more honorable or more generous" than Ticknor and Fields.[9] John Greenleaf Whittier scolded Fields for not remembering the capriciousness of women, but he predicted that the public's interest in *A Battle of the Books* would die in nine days.[10]

Fields did everything in his power to make Whittier's prediction a reality. The negative reviews of *A Battle of the Books*, which sold only about fifteen hundred copies, highlight the resources he could marshal to exert financial and social pressure. Hamilton not only lost seven hundred fifty dollars on the book; she also lost the power to negotiate any more than the "average" 10 percent with her new publisher, Harpers & Brothers. A shaken Fields left for Europe. Common wisdom said that given the heartache and publicity, Fields would have been better off paying Hamilton more, while she should have made her peace with less. Although neither combatant delivered a knockout punch, both left the ring battered. Throughout the ordeal, Annie had been alternately bewildered, defensive, angry, and wounded. Against reason, she had hoped to salvage a friendship she sorely missed. When she passed her old friend on Tremont Street, however, Hamilton pretended not to see her.

A Battle of the Books (1870)—"recorded by an unknown author for the use of authors and publishers"—took its epigraph from James Russell Lowell's *Biglow Papers*:

> "Why talk so much dreffle big, John,
> Of honor, when it meant
> You didn't care a fig, John,
> But jest for *ten per cent*?"

In a passage that mocks the self-puffery of editors who think themselves the handmaidens of genius, Hamilton writes:

> Had Messrs. Brummell & Hunt [Ticknor & Fields] gone into the grocery business, for instance, Homer [Whittier] would have been cobbling shoes in Haverhill, or at most, chronicling small beer in a country newspaper. Dante [Longfellow] would have been a lawyer in chambers. . . . Boccaccio [Hawthorne] . . . milking cows at Brook Farm. . . . and as Uncle Tom's Cabin would never have been built, the South would never have been provoked into rebellion; we

should have had no war and no greenbacks . . . and we should all have died comfortably in our beds.[11]

Hamilton's satire focuses in particular on the exploitation of women authors, who are told that "all women need to do is trust" and "all that men care to do is to protect." Justice, she writes, will come only "when writers deal with publishers, not like women and idiots but as business men with business men. . . . Under this law, there is no sex, no chivalry, no deference, no mercy. There is nothing but supply and demand; nothing but buy and sell."[12] Hamilton envisioned a day when women like the *Atlantic*'s Susan M. Francis no longer labored as editorial assistants and women-of-all-trades for a meager salary but instead worked with honor and fair reimbursement. It was to be a long time coming. In later years, Annie Fields would have her own battle over reimbursement with the *Atlantic*'s Horace Scudder.

The battle of the books resumed again under a later *Atlantic* editor—Thomas Bailey Aldrich—with the publication of Julian Hawthorne's memoir, *Nathaniel Hawthorne and His Wife* (1884). Julian's failure to mention Fields's role in furthering his father's career incensed Fields's friends. Aldrich hoped that when Thomas Wentworth Higginson reviewed the book for the *Atlantic*, he would "rap Julian on the knuckles for his shabby treatment of Fields." From the editor of the *Atlantic*, this hope was as good as a directive. Fields informed Higginson that "the literary history of Hawthorne that omits mention of J. T. Fields in connection with the publication of The Scarlet Letter & the later books is no history at all. The whole thing is a little piece of small revenge, growing out of a needless quarrel brought about years ago by the pestiferous Gail Hamilton." The attempt of authors and publishers to manipulate public opinion was of course nothing new. Agreeing with his editor, Higginson called Julian Hawthorne's omission of Fields a petty, "ungenerous whim."[13]

The Fieldses' relationship with Gail Hamilton was an anomaly. Hurtful and surprising as it was to Annie, it paled in relation to her deeply affectionate friendships with Stowe and her two favorite women from northern New England, Sarah Orne Jewett and Celia Thaxter. Jewett, who began writing for the *Atlantic* in 1869, would make a second home with Annie in Boston after James T. Fields's death in 1881. As one friend told the story, "before his death, Mr. Fields suggested Sarah Orne Jewett as a possible friend and companion for his wife in the future; and she gave Mrs. Fields great happiness, spending with her as much time as she could spare from her own delightful home in South Berwick, and adding her own peculiar charm to the house."[14] Annie and Jewett welcomed Thaxter whenever she could stay at Charles Street. Annie's friendship with Thaxter went back to the early days of her husband's editorship. Annie coddled her "Sandpiper," who found little time for herself or her writing while caring for her ailing mother and a disabled son. At the Fieldses' receptions and dinners, Thaxter came in contact with other writers, including Charles Dickens, who encouraged her career. When William Dean Howells first met Thaxter in 1860, he felt stunned by the "creature's beauty" as much as by her poetry: "how richly she made those sea-beaten rocks to blossom [he wrote of Thaxter's home on Maine's Appledore Island]. Something strangely full and bright came to her verse from the mystical environment of the ocean, like the luxury of leaf and tint that it gave the narrower flower-plots of her native isles."[15]

In 1873, Thaxter published *Among the Isles of Shoals*, chapters of which had appeared in the *Atlantic*. Her success brought visitors to the family hotel on Appledore, which locals—refusing to pander to the sensibilities of tourists—still called Hog Island. Thaxter's father, who had come up with the more felicitous Appledore, watched his hotel register grow in direct proportion to his daughter's fame. The *Atlantic* supplied, in addition to priceless free advertising, a steady supply of illustrious guests, from John Greenleaf Whittier to the James Lowells, from the Norwegian musician Olé Bull to the American Impressionist (Frederick) Childe Hassam. It was Thaxter's idea that Hassam drop his first name. His painting of her, titled *In the Garden*, hangs on the second floor of the Smithsonian American Art Museum's East Wing. The islands drew another type of tourist in 1873 after a local man named Louis Wagner broke into a house on nearby Smutty Nose Island and hacked to death its occupants, Anethe and Karen Christensen. Thaxter recounted the crime in her *Atlantic* essay "A Memorable Murder" (May 1875). Anita Shreve would return to the crime in her 1998 novel, *The Weight of Water*.

Many years after Hamilton pretended not to see Annie Fields on a Boston street, Harriet Prescott Spofford offered readers an alternative story to *A Battle of the Books*, which ignored Annie's many offices. Spofford opens *A Little Book of Friends* (1916) with a chapter on Annie and follows it with chapters on other notable women, including one on Hamilton. Returning to the fictional world of love and commerce on which Ticknor & Fields prospered, it continues Annie's tradition of commemoration. Spofford's version of the past, which also serves as a present corrective, differs radically from Hamilton's. It does not, for example, mention the disagreement that ended the women's friendship. Instead it pays tribute, in an age of Freud, to the beauties of female friendship and to an aesthetic that had gone largely out of fashion. With the First World War being waged in Europe, quarrels, petty or otherwise—not to mention books like *A Little Book of Friends*—would seem beside the point. Spofford stood witness to changes she could hardly have imagined when she attended the *Atlantic*'s farewell party for Stowe in 1859. Publishing had become a business like any other. Firms employed compositors, printers, binders, illustrators, distributors, agents, and advertisers. No longer could a house like Ticknor & Fields keep combined accounts of their book and stationers businesses.[16] Authors who delivered books into the outstretched arms of the public existed mostly in fiction—or the memoirs of Fields's successors. Gentlemen publishers were a thing of the past, and authors queued up like day laborers needing to sell their wares to the highest bidder.[17]

II

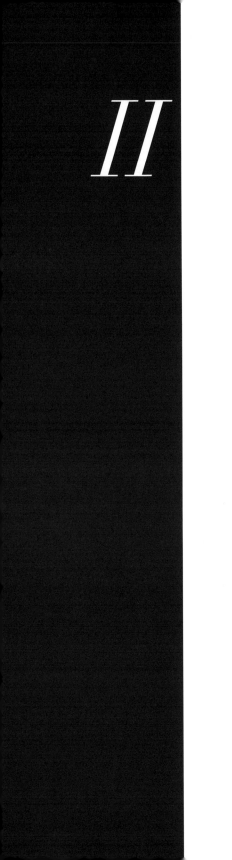

10

Henry David Thoreau, John Burroughs, and a Changing Magazine

The West is preparing to add its fables to those of the East.

HENRY DAVID THOREAU, "Walking," *Atlantic*, June 1862

IN THE EARLY 1860s, when the Civil War escalated and the nation's capital prepared for a possible onslaught of Confederate troops, the *Atlantic* had found inspiration in the majesty of the American wilderness and the nature writing of Henry David Thoreau. Offering both an escape from the daily horrors of war and a source of spiritual renewal, the wilderness reminded the nation of its shared destiny. Readers who followed Thoreau into the "marrow of nature" sought God in the natural world. Thoreau begins his *Atlantic* piece "Walking" with a disarming challenge: "I wish to speak a word for Nature, for absolute freedom and wildness, as contrasted with a freedom and culture merely civil—to regard man as an inhabitant, or a part and parcel of Nature, rather than a member of society. . . . There are enough champions of civilization: the minister and the school committee and every one of you will take care of that."[1] Thoreau's distrust of institutions and governments resonated, in later generations, with such influential leaders as Mohandas Gandhi, William O. Douglas, Martin Luther King Jr., and John F. Kennedy. More immediately, his essays, with their mix of anecdote and natural history, philosophy and poetry, won the praise of Ralph Waldo Emerson and of a man whom readers would affectionately call "the Grand Old Man of Nature," John Burroughs.

Thoreau's response to the natural world might be seen as the opposite of Oliver Wendell Holmes's embrace of the new technologies or Asa Gray's classification of plants, which Thoreau found depressingly scientific. Emerson thought Thoreau held a pagan's "key to every animal's brain, every plant, every shrub." He also had a touch of whimsy. When just a raven-haired girl, full of old Nick, Louisa May Alcott had romped through the woods with Thoreau as her tutor; he told her that fairies used cobwebs as little girls used handkerchiefs.[2] The *Atlantic* began a long tradition of publishing nature essays with Thoreau and Thomas Wentworth Higginson, who contributed essays on flowers and birds, later published in *Out-Door Papers*. Higginson had his disagreements with James Russell Lowell, whom he thought too finicky, but none of his complaints about Lowell matched those of Thoreau. Lowell and Thoreau could not have been more dissimilar. Despite Lowell's soliciting work from Thoreau by way of Emerson, he thought Thoreau a narcissist—and Thoreau, who suffered the indignities of Lowell's editing, returned the compliment. "I could excuse a man who was afraid of an uplifted fist," he wrote Lowell, "but if one habitually manifests fear at the utterance of a sincere thought, I must think that his life is a kind of nightmare continued in broad daylight."[3]

The young William Dean Howells met these literary lights on an 1860 trip to Boston. Lowell affected smoking jackets and Thoreau "fashionless trousers . . . let down too low" for "a quaint, stump figure of a man." Both had classical features, what Howells called noble faces with "a fine aquilinity of profile."[4] And both made him feel very green. Lowell teased him for wanting to claim the seventeenth-century English essayist Sir James Howell for an ancestor, while Thoreau made no effort whatsoever at conversation. As Howells's experience suggests, the two shared an arrogance that boded ill for collaboration. The irreparable break between the satirist and the "mystagogue"—as Lowell called Thoreau—occurred when Lowell deleted from "Chesuncook," part of *The Maine Woods*, a sentence about a pine tree that may have struck him as too romantic or likely to raise the hackles of orthodox readers: "It is as immortal as I am, and perchance will go to as high a heaven, there to tower above me still."[5] Thoreau caught the omission in the proof and asked that it be restored. Lowell ignored his request. "I have just noticed that that sentence was, in a very mean and cowardly manner, omitted," Thoreau wrote Lowell. "I do not ask anybody to adopt my opinions, but I do expect that when they ask for them to print, they will print them, or obtain my consent to their alteration or omission." Thoreau refused to be further "associated in any way . . . with parties who will confess themselves so bigoted and timid as this implies. . . . Is this the avowed character of the *Atlantic Monthly*?"[6] Lowell responded by delaying Thoreau's payment for "Chesuncook." In truth, he never came to terms with Thoreau, though he did not deny that Thoreau managed to write sentences "as perfect as anything in the language. . . . We have said that his range was narrow, but to be a master," Lowell admitted, "is to be a master."[7]

When James T. Fields succeeded Lowell, he had sought to repair the magazine's relationship with Thoreau. Fields, who had the advantage of also being Thoreau's book publisher, advised him to mine his copious lecture notes and journals. Wanting to provide for his family, Thoreau reworked four lectures before he died on 6 May 1862. Extracted from his journals, they appeared in the *Atlantic* as "Walking" (June 1862), "Autumnal Tints" (October 1862), "Wild Apples" (November 1862), and "Life without Principle" (October 1863). Other posthumously published essays included "Night and Moonlight" (November 1863), "The Wellfleet Oysterman" (October 1864), "The Highland Light" (December 1864), and "Winter Days" (January 1885).[8]

The deaths of great men and women always seem to mark eras' ends, or new beginnings. Thoreau's proved no exception. At the end of May 1862, after Confederate forces almost defeated the federal army at Seven Pines, Robert E. Lee assumed command of the Army of Northern Virginia from his predecessor, Gen. G. W. Smith, who had suffered a nervous breakdown. One of the bloodiest battles of the war, Seven Pines shook the nation's confidence. No magazine could repair a frightened union in a brutal war, but readers of the *Atlantic*'s June issue could and did take heart from a phrase from Thoreau's "Walking" that has since become the rallying cry of environmentalists: "In Wildness is the preservation of the world." Thoreau pointed the way toward a new utopia grounded in American experience and soil. "Hope and the future for me are not in lawns and cultivated fields, not in towns and cities," he wrote, "but in the impervious and quaking swamps."[9] "The American wilderness appealed because it was largely unscripted: "The valleys of the Ganges, the Nile, and the Rhine, having yielded their crop, it remains to be seen what the valleys of the Amazon, the Plate, the Orinoco—the St. Lawrence and the Mississippi will produce. Perchance, when in the course of ages, American Liberty has become a fiction of the past,—as it is to some extent a fiction of the present,—the poets of the world will be inspired by American mythology."[10]

Whether or not history has its roots in fictions vital to a nation's understanding of itself, Thoreau set the standard for *Atlantic* naturalists, who saw their field as part of a larger theological discussion about the nature of human beings and their relationship to the environment. Writing twenty years after Thoreau's death, John Burroughs was "not conscious of having any criticism to make of him," though he repeated the commonly held view that he might have borrowed too much from Emerson.[11] Burroughs suffered from similar comparisons to Thoreau. Henry James, for example, thought Burroughs a more sociable, less consequential Thoreau. In his day, however, Burroughs was a respected writer, who argued that science brought God closer by lessening fear of the unknown. "We lose the God of a far-off heaven," he wrote, "and find a God in the common, the near always present, always active, always creating the world anew. Science thus corrects our delusions and vague superstitions, and brings us back near home for the key we had sought afar. . . . We do not banish the mystery of the soul, we only bring it nearer home."[12] His commonsense mix of spirituality and science had broad appeal. John Burroughs Clubs sprang up like so many railroad stops from Massachusetts to California. On Burroughs's seventy-fifth birthday in 1912, schoolchildren laid roses at his feet and danced, while the American Museum of Natural History staged a parade of children costumed as his books.[13] Ironically Burroughs's own father, a hard-nosed religious bigot, read none of his son's essays.

Burroughs grew up near Roxbury, New York, and during the Civil War worked in Washington, D.C., as a clerk in the Treasury Office. Long an admirer of Whitman's verse, he ran into the poet there, and Whitman took him on his round of visits to wounded soldiers. The meeting seemed predestined. So completely did the men's interests, goals, and sympathies overlap that Sunday dinner at the Burroughs's became a regular fixture of Whitman's week. Burroughs later published a study of Whitman largely dictated by the subject himself (*Walt Whitman as Poet and Person*, 1867), and Whitman supplied the title of his 1871 collection of nature writings, *Wake-Robin*.

Burroughs had his first poem, "Expressions," accepted by the *Atlantic* in November 1860, after Lowell decided it had not been lifted from Emerson. Though he wanted nothing more than to write full time, he earned his living as a federal bank examiner until 1874, when he started a fruit farm and vineyard on the Hudson River in Ulster County. His wife, Ursula, would have preferred for him to remain at the bank, according to one biographer, who recounts how she disliked his littering the parlor with crumpled sheets of inferior prose.[14] Though the marriage lasted until Ursula Burroughs's death in 1917, Burroughs had a long liaison with a much younger woman, a physician named Clara Barrus. Burroughs made Clara his literary executor, and in 1920, the year before his death, she would publish *John Burroughs—Boy and Man.*

The appeal of Burroughs's prose lay in its lyrical rendering of precise observation. Does a bird or anything living creature signify nothing? he asked in "With the Birds" (*Atlantic,* May 1865). Using language that manages to be at once intimate and soaring, Burroughs wrote of a thrush he held in the palm of his hand: "I remember its strange ways, the curious look it gave me, its ineffable music, its freedom, and its ecstasy,—and I tremble lest I have slain a being diviner than myself. And then there is its freedom, its superior powers of locomotion, its triumph over time and space."[15] Nature in Burroughs's essays provides the stage and solitude, while the soul—as he stated in nearly every book—must furnish its own entertainment.

Burroughs came to see himself as a literary naturalist, who reproduced nature "tinged with the colors of the spirit."[16] His writings prompted readers like his friend Theodore Roosevelt to support sanctuaries for endangered birds and other wildlife when the popularity of plumes on women's hats threatened pelicans with extinction. But his career was not without contradictions. A friend of the entrepreneurs Harvey Firestone and Henry Ford, he came to forge his own compromises with the present. Written two years before the Spanish-American War, Burroughs's "The Poet and the Modern" (October 1896) presents Whitman as a poetic counterpart to a Firestone or a Ford:

> It was not for Whitman to write the dramas and tragedies of democracy as Shakespeare wrote those of feudalism, or as Tennyson sang in delectable verse the swansong of an overripe civilization.

> It was for him to voice the democratic spirit, to show it full grown, athletic, haughtily taking possession of the world and redistributing the prizes according to its own standards. It was for him to sow broadcast over the land the germs of larger, more sane, more robust types of men and women, indicating them in himself.[17]

Burroughs's essay reflected a growing sense of American purpose and entitlement from someone who, having dismissed automobiles for polluting the landscape, not only befriended industrial giants but accepted the gift of a Model T. Perhaps of all Burroughs's followers and friends, Whitman would have been least offended or surprised: "Do I contradict myself?" he writes in "Song of Myself": "Very well then I contradict myself."[18]

For many Americans living in areas scarred by recent battles or industry, the wilderness offered a reminder of America's exceptionalism. Fitz-Hugh Ludlow, who accompanied Albert Bierstadt to the Sierras, commemorated their stop at Bridal Veil with his *Atlantic* article "Seven Weeks in the Great Yo-Semite" (June 1864), while Bierstadt produced a spectacular painting of the falls (now in the North Carolina Museum of Art) that shows a sunlit veil of water streaming in a pool of light down from a towering ridge. The work of early painters of Yosemite such as Bierstadt, Thomas Moran, William Keith, and Thomas Hill captured the glories of the American wilderness for tourists, who traveled to see the wonders for themselves. The scenes these painters depicted later became part of the National Park system. Congress purchased Moran's painting *The Grand Canyon of the Yellowstone* in 1872 for ten thousand dollars. Following a tour of major American cities, it took its place in the Senate lobby of the Capitol.

The West's hold on the public's imagination had grown in the years after Lincoln's death because it seemed to augur, in the paintings of artists like Moran, a fresh start. In 1866, a historian of the Civil War, Charles Carleton Coffin, told *Atlantic* readers that "while we have been fighting for national existence, there has been a constant growth of the Republic. This is not wholly due to the power of democratic ideas, but owing in part to the native wealth of the country,—its virgin soil, its mineral riches." Coffin went on to write of the vast, unsullied region and its transformation as "pioneers of civilization" broke the "long solitude of the centuries" with "the buzzing of saws, the stroke of the axe, [and] the blow of the hammer and trowel." He looked forward to an era when the United States would lead the world through its commercial example. Coffin argued for the development of the West's seemingly endless supply of land and resources, which not only made the country less dependent on foreign nations but also lowered costs of common goods from coal to groceries. Beyond economic prosperity, technology promised to speed up the assimilation of immigrants by creating more jobs and giving them greater access to national life. "So ever toward the setting sun," he rhapsodized in the rhetoric of manifest destiny, "the course of empire takes its way,—not the empire of despotism, but of life, liberty,—of civilization and the Christian religion."[19]

As railroads made tourism and resettlement possible for more Americans, the drama of the future lay not in Boston, as postwar editors of the *Atlantic* realized, but beyond the Mississippi. In 1866, the magazine responded to the nation's shifting borders by hiring William Dean Howells, an Ohioan, which in those years meant a westerner. The magazine began broadening its definition of literary subjects and base of subscribers. As one writer explained, those who only knew about American frontier life through contemporary journals "can have little idea of the unwritten adventure in the vast Western prairie land, as rife with suggestion for the pen of the novelist and poet as are its Pacific circumvallations for the pencil of the artist."[20]

Fields had come to realize that the magazine needed to include writers and subjects outside New England if it was to reflect changes in American life. In 1870, for example, over half a million people resided in California. That figure increased more than a million by the turn of the century and nearly another million by 1910. Those associated with the *Atlantic* had, from its inception, seen it contributing to general education, which explains the discounts James Russell Lowell offered to teachers and postmasters. The aim succeeded to the extent that regional magazines such as *Land of Sunshine*, *Out West*, and *Overland Monthly* took the *Atlantic* for their model. But there were also those who objected to the *Atlantic*'s apparent monopoly on culture. In 1865, the Reverend I. N. Tarbox wrote a forty-page diatribe challenging high culture and the *Atlantic* in particular. He took exception to the magazine's exclusion of sentimental verse, even though such verses are "often read with moistened eye."[21] Exposing the limits of the magazine's commitment to democracy, he saved his best shot for last: America, he wrote, still awaits a great American magazine.

Perhaps the magazine's greatest challenge lay in defining an American literature rich and flexible enough to embrace a changing population with vastly different tastes. As one writer observed, "We are not yet a People; but we have great, vivid masses of popular life, which a century of literary expression will not exhaust."[22] In "Americanism in Literature" (January 1870), Higginson addressed fears about women's enfranchisement, big-business "brigands," and Chinese immigration before assuring readers that "we are equal to these things, and we shall also be equal to the creation of a literature. We need intellectual culture inexpressibly, but we need a hearty faith still more. 'Never yet was there a great migration that did not result in a new form of national genius.'" Higginson asked readers to forget the nightingale and the skylark in favor of the California jay, the Alabama yellowhammer, and the Minnesota common loon. They should look for writers rising from the carpet mills of Clinton and the granaries of Chicago, and above all should "look beyond our little Boston or New York or Chicago or San Francisco, and be willing citizens of the great Republic."[23]

II

William Dean Howells

DEMOCRACY AT WORK

Perhaps you are permanently engaged at "The Nation" bureau, and dont wish a Boston or Cambridge life, and it may be your present emolument is larger than I could offer you for the place to be filled in our establishment. . . . If you care to come East let me know, and tell me what salary will content you.

JAMES T. FIELDS
to W. D. Howells,
11 January 1866

WHEN JAMES T. FIELDS offered William Dean Howells twenty-five hundred dollars a year to be his assistant, Howells held out for another five dollars a week. He found it disquieting that Fields, who had rejected sections of his *Venetian Life* (1866), chiefly showed interest in his proofreading skills. He also knew that the *Atlantic* maintained an onerous standard of perfection: proofs went from the head reader to the editor, who checked every fact. If possible, they passed next to the author, then back to the editor, who accepted or rejected emendations before sending them on to the printer, the head reader, the editor again, the stereotyper (who made the plates), and finally back to the head reader for any corrections. But after consulting with James Russell Lowell, who brushed aside his reservations, Howells accepted Fields's proposal with the stipulation that he would succeed Fields as editor in chief.

The *Atlantic* had long been his bible, just as Boston had been his desired destination. In *Literary Friends and Acquaintance*, he wrote: "At Boston chiefly, if not at Boston alone, was there a vigorous intellectual life. . . . Every young writer was ambitious to join his name with theirs in *The Atlantic Monthly*, and in the lists of Ticknor & Fields, who were literary publishers in a sense such as the business world has known nowhere else before or since. Their imprint was a warrant of quality to the reader and of immortality to the author, so that if I could have had a book issued by them at that day I should now be in the full enjoyment of an undying fame."[1] His wife Elinor proved less enthusiastic about his leaving the *Nation*, a progressive weekly edited by the brilliant if bellicose E. L. Godkin (and still in business today), which promised, in its prospectus, to "wage war upon the vices of violence, exaggeration, and misrepresentation by which so much of the political writing of the day is marred." Elinor's reasons lay elsewhere. "It does seem retrograding," she wrote her father-in-law, "to go from New York to Boston."[2]

Howells's life had, in a sense, been pointing to the moment he joined the *Atlantic*'s staff. Certain in his twenties that he would be a poet, he had banked his future on an *Atlantic* acceptance and used all his ready cash to make his way to Lowell's doorstep. Lowell had looked him over, plied him with Madeira, and passed him on to Emerson, Hawthorne, and Thoreau. At the now legendary Parker House dinner, Oliver Wendell Holmes turned to Lowell with "sweet and caressing irony" and said of his friend's protégé: "Well, James, this is something like the apostolic succession; this is the laying on of hands."[3] The succession had to wait. During the Civil War, Howells served his country as consul at Venice—a plum received for having written a campaign biography of Abraham Lincoln. Returning to the United States, he accepted the job with the *Nation*. At a New Year's Eve party given by Bayard Taylor, an *Atlantic* travel writer with Ohio roots, he became reacquainted with Fields. Ten days later, Fields offered him the job.

Howells brought to the magazine his extensive experience as a journalist. Instead of Harvard, he attended a "university of the streets," where he saw a poverty of the spirit far more disheartening than any material disadvantages his family had known in backwoods Ohio. It made him want literature to speak for its time and place, even if that meant making poetry less "literary" and journalism more so.[4] Howells brought a unique perspective to the country's leading literary magazine. To him, nothing characterized the *Atlantic* more than its roots in New England Puritanism, and this he thought neither relevant nor vital to the new New England. In one of his most insightful criticisms of the region, he wrote: "The novel is a picture in which the truth to life is suffered to do its unsermonized office for conduct; and New England yet lacks her novelist, because it was her instinct and her conscience in fiction to be true to an ideal of life rather than to life itself."[5] Taking the *Atlantic*'s statement of purpose for his guide, Howells worked to make the magazine more democratic by drawing on writers from every corner of the United States. Yet Howells never forgot that the magazine owed its fame to its original founders; "it was not my part," he wrote, "to guard it against them." Printing nearly everything they sent, he "praised the gods" and swallowed hard.[6] At the same time, Emerson, Holmes, and Whittier proved easier to appease than his own family of would-be writers, particularly his youngest sister, Annie. "I know it will be next to impossible to make a reputation except as a contributor to *The Atlantic*," Annie wrote; "still I know your reasons for keeping me out, are convincing to you."[7]

Howells's previous work as an editor had not prepared him for the assault of friends who enclosed poems in letters asking about his health. He took as many poems as his conscience allowed from a fellow Ohioan John J. Piatt, his coauthor for a volume of poetry titled *Poems of Two Friends* (1859). In the years of growing fame, he remained loyal to early friends. When Lowell worried about having enough money to provide for his grown daughter, Howells reimbursed him above the going rate. He voted for Elizabeth Stuart Phelps's admission to the Academy of Arts and Letters, while poking fun at her style, and urged the admission of William Henry Bishop, who had not written a line in years. "Does a man cease to be an author because he no longer prints?" he asked. "I would have every man who has done good things . . . *welcomed* [underlined three times]."[8] Because of Howells's almost unfailing generosity, the magazine did not always live up to its commitment to feature "the best."

After Fields's resignation in 1871, Howells inherited a magazine that had an unofficial relationship with Harvard. With Lowell, Longfellow, Holmes Sr., and Louis Agassiz serving on the faculty, Ticknor and Fields might have appeared a university press. In 1867, Harvard granted Howells an honorary degree for his editorship of the *Atlantic*, which "endeared him personally to so many scholars." Nineteen years later, the president offered him the chair of foreign literatures previously held by Longfellow and Lowell. He declined this and other academic positions.

Modeled after English universities, Harvard had from its founding in 1636 sent forth ministers. The university changed radically with Charles Eliot's presidency (1869–1909). Enrollment tripled to three thousand students, and the faculty increased fivefold. In a community like Boston, men did business with those they knew at school, and a Harvard education assured certain social advantages. Fathers sent their sons there because their friends and their friends' sons went there. Francis Parkman thought that the *Atlantic*'s founder, Francis Underwood, never received adequate recognition because he was neither a "humbug" nor a Harvard man.[9]

Charles Eliot's appointment divided *Atlantic* contributors. Louis Agassiz, for example, considered him too young; others objected to his being a layman. Emerson hesitated until convinced by Eliot's *Atlantic* essay "The New Education" (February and March 1869). Proposing nothing less than a radical upheaval of the Harvard curriculum, Eliot argued for expanding elective offerings and raising standards for admittance and retention through a more stringent written examination process. His reforms honored performance over accidents of birth and class. A strong believer in living languages, including the study of English when "English" and writing were scarcely recognized subjects, he sought to equip students for what he called "an American man's life."[10]

Eliot took a provincial college and transformed it into a modern university by building its private endowment, professionalizing its programs, and replacing the ministers who had traditionally served on the Board of Overseers with alumni drawn from Boston's professional community. He won the battle to relax conduct codes for students but lost the one to abolish football, which he thought too close to war; and under his presidency, in 1879, Harvard admitted its first class of women.

James Russell Lowell applauded the changes in general education that prepared students "for the duties of life rather than for its business."[11] According to Holmes, who approved the medical school's new emphasis on the practical and experiential, Eliot had turned Harvard "over like a flapjack."[12] The question that Eliot asked *Atlantic* readers—and that Franklin D. Roosevelt and John F. Kennedy posed in their own ways—was "not how much our freedom can do for us unaided, but how much we can help freedom by our judicious education."[13] Eliot understood, as would John Dewey, the American psychologist and later *Atlantic* writer, that educational reform affected every aspect of society; and he imagined Harvard as the research institution it would become in the next century. "True progress in this country," he wrote, "means progress for the world."[14] A hands-on president, Eliot showed up on Howells's doorstep to repeat his request that the *Atlantic* editor offer a series of lectures on modern literature. To this invitation, Howells could not say no.

Howells's overhaul of the *Atlantic* struck someone like Lowell as being no less radical than Eliot's overhaul of Harvard. Though Elizabeth Stuart Phelps sold books in the tens of thousands, Howells no longer felt satisfied with her "gasping shuddering style."[15] Those at the *Atlantic* watched the drama of the marketplace as *Scribner's Monthly* absorbed *Putnam's* in 1870, to be taken over itself by the *Century* in 1881, the year Howells resigned his editorship. As every sign indicated, salvation lay—as the founders had hoped—in transforming a Boston magazine into an American magazine. "Without ceasing to be New England, without ceasing to be Bostonian, at heart," it continued to become, in Howells's hands, more "southern, mid-western, and far-western" in its sympathies.[16]

In the tradition of previous editors, Howells saw himself shaping American culture, which he mainly defined through literature. Under Howells, ironically, "Americanism" reflected the muses of Europe and Russia by way of French translations. In the early to mid-1870s, those eager for essays and fiction with European themes had an abundance of riches. They could read Henry James's story of an American artist in Rome, *Roderick Hudson*, or *A Passionate Pilgrim*, his novella about an American who pushes his claim to a country estate in England. Bayard Taylor, before being appointed minister to Germany in 1878, contributed "Autumn Days in Weimar," while President Lincoln's former secretary, John Hay, contributed *Castilian Days*, a travel book weighted toward politics. The *Atlantic*'s March 1871 issue took the reader from ancient Athens ("Women's Rights in Ancient Athens") to France ("Up and Downs of Bonapartes and Bourbons") and the Orient ("Looking for Pearls"). The article on women's rights in ancient Athens begged comparison with the present. In fact, it would have been difficult to find an issue of the *Atlantic* that did not set up a transatlantic dialogue through its content, and even more in its reviews.

In the mid-nineteenth century, reviewing remained an undeveloped art, designed primarily to sell books, and consisted largely of plot summary and moralities about "truth" or "beauty." The sheer number of reviews foisted on the public led even Howells to wonder whether the public cared for them as much as their editors thought, but, he added, "I have always said this under my breath, and I have thankfully taken my share of the common bounty."[17]

In the 1870s, the *Atlantic* might be seen as a cross between *Scribner's Monthly*, which cultivated a popular audience, and the more academic *North American Review*, which usually offered about a dozen reviews per issue. But that said, it is difficult to make distinctions when writers might publish in all three. *Scribner's Monthly* distinguished itself from the *Atlantic* by devoting approximately twenty pages to discussions of contemporary life, in sections such as "Topics of the Time" and "Home and Society." The *Atlantic* devoted about the same number to reviews of American and foreign literature. The February 1875 issue of the magazine contained, for example, twelve reviews, including "[Théophile] Gautier's Winter in Russia" and "[M. le Baron de] Hübner's Ramble Round the World." That same month *Scribner's* carried an omnibus review of British poets—Robert Buchanan, Dante Gabriel Rossetti, William Morris, and Algernon Charles Swinburne—by the American poet Edward Clarence Stedman, also an *Atlantic* contributor.

Howells, who did the lion's share of the magazine's early reviewing, used his reviews to wean the public away from sentimental or sensational fiction. He introduced them to the work of international writers such as Thomas Hardy, Ivan Turgenev, Émile Zola, and Leo Tolstoy, and American writers like John De Forest, who was known for his realistic portrait of the Civil War. Under Howells's leadership, the *Atlantic* forged an aesthetic that shaped the emerging field of American literary criticism and American novel-making for the next hundred years.

Howells found an early example of realism in Samuel Clemens's *Innocents Abroad*, which he reviewed favorably (December 1869). The author came to meet the anonymous reviewer, who had persistently referred to him as "Clements." Soon the two could be seen striding along Tremont Street talking nonstop and bursting into rowdy laughter. Fellow pedestrians scuttled out of their path, then turned to gawk at Clemens, a wild-looking man with a "crest of dense red hair," wearing his fur coat with the fur exposed, as it would be worn today—but certainly not then.[18] Howells came to feel that he knew his friend as well as anyone, which did not mean fully. Even though "Twain" signed many of his letters "Mark," Howells preferred his given name: Twain "seemed . . . to mask him from my personal sense."[19]

Twain would say that Howells set him on the "royal road to the public."[20] Understanding the power that reviews had in the new magazine age to make or break careers, Howells designed his to speak to both contemporaries and posterity. He knew that books lived as much on authors' personalities as on their contents, and his reviews of Twain frequently began with a miniature portrait of his friend. To Howells, Twain, no less than Henry James, embodied the future of American literature. In his review of *Tom Sawyer*, he predicted that "waves of emigration" extending across the continent would transform Americans' notions of their history and literature in ways as striking, sudden, and positive as the "feverish gallop to California." Knowing that Northern readers associated Missouri (and the Southwest generally) with the *Dred Scott* decision, Howells emphasized the humanity Twain saw in the "shabby little Mississippi River town" where Tom and his boy-gang rule. Howells could not write a review without furthering his campaign for greater realism in literature, and the review of *Tom Sawyer*, which praises the novel's "fidelity to circumstance," was no exception. Tom's St. Petersburg—"with its religiousness, its lawlessness, its droll social distinctions, its civilization qualified by its slave-holding, and its traditions of the wilder West which has passed away"—lives in popular imagination as an actual place. To Howells, "the study of literature as art will not best be pursued by an examination of the masterpieces of American literature, one or two exceptions being made, but as an exponent of American life it offers advantages which we suspect have been too much disregarded by students."[21]

Howells's reviews, with their intimate ruminations on the personal experience of reading itself, allow readers to understand books from the inside out. No matter how much Howells dissected a book's mechanical underpinnings, he remained in awe of an ultimately inexplicable magic. Twain captured the quality of his reviews when he told him that "as a rule, a critic's dissent merely enrages, & so does no good; but by the new art which you use, your dissent must be as welcome as your approval, & as valuable. I do not know what the secret of it is, unless it is your attitude—man courteously reasoning with man & brother, in place of the worn & wearisome critical attitude of all this long time—superior being lecturing a boy."[22] Howells himself explained that the best criticism "gives the critic, as well as the author, to the reader's knowledge."[23] Readers deserve to know, in other words, with whom they're dealing, since critics necessarily assert their personal tastes and prejudices.

At its *very* best, criticism gives a book back to its author in ways that the writer may not have fully understood. After Howells read and edited a final draft of *Tom Sawyer*, Twain "simply hunted out the pencil marks & made the emendations which they suggested."[24] Apart from advising him to cut the last chapter, Howells's most substantive help concerned the book's marketing: he convinced Twain to advertise it as a "boy book" and promised, at the propitious moment, to "start the sheep . . . jumping in the right places."[25] Twain would say of Howells: "He has a peculiar gift for seeing the merits of people, and he has always exhibited them in my favor. He has never written anything about me that I couldn't read six or seven times a day; he is always just and fair."[26] Howells himself saw criticism as a way for one mind to talk to another. He had a reputation for making his rejection letters, small masterpieces of tact and advice, seem like commendations. Again Twain said it best: small people thrive on belittling your ambitions, whereas, the great, the really great, have a gift for making you feel that you can become great too.[27] The *Atlantic* and its parent firm prospered from the men's friendship. Twain's *Innocents Abroad* (1869) sold seventy thousand volumes the first year, and *Roughing It* (1872) sixty-two thousand in four months. In 1875, the magazine serialized "Old Times on the Mississippi," better known by its subsequent title, *Life on the Mississippi*.

As Howells's power grew, so did his critics. The *Atlantic* came under attack for its championship of literary realism in the 1870s. Contributors writing in other veins, whether sentimental, Gothic, or historical, thought the new literary realism an umbrella to push the editor's personal agenda. Harriet Preston, a staple of the reviewing staff, minced no words when it came to Howells, whom she felt in need of deflation.[28] His editing of her review of James's novels removed, to her eye, the slightest hint of criticism. Preston's string of adjectives to describe Howells's character began with "provincial" and "intolerant" and ended with "dictatorial" and "dogmatic." In 1903, Preston negatively reviewed both Howells's *The Kentons* and James's *The Wings of the Dove* (January 1903). James, she accused of conveying "an impression of perpetual innuendo":

> But never, surely, in English drawing rooms or anywhere else, please God! did living beings actually converse after the manner of Mr. James's characters. His people never say anything outright, but carry on their "subtle" communion by means of whispered hints, re-

> mote suggestions, and the finely broken and shyly presented fragments of quite unspeakable epigram. They seldom complete even their own cryptic remarks, but start back as if scared by the sound of their own voices, and the possible dazzle of their own wit; while they shy, like frightened horses, from the faintest adumbration of a serious meaning.

Faulted for his "sociological" approach, Howells fared no better at her hands. Preston described a character in *The Kentons* as "the scum and spawn of a yeasty deep,—the monstrous offspring of barbarous and illicit social relations."[29] Asked as a courtesy if he wanted the review squashed, Howells told Bliss Perry, the *Atlantic*'s seventh editor, to print it.

Preston's response to Howells matched that of the novelist Constance Fenimore Woolson, who spoke for other contributors when she complained that the magazine contained too much of Mr. James and, by implication, too little of Miss Woolson. Yet between 1872 and 1882, the year after Thomas Bailey Aldrich succeeded Howells, Woolson published nine pieces in the *Atlantic*. Although Woolson considered herself a realist, *Atlantic* reviewers faulted her novels *Anne* and *East Angels* for excessive sentimentality, a charge commonly leveled at women writers. Aware of the criticism, Howells noted wryly that there was never too much of a good thing, if it was your good thing. Contributors, who assumed that Howells's preferred "real" stories about "real" people, had a right to be confused. Everyone knew that Howells hated books like *So Red the Rose*, which confined the multitude of human tragedies to unhappy love affairs. Those looking for a precise definition of a catchall term like "realism" (often defined as the opposite of sentimentalism) had to draw their own conclusions. Howells, for example, accepted sentiment as long as an author refrained from shamelessly manipulating readers' emotions, and he liked the fantastic if it exposed the strangeness of ordinary experience. Realism, he told an interviewer, "makes all things its province, the uncommon as well as the every-day affairs of human existence." Asked to list realistic books, he named novels as diverse as Herman Melville's *Moby-Dick* (1851), Rebecca Harding Davis's *Life in the Iron Mills* (1861), Twain's *Tom Sawyer* (1876), and James's *The American* (1877).[30] His own fiction, narrated in an unpretentious, slightly ironical voice, concerns daily incidents of middle-class life. To Theodore Dreiser, Howells's books were realism at its palest. To Mark Twain, they exuded life: "If your genuine stories can die," he told Howells, "I wonder by what right old Walter Scott's artificialities shall continue to live."[31] Scott, though long dead, remained a favorite author, especially with Southern readers.

While the magazine emphasized literature under Howells's leadership, it also increased the number of reviews and essays devoted to painting, architecture, and music. Topics included "the meaning of music" (October 1878), new books on art (July and August 1878), and the Society of Decorative Art ("Open Letters from New York, II," February 1878). William Foster Apthorp, a musician and later the program writer for the Boston Symphony Orchestra, advised Howells, who also sought original scores and lyrics. Welcoming collaborations between poets and musicians, he published "Sunset Song," a score by Julius Eichberg with Celia Thaxter's lyrics, in February 1877.

Of all Howells's innovations, "The Contributor's Club" proved to be the most popular, and also the most democratic to the extent that it opened the pages of the *Atlantic* to anyone who had an axe to grind. Conceived as series of short, anonymous pieces, along the line of letters to the editor, it returned to the days when subscribers enjoyed guessing who wrote what. Contributors received the same rate of pay in the Club as they did for articles or stories. Howells hoped the addition would boost sales by appealing to female readers interested in topical subjects and also by generating a little controversy. "If you know any bright women who are disposed to write in the Club," he told the poet Edmund Stedman, "invite them for me. I much desire the discussion of social matters."[32] Apart from being a testing ground for unknown authors, The Contributors' Club gave regulars additional space. "Spit your spite at somebody or something," he told Twain.[33] Perhaps most important for Howells, the Club helped him to sidestep conflicts of interest. Its anonymity, for example, allowed him to solicit a piece on Canadian Indians from his father, whom President Grant had rewarded for service to the Republican Party with a consulship at Quebec.

Howells announced The Contributor's Club at the beginning of his Editorial for the January 1877 issue and invited "all writers who have minds upon any ethical or aesthetic subject briefly to free them here, and while they will not wittingly suffer a personal spite to be wreaked, they will especially welcome the expression of intellectual grudges of every sort."

He wanted items of public interest that might otherwise go "unuttered in print."[34] Known for his unparalleled willingness to voice unpleasantries, Twain helped launch the Club by supplying a diatribe against Anna Dickinson, an antislavery orator turned actor-playwright. Twain objected to her histrionic portrayal of Ann Boleyn in a play of her own, *Crown of Thorns*.[35] A reporter for the *New York Times* predicted that the Club would restore the *Atlantic* to "the literary superiority of its palmiest days," and it certainly struck a chord with readers. Except for a brief interruption, it lasted for over sixty years, to June 1942.[36]

The Contributor's Club, which usually ran between ten and fifteen pages, can be seen in two entirely different ways. To some extent, its simulation of Boston club life reinforced the image of the magazine's elitism. However, from another perspective, the Club reached out to the country at large by asking readers to engage in conversation. Howells's conception of the Contributor's Club made it a relatively safe vehicle for controversial opinions precisely because they were the opinions of contributors, and therefore not attributable to the editor or the firm. Readers debated the merits of various books, the accuracy of French translations of Russian novels, the benefits of instituting a uniform system of spelling, and whether toasted cheese on bread should be called "rabbit" or "rarebit." Above all, the club focused on the emerging full-time profession of authorship, with advice from correspondents about preparing manuscripts and approaching publishers. One contributor, perhaps Twain, ranted about subsidized postal rates for book manuscripts: "Do you imagine that that 'author' lives who is poor enough to be willing to accept ten cents' worth of this charity of the United States government, with its burden of insecurity, when for a few cents added he can have the trusty services of the express companies? No, indeed. The fact is as I have stated it before: no one ever sends a book manuscript by mail."[37]

Desiring at once to entertain and provoke, writers like Twain pushed the limits of what the magazine usually tolerated. Though nothing stirred readers' ire more than articles that seemed anticlerical, he gleefully took on evangelists in a tongue-in-cheek review of the Rev. Edward Payson Hammond's *Sketches of Palestine*. Known as "the children's evangelist," Hammond wrote over a hundred hymns and tracts, including "Little Ones in the Fold" and "The Children's Guide to Heaven."[38] Twain quoted the opening lines of Hammond's poem, which described his wedding journey to the Holy Land. Written to the rhythm of Longfellow's *Hiawatha*, they read:

> Then they landed at Niagara.
> There they heard their Master calling,
> "Go and work within my vineyard,
> And my presence shall go with thee."
> Quickly they obeyed the summons.
> On the shore of Lake Erie.[39]

Twain wonders if Hammond paid critics to sing his praises. He brings up a touchy point. In January 1877, his friend Bret Harte was very much in the public's mind because of a scandal surrounding the reception of Harte's play *Two Men of Sandy Bar*. Apart from Twain, the play failed to impress anyone. A critic for the *New York Times* called it "the most dismal mass of [maudlin, mushy, aimless] trash that was ever put into dramatic shape before a New York audience."[40] In a letter to the *New York Tribune*, Harte responded to this and similar reviews by accusing the city's theater critics of taking bribes for favorable reviews. Pushed to name names, Harte ducked: "I would propose that those gentlemen who are aggrieved by my charge should bring an action against me."[41] Howells addressed the controversy in his first contribution to the Club in January 1877.

Although discussions in The Contributor's Club never strayed too far from literature, Howells gradually injected items that reflected his own liberal politics. When Henry Hilton excluded the prominent businessman Joseph Seligman from his Saratoga Grand Union Hotel because he was a German Jewish immigrant, the *New York Times* ran the headline "A Sensation at Saratoga." In response, a writer for The Contributor's Club—most likely Howells—observed that "it is comforting to Jewish hearts to see how the social thrust lately aimed at them has been resented by the free press. But does all this, I wonder, blind any thinking Jew to the wide difference between social justice and social preference, or tend to make him feel that he is the more welcome in the home circles of Christian families, supposing he cared to enter them."[42]

As this comment suggests, Howells's *Atlantic* reflected his growing concern with social inequities. In 1878, the magazine published Arthur G. Sedgwick's essay "Primitive Communism" (September), followed by Erastus B. Bigelow's "The Relations of Labor and Capital" (October),

Brooks Adams's "Oppressive Taxation of the Poor" (November), and "its remedy" (Adams, December). The first issue of the next year showed an increase in socially minded essays with Charles Dudley Warner's "Aspects of American Life," which claimed that the young men of the day were more conservative than those of old, and Goldwin Smith's "Is Universal Suffrage a Failure?" and "Workingmen's Wives." In January 1880, Howells began serializing his own *The Undiscovered Country*, a novel critical of religion when it seems akin to mesmerism, but sympathetic to Shakers, among whom he and his wife vacationed.

Although his successor would criticize Howells for publishing too much of his own work in the *Atlantic*, Howells understood the business of letters. In his essay, "The Man of Letters as a Man of Business," this man—who marketed his first novel, *Their Wedding Journey* (1871), as a courting book, complete with a white cover beribboned in blue—bluntly admitted that business "is the opprobrium of Literature."[43] Understanding did not prevent him from promoting his interests and those of his friends with the aplomb of a P. T. Barnum. If, in a perfect world, literature would neither be bought nor sold, it would, as Howells hoped, belong to everybody. A realist as well as an idealist, he saw most things from another perspective, and the business of literature proved no exception. At its worst, business turned artists into hucksters; at its best, it improved the overall quality of literature and kept magazines like the *Atlantic Monthly* afloat.

12

John Greenleaf Whittier's Seventieth Birthday

It was not given to all of us to be born in Boston, but when we find ourselves in *The Atlantic* we all seem to suffer a sea-change, and aesthetic renaissance; a livelier literary conscience stirs in us; we have its fame at heart; we must do our best for Maga's name as well as for our own hope; we are naturalized Bostonians in the finest and highest sense.

W. D. HOWELLS, Whittier Dinner Speech, 1877

ON MONDAY, 17 December 1877, the *Atlantic* threw a party that did double duty by celebrating John Greenleaf Whittier's seventieth birthday and its own twenty-year survival. William Dean Howells planned the event as if it were a grand opening of one of his farces—published for home entertainment in the *Atlantic*'s Christmas issue—at the Boston Museum. Ralph Waldo Emerson, Henry Wadsworth Longfellow, and Oliver Wendell Holmes agreed to play their venerated selves, with Mark Twain providing the comic relief. For this mustering of contributors from 1857 to 1877, the magazine got its publicity machine churning early. Readers of the *Boston Daily Advertiser* were privy to news of those who accepted or declined invitations, and as the day neared, it could confidently predict that the assembled company would be "the most notable that has ever been seen in this country between four walls."[1]

At six o'clock on the appointed day, guests gathered for cocktails in the Brunswick Hotel abutting Copley Square. At seven, they adjourned to the east dining hall to find their places and autograph seating charts commemorating their attendance. In honor of Whittier, the *Atlantic* had commissioned his portrait, which hung—garlanded with English ivy—behind the head table. To its left, a winter scene of his house in Amesbury, Massachusetts, recalled his most famous poem. "So days went on," he wrote in *Snowbound* (1866), "a week had passed / Since the great world was heard from last." Striking a chord with war-weary readers nostalgic for simpler times, in its first few months *Snowbound* sold twenty thousand volumes, or ten times what the usual collection of poetry sold.

The *Atlantic*'s publisher, Henry Houghton, presided at the dinner, and Howells acted as master of ceremonies. Lending "a reverend, almost holy air" to the cavernous room, Emerson sat at Whittier's right next to Longfellow. Oliver Wendell Holmes, Howells, and Charles Dudley Warner, Twain's neighbor and editor of the *Hartford Courant*, made up Houghton's left flank. It took nearly three hours for the guests to work their way through the menu, which started with raw oysters paired with a sauterne and proceeded through separate courses of soup, fish, capon, and mutton. The entrees included squabs *en compote* and fillet of beef in Madera sauce with a separate serving of game. Cheese, fruit, and coffee followed the pastries. If diners had not had their fill with the sauterne, sherry, Chablis, champagne (Dry Verzenay and Roederer Imperial), Burgundy, and claret, they could request a glass of cognac topped with flaming sugar.

At ten minutes past ten Houghton called his guests to order. The doors to the east room swung open, and a throng of women entered to take seats set up between the tables. The servers (mostly African Americans) took their stations along the back wall, where they, too, were allowed to witness the so-called "literary exercises"—or what organizers called "A Rich Feast of Reason."

Houghton addressed his opening remarks to the magazine's younger contributors. Look to the nation's primeval forests, he exhorted, to the prairies, rivers, and mountains of the West, the brooks and rivulets of New England, or the country in its entirety as it struggles with the "enfranchisement of a whole race from bondage." For twenty years, the *Atlantic Monthly* had stood for "the highest American culture in literature, the most impartial and independent criticism in science and art, and the freest discussion of politics, not from a partisan standpoint, but, as heretofore, in the cause of righteousness, truth, and common progress." With "the best business talent" and "the loftiest efforts of authorship" it would continue its domination. The audience rose to its feet and cheered.

Howells followed Houghton's introduction with an exuberant tribute to the magazine. He recalled what it had meant to him as a young man in the Western Reserve of Ohio, where the arrival of a new *Atlantic* drew a notice in the local paper. At the conclusion of Howells's remarks, Charles Eliot Norton acknowledged James Russell Lowell, then serving as minister to Spain. When the suitable moment arose, Oliver Wendell Holmes delivered his expected verses commemorating the occasion: "I'm a florist in verse," he said, "and what *would* people say / If I came to a banquet without my bouquet?" Suffering from a cold and almost overshadowed by praise of the magazine, Whittier managed to rasp out a brief thanks.

The evening might have been forgotten had Howells not arranged for Mark Twain to speak. Since their early days in Missouri and Ohio much had happened in the two men's lives, and their central roles at the *Atlantic* dinner signaled their success. "Clemens" had become Mark Twain, and along the way had married his Livy, moved from Elmira, New York, to Hartford, Connecticut, and fathered three children: a son named Langdon who died when only a year and a half, and daughters Susy and Clara. He had invented and patented *Mark Twain's Self-Pasting Scrapbook* and published, with Charles Dudley Warner (and some acrimony), the book that gave the Gilded Age its name. In 1876, *The Adventures of Tom Sawyer* assured his reputation, though its first-year sales of twenty-four thousand copies made him think it a bust. Howells had moved on too, in his craft and authority, but also in Cambridge—from Sacramento Street to Berkeley Street to a house on Concord Avenue. Between editing and reviewing, he produced several novels, a collection of poems, the Christmas farces, and a campaign biography of his wife Elinor's cousin, Rutherford B. Hayes—all this and his copious correspondence and services to friends, whose manuscripts he read on the side.

Neither man could quite believe his luck. Both had grown up ragged-Dick poor (to borrow from Horatio Alger's unlikely hero) in small-town America: Twain in the Hannibal, Missouri, he captures so evocatively in his fiction; and Howells in what he called "queer Ohio country," a landscape oddly reminiscent of New England, especially in the poignant light of late afternoon. By ten, he had done a man's work setting type in his father's print shop. The next year, he lived in a log cabin in the outpost of Eureka for difficult months, after his father gave up the editorship of Hamilton's *Intelligencer*. The equivalent of Twain's Hannibal, Hamilton would come to stand for a golden epoch in the boy's life. From there it would be Dayton, then Ashtabula, home of his father's newspaper, the *Ashtabula Sentinel*, an organ of the state's Republican Party. Each man could claim to be self-educated: Twain left school at thirteen following the death of his father; and Howells, who was in and out of school when not in the print shop, taught himself. Among his achievements, he learned Spanish by candlelight so he could read *Don Quixote* in its original language. In a parallel way, Twain—journeyman printer, cub pilot, prospector, and dueler—had, like Howells, written himself up and out of obscurity.

On the night of the Whittier dinner, Howells introduced Twain as a humorist "who never makes you blush to have enjoyed his joke; whose generous wit has no meanness in it, whose fun is never at the cost of anything honestly high and good."[2] With Twain about to perform, he could begin to breathe easier. The audience would soon be crying with laughter, for he knew with what care his friend prepared his speeches. He had seen him set "knife, spoon, salt-cellar, and butter-plate" on the dining table at Hartford, and a cue and nub of chalk on the billiard table, as mnemonic prompts for a particular twist of thought or phrase. Howells felt assured that Twain's speech would tease out every laugh, and he looked forward to glowing accounts of the event and priceless advertising in the next day's papers.

Twain's speech broke every expectation. It involved three tramps, or "deadbeats," who take advantage of a gullible miner by pretending to be the holy triumvirate of Emerson, Longfellow, and Holmes: "Mr. Emerson was a seedy little bit of a chap, red-headed. Mr. Holmes was as fat as a balloon; he weighed as much as three hundred, and had double chins all the way down to his stomach. Mr. Longfellow was built like a prizefighter. His head was cropped and bristly, like as if he had a wig made of hair-brushes. His nose lay straight down his face, like a finger with the end joint tilted up. They had been drinking, I could see that. And what queer talk they used!" The humor came partly from the absurdity of these descriptions. Anyone in the audience could see that Holmes was a featherweight and that Longfellow did have an unusually long nose. The burlesque had the tramps swilling the last drop of the miner's whiskey, cheating him at cards, stealing his boots, *and*, indignity of indignities, making him listen to their poetry.

Although observers agreed that Twain told his "eccentric tale" in his "usual characteristic drawling, stammering way," they agreed on little else. If we can believe the reporter for the Boston *Daily Globe*, his speech "produced the most violent bursts of hilarity. Mr. Emerson seemed a little puzzled about it [probably because he could not hear], but Mr. Longfellow laughed and shook, and Mr. Whittier seemed to enjoy it keenly."[3] Not so Howells, who spied Holmes doodling on his menu, as the silence gathered weight and deepened with each painful second. The impossible had happened: Twain stood "solitary amid his appalled and appalling listeners, with his joke dead on his hands." For once, Howells envied the abstracted Emerson his "Jovian oblivion."[4] Embarrassed by his friend's debunking of the magazine as much as the occasion, and miffed that an occasion he orchestrated had gone awry, Howells felt betrayed.

The dinner received its share of expected publicity, but not the kind the magazine wanted. The *New York Times* published the speech in its entirety (20 December 1877) without comment, while the *Boston Daily Globe* reprinted a paragraph from the *Cincinnati Commercial* entitled "Mark Twain's Offense against Good Taste" that began: "If amazement did not sit upon each brow in that assemblage as Mr. Twain went on with his extraordinary narrative, it was because courtesy restrained its expression. It would have read queer enough as a humorous sketch, but delivered, as it was, in the august presence of the men in whose lives there is nothing to suggest such an adventure in the remotest manner, it must have excited far other than humorous emotions."[5] The incident seems to have gained in importance after the fact, abetted perhaps by Howells's embarrassment and Twain's apologies the next day to the principals, who brushed the evening aside. Emerson remained mystified; Holmes, who was used to periodical derision, sympathetic; and Longfellow amused. Spying a photograph of Twain in Howells's study, Longfellow, shaking his head, said, "Ah, he is a wag!"[6]

Twain, who once remarked that he had been an author for twenty years and an ass for fifty-five, vacillated between defiance and abject humiliation at the failure of his performance. He would return twenty-three years later in his autobiography to "this calamity, this shipwreck, this cataclysm . . . the most disastrous thing that had ever happened in anybody's history" and in typical Twain fashion lay the blame away from his own doorstep. Given the faultlessness of the speech, the fault had to be in his listeners, "those majestic guests, that row of venerable and still active volcanoes" who failed to erupt with laughter. "Cruel time! To have made it impossible for him to turn those litt'ry immortals into pads of flowing butter."[7]

After the Whittier dinner, the *Atlantic* faced a bigger public relations fiasco than Twain's faux pas—and they had, among others, Gail Hamilton, James Fields's old nemesis, to blame. Although the magazine invited female contributors to other occasions, dinners remained sacredly male. The reasons for this practice ranged from convention to the memory of the dismal dinner for Harriet Beecher Stowe, which had grown in dreadfulness and hilarity with every telling. Continuing the tradition of all-male clubs, the *Atlantic* dinners had not kept pace with the times. Where were the women at the Whittier dinner? asked Frances Willard, the electrifying president of the Women's Christian Temperance Union and a friend of Hamilton. "The only reference to the gentler sex" concerns guests at the hotel, "but who had *earned* a seat at Whittier's own right hand?" Where *were* Stowe, Harriet Prescott Spofford, Gail Hamilton, Rebecca Harding Davis, Elizabeth Stuart Phelps, Ann Whitney, Louisa May Alcott, and Celia Thaxter? Her list continued for six lines. Even a supporter of women's suffrage like Colonel Higginson had overlooked them. "Some of us feel as if our own mothers had received a slight," Willard wrote. Echoing Whittier's protest against slavery with the line—"these things ought not so to be"—she signed her protest "A *Few* among Many."[8]

The absence of women at the dinner led one writer to claim that the *Atlantic* was the most masculine magazine in the country, by which she meant it was written by and for men.[9] Another sent fictional regrets from Stowe, Spofford, Davis, and Hamilton, the letter's likely author. Dear Mr. Houghton should know that they intended to start their own "maga" and have their own dinner. "Sufficient is it on these occasions to break bread, and, perhaps also heads."[10] The spoof ends with Houghton deciding to give a dinner two months hence in honor of Hamilton's seventieth birthday.

Two years after the Whittier dinner, women received invitations to a commemorative breakfast at noon (3 December 1879) in honor of the "Autocrat," Oliver Wendell Holmes, turning seventy. Julia Ward Howe sat at the head table. The aging abolitionist had become a bit of an embarrassment to friends for never refusing an opportunity to recite "The Battle Hymn of the Republic," during which she marched in place and clapped her hands, trumpeting, "Oh, be swift, my soul, to answer Him! be jubilant, my feet! Our God is marching on." Before she spoke, the male company raised their glasses to the women present. Howe addressed the guests by recounting a literary gathering the previous year in Paris to which women had not been invited. Whatever women may not be, she said, "they are people. It would seem to-day that they are recognized as literary people, and I am very glad that you gentlemen have found room for the sisterhood to-day, and have placed them so numerously here. I must say that to my eyes the banquet looks very much more cheerful than it would without them. It looks to me as though it had all blossomed out under a new social influence, and beside each dark stem I see a rose." She then read a Holmes-like "Tribute to Oliver Wendell Holmes," which builds to a crescendo after its relatively tame opening line: "Thou metamorphic god!"[11]

Frances Willard, ever alert to checks on women's equality, had captured the spirit of the *Atlantic* when she referred to it as a "guild," a word that conveys shared values, social exclusivity, and commercial advancement. Neither Louisa May Alcott nor Harriet Prescott Spofford felt like full members. Alcott complained that the magazine rejected her best work, and Spofford that Higginson wanted to change her into an entirely different kind of writer.

If nothing else, the Whittier and Holmes dinners challenged the *Atlantic*'s fiction of mutual prosperity. Not everyone suffered a sea change for the better at the *Atlantic*. Not everyone placed the magazine's interest above or on a par with self-interest. And not everyone was or wanted to be a naturalized Bostonian. Even a loyal employee like Howells wondered whether Boston values and a Harvard education would make his son a better man than his father and grandfather. From this perspective, Howells's irritation with Twain may have had less to do with the speech itself than with the realization that the idols of his youth might have clay feet, or that his response to Twain's talk had been misplaced. Perhaps more to the point, he had not held himself to a standard of friendship he shared with Twain. "The proper office of a friend is to side with you when you are in the wrong," Twain wrote from experience. "Nearly anybody will side with you when you are in the right."[12] Looking back at the night of the Whittier fiasco, Howells had to confront the "black-heart's truth" of having failed to perform that office for his best friend.[13]

13

Bret Harte to the Lions

In the early days I liked Bret Harte and so did the others, but by and by I got over it; so also did the others. He couldn't keep a friend permanently. He was bad, distinctly bad; he had no feeling and he had no conscience.

Mark Twain's Autobiography, 1924

IN HIS AUTOBIOGRAPHY, Henry Adams settled on 1870 as a pivotal year for fiction. This "fateful year . . . was to mark the close of the literary epoch, when quarterlies gave way to monthlies; letter-press to illustration; volumes to pages. The outburst was brilliant. Bret Harte led, and Robert Louis Stevenson followed."[1] Adams may have been right. He also included Guy de Maupassant and Rudyard Kipling, who lived for a time in the United States, but Stevenson died young after a life of illness, and Bret Harte's brilliance shone in an equally short blaze.

Harte had zigzagged through life working as an apothecary's helper, a miner, teacher, expressman, and clerk in the U.S. mint before becoming the country's most popular author for stories set in the West. Long after their friendship had cooled, Mark Twain described him as "a liar, a thief, a swindler, a snob, a sot, a sponge, a coward, a Jeremy Diddler"—the name of a confidence man in James Kennedy's 1803 play *Raising the Wind*.[2] Yet in 1870, the year that also signaled the first crack in their friendship, Twain counted Harte, whom he knew from his days in San Francisco when both wrote for the *Golden Era* and the *Californian*, to be a true friend. Referring to Harte's help with *Innocents Abroad*, Twain acknowledged that he "trimmed and trained and schooled me patiently until he changed me from an awkward utterer of coarse grotesqueness to a writer of paragraphs and chapters that have found a certain favor in the eyes of even some of the decentest people of the land."[3] Twain would come to resent comparisons of his work to Harte's. When Thomas Bailey Aldrich accused him of publishing an anonymous poem along the lines of Harte's "Plain Language from Truthful James," popularly known as "The Heathen Chinee," Twain demanded an apology, then, thinking better of it, protested that he was not "in the imitation business."[4]

Harte had first come to the attention of James T. Fields during the Civil War, when the *Atlantic* published his pro-Union piece "The Legend of Monte del Diablo" (September 1863). In the intervening seven years, Harte had started the *Overland Monthly*, a San Francisco magazine modeled after the *Atlantic*, which featured Twain and delighted the public with Harte's own "The Luck of Roaring Camp" and "The Outcasts of Poker Flats," whose "shaggy realism" gave birth to the modern Western. A reviewer for the *Atlantic Monthly* praised both the quality of Harte's magazine and his stories for presenting an honest view of the early West, rife with "rude pathos" and "poor, bewildered, sinful souls." Harte, he said, caught "the robust vigor and racy savor" of his characters' vernacular.[5] Years later, the critic Henry Seidel Canby would say that the "the literary West" spouted from his imagination. It was Bret Harte who made readers familiar with diamond-in-the-rough miners, gamblers, and prostitutes who have moments of true nobility.[6]

With the publication of "The Luck of Roaring Camp"—the story of miners who adopt the son of a sinful woman named Cherokee Sal—Harte became a celebrity worth courting. In 1869, Howells initiated a correspondence, hoping to cultivate Harte as an *Atlantic* regular. Harte responded by complimenting Howells on his travel book, *Venetian Life*: "I think you have such a rare faculty of not liking things in a likable manner," Harte wrote, isolating one of the key factors in Howells's success. "Any one can be charmingly enthusiastic, but so few can be even tolerably skeptical."[7] Harte's "Heathen Chinee" (1870) proved so popular that the Fields, Osgood edition of his *Poems* sold eleven hundred copies in five days. Harte followed his volume to Boston and dined at James Fields's invitation at the Saturday Club. There he met Henry Longfellow, James Lowell, Oliver Wendell Holmes, Ralph Waldo Emerson, Richard Henry Dana Jr., and Louis Agassiz, who quoted passages from "Truthful James":

> . . . it is not decent for a scientific gent
> To say another is an ass,—to all intent;
> Nor should the individual who happens to be meant
> Reply by heaving rocks at him, to any great extent.[8]

In March, Harte agreed to write exclusively for the *Atlantic*, now owned by James R. Osgood after Fields's retirement from publishing in 1871. Osgood agreed to pay Harte ten thousand dollars for twelve stories and poems at a time when reporters earned twenty dollars a week (or slightly over a thousand dollars a year) and a porterhouse steak ordered at an upscale San Francisco restaurant cost fifty cents. Harte carped that he had made "some pecuniary sacrifice for the sake of keeping my books in the one house, and of giving a preference to his earliest publisher. But I am satisfied. I hope you are."[9] At first his employers were satisfied. The *Atlantic* published one of Harte's immediately popular and widely anthologized stories, "The Poet of Sierra Flat" (July 1871), which looks slyly at the issue of authorship and gender when "the borned Poet" Milton Chubbuck turn outs to be a woman who "can jerk a rhyme as easy as turnin' jack." If Chubbuck owes his success to the "absolute vileness" of his "doggerel," Harte owes his perhaps to the story's humorous pushing of polite limits—Chubbuck leaves town with a cross-dressing actress who knows the secret of her suitor's gender.[10]

Harte came to Boston like a conquering hero. In the words of one friend:

> When he turned his back on San Francisco and started for Boston, he began a tour that the greatest author of any age might have been proud of. It was a veritable ovation that swelled from sea to sea; the classic sheep was sacrificed all along the route. I have often thought that if Bret Harte had met with a fatal accident during that transcontinental journey the world would have declared with one voice that the greatest genius of his time was lost to it.[11]

Watching the procession from the sidelines of Ohio, Howells's father worried that his son would be soon out of a job. Howells reassured him: "I should never suffer myself to enter rivalry with any one, but at any rate Harte's and my own lives are so divergent that we should not come into competition."[12] He turned out to be right, if naive about the ease with which an editor or a writer can stand outside the fray.

Before leaving for Europe, the Fieldses welcomed Harte to Boston. Annie Fields described the raven-haired stranger as "a dramatic, loveable creature, with his blue silk pocket-handkerchief and red dressing slippers, and his quick feelings."[13] Almost as an afterthought she added what would become a refrain in reminiscences about Harte: that he had an unusual disregard for time and money. "Why did you fool away your money paying debts?" Harte once asked John Hay, another *Atlantic* author and later secretary of state to both William McKinley and Theodore Roosevelt.[14] For many of Harte's Boston acquaintances, the matter of debts would point to the man's tragic flaw.

Elinor Howells, who hosted him on his trip east, had no warning that she would also be entertaining his wife and two boys. Arching an eyebrow at his foppish dress, which reminded Elinor of an actor playing a French marquis, she told her husband's sisters: "Of course they are not quite au fait in every thing, but they give you the idea of polished, cultivated people."[15] Elinor soon managed to turn a blind eye to Harte's attire for the enjoyment of introducing the nation's new literary light to her Cambridge neighbors. Her husband noted that the party they gave in his honor brought together "the genius and 'beauty' of Cambridge," with genius predominating.[16] Elinor had worried that all the women would fall in love with the visionary-eyed Harte before they learned he had a wife. Basking in the reception of his most recent *Atlantic* novella, *A Passionate Pilgrim*, Henry James assured a friend that he felt unintimidated by the author of the "Heathen Chinee."[17] The Howells's party marked the height of both the Howells-Harte friendship and Harte's use to the *Atlantic*, whose editor grew tired of prodding him for subpar material, which had to be passed on to the company's other magazine, *Every Saturday*.

Though Harte charmed nearly everyone he met, he presented a challenge to his editor. Taking umbrage at any criticism, even when he solicited it, Harte made it clear that he considered himself the final judge. "Many thanks for your good-natured commendation of my ballad," he wrote Howells, brushing aside questions about his unnamed sources and accented Spanish. "I would trust my ear rather than my dictionary or the dicta of any set of Yankee Professors who give three syllables to 'Joaquin.'"[18] Howells was offended, as only a man struggling with his conscience might be. Despite misgivings, he had conscientiously touted Harte in print and arranged for *Every Saturday* to put his picture on its cover.[19] Within two years of the Howellses' party, Harte's star had plummeted: his publisher had little motivation to continue his extravagant wages, and readers, trained to greater realism in fiction, complained that his characters were exceptions and his plots formulaic.[20]

Harte's strengths and weaknesses can be seen in his *Atlantic* poem "Grandmother Tenterden," set on the Massachusetts shore in 1800. Narrated by the title's grandmother, it tells the tale of her sailor-son who quarrels with his wife before being lost at sea, and who returns after death to kiss her goodbye. Witnessing the kiss, Grandmother Tenterden hardens her heart against her daughter-in-law:

> Now, when my darling kissed not me,
> But her—his wife—who did not wake,
> My heart within me seemed to break;
> I swore a vow! nor thenceforth spake
> Of what my clearer eyes did see.

Watching her daughter-in-law pine away, Grandmother Tenterden justifies her decision:

> One time I thought, before she passed,
> To give her peace, but ere I spake
> Methought, "He will be first to break
> The news in Heaven," and for his sake
> I held mine back until the last.[21]

However fantastic or sentimental the circumstances, Harte exposes not only the grandmother's self-delusion and jealousy—the hard narrowness of a certain New England type—but also the entrapments of family life. Assessing Harte's career several years later, Howells struggled to be fair:

> As a brother scribe I have myself watched his career with mingled joy and trepidation. When he first burst upon us, I was glad to have at least one author over-rated in this grudging world, where I could think of so much unrecognized merit within a stone's-throw of my own sequestered study; and I was also glad to have the public find

> out that it had overrated him, while I trembled lest he should prove himself as great as he was thought. I was always among the first to drop a crocodile tear upon his failures,—and they have been many and deplorable,—but though I can hate a brother writer as well as the next, I do love literature, and I am bound to own that some of Mr. Harte's best work, if not most of his best work, has been done since he came hither from California.[22]

Nonetheless, the subject of Harte troubled Howells, in part because the story of Harte's rise and fall seemed a cautionary tale to every writer who faced a blank page. Harte was just a year older than Howells, having been born in Albany, New York, in 1836. Like Howells, his education had been interrupted by frequent family moves. By age eleven, he supported himself by working odd jobs. At eighteen, he moved with his mother to California, where he scraped together a living—and almost got lynched for publicly condemning a massacre of Native Americans near Eureka, California—before accepting the editorship of the *Overland Monthly.* Although Harte would continue to write despite personal and financial setbacks, his fall in public favor seemed to have happened overnight. Howells looked at Harte, who seemed his own worst enemy, and thanked his stars for his loving wife—the Hartes were rumored to have their troubles—and a steady income. Howells would model Bartley Hubbard, the dodgy protagonist of his 1882 novel, *A Modern Instance,* partly on Harte and partly—he said with his usual honestly—on himself.[23]

Harte's parting from the *Atlantic* in 1872 came at a time when the firm experienced unforeseen expenses from a fire that raged through sixty-five acres of Boston's downtown in just twenty hours. Destroying the financial district, it stopped just short of Faneuil Hall and the Old State House. Sailors off the coast of Maine could see the sky lit by the fire's glow. Oliver Wendell Holmes spoke of giant buildings collapsing as if they were silently sinking into a "vast featherbed." From an upper window in Hovey's store on Summer Street, Holmes described a cityscape "flat to the water, so that we saw the ships in the harbor as we should have done from the same point in the days of Blackstone (if there had been ships then and no trees in the way)." Among the few tall chimneys still standing, he saw "piles of smoking masonry, the burnt stump of a flagstaff in Franklin Street," and groups of people trying to find where their businesses had been. The military and police tried to control looters as well as "crowds of people who have flocked in from all over the country."[24] At least twenty people died, and damages exceeded $73 million, or over $1 billion today.

More personally for *Atlantic* contributors, the firm lost whatever it had stored in various printing offices, binderies, and warehouses consumed by the fire or damaged by water. Howells, who recalled men using axes to free water-swollen paper from bins, immediately reassured contributors and readers that the magazine would survive, though the firm lost today's equivalent of about half a million dollars in presses, paper, stock, and plates.[25]

Harte's relationship with the *Atlantic* and its home city overlaps with the story of the Boston fire, for the magazine's losses would result in its sale to Henry Houghton in 1873.[26] (Five years later his company would acquire Ticknor and Fields and become Houghton, Osgood & Company.) The month of the fire, Harte and the lyceum impresario James Redpath (1833–1891) exchanged epistolary blows after Harte failed to appear for a scheduled lecture at the Boston Museum. Redpath announced that this was the third time "the 'Heathen Chinee' has insulted a Boston audience." The first had been his poor performance before Harvard's Phi Beta Kappa Society; the second, his no-show at the reunion of the Grand Army of the Potomac. Redpath decided that Harte needed to be "taught his place." The *Boston Daily Advertiser* escalated the feud by publishing Redpath's remarks and Harte's defense that he asked to postpone the lecture out of respect for victims of the fire. Harte wrote in explanation to his publisher, James R. Osgood: "Can it be possible that my omission to have anything more to do with him [Redpath] . . . will be construed into an insult to Boston! My hair rises with the thought."[27] Harte was both exasperated and puzzled to learn that his appearance fueled the rumors: "when they intimate that I am running on my good looks—save the mark! I confess I get hopelessly furious," he told his wife. "You will be amused to hear that my gold 'studs' have again become 'diamonds,' my worn-out shirts 'faultless linen.'" She would not have recognized the man they think "a handsome fop."[28]

Howells's association with Harte would be further complicated by his deep respect and affection for Twain. Howells and Twain understood one another. Having scrapped their way to success, both had fallen into the arms of women they considered their superiors, and they had no intention of self-destructing. Business cemented their friendship, which grew to include their wives and children. The couples exchanged photographs and organized overnights in Cambridge and Hartford. From 1873 to 1881, Howells visited Twain fifteen times in Hartford, and Twain stayed a dozen times in Boston and then at the Howellses' new house in the suburb of Belmont. In 1872, the year that Harte sold himself to the *Atlantic*'s publisher, Twain published *Roughing It.* He and Harte were still good enough friends for Harte to joke about his son Franky marrying Twain's newborn daughter, Susy—"provided her father does the right thing in way of dowry and relinquishes humor as a profession."[29] Harte actually lived with Twain at Nook Farm in Hartford during the fall and into the winter of 1876 as they collaborated on *Ah Sin,* a play meant to ride the popularity of Harte's "Heathen Chinee." The collaboration ended a friendship already strained by Twain's rise with *Tom Sawyer* and Harte's descent with the failure of *Gabriel Conroy,* which Twain had recommended to the American Publishing Company. Harte, who mocked the bourgeois excesses of Nook Farm, teased Livy in ways her husband found offensive. A successful run would have saved the day, but *Ah Sin* sank into oblivion after opening in Washington, D.C., and New York to good reviews. Game to try again, Twain offered Harte free board plus twenty-five dollars a week to collaborate on another play. Accusing Twain of exploiting his poverty, Harte broke off relations, warning: "I have kept a copy of this letter."[30]

Twain, from that time, systematically set about ruining Harte's character. By the night of the Whittier dinner, Harte's ship had sunk, or, to quote a Boston newspaper, Harte found himself "floating on the raft made of the shipwreck of his former reputation."[31] The *North American Review* panned his work; the *Cincinnati Gazette* quoted an anonymous source attacking his character: "Harte was absolutely devoid of a conscience. If his washerwoman had saved $500 by long years of careful industry, he would borrow it without the slightest intention of paying it back."[32] A little over a year after the Boston fire, Harte walked off the stage of the Tremont Temple in Boston into the arms of a sheriff who arrested him for failure to pay his debts. When he got down to his last twenty dollars, he resorted to writing jingles.

With the wolf at Harte's door, friends tried to get him a government appointment to China. Their efforts fell on the deaf ears of President Hayes, who knew Harte third hand, from a private letter that either his cousin, Elinor, or Howells had passed on from Twain, saying that "his wake is tumultuous with swindled grocers, & with defrauded innocents who have loaned him money. . . . He can lie faster than he can drivel pathos. . . . He is always steeped in whisky & brandy. . . . No man who has ever known him respects him."[33] When a post opened in Germany, Hayes again approached Howells to ask whether Twain's accusations about Harte were true. Howells responded artfully:

> He is notorious for borrowing and *was* notorious for drinking. This is *report*. He never borrowed of *me*, nor drank more than I, (in my presence) and yesterday I saw his doctor who says his habits are good, now; . . . From what I hear he is really making an effort to reform. It would be a godsend to him, if he could get such a place; for he is poor, and he writes with difficulty and very little. . . . *Personally*, I should be glad of his appointment, and I should have great hopes of him—and fears.[34]

Like Howells before him, Harte won his diplomatic appointment.

In his eloquent obituary, *My Mark Twain*, Howells would recall his early *Atlantic* days with Twain and Harte and state that nothing remained to him "of the happy time but a sense of idle and aimless and joyful talk-play, beginning and ending nowhere." Like Twain, he had dreamed of the moment they would be taken into the *Atlantic* circle, and with that achieved, they shared a fond if ironic response to Boston "illuminates."[35] History has treated Howells and certainly Twain more kindly than it has Harte, who, thanks to his former friend's vituperation, lives on as "Jeremy Diddler." Twain, on the other hand, has become the nation's beloved if cantankerous white-suited grandfather.

In 1896, the *Atlantic*, which had continued to publish friendly reviews of Harte's work, published a memoir by Mark Twain's one-time secretary, the poet and travel writer Charles Warren Stoddard, titled "Early Recollections of Bret Harte." As "one who knew California of old," Stoddard felt fortunate that Harte "came when he came, saw what he saw, and conquered as he unquestionably did conquer, and held fast the very spirit, if not the letter, of that Golden Age." Having befriended both Harte and Twain in that old California, Stoddard brings them together again on the occasion of a comprehensive edition of Harte's work. "Of American authors," he writes, "Bret Harte and Mark Twain have traveled farthest, and are likely to tarry longest. Whom would you substitute for these? Whom could you? In print each is as American as America."[36]

14

Straddling the Atlantic

HENRY JAMES

In life without art, you can find your account; but art without life is a poor affair.

HENRY JAMES, "Daniel Deronda: A Conversation," *Atlantic*, December 1886

OF THE MANY CONTRIBUTORS who supported and found support from the *Atlantic*, Henry James stands apart. James, who came into his own in the pages of the magazine, published stories, reviews, and novels through half a century—and with the Atlantic Ocean between himself and Boston. The second son of the eccentric Swedenborgian philosopher for whom he was named, James spent his peripatetic childhood traveling between the United States and Europe, where he studied with tutors in Geneva, London, Paris, Bologna, and Bonn. About people raised abroad like James and herself, Edith Wharton would say that they had been "produced in a European glass-house." They were "wretched exotics," none of them American; "we don't think or feel as the Americans do."[1] In 1864, the James family moved to Boston before putting down roots in Cambridge. James followed his older brother William to Harvard, where he studied law until literature announced itself as his calling.

Inheriting his father's wanderlust, James visited London in 1869 and made the acquaintance of artists and intellectuals, including George Eliot, William Morris, Gabriel Rossetti, and James Russell Lowell's friend Leslie Stephen. After extended periods in Paris, where he wrote letters for the *New York Tribune*, and Rome, James moved permanently to England in 1876.

His house in Rye, purchased in 1898, became a center for friends as different as Joseph Conrad and Stephen Crane.

Today the broader public knows James through films of his novels, notably Merchant-Ivory productions of *The Golden Bowl, The Bostonians,* and *The Europeans*. He holds a special place in the *Atlantic*'s pantheon of writers for a number of reasons, chief among them the many novels that explore the cultural and psychological differences between Europeans and Americans. To his contemporaries, James represented the quintessential artist, laboring at his craft to the exclusion of much else. In a May 1885 *Atlantic* review of a biography of George Eliot written by her husband, John Cross, James presents the author of *Middlemarch* as many saw James himself. The "creations" which "*possessed*" her and "brought her renown," James wrote,

> were of the incalculable kind, shaped themselves in mystery, in some intellectual back shop or secret crucible, and were as little as possible implied in the aspect of her life. What is remarkable, extraordinary and the process remains inscrutable and mysterious is that this quiet, anxious, sedentary, serious, invalidical English lady, without animal spirits, without adventures, without extravagance, assumption, or bravado, should have made us believe that nothing in the world was alien to her; should have produced such rich, deep, masterly pictures of the multifold life of man.[2]

Mere living might suit others, but, as James told H. G. Wells in 1915, "It is art that makes life, makes interest, makes importance, and I know of no substitute whatever for the force and beauty of its process."[3] In her letters to James, Wharton addressed him as "Cher Maître" because she bowed to his mastery of form. James's experiments with limited third-person narration places the reader in the consciousness of a narrator—him- or herself an actor in the story. The process allowed readers to see the narrator's process of thinking, the slow dawning of consciousness, accompanied by a loss of innocence.

James's first signed story, "The Story of a Year," appeared in the *Atlantic*'s March 1865 issue. Though melodramatic, it mimics and rejects the conventional endings of Civil War fiction by not having the pretty, young heroine immolate herself on the altar of her fallen lover's memory. Those who associate James with ambiguous prose and drawing-room dramas might be surprised to think of him beginning his career like any hack writer intent on boiling the pot, or plot. In 1871, the *Atlantic* serialized *Watch and Ward*, a novel that pushed conventional boundaries of fiction by having a bachelor adopt and groom a twelve-year-old girl for later marriage. A friend of the James family, Charles Eliot Norton, would have preferred for the beginning author to avoid sensation by pursuing his acquaintance with Homer and Virgil. Neither he nor James Russell Lowell, his coeditor at the *North American Review*, saw promise of a great career for James. That prediction fell to James's friend William Dean Howells, who bet on him "to do better than any one has yet done toward making us a real American novel."[4] James fulfilled that promise when *Daisy Miller* set readers on both sides of the Atlantic debating its heroine's morals. James told her story through the jaded eyes of an American expatriate named Winterbourne, who does not know how to interpret Daisy's flirtatious behavior any more than readers do. Readers fell into opposing camps: the "Daisy Millerites," who thought her virginal, and the "anti-Daisy Millerites," who knew her to be lost.[5] The argument soon extended to the manners of American girls generally.

Over the years, the *Atlantic* accepted as much work from James as it could reasonably print without seeming to be a vanity press. *Roderick Hudson* (1875), *The American* (1876–1877), *The Europeans* (1878), *The Portrait of a Lady* (1881), a dramatization of *Daisy Miller* subtitled "A Comedy" after being rewritten to end with Daisy and Winterbourne's engagement (1883), *The Princess Casamassima* (1885–1886), *The Aspern Papers* (1888), *The Tragic Muse* (1889–1890), and *The Old Things* (1896), later titled *The Spoils of Poynton*, all appeared in the magazine. If, with time, the young, dark-bearded author of controversial early tales like *Daisy Miller* bore little resemblance to the round-bellied author of *The Princess Casamassima*, who, according to critics, buried his tale of political intrigue and assignation under layers of woolly prose, the *Atlantic* remained respectful. The majority of its editors (though not all) stood by him, rightly predicting that his achievement would reflect on its own. Today a "Great Books" list of the hundred greatest novels lists Marcel Proust's *Remembrance of Things Past* first and James's *The Ambassadors* fourth. Mark Twain's *Adventures of Huckleberry Finn* ranks tenth. A similar Modern Library list places James's *The Wings of the Dove* and *The Ambassadors* at twenty-six and twenty-seven.[6] Such arbitrary lists have little value except to highlight the vagaries of taste and time, which in this case served James well enough, but if there were records of America's best-known, least-read authors, James might win the prize.

James has always been a writer's writer. His novels in the *Atlantic* formed the next generation's sense of what a novel was and was not. Willa Cather, who praised *Atlantic* readers for having some familiarity with French, took James as her example. "For me," she remembered, "he was the perfect writer . . . the foremost mind that ever applied itself to literature in America." "All students imitate," she told an interviewer, and "I began by imitating Henry James."[7] James's wish to render "the look that conveys . . . meaning, to catch the color, the relief, the expression, the surface, the substance of the human spectacle," foreshadowed Cather's belief that "realism" was "an attitude of mind on the part of the writer toward his material."[8]

The expatriated James might be thought of as an odd regular for a magazine that promised to advance the "American idea." In fact, the magazine went far beyond the British Isles to the rest of Europe in its continuing search for authors. And James, though too slow-moving for many twenty-first-century readers, provided a feast for nineteenth-century readers used to savoring long books. He had a large appeal for *Atlantic* editors and readers, who saw his straddling of the Atlantic as a strength because it fostered comparisons between Europe and the United States.

In his autobiography *Notes of a Son and Brother* (1914), James credited his detachment to his rootless early years. "The effect of detachment," he wrote, "was the fact of the experience of Europe."[9] Not surprisingly, his novels deal with themes that have bearing on his own life: liberation, entrapment, exile, and artistry. In *The Portrait of a Lady*, for example, Ralph Touchett experiments with his cousin Isabel Archer by convincing his father to make her a rich woman. From his sickbed, Ralph watches what she will make of the freedom money confers. Isabel's moment of recognition comes when she sees her husband sitting in the presence of her friend Madame Merle and realizes their intimacy. The marriage that she thought of as her own artistic experiment in changing human destiny has been false from its beginning, a convenience Madame Merle has contrived to benefit her daughter with Osmond. At Isabel's last meeting with Ralph, he tells her that he believes his gesture has ruined her. However, James would have readers see that in an odd way he has brought her into fuller if sadder understanding of herself. Having learned that freedom imposes its own restrictions, Isabel returns to the diminished life she chose. Whatever freedom James accords his protagonists comes with profound loneliness. To James, "the free spirit, always much tormented, and by no means always triumphant, is heroic, ironic, pathetic . . . and 'successful' only [in] having remained free."[10]

Apart from the many stories and novels he published in the *Atlantic*, James wrote a copious number of reviews, many of them unsigned. Along with those of Howells and other *Atlantic* critics such as J. T. Trowbridge, E. P. Whipple, Barrett Wendell, and Thomas Wentworth Higginson, James's reviews helped to formalize the aesthetics of literary studies. An *Atlantic* reviewer of James's *Partial Portraits* (1888)—which includes chapters on Emerson, Trollope, and Robert Louis Stevenson, as well as his landmark essay "The Art of Fiction"—called him an "excellent talker about books. . . . His knowledge is of the fullest, his resources of allusion and comparison are endless, [and] his demarcation of different schools of literature is exact."[11] James seemed "so perfectly at home in criticism," said another reviewer, that he found it hard to remember that he was also a productive novelist.[12] James saw the "critic's first duty" to be finding "some key to [an author's] method, some utterance of his literary convictions, some indication of his ruling theory."[13] Looking at books from both a reader's and a writer's point of view, he shared with other *Atlantic* reviewers the belief that art and criticism went hand in hand.

Despite his life abroad and his diminishing familiarity with American ways, James contributed to the *Atlantic*'s founding goal of shaping a national literature. From his perspective, "literary absenteeism" was "not a peculiarly American vice or an American virtue," but "an expression and a proof of the modern sense which enlarges one's country to the bounds of civilization."[14] Right or wrong, he could point to the long tradition of American expatriation, which extended back to travelers like Benjamin Franklin and James Fenimore Cooper. He could not, of course, have anticipated those who followed in the next century. Writers such as Ernest Hemingway, Gertrude Stein, F. Scott Fitzgerald, and Richard Wright thought of an apprenticeship in Europe as a rite of authorship. Unlike that war-weary generation of writers, James—heartbroken by America's refusal to enter World War I—denounced his U.S. citizenship in July 1915. For some Americans this gesture seemed like treason. James's loyal friend Howells disagreed. He defiantly titled the last essay he wrote "The American James."

The James-Howells relationship offers a glimpse into the working of the *Atlantic* and what amounts to the international politics of letters. Shrewdly predicting that James would have to create an audience if he were to continue to develop as an artist, Howells helped James as he helped Mark Twain by actively soliciting and reviewing his work. Howells's thinking about the novel and American fiction generally grew from his reading of James's evolving versatility. In January 1882, a reviewer for the *Atlantic*, who compared Howells's *Dr. Breen's Practice* to James's *Portrait of a Lady*, noted similarities in the two writers' focus on social forces and on characters typical of an entire class. The writer felt that James showed "how the complex and firmer life of the Old World acts upon Isabel, with her free and generous nature, and how the crude, experimental, yet largely ethical elements of New England society have conspired to confine and torture the honest spirit of Howells' Dr. Breen." The difference between the two authors lay in suggestions always seeming "to come from within, and to work outward" in James, while the process worked just the opposite in Howells, who was "frank, humorous, and sympathetic," if less "subtle and refined" than James.[15]

The men's success at stamping the *Atlantic* with their own imprints excited criticism as well as envy. In "Miss Grief" (1880), the story of a would-be Emily Brontë who labors in obscurity and dies from poverty and frustration, Constance Fenimore Woolson noted the extent to which "private relations" determine success.[16] Some readers thought Woolson's condescending male protagonist, a successful if far from brilliant writer, to be a slap at her friend James—or was it Howells?

In 1882, the two men found themselves at the center of an international slugfest when Howells claimed in *Century Magazine* that "the art of fiction has . . . become a finer art in our day than it was with Dickens and Thackeray." Dickens, Thackeray, Richardson, and Fielding, he wrote, are "great men," but men "of the past."[17] In their stead, Howells offered Henry James, the leader of a new school of American fiction, largely influenced by the French realism of Alphonse Daudet. It was not just that names like Howells and James had replaced those of Thackeray and Dickens, or that one national literature had superseded another. Howells jettisoned a whole system of values associated with British culture and represented by the Church, the aristocracy, Oxford and Cambridge, Epsom and Ascot.[18] To suggestions of a decline in the supremacy of British letters, the English novelist George Moore retaliated by mocking the lack of American originality: "James went to France and read Tourgenieff," he wrote. "W. D. Howells stayed at home and read Henry James. . . . [When] Henry James said, I will write the moral history of America, as Tourgenieff wrote the moral history of Russia—he borrowed at first-hand, understanding what he was borrowing. W. D. Howells borrowed at second-hand, and without knowing what he was borrowing."[19] From one perspective, Howells's *Century* review extended the sentiment of Emerson's Phi Beta Kappa address, or, to borrow Oliver Holmes's metaphor, it proved Howells's Emancipation Proclamation to Emerson's Declaration of Independence. From another, it underscored not only the transatlantic complexities of authorship and publishing in the late nineteenth century, but also the degree to which a country's national pride resided in its authors.

Like James, *Atlantic* contributors repeatedly returned to the question posed by the title of an unsigned May 1875 article, "What Is an American?" The author speculated: "Is he an Adams, a Jefferson, a Lincoln, a Barnum, a Butler, or a Fisk? Are Longfellow and Lowell, Hawthorne and Emerson, our representative literary men, or Bret Harte and his followers?"[20] Looking at *Atlantic* reviews, or the international focus of Henry James's serialized novels in the 1870s, a reader might be struck by the range of offerings about other cultures, which James and his friend and editor saw as contributing to larger discussions about American identity. This is perhaps most evident in James's travel writing for the *Atlantic*. "Why is it," he asks in "Recent Florence" (May 1878),

> that in Italy we see a charm in things which in other countries we should consign to the populous limbo of the vulgarities? If, in the city of New York, a great museum of the arts were to be provided, by way of decoration, with a species of veranda inclosed on one side by a series of small-paned casements, draped in dirty linen, and . . . the place being surmounted by a thinly-painted wooden roof, strongly suggestive of summer heat, of winter cold, of frequent leakage, those amateurs who had had the advantage of foreign travel would be at small pains to conceal their contempt.

The answer for James lay not in the veranda itself, or indeed in what was visible, but in "the historical process that lies behind it," in the accretion over time of the manners, values, rituals, and thinking that make one country this and not another.[21] Culture, for James, came best into relief through comparison, with Europe and America providing the other's measure. His own *depaysment*—as the French call a queasiness of soul in a strange place—both fed his art and formed its basis.[22] It seems fitting that a magazine that began by defining itself in comparison and opposition to English counterparts should count James among its most loyal contributors.

In 1904, the long-expatriated Henry James would board the *Kaiser Wilhelm II* and disembark in Hoboken, New Jersey. He had not stepped on native ground for over twenty years. The book that grew out of his visit, *The American Scene* (1907), captures the drama of returning to places changed beyond recognition or simply obliterated in the name of progress. James posed a number of questions about the workings of human memory and the relationship between history and place, but above all he wondered whether there is such an entity as an "American character," and how it might be found. James sought an answer in New York's Washington Square and the Bowery, at Grant's Tomb and in Central Park. He pondered New Hampshire's White Mountains and its summer watering holes. At Harvard's Union Hall, he gazed at John Singer Sargent's portrait of the philanthropist Henry Lee Higginson and felt transported, as if by magic carpet, face to face with the historical forces that led to Higginson's founding the Boston Symphony Orchestra. The mansions of Newport, the battlefield at Concord, Philadelphia's Eastern State Penitentiary, and the Confederate White House—these are just a few of the sites that James found alien. Allowing his mind to play freely, like a riffing jazz musician, he ruminated on the speech of American women, businessmen commuting on the Staten Island Ferry, and the spectacle of exceptional wealth—on anything that would distinguish America from his adopted Europe. In the end, he posed more questions than he perhaps answered, for though he believed it was better to know than to remain ignorant, true knowing involved surrendering himself to the finally unknowable welter of life. Perhaps it was impossible to grasp what America meant to him beyond its play on his imagination.

15

Clarence King, Scholar-Adventurer

While I looked the sun descended; shadows climbed the Sierras, casting a gloom over foothill and pine, until at last only the snow summits, reflecting the evening light, glowed like red lamps along the mountain wall for hundreds of miles. The rest of the Sierra became invisible. The snow burned for a moment in the violet sky, and at last went out.

CLARENCE KING, *Mountaineering in the Sierra Nevada*, 1872

WILLIAM BREWER, the field director of the California survey, looked long at the Sierra's highest peak, then back to his assistant, Clarence King (1842–1901), and shook his head: "A man might as well climb a cloud." That settled the matter for King, who went through life with an "audacity that invited disaster."[1] He decided then and there to ascend Mt. Whitney, which had been named after sighting by members of the California Geological Survey in 1864. Given other lives, King might have conquered continents or led a nation, but Louis Agassiz's Harvard lectures on glaciers had inspired him to desert the snug comforts of Cambridge and travel by wagon train and horseback through rough mining towns and rougher country, in search of Josiah Whitney, chief of the California Geological Survey.[2] King had to use every ounce of his silver-tongued eloquence to persuade Whitney to add him to his team. He had less trouble convincing Dick Cotter, a drover with the expedition, to join his climb of Mt. Whitney.

In the tangy, moist air of a California morning, the young men set off shouldering forty-pound packs, which threatened, once they reached higher altitudes, to drag them into oblivion. King, whose favorite literary hero happened to be Don Quixote, had no plan except accomplishing what Brewer had pronounced impossible. With no visible route and none of the sophisticated equipment of today's climbers, the two set off, knowing they would have to weave their way through a maze of towering pinnacles, chopping footholds up the sides of colossal boulders, and struggling through gorges and snowfields. The first night they made camp on a narrow granite shelf and tried to sleep as temperatures dropped to zero. Missiles of falling rock drove them from their shelter before dawn. The next day they lunched at thirteen thousand feet. To the west "stretched the Mount Brewer wall with its succession of smooth precipices and amphitheatre ridges. To the north the great gorge of the King's River plunged down five thousand feet." The Kern Valley opened below them "with its smooth oval outline, the work of extinct glaciers, whose form and extent were evident from worn cliff-surface and rounded wall; snow-fields, relics of the former névé, hung in white tapestries around its ancient birthplace . . . [and] the broad, corrugated valley [stretched], for a breadth of fully ten miles."[3]

Assessing their options, they realized they had one blind choice. Cotter declared they were "in for it now."[4] He braced himself against the mountain, then waved his companion forward. With the other end of the rope around his chest, King inched ahead, clutching shards of rock and wedging his fingers into crevices. They knew that if he lost his balance, both would die. As King told readers of the *Atlantic* (July 1871),

> I shouted to him to be very careful and let go in case I fell, loosened my hold upon the rope, and slid quickly down. My shoulder struck against the rock and threw me out of balance; for an instant I reeled over upon the verge, in danger of falling, but, in the excitement, I thrust out my hand and seized a small alpine gooseberry-bush, the first piece of vegetation we had seen. Its roots were so firmly fixed in the crevice that it held my weight and saved me.[5]

They reached their destination at exactly twelve noon. At the summit, King felt as though he had entered a vacuum drained of all sound. He and Cotter gazed out at a crazy quilt of peaks and discovered that they had not climbed Mt. Whitney after all. Unbowed, King rang his "hammer upon the topmost rock," the men grasped hands, and King officially christened their mountain Mount Tyndall, in honor of the English geologist John Tyndall.[6] He had already begun planning a future climb of Mt. Whitney, which he did a month after the first recorded ascent in 1873. When John

Muir climbed the mountain that October, he found a yeast can, which contained a note:

> Sept. 19th, 1873: This peak, Mt. Whitney, was this day climbed by Clarence King, U.S. Geologist, and Frank F. Knowles of Tula River. On Sept. 1, in New York, I first learned that the high peak south of here, which I climbed in 1871, was not Mt. Whitney, and I immediately came here. Clouds and storms prevented me from recognising this in 1871, or I should have come here then.
>
> All honour to those who came here before me.
>
> C. King

King included a "notice" written by another climber, Carl Rabe, on the sixth of September that year, which read: "Gentlemen, the looky finder of this half a dollar is wellkome to it." Muir, who replaced these records as well as the half dollar, made it clear that, having "spent ten years in the Sierras alone," he had never left his "name on any mountain, rock, or tree in any wilderness."[7]

Three years after persuading Whitney he should volunteer on the survey, King used his considerable eloquence with the U.S. Congress. They agreed to fund a survey of the proposed route of the Union Pacific railway along the Fortieth Parallel from eastern Colorado to California. At twenty-five, King headed the survey and began by studying the Comstock Lode in Nevada.

King had many gifts, not least among them a seeming freedom from self-doubt. A friend thought it "strange that the Creator . . . should have made only one" King, "when it would have been so easy to make more Kings."[8] With his unshaven cheeks, cropped light hair, stolid build, and blithe-blue eyes, King looked the national hero he became in 1872. Some said he saved the country from the brink of financial disaster when, in the last stages of the Fortieth Parallel survey, he heard rumors that the world's largest deposit of diamonds had been discovered in the West. Intrigued, he and his crew used their knowledge of the area to locate the secret mine. Accustomed to surviving on bacon, beans, and coffee, King rode day and night to a site near Fort Bridger, Wyoming, ascertained the falsity of the claim, and, braving a blizzard, spurred his horse toward San Francisco. There he met with the directors of the mining company, whose stocks had soared with news of the find. Insisting that the mine had been salted, King refuted the testimony of two other experts. The directors allegedly offered him a million dollars to delay his report a few days. King refused to wait a single hour, saying there was not enough money in California to prevent him revealing the truth. "But for King," an influential banker explained, "the free flow of capital for developing our mineral resources would have been set back for fifty years."[9]

The publicity surrounding the diamond hoax worked to King's advantage, making him a much-sought-after consultant and witness for mining companies. Dukes and duchesses extended invitations, as did the Rothchilds, the John Hays, and Henry Adamses. No group courted him more than politicians wrangling over funds for competing geological survey teams. William Dean Howells, King's editor and friend, commended him to President Hayes for his role in averting a national catastrophe and his mastery "of the last graces of Pike [County] dialect," which Twain included in his *Adventures of Huckleberry Finn*. He is, as you see, Howells wrote, "a charming and most civilized New Englander."[10] King called on Hayes the winter of 1879 and four months later assumed the first directorship of the U.S. Geological Survey (1880).

The *Atlantic* introduced King to thousands of readers, and he, in turn, introduced new readers to the field of geology and the glories of America's western wilderness. Chapters from *Mountaineering in the Sierra Nevada* (1872) ran in the magazine from May through August 1871. "Dedicated to Josiah Dwight Whitney and His Staff, My Comrades of the Geological Survey of California," the book reflected King's view that, though a science, geology embraced life's central religious, aesthetic, and moral issues. He described in the last of his *Atlantic* installments how a scientist feels "accountable for seeing everything, for analyzing, for instituting perpetual comparison, and as it were sharing in the administering of the physical world." This said, however, he went on to sing the praises of aimlessly luxuriating in nature: "No tongue can tell the relief to simply withdraw scientific observation, and let Nature impress you in the dear old way with all her mystery and glory."[11] King, who articulated in his own field Henry James's wish to be a naive reader again, liked to think that studying the earth trained the imagination, because, as he said, no person could look deeper into the ground than another.

Through the lens of his vast reading, King helped to make the American West familiar to educated easterners, while also communicating its singular beauty. When he first gazed upon Mt. Shasta, for instance, he wondered aloud, "What would [John] Ruskin, the most famous living critic of art, have said if he had seen *this*?"[12] As he struggled up the mountain, a line by James Russell Lowell kept echoing in his head: "burned out craters healed with snow." King could write as engagingly about the formation of the earth as he could about the boundaries between faith and science. He also had a writer's eye for details that bring characters to life. "It's all Bierstadt and Bierstadt and Bierstadt nowadays!" he recounts a would-be California painter complaining in "Wayside Pikes" (November 1871). "What has he done but twist and skew and distort and discolor and belittle and be-pretty this whole doggonned country? Why, his mountains are too high and too slim; they'd blow over in one of our fall winds. I've herded colts two summers in Yosemite, and, honest now, when I stood right up in front of his picture, I didn't know it."[13] Howells thought his friend should earn a living by writing. How many writers could make readers feel as if they themselves were hanging by little more than a fingernail on Mt. Tyndall?

Mountaineering in the Sierra Nevada cemented King's image with a public who thought its narrator a man of great physical energy, social standing, mental scope, training, and wit (to use Henry Adams's list).[14] In "Kaweah's Run," for example, King narrates his hair-raising ride from Visalia to Millerton on a nag that seems to spring wings to save him from bandits and almost certain death. Although King makes it to the nearest way station, it turns out to be a haven for his pursuers. His escape depends on his not awakening his host. Waiting until the middle of the night, he steals to the stable and disrobes: "In constant dread lest he [Kaweah] should make some noise, I hurried to muffle his forefeet with my trousers and shirt, and then, with rather more care, to tie upon his hind feet my coat and drawers."[15] After walking a quarter of mile, King decides it is safe enough to retrieve his clothes, and, with pistol cocked, gallops away.

King's characterization of himself as an American folk hero obscured the more troubling contradictions in his personality. Secretive and gregarious, imperious and generous, he possessed, as one friend noted, qualities not necessarily in harmony with one another. He had a gargantuan appetite for life, and his interests danced from "the rhythm of Creole gumbo to the verse of Theocritus, from the origin of the latest *mot* to the age of the globe, from the soar or slump of the day's market to the method of Lippo Lippi, from the lightest play on words to the subtlest philosophy."[16] He paid his first visit to the *Atlantic*'s printing office wearing a pith helmet in preparation for reading proof. To the editors of the magazine, he represented the best of what they called "the new California school" of vivid and graphic writing.[17] King cultivated the appearance of being unconventional. He once astounded the U.S. Commissioner of Mining Statistics by appearing for dinner, at his camp near the Great Salt Lake, formally dressed in crisp white linens and silk socks. His love of masquerade found expression in his collection of ecclesiastical objects and elaborate clothing—an embroidered and spangled matador costume, for instance—and, more dramatically, in his leading for thirteen years a double life as an African American named "James Todd." In 1888, passing as Todd, King married a former slave named Ada Copeland in a religious ceremony that was not legally binding. Ada attributed his absences to his purported work as a Pullman porter. King did not have to explain his blue eyes and sandy-colored hair, since federal law defined those who had one black great-grandparent as "black." King kept her and their five children ignorant of his real identity until just before his death.

King's last years were beset by financial failures and ill health. Visiting the lion house at the Central Park Zoo in 1893, he had a breakdown and was arrested for disturbing the peace. When he came before New York's State Supreme Court for sentencing, he agreed to a six-month stay in the Bloomingdale Asylum. There he fell under the authority of another *Atlantic* author, S. Weir Mitchell, famous for developing the rest cure, which Charlotte Perkins Gilman pilloried in her story "The Yellow Wallpaper." The indignity of King's final months deeply disturbed John Hay: "There you have it in the fact!" he told Henry Adams—"the best and brightest man of his generation, with talents immeasurably beyond any of his contemporaries; with industry that has often sickened me to witness it; with everything in his favor but blind luck; hounded by disaster from the cradle, with none of the joy of life to which he was entitled, dying at last, with nameless suffering, alone and uncared-for, in a California tavern."[18] Having hoped to recover some of his losses in California, King died in debt, leaving no provision for his wife and children. His friends conspired to keep his secrets. John Hay supported King's elderly mother and funneled money to Ada.[19] After Hay died, his widow, then his son-in-law, and finally his daughter saw that Ada's stipend was paid in full. The public learned of King's double life in 1933, when Ada sued his estate.

Despite his failings and contradictions—or perhaps because of them—King seemed to embody the spirit of America's West. He lives again as a character in Wallace Stegner's novel *Angle of Repose*, which presents him as a strong and mysterious force of nature. Students of geology know him as the author of the eight-hundred-page "geologic bible," *Systematic Geology* (1878), which set the standard for geological reporting. One admirer summed up its contribution by saying that "probably no more masterly summary of great truths of geology had been made since the publication of Lyell's Principles."[20] For most of his contemporaries, however, King had come as close as one could to achieving immortality through *Mountaineering in the Sierra Nevada*, a book that looks forward to John Muir's *My First Summer in the Sierra*. Oddly enough, King was wrong, and Muir—not a trained geologist—right, about the formation of the Sierra canyons. Muir, who first identified "living" or moving glaciers in the Sierras, attributed the peaks to glaciers carving canyons rather than to centuries of erosion.

King's sublime descriptions of the Sierras might be read as a counterargument to contemporaries who, in the name of progress, ignored the scars of railroad tracks, logging roads, and strip mining. He wrote at a time when people considered it almost "a religious duty" to make a pilgrimage to the mountains.[21] In an *Atlantic* essay titled "Mountains in Literature" (September 1879), Thomas Sergeant Perry tried to articulate the relationship between Americans and the landscape. "Even if we gaze at the mountains or at plains with other emotions," he wrote,

> it may be that in the complexity of civilization we have grown accustomed to finding whatever we please in the landscape, and that we read in it what we have in our own hearts. Perhaps, to take an example, the expanse of ocean, which, from association or emotion, expresses despair to one, and may express calm joy to another, is like a great mirror which images but what gazes at it. And so it may be with nature in general. Is it not possible, too, that our present enthusiasm about it is closely related to the modern feeling about music, of which very much the same thing is true?[22]

Perry spoke to the sublimity of the American landscape, be it the rocky coast of Maine, the painted desert, the Grand Canyon, the Tetons, or the redwood forests, which, in his mind, reflected whatever lay deepest in the hearts of its people.

The *Atlantic*'s founders had dedicated themselves to advancing "National Progress," but who defined that "progress," and what was its relationship to "an American idea"? While the country debated these questions, the *Atlantic* reflected a new reality. The issue containing King's "Kaweah's Run" (August 1871), for example, displayed how "national" the "eastern" magazine had become. To the same issue, John W. De Forest contributed a chapter from *Kate Beaumont*, a novel set in South Carolina, and Henry James the first installment of his New York novel *Watch and Ward*. With *Their Wedding Journey*, Howells began his chronicle of Isabel and Basil March, he from a small midwestern town, and she from Boston. Reviewers assessed Bret Harte's condensed novels and a series of pioneer biographies from the Ohio Valley. Realizing that they could only speak to and for the country as far as they knew it, contributors who had taken the notion of an American culture for granted now thought in terms of cultures, plural—intra- as well as international.

16

The Gilded Eighties

Civilization is the lamb's skin in which barbarism masquerades.

THOMAS BAILEY ALDRICH, *Ponkapoag Papers*, 1903

THE PERIOD BETWEEN Reconstruction and the so-called Progressive Era owes its name to Mark Twain and Charles Dudley Warner's satiric novel about political corruption and cupidity, *The Gilded Age* (1873). "What is the chief end of man?" Twain asked in the 1870s, "—to get rich. In what way?—dishonestly if he can; honestly if he must."[1] The name "Gilded Age" emphasizes appearance over substance, the counterfeit over the genuine. The period when the United States rose as an industrial and world power, it was, to quote the art historian Wayne Craven, "gilded," not "golden": "The gilt of the Gilded Age pertained to that part of American society created by this country's first millionaire society."[2] Ironically, the country owes many of its great institutions to a generation of robber barons. Andrew Carnegie endowed the Pittsburgh museum that bears his name; and J. P. Morgan's son, Pierpont, assembled a magnificent library that testifies to his father's love of books. Henry Clay Frick's New York mansion, erected on the profits of steel and coke, houses his collection of exquisite paintings and Renaissance gilt bronzes.

Though no industrialist herself, Isabella Stewart Gardner shared the dream of creating a museum that would both enrich and educate the public. Living "at a rate and intensity . . . that makes other lives seem pale, thin and shadowy," Gardner built the Boston museum that now bears her name.[3] Between 1894 and

1903, the year she opened the mansion she called "Fenway Court" to the public, Gardner would spend over a million dollars—an immense amount in those times—amassing the country's largest private art collection. Think of it, she wrote a friend: "I can see that Europa, that Rembrandt, that Bonifazio, that Velázquez . . . anytime I want to."[4] Modeled after a Venetian palazzo overlooking the Grand Canal, Fenway Court sits on reclaimed swampland. Although the *Boston Herald* dismissed Gardner's achievement as a woman's whim, it won accolades from unlikely sources. "As long as such a work can be done," Henry Adams told her, "I will not despair of our age."[5] Henry James, having incinerated a houseful of priceless furniture in *The Spoils of Poynton* (serialized in the *Atlantic* as "The Old Things," 1896), found himself stymied by the "attempt to tell the story of the wonderfully-gathered and splendidly-lodged Gardner Collection. . . . It is in presence of the results magnificently attained, the energy triumphant over everything, that one feels the fine old disinterred tradition of Boston least broken."[6]

As James implies, Gardner's "energy triumphant" surprised everyone. In the first place, she was a woman, and no other woman had the means or the daring for such a project—though she left the choosing and acquisition of her paintings to the not always reliable art historian Bernard Berenson. Gardner's accomplishment, like those of Frick and Morgan, suggests the place of art and art collection in the Gilded Age but also the growing separation in America between the extraordinarily rich and the hungry poor. Bliss Perry, a later editor of the *Atlantic*, recalled a lunch at Annie Field's house that captures the spirit of the age. During lunch, Isabella Gardner charmed the other guests with stories of her travails with the Italian workmen. No detail escaped her attention. Her craftsmen grumbled about her daily, sometimes hourly interference, then threatened to strike. Habituated to command, Gardner refused to negotiate. She fired the chief stonemason for lying, and the electrician for stealing. After chastising the floor layers for loafing, she caught them mimicking her, and with a wave of her hand banished them from the premises.

Perry found "something exhilarating in this picture of a lone Yankee woman subduing the insurgent sons of Italy by sheer pluck and will power." Another guest reacted differently. William Dean Howells, who knew what it was like to work for pennies, had trouble controlling himself. His anger at Gardner was partly anger at himself for laughing politely at the tale of her epic struggles and their preordained outcome. The lunch ended amicably enough, but when Howells and Perry were safely ensconced in their cab, Howells "broke out in bitter denunciation of the arrogance of wealth."[7] Perry attributed his invective to the years he spent in Venice as U.S. consul and to his respect for Italian craftsmen. It did not occur to him that Howells equated his own labors for literature with those of a master stone mason or that Gardner's Fenway Court seemed an unbridled expression of capitalism, the Boston equivalent of a pharaoh's pyramid.

An era of "conspicuous consumption," political partisanship, and industrial growth, the Gilded Age prompted the rise of populism and other reform movements. *Atlantic* reviewers were quick to note that literature reflected growing social tensions. In January 1881, the month that Howells officially resigned his editorship, the magazine reviewed a cluster of "political novels"—among them *Bricks without Straw*, Albion W. Tourgée's bitter account of Reconstruction, subverted by violence, fraud, and the retraction of civil rights for freed blacks. His review followed another on Émile Zola's *Le roman expérimental*, in which Zola argued that the French naturalists' production of "true documents" would eventually result in a "better society."[8] In March, the *Atlantic* carried a controversial article by a former lawyer turned journalist, Henry Demarest Lloyd, titled "Story of a Great Monopoly." The press called Lloyd, whose father-in-law was an owner of the *Chicago Tribune*, "the millionaire socialist." A strong opponent of bribery and corruption, and a model for younger reformers such as Clarence Darrow and John Dewey, Lloyd had been instrumental in removing the Tammany boss, William Tweed, from office. As mayor of New York, Tweed filched millions of dollars in kickbacks from those seeking jobs, benefits, and contracts. In 1873, he received a twelve-year prison sentence for embezzlement of public funds, which an appellate court reduced to one year. Facing other charges after his release, Tweed fled to Spain, only to be extradited to the United States. He died in prison.

In "Story of a Great Monopoly," Lloyd claimed that Rockefeller's Standard Oil was in cahoots with the railroads. By refusing transport to smaller producers or granting it at exorbitant prices, the railroads conspired with Standard Oil to drive the company's competitors into bankruptcy. Anticipating Lincoln Steffens's argument in *The Shame of the Cities* (1904), Lloyd told *Atlantic* readers that "Standard has done everything with the

Pennsylvania legislature, except refine it. . . . America has the proud satisfaction of having furnished the world with the greatest, wisest, and meanest monopoly known to history." Calling for the regulation of railroads and the establishment of a national board to hear citizens' complaints, Lloyd identified the cornerstones of capitalism as "fortune, power, precedence, [and] success." According to Lloyd, the states had failed to regulate commerce. "The United States must succeed, or the people will perish."[9] He would call the book that grew from this exposé of the Standard Oil Company *Wealth against Commonwealth* (1894). It paved the way for the Interstate Commerce Act (1887) and the Sherman Antitrust Act (1890) and buttressed the claims of Ida Tarbell's muckraking *History of Standard Oil* (1904). In 1911, the U.S. Supreme Court would order the dissolution of Standard Oil into thirty-four independent companies. The decision broke the monopoly but made John D. Rockefeller, who owned a quarter of these companies' surging shares, the richest man in the world.

Although public interest in Lloyd's *Atlantic* article increased sales of the March 1881 issue seven times over, the *Atlantic* needed a string of similar successes to push its circulation above 12,000, while *Harper's* enjoyed a circulation of 100,000, and the *Century*, the successor to *Scribner's*, 210,000 and rising.[10] The *Century* owed its popularity to a number of factors, including its coverage of New York City, its focus on history, and a chatty tone.[11] In August 1885, the *Century*'s table of contents included, apart from installments of Howells's *The Rise of Silas Lapham* and James's *The Bostonians*, articles on "typical dogs," housekeeping, a number of short reviews, light "Bric-a-Brac" pieces with titles like "A Lesson in Tennis," and recollections of Civil War veterans—part of its spectacularly successful series on the Civil War. Planned for one year and lasting three (1883–1886), the series had been designed to clear "up cloudy questions with new knowledge and the wisdom of cool reflection." Instead it elicited so many passionate responses and supporting documents from readers that the editors created a supplementary department called "Memoranda on the Civil War."[12] The *Century* both engaged and catered to readers. Its habit of breaking regular columns into short sections made reading easier for those who read between other tasks, while its wider choice of types of fiction and its numerous illustrations appealed to a cross section of middle-class readers. The same issue of the *Atlantic* had narrower offerings. Apart from The Contributor's Club, readers could choose among a smattering of poems; four stories; a travel piece by Charles Dudley Warner; essays on education, Buddhism, history, and literature; an imaginary conversation between Shakespeare and Anne Hathaway in the spirit of Walter Savage Landor; and ten reviews. With a limited budget, the *Atlantic* could augment its pages less expensively with essays and reviews than with fiction.

The tone of the *Century* further differed from that of the *Atlantic* in emphasizing "social and domestic moralities" over self-education.[13] As editor, Richard Watson Gilder allowed "no vulgar slang; no explicit references to . . . the generative processes; no disrespectful treatment of Christianity; no unhappy endings for any work of fiction"—but untold social connections.[14] He once recommended an essay on Catholic Church music to the *Atlantic* by giving the young author's pedigree: the daughter of W. Bayard Cutting, she was married to "the young lawyer just appointed by President Roosevelt Auditor of Porto Rico." Her father is "Samuel Gray War whose family have represented the Barings so long, who was a friend of Emerson and one of the creators of Lenox, for it was through him that Hawthorne was brought there."[15] Walt Whitman captured the central paradox of the *Century* when he wrote: "It is so sort of fussy, extra-nice, pouting"—but then again, "those very limitations were designed—maybe rightly designed."[16]

Much as Gilder admired Twain, he did not hesitate to cut passages from *Huckleberry Finn* that might strike readers as violent or coarse. If he were alive today, he would probably support the decision of NewSouth Books to substitute the word "slave" for "nigger." The *Century*'s column titled "Topics of the Times" made a point of commenting on contemporary manners and morals. In the wake of recent anarchist activity, Gilder asked Howells to reconsider a line in *The Rise of Silas Lapham*, in which a character mentions "applying dynamite to those rows of close-shuttered, handsome, brutally insensitive, houses." Howells changed the text to read "nothing but the surveillance of the local policeman prevents me from *personally affronting* [italics mine] those long rows of . . . houses."[17] Gilder told disgruntled contributors that he considered it his "duty to go slowly and make as few mistakes as possible."[18]

Gilder's concerns about the tone of his magazine reflected both unstable times and shifting mores. After passage of the Comstock Act in 1873, for example, editors like Gilder had to contend with laws that made it illegal to send any "obscene" material through the U.S. mail. Offending material ranged from contraceptives and pornography to medical textbooks—and Leo Tolstoy's *Kreutzer Sonata* (1889), a study of lust. The year his act passed, Anthony Comstock organized the New York Society for the Prevention of Vice. Publishing houses and book distribution centers soon found themselves the subject of unwanted headlines. As the first two decades of the twentieth century unfolded, Comstock himself would become an object of derision among intellectuals for his 1906 raid on the Art Students League of New York and his attack, seven years later, on Paul Chabas's nude painting *September Morn*. In the meantime, editors and writers tested the limits of public tolerance at their own peril.

Thomas Bailey Aldrich, who followed Howells as editor of the *Atlantic* in 1881, had no intention of offending readers or challenging censors when he accepted an eight-part serial from the English novelist Thomas Hardy, whose critically acclaimed novel *Far from the Madding Crowd* had boosted the sales of Ticknor and Fields's *Every Saturday* in its dying days. Hardy expressed his pleasure at "sailing" in the *Atlantic*'s ship: "*The Atlantic* is, I need hardly say, a magazine for which I have long had a great liking and respect."[19] He promised to meet all deadlines and proposed ensuring the manuscript against loss by sending a second copy of each installment in a separate mailing.

The reception of *Two on a Tower* defines what the public was and was not willing to accept in "realistic" fiction, especially when it undermined myths about woman's nature. The plot, inspired by Hardy's sighting of a comet, had the earmarks of a potboiler. Lady Constantine falls in love with a young astronomer, Swithin St. Cleeve, during her husband's absence in Africa. After receiving word of her husband's death, they marry, then learn that their marriage predated Lord Constantine's passing by two weeks. The fact allows Swithin to accept a legacy that requires him to remain unmarried until this twenty-fifth birthday. The two agree that they will marry once Swithin inherits and that he will use the intervening four years to further his scientific studies. After Swithin leaves on an extended scientific expedition, Lady Constantine realizes she is pregnant. Desperate to avoid scandal, she accepts the proposal of a visiting bishop. Hardy spares Swithin—who returns to find his "wife" a widow as well as a mother—any hard decisions by having her die. Harriet Preston led a chorus of critics who thought that Hardy's "pathological study" of Lady

Constantine "fit only for a professional book," and his use of the bishop a reproach to the church. Aldrich privately conceded that the concluding chapters "were not quite in the line of *The Atlantic*. . . . The American public, like the English public, sometimes strains at a gnat, though its usual diet is camels whole."[20] Nevertheless, he lobbied for a second novel from Hardy, who continued to test the limits of publishable fiction with *Tess of the D'Urbervilles* (1891) and his last novel, *Jude the Obscure* (1895). The Bishop of Wakefield found *Jude* so "obscene"—its heroine defies convention by living with Jude and bearing his children out of wedlock—that he publicly burned a copy. Returning to poetry, Hardy thought his novels too far ahead of their time to win favor with readers, who may have found his unbearably bleak vision of life more disturbing than the flouting of public morality.

Those connected to the *Atlantic* winced once again when the magazine's first editor, James Russell Lowell, confided his reservations about *Two on a Tower* to Julian Hawthorne, who turned around and sold his remarks as an interview to the *New York World* (24 October 1886). The report caused a stir because Lowell had been until 1885 minister to the court of St. James. After the firestorm died down, Lowell wrote that the expression "Save me from my friends must be stretched, it would seem, to take in their children also."[21] Hawthorne claimed that apart from calling the Prince of Wales monstrously fat and belittling his use of speechwriters, Lowell had disparaged Hardy for being "small and unassuming in appearance—[he] does not look like the genius of tradition."[22] Another man might have laughed off the observation; not Hardy, whom friends knew to be morbidly sensitive about his appearance. The gratuitous insult stung doubly because Hardy had always loyally supported Lowell against detractors. According to Edmund Gosse, Hardy might as well have received an unsportsmanlike kick in the stomach. In any case, he was deeply hurt. Lowell disowned the interview, hedging his denials by saying he had never commented on the Prince of Wales's weight. About Hardy he remained suspiciously silent. Gosse, a friend of both men, advised Lowell to repudiate the attribution more vigorously; Hardy should be assured privately that Hawthorne had misrepresented his remarks.[23] On one point everyone agreed: the embarrassment was like "a dead rat in the wall—an awful stink and no cure."[24] Even Lowell's old adversary Thomas Wentworth Higginson sent a note of commiseration. If nothing else, the incident highlighted the intricate transatlantic network of *Atlantic* authors.

Morals and manners may have embarrassed magazines like the *Century* and the *Atlantic*, but through the 1880s the problems exposed by muckrakers such as Lloyd and Ida Tarbell cut deeper into the body politic. Though publishing articles by Jacob Riis and other reformers, they addressed issues of poverty and discontent in fiction. The year 1885 happened to be a banner year for American fiction, with the *Century* serializing Howells's *The Rise of Silas Lapham* (November 1884–August 1885), along with three excerpts from Mark Twain's *Adventures of Huckleberry Finn*.[25] A master promoter, Twain timed his pieces to come out during his much-touted lecture tour with the New Orleans writer George Washington Cable.

From September 1885 to October 1886, the *Atlantic* published Henry James's *The Princess Casamassima*, the story of an illegitimate bookbinder and a would-be assassin with the unusual name of Hyacinth Robinson. Robinson, whose French mother murdered his father, an English lord, embodies the conflict between the classes and the masses. James explained in the preface to his novel that he wanted to create a working-class protagonist who, appreciating "freedom and ease, knowledge and power, money, opportunity, and satiety," had "every door of approach shut in his face."[26] Such a man, he argued, has the making of an assassin. James envisions a vast network of terrorism, "peopled with a thousand forms of revolutionary passion." These include the grumblings of workers aired in bars; the ambitions of a radical, Paul Muniment, who ends his career as a conservative member of Parliament; the manipulations of an international CEO of terrorism, Diedrich Hoffendahl; and the political dilettantism of the Princess Casamassima.[27]

Invited to the princess's country estate, Robinson has a revelation. "I may have helped you to understand and enter into the misery of the people," he tells her, "but you have led my imagination into quite another train. . . . The monuments and treasures of art, the great palaces and properties, the conquests of learning and taste, the general fabric of civilisation as we know it, based, if you will, upon all the despotisms, the cruelties, the exclusions, the monopolies and the rapacities of the past, but thanks to which, all the same, the world is less impracticable and life more tolerable."[28] Robinson's awakened sense of beauty leads him to think that life may be worth living. But with either the hangman's noose or a comrade's bullet in his future, he turns his gun on himself.[29]

James's novel appeared at a time when the public struggled to understand a wave of bombings at Euston Square, London Bridge, the House of Commons, and the Tower of London. In 1885, the founder of the English Anarchist Circle, Henry Seymour, brought out the first issue of the *Anarchist.* The Russian revolutionaries Prince Peter Kropotkin and Sergei Mikhailovich Kravchinski, better known as "Stepniak," lived in London.[30] Although readers understood that James's creation of an international terrorist leader had real-life counterparts, *The Princess Casamassima* failed to resonate with readers, who disliked the increased introspection and uncertainty of James's vision. But James's extraordinary book anticipated later works, such as Joseph Conrad's *The Secret Agent*, and should have alerted Americans to threats in their country and abroad.

The subject of James's novel struck closer to home on 4 May 1886, when protesters in Chicago's Haymarket Square demanded an eight- instead of a twelve-hour workday. As police tried to break up the demonstration, someone threw a bomb into the crowd, and officers responded by firing. When the "riot" ended, eleven people were dead, including four policemen. Anarchist leaders who had sponsored the demonstration found themselves accused of inciting violence. Of the eight accused, one committed suicide, four were hanged, and three were pardoned after seven years in prison. Henry Demarest Lloyd and William Dean Howells were among the few who risked not only their reputations but also their livelihoods to protest what they saw as an unwarranted rush to judgment. The governor of Illinois, John P. Altgelt, agreed when he pardoned the surviving anarchists. George Frederic Parsons captured the American public's mood after the Haymarket riots when he told *Atlantic* readers that "freedom of speech is never more than relative, and that if we are to avoid the necessity of putting down anarchist riots we must see to it that the dissemination of anarchist doctrine is prevented."[31] He worried that modern socialists tended to place class loyalties above a love of country.

17

Thomas Bailey Aldrich, Guardian at the Gate

This is the story of a bad boy. Well, not such a very bad, but a pretty bad boy; and I ought to know, for I am, or rather I was, that boy myself.

THOMAS BAILEY ALDRICH, *The Story of a Bad Boy*, 1869

THOMAS BAILEY ALDRICH published his *Story of a Bad Boy* (1869) in a Ticknor and Fields publication for children called *Our Young Folks*, meant to compete with *Youth's Companion* and cultivate a new generation of *Atlantic* readers. His book about Tom Bailey's childhood growing up in Portsmouth, New Hampshire, owed a debt to Thomas Hughes's immensely popular book set in Victorian Britain, *Tom Brown's Schooldays* (1857). Both return to a time of life when a boy's first loyalty belongs to other boys. Tom Bailey's world extends just a few blocks, but those blocks offer endless opportunity for mischief. Told by Tom himself, the novel assures young readers that the terrors of childhood have a natural way of righting themselves and that soon a scapegrace like Tom will become a well-respected Thomas like his author—an ending that Mark Twain rejected for Huck Finn.

Aldrich came to the editorship of the *Atlantic* by way of its eclectic sister- publication, *Every Saturday*. Devoted to publishing the best of foreign literatures, the Ticknor and Fields weekly had almost gone up in flames with the Great Boston Fire of 1872, yet managed to limp on until, three years later, the cost of illustrations in a harsh recession sealed its fate. The reciprocal relationship between the publishing house, which needed to appeal to a broader audience than the *Atlantic*, and the *Atlantic* itself, which fed the house and its authors, would determine to some extent Aldrich's unwillingness to take risks. The *Atlantic* had changed hands a number of times when, in 1880, it became the property of Houghton, Mifflin & Co. and moved into the former parlors of the Woman's Club at No. 4 Park Street. In September, Aldrich took over a little back room overlooking the Old Granary Burying Ground, "where, as he liked to joke, lay those who would never submit any more manuscripts." Aldrich worked as his dog Trip drifted in and out of sleep before the coal fire. When Trip ate a dropped sonnet, his master wondered how he could have developed an appetite for doggerel.[1] Often, Aldrich's jokes had a target. This one reflects his dislike for poets like James Whitcomb Riley (sometimes called "the children's poet"), whom Aldrich was not above parodying with doggerel of his own:

Ma and me's asked out to dine
And I have dot a sickly spine,
But I don't mind a sickly spine
'S long as I am asked out to dine.[2]

Distancing himself from Howells, Aldrich weighed his scales in favor of poetry like his own, or perhaps any poetry that realistic fiction had overshadowed. At the same time, he intended to cultivate more foreign contributors, whom *Every Saturday* had profitably pirated. In the fall of 1881, after he assumed the editorship, Houghton Mifflin signed an agreement with Mssr. Ward, Lock & Co. to distribute the *Atlantic* in England.

Aldrich spent six hours a day in his office, whereas Howells, who preferred to work at home, had allotted himself one afternoon a week. The men also differed in style. Henry James voiced the general feeling that the *Atlantic* had "bought," in the slight, golden-haired Aldrich, a "gilded youth." He was considered—and apparently considered himself—the most handsome of literary men, "having a well-proportioned figure, a delicately florid complexion, a finely molded rather square face with a moustache and strong intellectual features. In dress he was always *biensoigné*, even fastidious."[3] Aldrich had grown up almost as poor as Howells, yet he appeared to know practically nothing of "the domestic tribulations . . . of the usual householder in this ill-served land" and cared little about bringing them into the homes of *Atlantic* readers.[4] His wife, Lilian, whom Mark Twain called a "strange and vanity-devoured, detestable woman," added force to those who thought him a frightful snob. Twain's dislike of

Mrs. Aldrich went back to the time Aldrich brought him home for dinner, and Lilian, thinking Twain drunk, refused him so much as a cup of tea. Nonetheless, the men became fast friends, which didn't stop Twain from noting that "Aldrich was so vain that he thought the sun rose for the sole purpose of shedding light on his writing." On second thought, he called Aldrich the second-vainest man in the world. The first was Twain himself.[5]

While "the great little T. B. Aldrich"—as James called him—escaped the worst sins of too much power, his obvious self-satisfaction rankled critics.[6] Aldrich had partisans in Howells and in Twain, who forgave Aldrich's praise of Bret Harte, if not his marriage to Lilian. A ferocious friend as well as a ferocious enemy, Twain bowed to Howells as a humorist and to Aldrich as a raconteur. Listening to Aldrich made him feel like the dark side of the moon to Aldrich's bright face. Not, he added, that Aldrich didn't have his faults, the biggest being his disinclination to curse. In the days when friends exchanged photographs, Twain once sent Aldrich a picture of himself every day for a week. Aldrich returned the compliment with a warning that the police swept down upon materials of this sort. The perpetrator—"known to the police as Mark Twain, alias 'The Jumping Frog,' a well-known California desperado"—risked arrest. Aldrich signed his letter "'T. Bayleigh, Chief of Police,' and on the outside of the envelope he wrote that it would be useless for that person to send any more mail-matter, as the post-office had been blown up."[7]

His sense of humor notwithstanding, Aldrich wrapped the *Atlantic* in a high seriousness that made it appear hostile to innovation. Coverage of topics like anarchism in the 1880s too often received glancing treatment in reviews instead of full articles, though Aldrich had, in the wake of the Haymarket riots, tried to secure an essay from Terence Powderley, head of the Knights of Labor, a labor organization that rejected violence. More usually, the articles skirted difficult issues and, as with the reviewer of Stepniak's *Russia under the Tzars* (August 1885), said more about a book's cover than its contents. The problem lay less in the contributors' awareness of current events than in the treatment of them. In contrast, the July 1887 issue of the *North American Review* contained essays by the economist Henry George and a dead president touched by scandal, James A. Garfield—baring his finances to show that he had not profited from public office—as well as pieces titled "Land Stealing in New Mexico," "English Women as a Political Force," and "Why Am I a Free Regionalist?" Offering similar pieces, *Harper's* published a regular feature titled "Monthly Record of Current Events" and a series called "Social Studies," which that month debated the future of corporations. While the *Atlantic* published essays on censorship ("Count Tolstoi and the Public Censor") and the regulation of railroads ("Is the Railroad Problem Solved?") in July 1887, their number signaled a decrease in social and political commentary after Howells's editorship.

Aldrich's limitations became those of the magazine, bringing it close to "the literary equivalent of tufted furniture and gas chandeliers."[8] Poets hoping to publish in the *Atlantic* would have done well to take his poem "Realism" as a warning:

> Romance beside his unstrung lute
> —Lies stricken mute.
> The old-time fire, the antique grace,
> You will not find them anywhere.
> To-day we breathe a commonplace,
> Polemic, scientific air:
> We strip Illusion of her veil;
> We vivisect the nightingale
> To probe the secret of his note.
> The Muse in alien ways remote
> —Goes wandering.[9]

J. P. Logan expressed Aldrich's belief that poetry belongs to a few gifted souls "whose heart and imagination have fed on abstract ideals, on visionary gleams of nature and life": its appeal is "special and exclusive"; its practice requires a remove from the hurly-burly bustle of everyday life.[10] Aldrich's inclination would have been to publish four poems a year, the number, he estimated, of undeniably fine poems among the bales of chaff.[11] His snobbery about poetry highlights the more open or democratic quality the magazine had under Fields and Howells. Now those who complained that he favored poems with classical allusions, like James Russell Lowell's "Credidimus Jovem Regnare," demanded fair hearing. One rejected author called Aldrich "a vulgar, unblushing Rascal" after the office returned his manuscript in its original wrapping. Such treatment, he wrote, deserved to be punished by a public horsewhipping.[12] Established authors felt similarly aggrieved. The reformer John Jay Chapman complained of

> these Aldriches who think style is the means of saying things well! . . . What better proof could we have of how thoroughly the plagiarists have overcrawled the world? "Use beauty-wash!" they cry—patent Italian sonnet-varnish—the only thing that has stood the test of time. Use the celebrated "Milton finish" for odes, epics and epitaphs. . . . "Use Shakespolio, Wordworthene, and Racine—they never vary and are Reliable"—Is it a wonder a man will not arrive anywhere if he spends all his life getting forward and backward over his style.[13]

To a great extent Aldrich's critics were right. He did not so much introduce a new standard for verse as endorse traditional forms and subjects. Aldrich continued to welcome poetry from Holmes and Lowell, while the two great poets of the century, Emily Dickinson and Walt Whitman, got—as they did from most magazines—short shift, or, with Dickinson, posthumous recognition. The *Atlantic*'s editors and reviewers could not understand Walt Whitman, though the magazine published two of his early poems—"Bardic Symbols" (1860), better known by the title "As I Ebb'd with the Ocean of Life," and "Proud Music of the Sea" (1869), for which it paid one hundred dollars. Howells had trouble seeing Whitman's lines as poetry, while Aldrich thought him little more than a conventional poet who "as the voice of the 19th century . . . will have little significance in the 21st. That he will outlast the majority of his contemporaries, I haven't the faintest doubt—but it will be in a glass case or a quart of spirits in an anatomical museum."[14] In September 1882, Aldrich approved an anonymous review of Whitman's 1881 edition of *Leaves of Grass* (September 1882), which, noting his "stained and distorted" views of human sexuality, ended with one of the greatest miscalculations in literary history—that "the book cannot attain to any very wide influence."[15]

Oliver Wendell Holmes philosophically remarked of literature that "there is room for everybody and everything in our huge hemisphere. Young America is like a three-year-old colt with his saddle and bridle just taken off. The first thing he wants to do is to roll. He is a droll object, sprawling in the grass with his four hoofs in the air; but he likes it, and it won't harm us."[16] Holmes notwithstanding, the magazine did not embrace Whitman until Bliss Perry, a Whitman scholar, became editor at the turn of the twentieth century. In 1904, Perry published his lecture "An American Primer" (April 1904), which celebrates Whitman's verbal exuberance.

Thomas Bailey Aldrich inherited a magazine that had become an institution. When the *Critic* polled readers for the names of forty living "Immortals" of the "sterner sex," Holmes, Lowell, Whittier, Bancroft, and Howells headed the 1884 list, with Aldrich, Harte, James, Twain, and Asa Gray in the top twenty-one.[17] The twenty-three-year-old George Santayana felt differently. In 1883, the year he celebrated his twentieth birthday, he said that no city appeared more genteel than Boston, and no magazine more expressive of its birthplace than the *Atlantic*, that bastion of aging antislavery and social liberals—with Harvard educations like his own.

In a sense, Aldrich guided the magazine back to a previous generation in poetry, while, mainly for financial reasons, seeking out a new generation of writers who would remain with the magazine after he left. Sarah Orne Jewett, who had a long, profitable relationship with the *Atlantic*, published *A Country Doctor* (1884), *The Country of the Pointed Firs* (1896), and her last novel, *The Tory Lover* (1901). *A Country Doctor* was one of three *Atlantic* novels about female physicians struggling to reconcile their personal and professional lives. Coincidental similarities between Howells's *Dr. Breen's Practice* (1881) and Elizabeth Stuart Phelps's *Dr. Zay* (1882) caused some concern in Park Street until Howells published a letter relating how he and Phelps had discovered the potential conflict and brushed it aside.

Like other regional writers, Jewett bemoaned the slow death of rural America through urbanization. She set "The Foreigner" (August 1900) in a town modeled after her own South Berwick, Maine, which had seen the collapse of its shipbuilding and textile industries. "The Foreigner" of Jewett's title refers to the French widow of a local sea captain, isolated by both her native language and her Catholic religion. The narrator regrets that she had not genuinely befriended the foreigner until the moment of her death, while the reader understands that the memory of the foreigner has become part of the town's history. The *Atlantic* published more than forty contributions from Jewett, who, under Aldrich, received thirteen dollars a page. Jewett's rate of compensation led Annie Fields to demand the same rate from Aldrich's assistant, Horace Scudder, who had no tactful way of saying that the firm did not think her worth more than ten.[18]

Apart from Jewett, the Tennessee writer Charles Egbert Craddock (Mary Noailles Murfree) found a home at the *Atlantic*. When Aldrich invited Murfree to Boston in 1885, he expected to greet the burly mountaineer who wrote with such a decisive, heavily inked script. Although Howells had picked Craddock up at the train, neither he nor the *Atlantic*'s staff forewarned Aldrich, who thought he was hallucinating when little Mary Murfree, lame since birth, came forward to take his hand. Between 1881 and 1890, the *Atlantic* serialized Murfree's *The Prophet of the Great Smokey Mountains*, *The Despot of Broomsedge*, *His Vanished Star*, *The Mystery of Witch-Face Mountain*, and *The Juggler*. Like Jewett, Murfree focused on a rural section of the country that increasingly drew tourists, folklorists, and developers. *The Prophet of the Great Smokey Mountains* begins with hyperbole to rival any of Albert Bierstadt's paintings of the Alps or Yosemite. "Always enwrapped in the illusory mists, always touching the evasive clouds, the peaks of the Great Smoky Mountains are like some barren ideal, that has bartered for the vague isolations of a higher atmosphere the material values of the warm world below."[19]

The greatest coup for Aldrich's *Atlantic* may have been the discovery of Charles Chesnutt, whose story "The Goophered Grapevine" (August 1887) he selected from a pile of submissions. Neither he nor his associates knew anything about the author, who turned out to be an African American lawyer. Chesnutt became one of Aldrich's favorites. The *Atlantic* published "Po' Sandy" (May 1888), "Dave's Neckliss" (October 1889), "Hot-Foot Hannibal" (January 1899), "The Bouquet" (November 1899), and "Baxter's Procrustes"(June 1904), a send-up of San Francisco's exclusive Bohemian Club.

Chesnutt described himself and his work as "the first contribution by an American of acknowledged African descent to purely imaginative literature. In this case the infusion of African blood is very small—is not in fact a visible admixture—but it is enough combined with the fact that the writer was practically brought up in the South, to give him knowledge of the people whose description is attempted."[20] Chesnutt, who won wide recognition as an expert on matters of race, offered *Atlantic* readers an alternative to Joel Chandler Harris, famous for his tales of Uncle Remus.

Chesnutt's "Goophered Grapevine," for example, follows the shifting balance of power between a former slave named Uncle Julius and an Ohioan couple who want to buy Julius's old home and market grapes. Julius tries to discourage them from purchasing the plantation by telling them the grapes are conjured "en deyain' no tellin' w'en it's gwine ter crap out." Julius seems to be the only living soul left who knows which vines were planted after the curse and therefore safe to eat. The narrator buys the plantation after he learns that Uncle Julius derives "a respectable revenue from the neglected grapevines. This, doubtless, accounted for his advice to me not to buy the vineyard, though whether it inspired the goopher story I am unable to state. I believe, however, that the wages I pay him for his services are more than an equivalent for anything he lost by the sale of the vineyard."[21] "The Goophered Grapevine" shows the narrator's assumptions about race working to Uncle Julius's advantage. To some extent, the relationship between Uncle Julius and the narrator, who fails to see Julius for the tactician he is, foreshadows the relationship between Chesnutt and early critics, who ignored his technical sophistication and hailed him as an accomplished dialect writer. Uncle Julius they characterized as "shrewd, wily, picturesque, [and] ingratiating."[22]

Chesnutt's fiction works by indirection to expose the tenuous nature of identity and the inherently racist structure of American society. These themes inform his well-known *Atlantic* story "The Wife of His Youth" and his novel *The Marrow of Tradition*. Howells reviewed *The Marrow of Tradition* for the *Atlantic* and praised Chesnutt's characters: "They are like us because they are of one blood by more than a half, or three quarters, or nine tenths. It is not, in such cases, their negro blood that characterizes them; but it is their negro blood that excludes them."[23] After reading *The Marrow of Tradition*, based on the Wilmington, North Carolina, Race Riot of 1898, Howells admitted his naïveté: "Good Lord!" he said of Chesnutt, "How such a negro must hate us."[24]

Despite discoveries like Chesnutt, Aldrich alienated writers whom his publisher, Henry Houghton, personally supported. Aldrich declined commissioned articles from Woodrow Wilson and Marion Crawford, as well as Houghton's friend Daniel Gilman, the president of Johns Hopkins University. After an embarrassed Houghton made his displeasure known about Gilman's treatment, Aldrich resigned, then withdrew his resignation, and finally resigned again in June 1890. He could hardly have known that a century after his death his poem titled "At the Funeral of a Minor Poet" would carry an unintended poignancy.

> Not great his gift; yet we can poorly spare
> Even his slight perfection in an age
> Of limping triolets and tame rondeaux.
> He had at least ideals, though unreached,
> And heard, far off, immortal harmonies,
> Such as fall coldly on our ear today.[25]

Aldrich lived until 1907, the year that marked the fiftieth anniversary of the *Atlantic Monthly*. "Aldrich is dead!" William Stanley Braithwaite announced: "Death taking him, still leaves his deathless fame."[26] Mark Twain's assessment proved more accurate: "His prose was diffuse, self-conscious, and barren of distinction in the matter of style. . . . His fame as a writer of verse is also very limited, but such as it is it is a matter to be proud of. It is based not upon his output of poetry as a whole but upon half a dozen small poems which are not surpassed in our language for exquisite grace and beauty and finish."[27] In 1908, Lilian Aldrich asked Howells and Twain to attend the dedication of his house to the city of Portsmouth. Twain agreed, even though he disliked the widow. Looking down at his black suit and shaking his head, Twain told those gathered that Aldrich would not have wished to see his friends in mourning: "When it came to making fun of folly, a silliness, a windy pretense, a wild absurdity, Aldrich the brilliant, Aldrich the sarcastic, Aldrich the merciless, was a master."[28] The same could not be said about his editorship of the *Atlantic*, the high seriousness of which left little room for laughter or experimentation. However, when compared to other magazines—to quote the *Nation*—the *Atlantic* flew "the flag of belles-letters, and will . . . till the tattered ensign goes down with the ship or is safely stored in some museum library."[29]

18

In the Wake of Louis Agassiz

When I first met Louis Agassiz . . . I was at once his captive.

The Autobiography of Nathaniel Shaler, 1909

TWELVE YEARS AFTER Louis Agassiz died, the *Atlantic* reviewed Elizabeth Agassiz's two-volume edition *Louis Agassiz: His Life and Correspondence* (1885). The end had come peacefully to the people's scientist, who was buried in Cambridge's Mount Auburn Cemetery. It seems fitting that trees sent from his native Switzerland shade his grave, marked by a twenty-five-hundred-pound boulder from Aar, the site where he had first imagined vast sheets of glacial ice moving south and covering the entire northern hemisphere as far as the Mediterranean and Caspian Seas.[1] His wife took comfort in thinking the gravesite united "the land of his birth and the land of his adoption."[2] She was not the lone angel at his grave. Boston newspapers published special editions bordered in black, and James Russell Lowell and Oliver Wendell Holmes wrote elegies. Holmes paid tribute to the generation of scientists that Agassiz sent out like missionaries, including Stanford's first president, David Starr Jordan, the country's leading ichthyologist, and Harvard's dean of science, Nathaniel Shaler. "God bless the great Professor!" Holmes had written in "Farewell to Agassiz": "And Madame, too, God bless her! / Bless him and all his band, / On the sea and on the land."[3]

As Holmes's verses indicate, Agassiz's influence had extended far beyond the walls of his laboratory. How many teachers have inspirited the general public with a love of scientific inquiry? Schoolboys brought him odd-looking specimens of fish; farmers, nests of turtles' eggs; and woodsmen, families of rattlesnakes. Agassiz had taken these offerings with the same enthusiasm he showed the tobacconist whose munificence funded the Anderson School of Natural History on Penikese Island (in Buzzards Bay, Massachusetts), or the officers of the government who placed at his command the resources of the Coast Survey.[4] No matter what their views of evolution, amateur scientists loved him because he could laugh at himself. He liked to tell students how he had spent hours trying to unlock the mystery of "an old pair of leather pantaloons" he mistook for a rare specimen.[5] "He was so human," Lowell wrote in his ten-page elegy, which recounts the shock of reading "three tiny words . . . *Agassiz is dead!*"[6]

In the dozen years between Agassiz's death and the publication of his letters, scientists grappled with and generally accepted Darwin's findings, so vigorously defended by Agassiz's respected opponent, Asa Gray. The change marks a seismic philosophical shift, from the platonic idealism Agassiz advanced—that reality is a mirror of higher truth—to the world of chance central to Gray's understanding of the transmutation of species. But Agassiz's reputation had exceeded the measure of his scientific peers. It mattered less, William James had written his father from South America during the 1865 expedition along the Amazon, that the great professor uttered "a greater amount of humbug. . . . No one sees farther into a generalization than his own knowledge of details extends, and you have a greater feeling of weight and solidarity about the movement of Agassiz's mind, owing to the continual presence of this great background of special facts, than about the mind of any other man I know."[7] As compelling as a Southern Baptist preacher at his best, Agassiz had led a movement that brought American science into the twentieth century. Advancing the goals of higher education and public welfare, he is still remembered by visitors to any of the institutions he and his acolytes founded, most notably the Museum of Comparative Zoology, now part of Harvard's Museum of Natural History.

Elizabeth Agassiz, who outlived her husband by more than three decades, was formidable in her own right. She raised her widowed stepson's children and presided over the first class of women scholars at the Harvard Annex. When editing her husband's letters, she made a strategical choice not to rehash old war stories about scientific skirmishes; instead she focused on his contributions to humanity at large. At first her omission caused the *Atlantic*'s reviewer a moment's pause for leaving so much of the record blank. Reconsidering, he decided that Agassiz had been "too large" to be remembered as a mere scientist. Instead the reviewer let Agassiz sum up his own character with a statement that underscores his love of his adopted people: "Naturalist as I am, I cannot but put the people first, the people who have opened this part of the American continent to European civilization."[8]

As Holmes noted, Agassiz's greatest contribution to science might have been the students he taught. Alpheus Hyatt, Frederick Ward Putnam, Edward S. Morse, Addison Emery Verrill, Albert Ordway, and Samuel H. Scudder all went on to distinguished careers in fields as varied and related as zoology, paleontology, archaeology, and ethnography. Verrill served as curator of the Peabody Museum, and Morse of the Museum of Fine Arts's Japanese ceramics collection; Scudder edited the journal *Science*. These men dined out for years on stories about their former teacher, an inveterate whistler, who would plant himself before them with feet spread, a cigar lodged firmly between his teeth and a fish specimen in each hand. Friends and relatives had slightly different memories, but they all remembered the ever-present odor of fish, which followed these young scientists home from the laboratory to the city's most exclusive drawing rooms.[9]

Among Agassiz's group of gifted students, Nathaniel Shaler (1841–1906) emerged as Agassiz's heir apparent. Shaler had come to Boston at eighteen from Kentucky after studying classics with a German tutor. As a Southerner from a slaveholding family who also served in the Union army, he brought an unusual perspective to the study of geography and racial identity. Bristling like his mentor "with points and vivacity," he taught natural history to over seven thousand Harvard undergraduates before becoming dean of the Lawrence Scientific School in 1891.[10] He too saw himself as the people's professor, and what better venue for his publications than Agassiz's, the *Atlantic Monthly*? Shaler proved a mainstay of the magazine from the 1880s through the 1890s. Though trained as a paleontologist and geologist, he published articles on a wide range of topics, from education, history, and travel to the improvement of the nation's highways, and the ever-inflammatory issue of race. He brought the findings of his career together in his three-volume *The United States of*

America (1894), based on experiences with the U.S. Coast and Geological Surveys as well as the Kentucky Geological Survey, which he directed.

Shaler's contributions to the *Atlantic* reflected the emergence of sociology as a formal academic discipline. They also complicate its support of minorities, notably African Americans, immigrants, Jews, and American Indians. To give a sense of scientific thinking about race in Shaler's era, the founder of American anthropology, Lewis Henry Morgan, measured human progress on a three-rung ladder, climbing upward from savagery to barbarism to civilization. This tier wedged people from China and India above American Indians and Australian aborigines. Some cultural evolutionists believed that each racial group passed on to their offspring "germ cells" or "germ plasma" (Shaler, who shared this view, called them "seeds"), which determined factors such as social behaviors and intelligence.[11] The national narrative that grew from this mix of ideology and science attributed the flowering of American democracy to its Teutonic roots, an irony in view of the imminent world war.

As with Agassiz, Shaler's interdisciplinary approach to science lent itself to a blurring of the boundaries between pure and applied science. Like many of his contemporaries, he appears to have been preoccupied with creating anatomies and pigeonholing assorted elements of the natural world into discernible categories. This ubiquitous urge, which suggests how near scientists felt to "unlocking Nature's secrets," helps to explain their anxiety about the muddle of contemporary life. Shaler's habit of touching on eugenics in nearly every essay he published in the *Atlantic* typified the writing of his time. In an article about Martha's Vineyard, he examined the island's oldest male residents, with their peculiarly strong bodies and great lungs, as types that performed a crucial role in the building of "our Anglo-Saxon or Gothic civilization."[12] His "Natural History of Politics" (March 1879) explored the tensions between individualized local cultures, the physical properties of which produce different peoples: Virginia, for example, giving rise to soldiers and statesmen, and New England to men "of science, letters, and economics," and the need of a national government to impose uniformity.[13]

Shaler brought to his discussions of race, particularly his discussions of American blacks, the diverse perspectives of scientist, "enlightened" Southerner, and would-be statesman, who did not want readers to suppose that he disliked Americanized Africans. "On the contrary," he explained in *The Neighbor* (1904), "I am very much attached to them, for I find that they are in their simple human nature as likable a people as my own . . . [and] as a whole, very human." Incredible as it may seem, Shaler saw his *Atlantic* essays and a book like *The Neighbor*, which includes a chapter on what was called the "Hebrew Problem," as "a plea for a larger understanding of the differences between men."[14] In 1886, he told *Atlantic* readers that America's greatest challenge lay in reconciling the races: "Let them ['every intelligent negro and white of this country'] see that the task is as difficult as it is noble; let them feel that the work to be well done demands the best efforts of every one who can lift his soul to the level of high duty."[15] But however liberally Shaler meant his essays to be read, supporters of anti-immigration laws and Jim Crow could cite his findings—as they had Louis Agassiz's—to support the belief that blacks belonged to a separate species. "The truth is that a man is what his ancestral experiences have made him," Shaler wrote. "He is but the momentary expression of the qualities bred in his race for immemorial ages. No sound national policy can afford to ignore the truths of inheritance."[16] Judged by scientists like Shaler and other leading scholars to be intellectually, socially, and morally inferior to whites save in their capacity for physical labor, black Americans saw hopes of full citizenship fade.

During Aldrich's editorship of the *Atlantic*, Shaler published three articles that might be seen as parts of a larger working treatise on the country's "Negro Problem." He called the first "The Negro Problem" (1884) and followed it with sequels titled "Race Prejudices" (October 1886) and "Science and the African Problem" (July 1890), which argued that education was the single most immediate necessity of blacks. In "The Negro Problem," Shaler writes as an apologist for American slavery ("the mildest and most decent system of slavery that ever existed"), at the same time claiming the conversion of an African into an American citizen as "the most wonderful social endeavor that has ever been made by our own or any other race."[17] Shaler's *Atlantic* articles illustrate the knotty double-speak that characterizes the magazine's coverage of science when the international scientific community and ordinary citizens tried to come to terms with the implications of evolution for racial and social spheres.[18] In a politically liberal magazine like the *Atlantic*, they exemplify the depth of slavery's unhealed divisions and the ongoing struggle to set things right.

Shaler's conclusions were in keeping with the tone and beliefs of the

Atlantic's other major scientific contributor, John Fiske, the American flag bearer of evolutionary growth in the march toward achieving that ambiguous goal of "National Progress." On one of his Saturday excursions to the Old Corner Bookstore of Ticknor and Fields, Fiske had discovered a prospectus announcing the publication in quarterly numbers of Herbert Spencer's philosophy, to be sold by subscription. His soul caught fire reading books on sociology and psychology by this polymath, who may be best known for the phrase "survival of the fittest." "I consider it my duty to mankind as a Positivist to subscribe," he told his mother, "and if I had $2,000,000 I would lay 1,000,000 at Mr. Spencer's feet to help him execute this great work."[19] He would tell Spencer when they met that his influence could be seen in Fiske's every word. So "inextricably" had Spencer's thinking become "intertwined" with his own that Fiske scarcely knew "whether to credit" himself or Spencer.[20]

Born Edmund Fisk Green (1842–1901), Fiske added an "e" to his middle name when he dropped "Green." This act of self-invention at age fifteen would characterize his career, which began in law and burgeoned into science and history. A tall, burly man with a large head and a full, rather carelessly kept brown beard, Fiske had a reputation for never doing anything in moderation, whether eating, working, singing, smoking, or talking. He had a photographic memory and a compulsive need to exhaust a topic to his own satisfaction. Asked a question, he could—and would—deliver a perfectly constructed lecture on the subject that might not end until his last listener had nodded off. Mark Twain described him as "a spotless and most noble and upright Christian gentlemen" who swore once by indirection. When Fiske's wife complained that their son had called his aunt Mary a fool and his aunt Martha a damned fool, she did not get the response she expected: "Oh well," he said, "it's about the distinction I should make between them myself."[21]

Fiske's association with the *Atlantic* dated back to William Dean Howells's editorship, when the two men were neighbors in Cambridge and drinking partners at the Tavern Club. Howells serialized Fiske's *Myth and Myth-Makers* (1872), with its groundbreaking opening chapter on the origins of folklore. Fiske dedicated the book to Howells "in remembrance of pleasant autumn evenings spent among were-wolves and trolls and nixies." After Howells's departure as editor, Fiske contributed nearly fifty articles to the magazine, many of them on the history of colonial

America. A prodigious worker, he published nine volumes in fourteen years, quite apart from giving nearly fifteen hundred lectures and cranking out four potboilers. Critics complained about Fiske's superficial treatment of people and events, on the one hand, and praised his accessibility and humor, on the other.[22] Various chapter titles of *The Critical Period of American History, 1783–1789* (1888), such as "Drifting toward Anarchy" and "Germs of National Sovereignty," convey the evolutionary underpinnings of his work. Fiske belonged to a group of late nineteenth-century historians, including George Bancroft and Brooks Adams, who embraced the theories and terminology of science. A "scientific historian" like Fiske studied "evolution in order to find a correct methodology. "When one has frequent occasion to refer to the political and social *progress* of the human race," he explained, "one likes to know what one is talking about."[23]

American writers such as Ellen Glasgow and Theodore Dreiser shared Fiske's enthusiasm for Herbert Spencer. Glasgow incorporated her reading of Spencer's *First Principles* into her life's work, a social history of the rise of the middle class in Virginia from the Civil War to World War II. Dreiser recalled having his worst suspicions about life verified by his discovery of Spencer:

> Up to this time there had been in me a blazing and unchecked desire to get on and the feeling that in doing so we did get somewhere; now in its place was the definite conviction that spiritually one got nowhere . . . that one lived and had his being because one had to, and that it was of no importance. Of one's ideals, struggles, deprivations, sorrows and joys, it could only be said that they were chemic compulsions, something which for some inexplicable but unimportant reason responded to and resulted from the hope of pleasure and the fear of pain. Man was a mechanism, undevised and uncreated, and a badly and carelessly driven one at that.[24]

Rebecca Harding Davis, Frank Norris, Stephen Crane, and Sherwood Anderson all claimed the same sense of impotence in the face of random forces. *Atlantic* writers Abraham Cahan and Jack London similarly assumed a scientific explanation for human behavior. Titles such as Gilbert Parker's "The Battle of the Strong" (April 1898) and S. M. Crother's "The Evolution of the Gentleman" (May 1898) suggest the degree to which the language of scientists had permeated American literature.

Despite the work of Oliver Wendell Holmes and of early science fiction writers the *Atlantic* might be said to have accepted science while largely overlooking technology. Howells, whose life seems a register of American change, had joined the approximately 10 million people attending the Centennial Exposition held in Philadelphia from 10 May to 10 June 1876, and he found its vision of the future unsettling.[25] Proof of American ingenuity and energy, the Corliss Engine, "an athlete of steel and iron," made him tremble.[26] By 1900, when Henry Adams stood before the dynamo at the Paris exhibition, he knew that there was no going back to the world of his youth. The adjustments such energy brought had their counterpart in Darwin's theories. In the third-person writing he adopted, Adams said: "The planet itself seemed less impressive, in its old-fashioned, deliberate, annual or daily revolution, than this huge wheel, revolving within arm's length at some vertiginous speed, and barely murmuring. . . . No more relation could he discover between the steam and the electric current than between the Cross and the cathedral." Seeing "an absolute *fiat* in electricity as in faith," Adams decided the forces were interchangeable but not reversible.[27]

The *Atlantic*'s uneasy relationship with technology can be seen in its giving little or no mention to the discovery of electromagnetic waves or the invention of machines that changed people's lives, including the internal combustion engine, washing machine, elevator, bicycle, machine gun, Brownie camera, and telephone. Even a new symbol of American ingenuity like the Brooklyn Bridge, the so-called eighth wonder of the world, received only passing mention in its pages. As early as 1858, the magazine's ambivalence toward technology found expression in a short story by Fitz-James O'Brien titled "The Diamond Lens." O'Brien recounted the tale of a scientist who resorts to murder to acquire a diamond lens for his microscope. The lens is so powerful that it reveals the figure of a lovely woman in a drop of water. When the scientist fails to keep the water from evaporating, his vision of the woman dies. The loss drives him insane, and he ends his days lecturing as "Linley, the Mad Microscopist." The story, which many thought the work of Edgar Allan Poe, proved a sensation. In 1891, the *Atlantic* would publish a curious tale by Walt Whitman's friend William Douglas O'Connor titled "The Brazen Android" (April and May). O'Connor originally wrote the story in 1857, a year before the *Atlantic* published "The Diamond Lens." Thirty-four years later, anxieties that fed O'Connor's story, including the Panic and the *Dred Scott* decision, took new but no less intense forms. The android in his story—designed to scare a despotic king into sharing power—talks with the aid of a hidden, steam-driven phonograph.[28] The plot fails when a scholar, fearing that the android will be the first of a new race, conjures a spirit to inhabit the android. Either magically (by the spirit) or naturally (by lightning), the android explodes. In either case, though neither is necessarily more comforting, technology has been marshaled by stronger forces.

O'Connor's story might be seen as responding to the phenomenon commonly known as "future shock." "The Brazen Android" pointed toward a future ruled by sentient machines. The world's long-rising anxiety about the misuse of science and technology and its impact on ancient systems of belief and governance would find expression in H. G. Wells's 1898 science fiction novel *The War of the Worlds*, in which Martians invade England. Whether commenting on British imperialism, science run amok, miscegenation, or evolution producing monstrous octopuslike creatures, the novel captures the possibility of human impotence in the face of unpredictable, overpowering change.

19

A Magazine in Decline and Ascension

I first saw the light in the city of Boston in the year 1857.

EDWARD BELLAMY, *Looking Backward*, 1888

THE *ATLANTIC*'S PUBLICATION of Edward Bellamy's short stories "The Blindman's World" (November 1886) and "At Pinney's Ranch" (December 1887) pointed toward the next century, though Bellamy did not become a household name until the publication of his socialist-inspired, utopian romance *Looking Backward, 2000–1887*. At that time surpassed in sales only by *Uncle Tom's Cabin* and *Ben Hur*, *Looking Backward* inspired a populist movement called "Nationalism," which sought "to reconcile peacefully an unreasonable capitalist class to an embittered laboring class."[1] Bellamy himself participated in the Nationalist Club of Boston, where members met to discuss the implementation of his ideas, among them the nationalization of industry and the economic equality of all citizens, including African Americans and women. Though socialistic in principle, Bellamy wanted to avoid any suggestion of the red flag, free love, or atheism, which may have prompted Thomas Wentworth Higginson to joke that a Bellamy "Nationalist" could be identified by the cigar between his lips and the wine glass in his right hand.[2]

One year after the publication of *Looking Backward*, the World's Fair opened in Paris, commemorating the hundredth anniversary of the storming of the Bastille. Inspired perhaps by the Bastille, which figures so largely in French history, the *Atlantic*'s anonymous representative focused on the fair's replicas of troglodyte caves, central African huts shaped like beehives, a Hindi palace, and the hostel of Henri II as if they mapped civilization's march toward the Eiffel Tower now proudly standing at the entrance to the fair. Exhibitions like the one in Paris—where the *Gallerie des Machines* marked the beginning of a new epoch in human history—provided an opportunity for assessment of everything from the relative achievements of the sexes to that of nations.

Twenty-eight million people attended the exposition in Paris, which showcased Buffalo Bill, Annie Oakley, and—winner of the *Grand Prix*—Heineken beer. Nearly the same number of people, over 27 million, or half the populace of the United States, spent their fifty cents to attend the Columbian Exposition in 1893. Chicago hosted the fair, which transformed more than a thousand acres along Lake Michigan into instant parks and boulevards, canals, and colonnaded Beaux Arts buildings. Visitors could travel on a moving sidewalk or survey the city from a seat on the very first Ferris wheel. Exhibits included a map of the United States made entirely of pickles. Mary Cassatt's mural *A Modern Woman* greeted visitors at the entrance to the Women's Pavilion.

For all practical purposes, the Chicago Fair comprised two separate fairs. One took place on the midway, the mile-long alleyway of wonders, which included Little Egypt, "the Bewitching Bellyrina," and the corpse of a Comanche warrior, said to be the last survivor of Little Big Horn. The other took place in the White City, a central conclave of white stucco buildings that glowed like benevolent ghosts in the electrified dark. Touted as a model of efficiency and cleanliness, the White City promised a future in which art and industry worked hand in hand to turn the masses into the classes. As if to dispel such overweening pride, or as fate would have it, the United States entered a depression that lasted four years and put 2.5 million people out of work.

Frederick Douglass went to the same exposition as the architect Henry Van Brunt and came away with a more discouraging view of the future. Like other African American leaders, he objected to the symbolism of a "white" city sending forth its civilizing rays when he saw that African Americans entered the fairgrounds as second-class citizens. On "Colored People's Day," a day dedicated to recognizing the contributions of African Americans, the organizers offered every black visitor a free watermelon. Once through the gate, African Americans expected to see exhibits explaining the enormous strides they had made since emancipation. Instead they were channeled past African villages, inspired perhaps by the enormously popular *village nègre* at the Paris exhibition, where crowds had gawked at hundreds of indigenous people. Douglass accused the organizers, all white, of deliberately presenting his people and their ancestors as repulsive savages devoid of the invention and artistry attributed to Europeans. The exclusion of African Americans from the planning of the fair, he argued, reflected their political, fiscal, and social exclusion from America itself. He and other African Americans, including Ida B. Wells, distributed a corrective pamphlet titled "The Reason Why the Colored American Is Not in the World's Columbian Exposition." It contained shocking statistics on racial violence and a photograph of a lynching.

Van Brunt, who reported on the Columbian Exposition for the *Atlantic*, remained unaware of any omissions, misrepresentations, or injustices. For him, the racial issue seemed moot. Having weathered the politics of designing Harvard's Memorial Hall, he marveled that the White City had come about through the efforts of unusual prophets—bank presidents, manufacturers, merchants, and lawyers. To him, the fair symbolized "the establishment of a great movement of civilization," appropriately realized in America's heartland. Predicting that the fair would teach midwesterners a lesson in civilization, he wrote: "They will discover that . . . by cultivating the arts which are not practically useful, their lives may be made much better worth living, more fruitful, more full of real enjoyment, and larger in every respect. They will be suddenly confronted by new ideals and inspired by higher ambitions."[3] Like Van Brunt, nearly everyone who attended the exposition commended its emphasis on education. Frances Burnett Hodgson, author of *Little Lord Fauntleroy* (1886) and later *The Secret Garden* (1911), urged parents to take their children to the exposition because a week there rivaled any course a university might offer.

In one way or another, the *Atlantic* itself had always been committed to education, in both its contents and its advocacy for better schools and curriculum. Horace Scudder, the magazine's fifth editor (1890–1898) and a member of the Massachusetts School Board, was passionate about public education, and his fervor gave the magazine a renewed purpose as well as a new coherence. In 1893 alone, the *Atlantic* carried Edward Everett Hale's "My College Days" (April), Justin Winsor's "The Future of Local Libraries" (June), Edward S. Morse's "If Public Libraries, Why

Not Public Museums" (July), Eugenia Skelding's "The First Principal of Newnham College" (August), and Scudder's own "School Libraries" (November). A tireless worker, Scudder believed that even hack work for Houghton Mifflin contributed "to the development of American culture and character."[4]

Piqued at Henry Houghton accepting his resignation, Thomas Bailey Aldrich did not make it easy for his successor, who looked a bit like an orthodox rabbi. "Why is Horace Scudder greater than Moses?" Aldrich asked. The answer: "Moses dried up the Red Sea once only; Scudder dries up *The Atlantic* monthly."[5] Annie Fields and Sarah Orne Jewett joined Aldrich, applauding any wit at Scudder's expense. "What a strange world this is!" Jewett remarked, "full of scudders and things."[6] Fields and Jewett had known Scudder since he first went to work for the magazine in 1863 and unfairly characterized him as an old-fashioned, earnest plodder who read the New Testament in the original Greek each day.[7] The situation recalls Henry Adams and his wife occupying what many thought of as a second White House during Rutherford B. Hayes's administration and mocking everything in Hayes's presidency. When the *New York Times* touted Horace Scudder's "high intelligence, flawless integrity, and social prestige," Annie Fields and her circle were buying none of it.[8] Jewett took her business elsewhere until Scudder wooed her back by paying more—thirty-five dollars for a thousand words—though publishing her less.

Scudder came from a Boston family and, after graduating from Williams College, taught in New York City. Believing that America needed "an insistence on the high ideals of literature and life," he had lusted after the editorship of the *Atlantic* for years.[9] He felt particularly hurt when Henry Houghton offered the job to Aldrich after Howells resigned, and as Aldrich's assistant ran the magazine during the editor's summer sojourns in Europe. In June 1890, Scudder could finally allow himself a little private fun at Henry Houghton's expense. "Yesterday," he confided to his diary,

> Mr. Houghton told me that Aldrich had resigned the editorship of *The Atlantic*, and proceeded to speak of me in connection with the work. I said, smilingly, you have not asked me to take the place. "No," he said, "some things we don't ask. I believe I never asked Mrs. Houghton to marry me." I think it not unlikely, for his habit of mind

> is so ineradicably indirect that I can easily think of him talking an hour to Miss Manning, and at the end of it, her finding herself engaged to him.

Scudder, who wanted nothing more than a chance "to keep the magazine at the front of American literature," required no courting: his heart beat "quicker at the thought of serving God in this cause of high, pure literature."[10] Houghton offered Scudder the job not because he wanted to support his service to God and literature, but because he knew that Scudder's commitment to the firm was second only to his own. If editing a national magazine was not enough work, Scudder also oversaw the Riverside Literature series and headed the firm's trade department. He accomplished all this and more, while suffering from a mysterious illness that left him completely deaf for extended periods of time. At the office, he used an ear trumpet, and colleagues communicated with him through notes.

Convinced that the teachings of great literature would improve both the tenor and the quality of American education and hence American life, Scudder took on the editorship with the spirit of a crusader marching off to Jerusalem. He inherited a magazine in decline, as competitors such as *McClure's*, *Cosmopolitan*, and *Munsey's Weekly* pushed the floundering *Atlantic* toward finer self-definition.[11] In 1887, Charles Scribner's Son had started another magazine also called *Scribner's*, designed to compete specifically with literate monthlies like the *Atlantic* and priced ten cents less an issue. Perhaps of equal importance in assessing the *Atlantic*'s crisis was a shift in public perception. Weary of freelancing and wanting the security of a steady paycheck, Howells accepted a job with *Harper's* in 1886. His move to New York symbolically marked a shift in the country's literary capital. As Boston struggled to retain its cultural coin, so did its signature magazine. Oliver Wendell Holmes, who received four thousand dollars a year to write exclusively for the *Atlantic*, remained loyal.[12] Realizing that the magazine had trouble keeping writers who could earn more elsewhere, he made a civic pitch to James Russell Lowell to publish in the *Atlantic*:

> I do know that Mr. Houghton has treated me very liberally, that he is an exact man of business, that he takes a pride in *The Atlantic*, which I suppose in a literary point of view is recognized as the

> first of the monthlies, and that he is very anxious to see you again in the pages of the old magazine you launched so long ago. . . . Other things being equal, you might perhaps prefer to publish in Boston, and add to the prestige of the city and the University.[13]

Houghton's "liberality" notwithstanding, he handcuffed the *Atlantic*'s editors by setting non-negotiable rates of payment. The *Century* could pay double the *Atlantic*'s ten dollars a page for nonfiction and twenty for fiction, though the *Atlantic* recognized special cases, paying Howells, for example, fifteen dollars a page on acceptance rather than making him wait for publication.[14] With a few rare exceptions, Houghton's business office routinely rejected requests for higher pay. This provoked reliable contributors such as Charles Eliot Norton, James, Jewett, and Higginson to find second and third homes with the editors of *Harper's Monthly* and the *Century*.

Scudder aimed to make the magazine more topical by fulfilling the promise of its subtitle to cover politics, which he defined as any subject having "a direct bearing upon the life of the country." The magazine was to remain nonpartisan: "There is always a right side," he thought, "and there are after all few questions of importance which cannot be discussed independently of party lines."[15] Howells praised Scudder's willingness to publish Walter Crane's "Why Socialism Appeals to Artists" (January 1892). Scudder increased the magazine's offerings of social and political essays, with topics ranging from the pros and cons of women's suffrage to the plight of American Indians and immigrant Jews. A measure of the new editor's foresight was his asking for articles from two future presidents of the United States. Theodore Roosevelt and Woodrow Wilson were both good writers of very different sorts, Roosevelt asserting his knowledge of a wide range of topics and Wilson studiously arguing finer points of political history.

Having come to the *Atlantic* not many years after its founding, Scudder stood witness to the relentless passing of the old guard. Emerson had died in April 1882, the month after the magazine published Edmund C. Stedman's farewell verses, "On a Great Man Whose Mind Is Clouding."

> THAT sovereign thought obscured? That vision clear
> Dimmed in the shadow of the sable wing,
> And fainter grown the fine interpreting

Which as an oracle was ours to hear?
Nay, but the gods reclaim not from the seer
Their gift,—although he ceases here to sing,
And, like the antique sage, a covering
Draws round his head, knowing what change is near.[16]

Emerson's death, a month after Henry Wadsworth Longfellow's, marked a long closing chapter in the history of the magazine. James Russell Lowell fell next (1891), followed by John Greenleaf Whittier (1892), Oliver Wendell Holmes (1894), and Harriet Beecher Stowe (1896).

Despite Scudder's forward glance, each death provided an occasion for the magazine to mythologize its past and make a case for its present importance. Holmes eulogized Lowell as a patriot and poet: "He loved New England,—people, language, soil."[17] Anticipating his own death, Whittier addressed his goodbye to Holmes (September 1892):

Thy hand, old friend! the service of our days,
In differing moods and ways,
May prove to those who follow in our train
Not valueless nor vain. . . .
The hour draws near, howe'er delayed and late,
When at the Eternal Gate
We leave the words and works we call our own,
And lift void hands alone.[18]

Two months later (November 1892), Holmes found himself acknowledging Whittier's passing: "Thou, too, has left us":

. . . Lift from its quarried ledge a flawless stone;
Smooth the green turf and bid the tablet rise,
And on its snow-white surface carve alone
These words,—he needs no more,—HERE WHITTIER LIES.[19]

The toll continuing, Scudder noted that references to the magazine's first supporters now required "the past tense."[20] After Stowe's death, the *Atlantic* published Annie Fields's memoir titled "Days with Mrs. Stowe" (August 1896) and Charles Dudley Warner's tribute "The Story of Uncle Tom's Cabin" (September 1896). In November 1896, subscribers received the first installment of Thomas Wentworth Higginson's *Cheerful Yesterdays*, reminiscences of Boston and Cambridge, with a chapter titled "Kansas and John Brown."

It went without saying that the canonization of the *Atlantic*'s earliest contributors meant a steady stream of sales for its parent company. Scudder edited books by and about Whittier, Lowell, Longfellow, Thoreau, Henry Houghton, and the travel writer Bayard Taylor. In "spare" moments, he compiled "masterpiece" collections of British and American literature that featured *Atlantic* writers and anticipated Barrett Wendell's *A Literary History of America* (1900) and E. C. Stedman's *An American Anthology* (1900). With an eye toward history, Houghton Mifflin had the Riverside Press semiannually bind about five thousand volumes of the magazine. In physical form, the volumes had the cultural authority, and certainly the heft and length, of Victorian novels.

In "Authorship in America" (June 1883), Scudder offered a canon of American literature that was composed, not surprisingly, of *Atlantic* authors. Making the best literature part of the average schoolchild's curriculum had not been possible, he explained, because there had been "no native literature at the service of the schools. Now, the accumulation of a body of prose and poetry, with its origin in national life, has become a substantial foundation upon which a love of literature may be built."[21] Scudder had no intention of letting *Atlantic* authors go out of print. Generations of students who hated reading Longfellow's *Evangeline* had Scudder to thank for making the poem a staple of school readers. Nevertheless, Scudder's sensibility and training had convinced him that literature offered the best training for citizenship—a conviction that had inspired James Russell Lowell to offer discounted subscriptions to teachers. In the 1890s, the *Atlantic* crusaded for a common language, thought crucial to creating a common sense of nation. "The perils which beset us now in the industrial world," he argued, foreshadowing E. D. Hirsch's argument for core knowledge, are augmented by this lack: "A common literature is essential to any true community of ideals; and in the work of producing a homogenous nation out of the varied material which different races, different political orders, and different religious faiths have contributed since the war for the Union,—a work which is largely committed to the public schools,—there is no force comparable to a great, harmonious literature." Scudder's belief that literature would bring about "the nationalization of the American people" did not prompt him to ask directly, "Which literature?," because Scudder and the *Atlantic* operated on the principle that the hope of the country lay in finding likeness, not difference.[22]

III

20

From the Far East to Mars

LAFCADIO HEARN AND PERCIVAL LOWELL

I suppose you must know, or feel, that any one who wishes to be purely *himself*, must be isolated in all countries.

Quoted in NOBUSHIGE AMENOMORI, "Lafcadio Hearn the Man," *Atlantic*, October 1905

WHEN LAFCADIO HEARN (1850–1904) entered a room, people tried not to stare. A slight man with one blind eye and the other bulging from strain, he looked all wrong. The daughter of the renowned Orientalist Ernest Fenollosa remembered his visit in Tokyo. Apart from Hearn, the company included the Asian scholar Sturgis Bigelow and Percival Lowell, author of *The Soul of the Far East* (*Atlantic*, September–December 1887). Fenollosa's daughter thought Hearn a repulsive-looking man with a beautiful voice: "He was totally blind," she wrote erroneously, "and his food landed in strange places, much to my delight."[1] Hearn may have had some revenge, for the meal came to a crashing halt when plaster fell from a nearby hall ceiling and a six-foot snake wriggled free of the debris. The butler killed the snake, and Bigelow led the company in three cheers.

Lafcadio Hearn published over twenty essays in the *Atlantic* with titles such as "At the Market of the Dead" (September 1891), "In a Japanese Garden" (July 1892), "The Japanese Smile" (May 1893), "The Genius of Japanese Civilization" (October 1895), "Out of the Street: Japanese Folk-Songs" (September 1896), and the reverie called "Dust" (November 1896). These essays, consolidated into books, formed part of the Houghton Mifflin list. *Glimpses of Unfamiliar*

Japan (1894) and *Out of the East: Reveries and Studies in New Japan* (1895) opened the East to Western readers who seemed to have an insatiable curiosity about its exotic people and customs. The reviewer for the *Atlantic* thought Hearn had been born "to be the mouthpiece of races so alien to ourselves that they live the poetry they do not talk about."

Praising Hearn's genius as a poet, he declared his "service to science" equally unique. Between 1895 and 1897, Hearn published *Out of the East: Reveries and Studies in New Japan* (1895); *Kokoro: Hints and Echoes of Japanese Inner Life* (1896); and *Gleanings in Buddha-Fields: Studies of Hand and Soul in the Far East* (1897). In Japan, according to the *Atlantic* reviewer, Hearn discovered a civilization as rich as "ancient Rome," flush with "military success" and on the brink of modernization.[2] Readers may or may not have seen parallels between Japan and the United States, fighting its own war in the Philippines. Hearn, who protested any kind of racial bias and whose last novel, *Youma* (1890), dealt sympathetically with a slave rebellion, believed that ethical behavior demanded tolerance for people and cultures not one's own. Like Horace Scudder, he valued what he called moral over intellectual beauty and worried that Japanese enamored of Western ways would adopt Western values.[3] In terms of armies, navies, and planned occupations of their neighbors, they already had.

Apart from education, Hearn had little in his background to make him either a scientist or a poet. Born to a Greek mother, who named him for her Ionian island, and an Irish father serving as an army surgeon, he spent a Dickensian childhood in the custody of an Irish aunt, who believed that locking children in closets cured a fear of the dark. Hearn lost his left eye in a sports scuffle at St. Cuthbert's College in England. Morbidly self-conscious after the injury, he met the world with an averted face. At seventeen, he was forced to withdraw from school when a family friend nearly beggared his aunt by exploiting her investments. Sent to Cincinnati to look up a long-lost relative, he received a few dollars and was told not to come again. After a hand-to-mouth year of living on the streets, in which he nearly starved to death, he convinced the printer of a local trade journal to take him on. This job led to his next as a hack reporter for the daily *Cincinnati Enquirer*, where he made a specialty of lurid stories about the city's misfits. Hearn earned a reputation for his coverage of the Tanyard murder trial, in which the jury found a father and son guilty of shoving the daughter's seducer into a hot baking oven. In a city prohibiting mixed marriages, Hearn challenged the law by marrying a freed slave. Their relationship did not last, nor did his job with the *Enquirer*. For a time, he worked for one of the *Enquirer*'s competitors, the *Cincinnati Commercial*, before moving in the late seventies to the warmer climes of New Orleans, a city known for its more relaxed attitude toward interracial socializing.

In New Orleans, Hearn opened and quickly closed a restaurant called The Hard Times. (He later wrote a Creole cookbook.) Fluent in French, he translated works by Guy Maupassant, Gustave Flaubert, and Pierre Loti and learned everything he could about Creoles and their culture. All the while, he was developing his elliptical style and turning out books that showed a growing interest in Asia. After lonely times in the French West Indies, Philadelphia, and New York, during which he published *Stray Leaves from Strange Literatures* (1884), *Some Chinese Ghosts* (1887), and *Chita* (1889), he packed up the unsold copies of his cookbook and accepted an assignment from *Harper's* that would take him to Meiji, Japan.

In 1890, Hearn sailed from New York to begin again. He married a woman from a Samurai family named Setsu Koizumi, fathered four children, taught in schools and what is now Tokyo University, and became Yakumo Koizumi, a Japanese citizen. The writing continued but came hard. "Work with me is a pain," he said, "—no pleasure till it is done":

> It is forced by necessity. . . . Unless somebody does or says something horribly mean to me, I can't do certain kinds of work. . . . When I begin to think about the matter afterwards, then I rush to work. I write page after page of vagaries, metaphysical, emotional, romantic,—throw them aside. Then next day, I go to work rewriting them. I rewrite and rewrite them till they begin to define and arrange themselves into a whole,—and the result is an essay; and the editor of *The Atlantic* writes, "It is a veritable illumination,"—and no mortal man knows why, or how it was written,—not even I myself,—or what it cost to write it.[4]

Throughout his life, Hearn remained fascinated by the workings of perception. Why does one person hear the singing of grasshoppers and another unbroken silence? Trying to articulate his response to Japan, he wrote to his future biographer Elizabeth Bisland: "This is a domesticated

Nature, which loves man, and makes itself beautiful for him in a quiet grey-and-blue way like the Japanese women, and the trees seem to know what people say about them,—seem to have little human souls. What I love in Japan is the Japanese,—the poor simple humanity of the country. It is divine. There is nothing in this world approaching the naive natural charm of them. No book ever written has reflected it."[5] *Atlantic* readers, in turn, loved Hearn's minute descriptions of Shinto shrines, samurai legends, jujitsu, and marketplaces, which displayed strange sea creatures and bean curds of every imaginative texture. He made them feel as if they saw the places and knew the people themselves. In this respect, he lived up to his own wish to be "a literary Columbus."[6]

Americans had been fascinated with Japan since Commodore Perry's black ships landed at Kurihama in 1853. Perry's second voyage led to the Convention of Kanagawa (1854) and the opening of Japan's fortressed ports to Western trade. Six years later, Japan sent a delegation to Washington, D.C. Trade agreements between the United States and Japan resulted in a flow of travelers, goods, and ideas between the countries. In 1868, when revolution in Japan wrested power from the shoguns and restored the emperor, ancient samurai families were reduced to beggars. They sold whatever was valuable, and many of the country's great collections of prints, lacquerware, pottery, textiles, and bronzes went to foreign connoisseurs like Edward S. Morse and Sturgis Bigelow, for the Boston Museum of Fine Arts Asian collection. At the same time, Western missionaries and teachers tried to impress upon the Japanese the superiority of Christian theology and culture. Japanese students who studied abroad viewed the ancient arts with shame, while at home their fathers hung up their swords and kimonos—or donned top hats to waltz. Save for the efforts of Japanophiles, arts like Noh would have disappeared. Following Ernest Fenollosa, Bigelow, and Percival Lowell, Hearn taught the Japanese the importance of their own culture, which *Atlantic* readers valued precisely because it offered an alternative to modern ills. What the emperor said of Fenollosa, who dreamed of a utopian fusion of Eastern and Western cultures leading to a new world order, applied to all of these early Western enthusiasts: "You have taught my people to know their own art."[7] If Hearn and other Japanophiles could be accused of nostalgia, they also recognized, earlier than most, the connection between Japan's rapid industrialization and its military ascension.[8]

The transfer of culture flowed from East to West as well as from West to East. As Whittier's hymn for the 1876 Centennial suggests,

> Thou, who hast here in concord furled
> The war flags of a gathered world,
> Beneath our Western skies fulfill
> The Orient's mission of good will,
> And, freighted with love's Golden Fleece,
> Send back the Argonauts of peace.[9]

Gilbert and Sullivan's comic operetta *The Mikado, or The Town of Titipu* (1885) ran for 672 performances at London's Savoy theater, feeding the craze of "Orientalism." John LaFarge, Henry Adams, James McNeill Whistler, and John Singer Sargent are just a few of the countless artists to find an antidote to the "exhausted" West in the sensual possibilities of Asian art. Lucky for once in his life, Hearn arrived at a key time to describe Japan's mysteries for readers around the world.

In an 1893 *Atlantic* essay on Westerners' misinterpretation of the Japanese smile, Hearn told the story of a samurai who greeted his employer's every insult with a smile. Incensed by that smile, the employer struck his elderly servant, and in an instant as swift as the samurai's drawing of his sword, he saw the old man transformed into a youthful warrior. The samurai cowed his master by swashing his sword before sheathing it and smiling. The next day the employer received word of his suicide. Honor forbade the servant from killing a man he had agreed to serve and from whom he had borrowed money. As a samurai, he could not live with the shame of an unavenged insult. Hearn protested that since ancient times, national government in the East "has been based on benevolence, and directed to securing the welfare and happiness of the people. No political creed has ever held that intellectual strength should be cultivated for the purpose of exploiting inferiority and ignorance."[10] The same could not be said of the West, where emphasis on the individual ran contrary to collective interests: "Individualism is to-day the enemy of education, as it is also the enemy of social order," he wrote in "The Genius of Japanese Civilization" (October 1895); "citizens should be formed for society not the other way around."[11]

Like many of his contemporaries in the decades after Charles Darwin and Herbert Spencer, Hearn confronted the possibility of a godless universe. "Transmigration—transmutation: these are not fables!" he rhapsodized in the *Atlantic* essay "Dust" (November 1896): "What is impossible? Not the dreams of alchemists and poets; dross may indeed be changed to gold, the jewel to the living eye, the flower into flesh. What is impossible? If seas can pass from world to sun, from sun to world again, what of the dust of dead selves—dust of memory and thought? Resurrection there is, but a resurrection more stupendous than any dreamed of by Western creeds. Dead emotions will revive as surely as dead suns and moons."[12] Though not quite a convert like Fenollosa and Bigelow, Hearn saw in Buddhism a philosophy that embraced contrary forces and in doing so offered a faith more congruent with life's pain and impermanence. Life, he wrote in "The Genius of Japanese Civilization," "is but one momentary halt upon an infinite journey . . . all attachment to persons, to places, or to things must be fraught with sorrow [and] . . . only through suppression of every desire—even the desire of Nirvana itself—can humanity reach the eternal peace."[13]

In Buddhism Hearn found a confirmation of his experience of life's permanent instability. A man uncomfortable in his own skin, a man who never felt at home anywhere on earth, he saw his natural condition—indeed the condition of humankind—as a state of perpetual exile. In Japan, where few Westerners could hope to master the language or a complex system of manners, his oddities seemed the product of his foreignness and therefore less odd. Although Hearn showed his respect for the Japanese by taking a Japanese name, he paid, as Henry James said of all exiles, with his person. Before Hearn died, he requested that his ashes be buried with no fanfare in an ordinary box on a tree-covered hill. This request fell on deaf ears; the people he had adopted as his own honored him with a formal Buddhist ceremony. If to a lesser extent today, he remains a national treasure to the Japanese. Children can still read his essays in school, and pilgrims can tour his house in Matsue, where he lived his first year in Japan, or decorate his gave at the Zōshigaya Cemetery in Tokyo with haikus and flowers.

Atlantic readers familiar with the work of Hearn would also have known the work of Edward H. House and Percival Lowell. A friend of Walt Whitman and an enemy of Mark Twain, with whom he wrangled over copyright infringement, House spent thirty years in the East. The *Atlantic* serialized his novel *Yone Santo* from January to June 1888.

House hoped that it might lessen Westerners' arrogance toward Asians. Hearn had only a glancing familiarity with House, having chanced upon one of his earliest *Atlantic* essays on Japan, which remarked on how the Japanese delight in Western cookery and spirits.[14] Instead he credited his fascination with Japan to Pierre Loti's *Japoneries d'automne* (1889) and Percival Lowell's *Occult Japan*, later subtitled "*or The Way of the Gods, an Esoteric Study of the Japanese Personality and Possession*" (1894).

Percival Lowell (1855–1916) survived Lafcadio Hearn by a dozen years and died worth $16 million. No less an eccentric, though far more personable, he too cherished his independence. Eccentricity seems to have been a Lowell family trait that perhaps found its most extravagant expression in Percival's younger sister, Amy—a stout, cigar-chomping, thin-lipped New Englander with a flair for verse. Percival's tastes included fine wines, polo, London tailors, the classics in their original Greek and Latin, detective stories, dressing up as Santa Claus at Christmas, the obedience of subordinates, and liberated women. Neighbors once witnessed him kicking his butler down the front steps of his Boston house and punting the man's suitcase after him. The quintessential Boston Brahmin, he had money, brains—James Russell Lowell called his cousin "the most brilliant man in Boston"—and something not wholly inherited, a charisma that one observer compared to "a powerful magnetic field."[15] He was, in other words, the opposite of Hearn, owning or dominating every room he entered. These qualities, and his friendship with Sturgis Bigelow, led to his serving on a special trade mission to Korea in 1883 (the first from any Western power to the Hermit Kingdom), which ended successfully with an agreement between the United States and Korea, and also with *Chosön* (1885), a book that Lowell wrote after a few weeks in Korea and that established his reputation as a specialist on the Far East.

Hearn's initial respect for Lowell later turned to repulsion. He hated Lowell's "show-me" attitude, which he judged "painfully unsympathetic," if not "Mephistophelean."[16] It troubled him to think, for instance, of Lowell cold-bloodedly sticking pins into mystics to see the depth and authenticity of their trances. Despite Lowell's ten-year residency in the East and his flirtation with its mysteries, he was ultimately a scientist driven to scrutinize rather than accept the unknown. Hearn had become understandably territorial about Japan. The *New York Times* reviewer of *Occult Japan* weighed the work of both men by calling Hearn a "grave poet" and

Lowell a "gay philosopher," though in different circumstances the descriptions could just as helpfully have been reversed. In the reviewer's opinion, Hearn had been "unduly impressed" by the Shinto religion, whereas Lowell viewed the subject as an entomologist might a bug: he captured it, dissected it, and disseminated his findings.[17] The reviewer argued that, read together, these two writers presented the most complete picture of this still largely unknown country.

For all their differences, Lowell matched Hearn's intensity and restlessness. Since first presented with a telescope in childhood, he had looked with curiosity at the heavens. Lowell brought to his study a background in mathematics that at one time led Harvard to offer him a professorship. Learning that Harvard intended to build an observatory in the southwestern United States, he staged a coup d'état, effectively commandeering the directorship of the project and two Harvard astronomers, whose salaries he agreed to pay from the private fortune he had made in his first career as a businessman. A part owner in the Union Pacific Railroad, he would arrange for the train to San Francisco to make an unscheduled stop for him in Flagstaff, Arizona. In Flagstaff, Lowell lived in a mansion he named "Mars Hill." After a long-term affair with his secretary, the free-spirited Wrexie Leonard, Lowell unaccountably married his Boston neighbor, a Tartar of a woman named Constance Savage Keith who earned a living dabbling in real estate and decorating. The bride was forty-four, the groom fifty-three. They lived in Flagstaff, where Wrexie continued as Lowell's secretary. After his death, she published a memoir titled *Percival Lowell: An Afterglow.*

Lowell became famous for issuing weather reports from Mars and hypothesizing—to the scorn of professionally trained astronomers—that the planet had experienced a catastrophic drought, as evidenced by a visible system of canals, designed to channel water from its polar caps to valleys. In 1877, the Italian astronomer Giovanni Schiaparelli had used the word *canali* to describe irregularities on the surface of the planet. The Italian word refers to grooves or channels, but English speakers understood it to mean "canals." Looking at the *canali*, Lowell imagined a highly evolved, peace-loving nation. A credible scientist who served on Harvard's Committee on Mathematics, Physics, and Chemistry, he gleefully took on naysayers in the pages of the leading scientific journals. The *Atlantic*, however, serialized his first book on the planet, simply titled

Mars (1895). In quick sequence there followed—if not in the *Atlantic*—*The Annals of Lowell Observatory* (vol. 1, 1898; vol. 2, 1900), *The Solar System* (1903), *Mars and Its Canals* (1906), *Mars as the Abode of Life* (1908), and *The Evolution of Worlds* (1909).

To his third career as the founder and director of his Flagstaff fiefdom, Lowell brought the skill he had acquired in Japan of looking at things fresh, or what he termed "topsy-turvy." (On his honeymoon, he went up in a hot air balloon to get a sense of what the network of canals on Mars, represented by paths in Hyde Park, might look like from space.) On clear nights, he could be heard climbing the observatory's staircase to his state-of-the-art Clarke telescope, through which he gazed to first light. Sphinxlike, the planet appeared as unknowable as Japan. Lowell had once explained his desire to go to Noto, a peninsula on the western coast of Japan, "just because it was not known!" He itched "to tread what others had not already effacingly betrodden," and the more he looked and longed and turned the color of its vowel around his mouth, the more he felt Mars to be an otherworldly Noto.[18]

Mars offered a new wilderness, or, in Lowell's case, the promise of a more ordered civilization, one that had much to teach those on earth at the turn of a new century. Interest in the exotic spoke to a contradictory yearning for change and stasis. Like Hearn, Lowell sensed a shadow self in Japan. In a passage from "Noto," describing his goodbye to a kind innkeeper, he captures the mutability of self and the sorrow of endings:

> There is a touch of pathos in this parting acquiescence in fate. If it must be so, indeed! I wonder did mine host suspect that I did not all leave,—that apart of me, a sort of ghostly lodger, remained with him who had asked me so little for my stay? Probably in body I shall never stir him again from beside his fire, nor follow as he leads the way through the labyrinth of his house; but in spirit, at times, I still steal back, and I always find the same kind welcome awaiting me in the guest room in the ell, and the same bright smile of morning to gild the tiny garden court. The only things beyond the grasp of change are our own memories of what once was.[19]

Four years after the publication of Lowell's essay on Noto, China ceded Formosa (Taiwan) to Japan in a treaty ending the Sino-Japanese war, and Korea became a Japanese protectorate, while Japan's rising military might and rapid modernization began to threaten Western dominance.

As Hearn predicted, Japan's rising militarism paralleled its increasing Westernization. Many in Japan reacted negatively to casting off traditional dress, and with it centuries of tradition. Lowell, for example, witnessed a backlash against modernization and an assertion of cultural authority when the reformer Mori Arinori died at the hands of an assassin who held him responsible for the desecration of a shrine. In "Fate of a Japanese Reformer" (November 1890), Lowell wondered at the public's veneration of the murderer, who "executed his plan with all the old-time samurai bravery. He had done it as a samurai should have done it, and he had died as a samurai should have died. . . . The substitution of a kitchen knife for a knightly katana was shown to have been made with the express intent of casting obloquy upon its victim."[20] Japan and Mars: in a sense they were interchangeable for Lowell's purpose of viewing "our own humanity in some mirth-provoking mirror of the mind,—a mirror that shows us our own familiar thoughts, but all turned wrong side out."[21]

Although he was first and foremost a scientist, Lowell had, like his sister Amy, a poetic streak. In an extended argument for *Atlantic* readers that surveyed the atmosphere, water, canals, and oases of Mars, he leapt to the astonishing conclusion that human beings are not alone in the cosmos, but merely a link in a chain of life:

> A mind of no mean order would seem to have presided over the system we see,—a mind certainly of considerably more comprehensiveness than that which presides over the various departments of our own public works. Party politics, at all events, have had no part in them; for the system is planet wide. Quite possibly, such Martian folk are possessed of inventions of which we have not dreamed, and with them electrophones and kineto-scopes are things of a bygone past, preserved with veneration in museums as relics of the clumsy contrivances of the simple childhood of their kind. Certainly, what we see hints at the existence of beings who are in advance of, not behind us, in the race of life.

Conceding that further answers would have to await the future, Lowell advised readers to be outliers, by which he meant they should free their minds of shackles and shed local points of view. Above all, they must recognize the possibility of other people undergoing a similar process of liberation. Lowell stopped short of suggesting a mass movement or the dawning of a new era. He remained content with a simple recognition of humanity's shared kinship. "If astronomy teaches anything, it teaches that man is but a detail in the evolution of the universe. . . . He learns that though he will probably never find his double anywhere, he is destined to discover any number of cousins scattered through space."[22] Instead of the cousins, Lowell discovered water on Mars. He was sure of its presence in the canals and of its importance to Martian civilization. It took almost a century for scientists to call him right—at least about the water on Mars.

Lowell did not abandon the search for interstellar relatives, concentrating in his last years on discovering a Planet X. Following his death in November 1916, his wife Constance fired her rival, Wrexie, and began a protracted, costly battle for control of the endowed laboratory. In 1930, astronomers at the Lowell Observatory discovered Planet X. After much wrangling with Constance, who insisted it be named "Constance," the astronomers named Planet X "Pluto," incorporating Lowell's initials, "PL." Given its recent downgrading to a dwarf planet, Pluto provides a fitting legacy for a man who thought the world turned upside down. Lowell's passion for Mars found popular expression in the science fiction or speculative writing of the time. Besides *The War of the Worlds* (1898), readers could enjoy George du Maurier's *The Martian* (1897) and Edgar Rice Burroughs's Lowell-inspired Mars books, including *A Princess of Mars* (1912). To Hearn, however, Lowell remained a man who grew too tall to "see anything near him clearly," and though the opposite might be said about Hearn, both men managed to see more and better than others could.[23]

The spiritual awakening that Western travelers sought in Japan led many Americans to dabble with automatic writing, palmistry, and séances, which may explain some of Hearn and Lowell's popularity. Even someone as levelheaded as William Dean Howells caught the fever. In an end-of-the-century *Atlantic* essay titled "On Coming Back," he voices what would become an increasing worry about the mutability of self.

> If we come back, it is as ghosts . . . though it is generally supposed there is but one ghost, actual or potential, to each personality, my experience is that there are at least a dozen to each of us, formed

> of our cast qualities and forces. I have known quite that number of my own, but I will merely instance my Boston ghost, which was evolved mainly during my relation to this magazine, and which I abandoned to it fifteen years ago, without an attempt to resume it since. Now that I come to the old place where I was once at home, and very substantial, I feel myself strangely thin, and, as I may say, flittering, with a lax hold upon my own thoughts, and a tendency to sway and waver in the reader's breath, as if there were nothing of me but that ghost.[24]

Here Howells's own ghostly self sounds like that of Lafcadio Hearn. His practical self, however, looked in another direction. Who, for example, would lead the *Atlantic* into the new century? What kind of magazine might it become? For what did it stand? And who would read it? Howells himself was aging, and the founding generation he had known, loved, and respected had begun to say its goodbyes, but one thing remained clear: The *Atlantic Monthly*, having addressed with conviction the troubles and confusion of American life for nearly four decades, would find no dearth of subjects in an unknown future.

21

Booker T. Washington and W. E. B. Du Bois

I was ready to admit the best of men might fail. I meant still to be the captain of my soul, but I realize that even captains are not omnipotent in uncharted and angry seas.

W. E. B. DU BOIS, *Autobiography*

ON A DISMAL Monday evening, 22 January 1906, an estimated five thousand people made their way to Carnegie Hall for a fundraiser in honor of Tuskegee Institute's silver jubilee. Opened just fifteen years before, yet stretching imaginatively back to the Italian Renaissance, the hall's elaborate, marbled interior presented a dramatic contrast to Tuskegee's functional, student-built structures. Even with the drizzly, bone-chilling cold, the line for seats stretched two blocks north toward Central Park. Mark Twain's secretary assumed that these hearty souls in brilliant gowns and evening dress had come to hear Twain. Twain thought they came to vex him by confiding how they had known his beloved mother in Arkansas, New Jersey, California, or Jericho—any place she had never stepped foot. But not denying Twain's enormous draw, the night belonged to the charismatic black leader, Booker T. Washington.

Most of the attendees would have known Washington from his autobiography, *Up from Slavery* (1901), or essays in newspapers and magazines like the *World* and the *Atlantic*. Washington (1856–1915) spent his earliest years on a hardscrabble tobacco farm in southwestern Virginia. He learned that he was free three years after the issuing of the first Emancipation Proclamation. As he stood outside the main house listening to a strange man read the Proclamation, he saw tears streaming down his mother's face. Washington was nine years old when the family traveled to Malden, West Virginia, where he worked in the local salt mine. Rising at four in the morning, the boy clocked a full day before attending afternoon classes. His lot improved when a townswoman employed him as a houseboy. At sixteen, he bid the world he knew goodbye and set off on a four-hundred-mile trek, hoping to talk his way into the Hampton Normal and Industrial School. A historically black institution, Hampton had been founded, despite prohibitions against teaching slaves to read and write, on the eve of the Civil War. Hampton required that students learn a trade as well as a profession. Arriving on its doorstop starving and in rags, Washington had to clean a room well enough to prove his right to stay. And stay he did, working as a janitor to pay his board, and learning to value, as he would later say, a job in a factory more than a seat in an opera house.

After graduation, Washington earned a degree at Wayland Seminary in Washington, D.C., before accepting the principalship of a new school in Tuskegee, Alabama. At Tuskegee, he hoped to train a generation of students who would transform the South, both industrially and spiritually. The doctrine of physical and moral hygiene he took from Hampton appealed to liberal whites who were wary about their responsibilities for, and relationship to, former slaves in the post-Reconstruction era. Speaking to a biracial audience in his 1895 Atlanta Compromise address, Washington proposed that whites and blacks could remain "in all things that are purely social . . . as separate as the fingers, yet one as the hand in all things essential to mutual progress."[1] Washington believed in working quietly through political channels and the courts to end segregation. In a posthumously published 1915 article for the *New Republic*, he summarized his argument against segregation: "The courts in no section of the country would uphold a case where Negroes sought to segregate white citizens. This is the most convincing argument that segregation is regarded as illegal, when viewed on its merits by the whole body of our white citizens."[2]

In the twenty-five years between Tuskegee's founding and Washington's speech at Carnegie Hall, promises had been made and broken to African Americans, who had expected the same protections guaranteed to every citizen. As Washington entered Carnegie Hall, a messenger handed him a note from Thomas Dixon Jr., author of the immensely popular white supremacist novel *The Clansman*. Dixon said that he would contribute ten thousand dollars to Tuskegee's endowment in exchange for a few words from Washington himself. He wanted Washington to guarantee that neither he nor the interests he represented sought social equality or the amalgamation of the races.

The Dixons of the world provide a measure for gauging the spirit of the gathering at Carnegie Hall. Among Washington's supporters was the former American ambassador to the Court of St. James, Joseph Choate. In comparison to Dixon, Choate exemplified the thinking of white liberals. Introducing Washington, he said, "It is not the educated negroes who make themselves enemies to the South; it is uneducated negroes. The desire for these Tuskegee can satisfy." Choate noted the expanded opportunities available to blacks, who were "making the most of it."[3] Washington's development of Tuskegee struck many as just short of miraculous. Twain, who estimated the value of the school's property at a million and a half dollars, credited Washington with raising, in his twenty-five years at Tuskegee, many hundreds of thousands more, which brought the school's endowment to a million dollars.[4] When Tuskegee marked its twenty-fifth anniversary in 1906, participants included the U.S. secretary of war, William Taft; the president of Harvard, Charles Eliot; and the plutocrat Andrew Carnegie.

Twain first met Washington at a Fourth of July celebration in London hosted by Ambassador Choate. Since that day, the two had talked a number of times, but Twain—who described "race" as a state of mind and racism "a fiction of law and custom"—still had not noticed the color of Washington's eyes.[5] The night of the Carnegie Hall benefit, he suddenly realized that Washington "was a mulatto and had blue eyes. I didn't notice it until he turned . . . and said something to me. . . . How unobservant a dull person can be! Always, before, he was black, to me, and I had never noticed whether he had eyes at all, or not."[6] The anecdote recalls a much later one from another *Atlantic* writer named Mary Austin (1868–1934), best known for her studies of the desert and fascination with American Indians. The first African Americans she dined with were James Weldon Johnson and his wife, Grace. When Johnson passed her the bread she noted how black his hand looked against the white plate, and thought, "I am eating dinner with a black man!" She felt she should be astonished, until an inner voice said, "Well, I don't see it," meaning his color, and looking again she decided that she did not in fact see his hand as being any different from her own.[7] Twain realized that he had experienced the visual equivalent of turning a deaf ear, while Austin, who effectively dyed Johnson white, made a conscious decision to see only what she thought important. These related responses to color come from a man who felt shamed by his race's behavior—"We have ground the manhood out of them, and the shame is ours, not theirs, & we should pay for it"—and by a woman who thought the history and art of African Americans central to American life.[8] Over a decade apart, they call to mind how much rather than how little race mattered in a nation long obsessed with what was commonly called "the African" or "the Negro" Problem.

Many of the *Atlantic*'s contributors assumed that the lasting solution to racial inequities, apart from full enfranchisement, lay in education. Washington shared the *Atlantic*'s position when he appealed to his audience's sense of justice. As he told the audience at Carnegie Hall: "No two groups of people can live side by side where one is in ignorance and poverty without its condition affecting the other. The black man must be lifted or the white man will be injured in his moral and spiritual life. The degradation of the one will mean the degradation of the other."[9]

Washington's contributions to the *Atlantic* gave readers an opportunity to assess the "Negro Problem" from the "other's" point of view. He began his well-known essay "The Awakenings of the Negro" (September 1896) with two personal anecdotes. Both are what Henry James would call the *données* of larger stories. First, he remembered the impression made upon him when, as a boy, he saw a young colored man who had several years' worth of education sitting in a "common cabin in the South" studying a French grammar. Second, he told of riding on the outer edges of a Southern town and hearing the sound of a piano rising from squalid surroundings. Washington did not need to give more details. Readers could appreciate the hours of practice, the number of meals skipped, or the extra hours of labor required of the entire family to support one poor person's mastering a foreign language or musical instrument.

But these experiences led Washington to a surprising conclusion, especially for those who believed in the ennobling powers of culture. Tallying the four or five dollars a month it takes to rent a piano, he blocked his ears to expensive luxuries, to the rising strains of Brahms or Bach, and wondered, instead, how the girl's accomplishment contributed to the cardinal needs of the 7 million African Americans living in rural poverty. How could playing the piano or mastering French provide necessities such as food, clothing, and shelter? How could it teach proper habits or, more crucially, improve race relations? It could not, he argued, but vocational training could. At Tuskegee, for example, male students cultivated 650 acres of land, and female students contributed by making, mending, and laundering their work clothes. Washington assured *Atlantic* readers that "fortified at Tuskegee by education of mind, skill of hand, Christian character, ideas of thrift, economy, and push, and a spirit of independence," students would return to their communities and show others how to "lift themselves up."[10] Following the suggestion of the *Atlantic*'s assistant editor, Walter Hines Page, who saw the problem of poverty largely in terms of class, Washington broadened his argument for industrial education to include poor whites as well as Southern blacks.

Washington stated hard truths as he saw them. Despite a boom in black-owned small businesses during Reconstruction, many professionals had a hard time sustaining their practices. In "The Case of the Negro" (November 1899), he explained: "I do not believe that the world ever takes a race seriously, in its desire to share in the government of a nation, until a large number of individual members of that race have demonstrated beyond question their ability to control and develop their own business enterprises."[11]

Although white America responded to Washington as if he were the single spokesman for his people, opposition to his leadership had grown among more militant African Americans since the Supreme Court's "separate but equal" ruling in *Plessy vs. Ferguson* (1896). Many blacks resented Washington's stump representations, which seemed to categorize them as illiterate and in need of white handouts. Resentment festered about his vetting of candidates for government appointments and the favors extended to loyal soldiers.

The question may not have been whether Washington had detractors but who among them had the courage to take him on. The man who did—W. E. B. Du Bois (1868–1963)—came from a vastly different background than Washington. A Northerner whose family had been free for over a hundred years, he attended Fisk College and studied in Berlin before receiving a PhD in history from Harvard in 1895—the first granted to an African American. At Harvard, Du Bois studied the art of prose writing with the literary historian Barrett Wendell and the fundamentals of psychology with William James. He also read and digested works by earlier philosophers, such as the English giants—Locke, Berkeley, and Hume—and those by the philosopher George Santayana. His education included a class with the scientist Nathaniel Shaler, who expelled a student for refusing to sit next to Du Bois in class.

After leaving Harvard, Du Bois taught Latin and Greek at Wilberforce University, went on to teach sociology at the University of Pennsylvania, and later established Atlanta University's Department of Sociology. On his twenty-fifth birthday, while a doctoral student at the University of Berlin, Du Bois had made a half-drunken but nonetheless solemn vow, ceremoniously sealed with incense and candles, to work for "the rise of the Negro people."[12] In the 1890s, he published a number of books meant to augment the historical record: *The Suppression of the African Slave Trade* (1896), *A Program of Social Reform* (1897), *The Study of the Negro Problems* (1898), and *The Philadelphia Negro* (1899). These he followed with many more, including a biography of John Brown (1909) and his powerful best-known work, *The Souls of Black Folk* (1903). We want, he proclaimed in opposition to Washington's policies of social and political accommodation outlined in the Atlanta Compromise, "every single right that belongs to a freeborn American," the right to vote, to work, to educate our children, and *rise*."[13]

Lecturing, cajoling, scolding, and challenging his country to live up to the democratic principles of its Constitution, Du Bois stayed true to the oath he had taken so many years before in Berlin. In the 1890s, he published two influential essays in the *Atlantic*: "Strivings of the Negro People" (August 1897) and "A Negro Schoolmaster in the New South" (January 1899). The first essay, which became part of *The Souls of Black Folk*, contained his often-quoted explanation of what it feels like to be black in America.

> Between me and the other world there is ever an unasked question: unasked by some through feelings of delicacy; by others through the difficulty of rightly framing it. All, nevertheless, flutter round it. They approach me in a half-hesitant sort of way, eye me curiously or compassionately, and then, instead of saying directly, How does it feel to be a problem? they say, I know an excellent colored man in my town; or, I fought at Mechanicsville; or, Do not these Southern

> outrages make your blood boil? At these I smile, or am interested, or reduce the boiling to a simmer, as the occasion may require. To the real question, How does it feel to be a problem? I answer seldom a word.[14]

In "Strivings of the Negro People," Du Bois described the first time he felt an unbridgeable divide between himself and others. He was just a schoolboy when he and his classmates decided to exchange visiting cards and a new girl haughtily refused to accept his. He knew then that he "was different from the others . . . shut out from their world by a vast veil. . . . Why did God make me an outcast and a stranger in my own house?" he asked. Du Bois gives the sense that he, like the reader, must work his way toward an answer in small, painful, yet revelatory increments. "The Negro," he explains,

> is a sort of seventh son, born with a veil, and gifted with second-sight in this American world,—a world which yields him no self-consciousness, but only lets him see himself through the revelation of the other world. It is a peculiar sensation, this double-consciousness, this sense of always looking at one's self through the eyes of others, of measuring one's soul by the tape of a world that looks on in amused contempt and pity. One ever feels his two-ness,—an American, a Negro; two souls, two thoughts, two unreconciled strivings; two warring ideals in one dark body, whose dogged strength alone keeps it from being torn asunder.[15]

The passage describes a tenuous balance of impotence and power. In his vision of a distorted-mirror world, blacks see themselves through white eyes. No matter how many times they look again, the false image stares back. For Du Bois, this schizophrenic split grants African Americans—at great psychic cost—a knowledge of whites that exceeds whites' knowledge of them. In a final passage, he turns eloquently to the burden borne by African Americans "in the name of an historic race, in the name of this the land of their fathers' fathers, and in the name of human opportunity." He reminded readers that Africans did not come empty-handed to American shores. Their folktales and those of native tribes are more American than those of Grimm and Anderson, while the "sweet wild melodies" of spirituals constitute the only "true American music."

Du Bois offered his people as "the sole oasis of simple faith and reverence in a dusty desert of dollars and smartness."[16] If the essay suggests that Du Bois held whites responsible for the conditions inhibiting black progress, it also underscores values whites shared with African Americans. Responses to Du Bois's essay—and eventually to *The Souls of Black Folk*—differed widely among *Atlantic* readers, who either thought his rhetoric incendiary or wanted to apologize for slavery.

The second essay Du Bois contributed to the *Atlantic* recounts his experiences teaching school in rural Tennessee, where he had few books and the barest of classrooms. His desk consisted of three boards, and his chair had to be returned to his landlady each night. Some of Du Bois's pupils knew about slavery and the war solely through childhood tales. Education not only made them desire better lives; it made them fuller, more mindful human beings. When Du Bois returned to the area fifteen years later, he found his favorite pupil dead from overwork, her brother an escapee from jail, and her younger sister caring for her bastard child. Heartbroken by "all this life and love and strife and failure," he left for Nashville aboard the Jim Crow section of his train.[17]

In a 1902 *Atlantic* essay titled "The Training of Black Men," Du Bois explained that racial harmony could exist only between equals. By this time, Washington showed signs of wanting conciliation. In 1899, for instance, he quoted Frederick Douglass to *Atlantic* readers to prove his point that property "will purchase for us the only condition by which any people can rise to the dignity of genuine manhood; for without property there can be no leisure, without leisure there can be no thought, without thought there can be no invention, without invention there can be no progress." He conceded that "material development was not an end, but merely a means to an end. As Professor W. E. B. Du Bois puts it, the idea should not be simply to make men carpenters, but to make carpenters men."[18] Washington lived by this philosophy in his dealings with the *Atlantic*, telling his astonished editor that he didn't write for money.[19] Ever hopeful and urging the highest standards for citizenship, for whites as well as blacks, he looked toward a future in which his race would no longer be confined to jobs in agriculture, domestic service, and mechanics.

The future seemed far off to Du Bois, who acknowledged the failure of governmental policies to lessen racial divisions and wrote that prejudice "cannot be laughed away, nor always successfully stormed at, nor easily abolished by act of legislature." With a gesture of compromise to Washington, he granted that industrial schools like Tuskegee had helped to improve the standard of living for many blacks, before leaving readers with this poignant image:

> I sit with Shakespeare and he winces not. Across the color line I move arm in arm with Balzac and Dumas, where smiling men and welcoming women glide in gilded halls. From out the caves of Evening that swing between the strong-limbed earth and the tracery of the stars, I summon Aristotle and Aurelius and what souls I will, and they come all graciously with no scorn nor condescension. So, wed with Truth, I dwell above the Veil. Is this the life you grudge us, O knightly America? Is this the life you long to change into the dull red hideousness of Georgia? Are you so afraid lest peering from this high Pisgah, between Philistine and Amalekite, we sight the Promised Land?[20]

In 1901, the White House, if not the Promised Land, opened for a brief time. That year, President Theodore Roosevelt invited Booker T. Washington to advise him on matters of race. Their talks extending to the dinner hour, Roosevelt asked his guest to dine with him. The papers, getting wind of his schedule, had a field day. A typically incendiary headline in the South read: "Roosevelt Dines [with] a Darky." Editorials insisted that no self-respecting Southern woman would ever again grace the president's table. Senator Ben "Pitchfork" Tillman, a white supremacist from South Carolina, prophesized that this single dinner would necessitate the "killing of a thousand niggers in the South before they will learn their place again."[21] The furor, which caused the White House to deny Mrs. Roosevelt's presence at the dinner, incensed Mark Twain. Washington, he wrote in his journal, was "a man worth a hundred Roosevelts. The president was not worthy to untie his shoe-latchets."[22] The unfortunate meeting lessened Washington's power by making it harder for him to raise money from white donors, who worried about his pushing for social equality. And tragically, through the coming decades, a thousand blacks, and more, did die from lynching.

When teaching at Atlanta University, Du Bois had seen the burned knuckles of a black farmer named Sam Hose displayed in a store window. Among the two thousand men, women, and children who witnessed

Hose's hanging, burning, and mutilation were people who took pieces of his mutilated body for souvenirs. Washington had hoped that policies of accommodation and segregation, and the voices of incensed whites shamed by the "awful horror of mob violence," would decrease the racial carnage.[23] Between 1885 and 1910, however, the NAACP (founded in 1909) estimated that 2,425 lynchings occurred in the United States—105 of them in the year Washington dined with Roosevelt. That same year a black politician named George H. White resigned his congressional seat. White would be the last African American congressman to serve in the U.S. House of Representatives for the next twenty-eight years. And worse would come. Ordinances passed in Baltimore, Dallas, Richmond, and other American cities redlined or segregated neighborhoods by race. Racially designated facilities and workspaces in the nation's capital followed. It was cold comfort that, for one moment on 16 October 1891, manners had trumped politics. No matter that Roosevelt considered Africans Americans responsible for their lot. When he met Washington, common decency ruled, and for the space of an hour the country might have glimpsed its future. In the face of the firestorm that followed, Roosevelt would continue to consult Washington, though not at a time when a meeting could extend into lunch or dinner.

In *The American Scene*, Henry James singled out W. E. B. Du Bois for his belief in a "Talented Tenth," which echoed James's own wish, expressed in the preface to "Lady Barbarina," for "some eventual sublime consensus of the educated": "There," James announced, "is the personal drama of the future."[24] The *Atlantic* had been founded by people who believed in education no less than Washington and Du Bois did. For all they might have thought themselves an equivalent of the "talented tenth," they also believed in democracy, which, in the 1890s, the *Atlantic* furthered with its endorsement of Washington and Du Bois. The editors needed no convincing that African Americans were, to borrow an earlier phrase from Douglass, a "permanent part of American society."[25]

22

Progressive Politics under Walter Hines Page

We all think when we are young that we can do something with the mummies. But the mummy is a solemn fact, and it differs from all other things (except stones) in this: it lasts forever.

WALTER HINES PAGE, letter to the *State Chronicle*, 1886

WALTER HINES PAGE (1855–1918) was the last *Atlantic* editor to have personal memories of the Civil War. Growing up in Cary, North Carolina, the lanky boy with nut-colored curls and Huck Finn innocence wandered down to the train station with his best friend, an African American named Sam. There they saw the train halt and a large box containing the body of a Confederate soldier laid gently in the shade. A man told them that Billy Morris had come home to his parents. The boys tended the coffin while the man fetched the Morrises. In the hour or more that it took for old Mr. Morris, still covered with lint from the cotton gin, and his suddenly aged wife to come, Walt Page became aware of the world's wrongs. At Billy Morris's funeral the minister prayed for Southern victory. Listening to the women weep, Page felt guilty, wondering whether his doubts about the Cause had helped determine Billy's fate. Mrs. Gregory, a neighbor, cried, "It'll be my John next," and sure enough, his coffin followed Billy's.

As more coffins arrived and more women donned mourning, starved and wounded soldiers straggled home. The shoemaker Mr. Sanford looked so thin that Page thought he might disintegrate before his eyes; Mr. Larkin and Joe Tatum limped into town on crutches; and one man arrived minus a cheek and ear. Young Walt and Sam still went fishing on the riverbank, but instead of waiting silently for their catch, they spoke in hushed tones of battles and bodies.[1]

Page left Cary for college, and later landed a job as a cub reporter for the *St. Joseph Gazette* in Missouri. He rose quickly to editor before leaving to join the staff of the *New York World*. From there he moved first to the *Raleigh State Chronicle* and then to the *Forum*, where he raised circulation and caught Horace Scudder's attention at the *Atlantic*. Page, who came to the magazine as both its assistant and acquisitions editor, succeeded Scudder in 1898. Scudder had two hesitations about Page. He worried about trusting the magazine to such a young man. (Page, at forty-three, was seventeen years younger than Scudder.) And he worried about having a Southerner at the helm, though Page, having little patience with tradition for tradition's sake, hardly seemed "Southern." Blaming the South's woes on Confederate hero-worship, Page rejected all forms of what he called "mummified" thinking. To his mind, the *Atlantic* had strayed from its vision as a political force, and he meant to get it on track.

Page's politics were complicated. He editorialized about the Populist menace in October 1896, fearing it would bring mob rule. Despite childhood memories, he supported the Spanish-American War, reinstating the American flag from Civil War days on the *Atlantic*'s June 1898 cover. His support of the war troubled a core of anti-imperialists associated with the magazine, including William Dean Howells, Mark Twain, and Charles Eliot Norton, who begged his students not to volunteer their service. Rejecting an antiwar article from E. L. Godkin, Page drew his line between "the intelligent classes who criticize and predict disaster, and the men who must take those tasks in hand."[2] *Atlantic* writers supporting the war assumed the moral superiority of the United States and its responsibility toward those colonized. Page himself called it a "necessary act of surgery for the sake of civilization."[3]

As a man whose family had at one time owned a few slaves and who had not wholly shed the prejudices of his caste and training, Page found it disconcerting to enter the office every day to work under the gaze of William Lloyd Garrison's portrait. Garrison's son, employed at the *Atlantic*, often invited African Americans to visit and consult with him about personal and political matters. According to Page's biographer, Burton J. Hendrick, another *Atlantic* staffer recounted an incident when Page told Garrison that one of his "niggers" waited outside for an audience. "I very much regret, Mr. Page," came the response, "that you should insist on spelling 'Negro' with two 'g's.'"[4] Ellery Sedgwick, a future *Atlantic* editor, described Page as foursquare, pragmatic, and impatient of failure. Devoted to family, country, and the craft of editing, he remained immune to social and literary subtleties. Page made his presence felt in Park Street, first with the odor of tobacco that permeated every floor, and second by replacing the editor's traditional desk with a long worktable.

These changes were, of course, superficial. The deep differences between the old guard and the new centered on the definition of the magazine, its cultural mission, and the future of publishing. Page had little respect for what didn't sell. Why publish the best if no one reads it? Favoring action to aesthetics, he solicited articles from Theodore Roosevelt, Jacob Riis, the revolutionary prince Peter Kropotkin, Frank Norris (then a war correspondent in Cuba), and Woodrow Wilson, who would appoint him ambassador to Great Britain in 1913. As if Scudder's opposite, Page disliked the "yak-yak" of literary reviews, the number of which he decreased along with the magazine's offerings of poetry. He widened the division between the magazine and the publishing house by serializing fewer novels. His tastes, determined by copies sold, ran from Mary Johnston's historical romances to Jack London's unforgiving story "An Odyssey of the North" (January 1900). After reading Johnston's manuscript of "Prisoners of Hope"—in which the beautiful Lady Jocelyn Leigh takes an American husband on sight to avoid marrying the brutal Lord Carnal—Page boarded a train to Richmond to secure another serial. He left with *To Have and to Hold*, set in colonial Virginia, which doubled sales of the sluggish *Atlantic* before skyrocketing to the head of best-seller lists. He also solicited work from Kate Chopin, whose stories of Creole life in Louisiana—"Nég Créol" (July 1897), "Tante Cat'rinette" (September 1894), and "Althenaise: A Story of a Temperament" (August and September 1896)—opened a world of complex interracial issues for *Atlantic* readers. Largely remembered today for *The Awakening* (1899), Chopin presented men and women gripped by amoral passions and forces beyond their control.

Although he sought out women contributors like Johnston, Page found them tiresome and time-consuming. "Their imaginations are more easily excited by the hope of success, and few of them have had business experience," he wrote in his memoir, *A Publisher's Confession* (1905). "They want to be fair and appreciate frank dealing. Yet they like to have everything explained in great detail."[5] Mary Johnston's friend Ellen Glasgow came first on his list of female nuisances. As she worked on her second novel, she told Page: "It is going to be worth my while and worth your while, and if I send it to you and you do not want it for *The Atlantic* you will be very blind and I shall be very wrathful."[6] He did not bite and later told her she would have been better off burning the manuscript.

Exhorting contributors to put all effort into the piece in hand, Page reminded them that the *Atlantic*'s audience lay outside a hallowed circle of editors. Perhaps most important, he brought the practices of newspaper publishing to Park Street by sending reporters on assignment and soliciting articles on specific topics. He wanted the magazine known for its stands on contemporary issues. The novelist Frank Norris, who had reported on the Boer War, contributed a short piece about Cuban refugees of the Spanish-American War at El Caney waiting for the one Red Cross doctor to distribute food. Describing the main meal of the day, *la comida*, he writes: "It means 'food;' not breakfast, dinner, or supper, not food in dishes and served by a waiter in the hotel, not a polite knife-and-fork affair in any sense of the word. Comida is downright nourishment, sordid, vulgar nutriment, of the kind that fills empty stomachs after a three days' abstinence,—the kind that we ladled out of camp kettles to six thousand starving refugee children at Caney during the second day's truce. This is comida."[7]

Norris's contribution exemplifies what Page wanted: brisk, clear writing that eschewed artsy, introspective flourishes. Contributors needed to *show* the relevance of the piece to the reader. Scholarly treatises on literature and philosophic ruminations became unwelcome at the *Atlantic*, as were articles on mysticism (a personal pet peeve of Page) and religion. He hoped to woo young readers by banning quotations from Greek and Latin, a change that also reflected a decreased emphasis on the classics in American education. According to one *Atlantic* writer, the "invasion of journalism" (July 1900) promised to change the way Americans communicated or thought. Another contributor saw journalism becoming "the basis for literature" (February 1900).

By devoting all his energies to the magazine, Page as good as stamped it "mine." As he explained to one writer: "What we should like is a record of social betterment, that is to say, the most striking and specific facts which show to what extent the mass of the people in the United States has improved during the century."[8] He toured the South to get a range of opinion from African Americans and people of different classes. Henry James ranked high among the authors who exasperated him for stirring "no emotion" except weariness. "The professional critics who mistake an indirect and round-about use of words for literary art will call it an excellent piece of work; but people who have blood in their veins will yawn and throw it down—if, indeed, they ever pick it up."[9] The magazine limited rather than ended its association with Henry James, as Page tilted the *Atlantic* away from literature toward politics. No one seems to have noticed that he also began to shift the focus of the magazine from Boston toward New York, seeking contributions, for example, from the socialist writer Abraham Cahan and the journalist Hutchins Hapgood.

Page, who became a partner in Doubleday, Page and Company, made many changes but served as editor in chief only one year. In that time he doubled the number of articles on politics, economics, and pressing social issues, while arguing that literature, especially the realistic fiction he himself favored, had always tackled these subjects. His *Atlantic* featured Woodrow Wilson and Wilson's predecessor, Theodore Roosevelt, political men with a talent for words. Describing Roosevelt's conversation for *Atlantic* readers, John Burroughs wrote:

> What a stream of it he poured forth! and what a varied and picturesque stream,—anecdote, history, science, politics, adventure, literature; bits of his experience as a ranchman, hunter, Rough Rider, legislator, Civil Service commissioner, police commissioner, governor, president—the frankest confessions, the most telling criticisms, happy characterizations of prominent political leaders, or foreign rulers, or members of his own Cabinet; always surprising by his candor, astonishing by his memory, and diverting by his humor.[10]

The *Atlantic* had followed Roosevelt throughout his career, praising his efforts, in 1892, to stop political parties from dunning governmental employees for campaign contributions, and covering the 1912 presidential election that pitted him against his own party's candidate, William Taft. When Taft won the Republican nomination, Roosevelt ran under the auspices of the Bull Moose Party, paving the way for a Woodrow Wilson victory. Wilson, who had witnessed Jefferson Davis bound in chains and marched through his hometown, went on to become a student of government, the executive branch in particular. Like Abraham Lincoln, who measured the *Atlantic*'s influence in lives saved, Wilson saw the magazine as an entrée to the halls of power, if not the White House itself. The magazine introduced him to a wide swath of the electorate, and more crucially educated them to the desirability of a Wilson candidacy.

In articles with titles such as "Responsible Government under the Constitution" (April 1886), "Character of Democracy in the United States" (November 1889), "A Literary Politician" (November 1895), and the complimentary "Mr. Cleveland as President" (March 1897), Wilson argued for placing more concentrated authority in the office of the president. "Government is action," he wrote in November 1889,

> and I believe that unless we concentrate legislative leadership,—leadership, that is, in progressive policy,—unless we give leave to our nationality and practice to it by such concentration, we shall sooner or later suffer something like national paralysis in the face of emergencies. We have no one in Congress who stands for the nation. Each man stands but for his part of the nation; and so management and combination, which may be effected in the dark, are given the place that should be held by centred and responsible leadership, which would of necessity work in the focus of the national gaze.[11]

As president of Princeton University from 1902 to 1910, governor of the state of New Jersey from 1911 to 1913, and president of the United States when Taft and Roosevelt split the Republican ticket in 1912, Wilson lived up to his own pronouncements by overhauling the banking system, curtailing monopolies, reducing tariffs, protecting consumers from unfair business practices, limiting the workday of child laborers, providing compensation for injured workers, and supporting women's right to vote.

Wilson's contributions to the *Atlantic* were not limited to politics. Both he and Roosevelt published essays on literature and the broader culture, Wilson writing about "the author himself" (September 1891), for example, and Roosevelt, then U.S. Civil Service Commissioner (1889–1895), on reforming the service to reward merit rather than political cronyism. In "The College Graduate and Public Life" (August 1894), the Harvard-educated Roosevelt argued that honor binds the college man "to take an active part in our political life, and to do his full duty as a citizen by helping his fellow-citizens to the extent of his power in the exercise of the rights of self-government. . . . And while he must show the virtues of uprightness and tolerance and gentleness, he must also show the sterner virtues of courage, resolution, and hardihood, and of desire to war with merciless effectiveness against the existence of wrong."[12] As assistant secretary of the navy, Roosevelt had advocated if not forced war with Spain. He emerged from the Battle of San Juan Hill a national hero. As president, following the assassination of William McKinley, he would add to the Monroe Doctrine a corollary giving the United States, and the United States only, the right to intervene in South American politics. It seems ironic that a man whom many associate with the slogan "speak softly and carry a big stick" would provide the model for children's "teddy bears."

Roosevelt's contribution was unique for its obvious grandstanding and self-promotion. Bliss Perry remembered two occasions when, after their cigars were lit, the anti-imperialist Charles Eliot Norton launched into "an elaborate analysis of Theodore Roosevelt. In both instances, he began with: 'Of course the man is a Barbarian.'"[13] Too often substituting "instinct for intellect," Roosevelt troubled the conscience of literary men and women, who disliked his politics (or the idea of hunting) but appreciated him as a fellow writer. On the subject of Roosevelt, and perhaps Roosevelt only, Henry James and Mark Twain agreed. James thought Roosevelt the "monstrous embodiment of unprecedented and unresounding noise," while Twain parodied his hunting exploits with invented newspaper headlines such as "Ate All the Game, Except a Wildcat, and That Had a Narrow Escape" and "Charged Into the Canebrake after Bear and Hugged the Guides after the Kill."[14] He couldn't understand how Roosevelt could be the worst U.S. president but the most admired. Had Roosevelt known Twain's opinion of him, he would not have taken it well. In 1905, the *Atlantic* initiated a series of letters to famous statesmen, written by Rollo Ogden, comparing what candidates said before they were elected with "their words and actions after they assumed real political responsibility." The first was a letter addressed to Theodore Roosevelt. The letter so incensed the president that he had the offending pages torn out of the White House's copy of the magazine. Henry Cabot Lodge informed Henry Houghton of his boss's response, and Houghton asked Page's successor, Bliss Perry, to send a formal apology. Perry offered to resign, but George Mifflin persuaded him to stay on. Perry returned the favor by abandoning the series.[15]

To Jacob Riis, Roosevelt was larger than life—masculine, independent, and naturally aristocratic. The meeting between the two men proved to be one of those fateful encounters that had a profound effect on the lives of others. As an immigrant, Riis had been forced to seek shelter in doorways or the Church Street police station, where another tramp robbed him of his last link to home, a gold locket containing a precious lock of hair. When Riis reported the crime to the policeman on duty, he was dismissed from the station with a kick in the pants. Riis's dog had patiently waited for him through the night and, witnessing Riis's indignity, attacked his attacker, who "seized the poor little beast by the legs, and beat its brains out against the stone steps." "The outrage of that night" fed Riis's efforts to provide decent housing for New York's poor and to eradicate the abuses of police-run lodging houses like the one on Church Street. When Roosevelt, who accompanied Riis on walks through Manhattan's Lower East Side, heard this story, he got visibly angry. "They did that to you?" he asked, clenching his fists. He promised to "smash them to-morrow." And as commissioner of police, he kept his promise, closing all police lodging houses on 15 February 1896. After twenty-five years, Riis wrote, his dog was finally avenged.[16]

Never one to rest with victory, Riis took his case to the public. He understood the power of pictures and illustrated his articles with the faces of the poor themselves. Photographs like "5 Cents a Spot," which revealed people cramped promiscuously together trying to get a few hours' sleep, were made possible by the new technology of magnesium flash powder. By way of the newspapers, his photographs brought the poor willy-nilly into middle-class parlors. Riis became a popular lecturer, famous for his lantern-slide pictures of "how the other half lives," the title of the 1890 book that originally brought him to Roosevelt's attention and began the mutual admiration. In his introduction to Riis's autobiography, *The Making of an American* (1901), Roosevelt wrote, "If I were asked to name a fellow-man who came nearest to being the ideal American citizen, I should name Jacob Riis."[17]

Riis's essays in the *Atlantic* came without his trademark photographs of stunned countenances or of bedraggled laundry flapping from tenement porches like white flags—but they opened with every bit of power.

In "Out of the Book of Humanity" (November 1896), Riis told the story of Isaac Josephs, slipper-maker, who sat up "on the fifth floor of his Allen Street tenement, in the gray of the morning, to finish the task he had set himself before Yom Kippur." He worked without sleep or food for days to finish the two dozen slippers that would allow his family to observe the holiday. It took three years for him to save enough money to bring his wife and two children to America, and this Yom Kippur, the holiest day in the Jewish calendar, celebrated their reunion. Toward morning, he dozed off, and waking with a start upset an oil lamp: "The slippers, the slippers! If they were burned, it was ruin. There would be no Yom Kippur, no feast of Atonement, no fast,—rather, no end of it; starvation for him and his."[18] Panicking, he beat the fire with his bare hands, yet the fire flared more fiercely, snaking its way toward the finished slippers. Blocking its path with his body, he cried out. His wife dashed in and smothered the fire with a blanket. Yom Kippur was saved. Riis followed the story of Isaac Josephs with a section called "Lost Children," little ones scooped away to children's homes and sometimes sent to other states, where no one spoke their language. Writing at a time when Congress wanted to restrict immigration of certain minorities thought to be less intelligent, Riis described the look of comprehension that transformed the face of one seemingly dim boy when he heard his native dialect. He detailed the unending labor of an eight-year-old tailor named Paolo who managed to get an education and graduated with a fellowship that would allow him to take his mother to their native land. Riis spared readers nothing. On his way home, Paolo died in a train accident still clutching his blood-stained diploma.

Paolo gave *Atlantic* readers an opportunity to attach a face to the slum's shocking statistics of death and disease. "In 1880," Riis explained with statistics instead of pictures, "the average number of persons to each dwelling in New York was 16.37. In 1890 it was 18.52; in 1895, according to the police census, 21.2. The census of 1900 will show the crowding to have gone on at an equal if not at a greater rate."[19] According to Riis, the slums doomed generations to ignorance and helpless poverty. Victims of their environment and exploited by predatory employers, landlords, and Tammany Hall politicians, the poor spent their days deprived of light and air. One of every five tenement babies died from diseases in their own homes, which social workers referred to as "infant slaughter houses." Women who could make more than a dozen pairs of pants a day might make sixty cents. Despite these conditions, Riis saw and helped to bring about significant improvements. In the twenty-nine years since he spent the night at the police lodging house, "Bottle Alley is gone, and Bandits' Roost. Bone Alley, Thieves' Alley, and Kerosene Row,—they are all gone."[20] But work remained, he reminded readers: every citizen deserved access to public baths and parks and education.

At the same time, he argued that misplaced charity did more harm than good. The solution to the slums lay in treating workers fairly by ensuring eight-hour workdays, safe and hygienic surroundings, and fair wages. His focus on charity formed part of a larger nineteenth-century discussion about its ills and benefits. How much charitable work was merely a diversion for the rich, some of whom toured the slums as if going to the theater? Did donating money constitute true charity, or did philanthropists need to work alongside the poor as Leo Tolstoy worked in the fields? To Thomas Bailey Aldrich, Tolstoy's altruistic call in "Que faire" (trans. 1887) threatened all that American capitalism had achieved. Reformers such as Jane Addams, who published an *Atlantic* article titled "The Subtle Problems of Charity" (February 1899), and Charles Richard Henderson, who argued for a scientific approach to giving (February 1900), rejected the idea that capitalism would lead to the elimination of poverty or that the poor were prone to alcoholism and criminality. The public worried about creating a class of professional beggars, about race wars, and about masses of foreigners changing the complexion of American society. Such fears fed movements to restrict immigration, sterilize the mentally disabled, and criminalize miscegenation statutes. Apprehensive about demographic prophecies, Teddy Roosevelt called on white mothers to have more babies. His daughter Alice responded by forming the Race Suicide Club, a group that exchanged information about birth control.

Riis assumed that his readers wanted to find a lasting and just solution to urban ills. One of his most influential *Atlantic* articles, "The Genesis of the Gang" (September 1899), argued that environment largely determined human behavior. "Jacob Beresheim was fifteen when he was charged with murder," Riis reported, and wondered whether he would get "the chair": "Of his crime the less said the better. It was the climax of a career of depravity that differed from other such chiefly in the opportunities afforded by an environment which led up to and helped shape it. My business is with that environment. The man is dead, the boy in jail.

But unless I am to be my brother's jail keeper, merely, the iron bars do not square the account of Jacob with society." Jacob represented for Riis a class of street boys growing up in darkness, discouragement, and dirt. Without the benefits of school or church, they knew authority as the oppressive eye of the landlord and neighborhood police. Deprived of a childhood and of the chance to develop moral character through play, boys like Jacob, who found a substitute family in gangs, were time bombs destined to explode. Riis compared the organization of these gangs to ward politics ("Of what gang politics means every large city in our country has had its experience") and warned of their allure for middle-class youngsters who wanted to live the adventures they followed in dime novels.[21]

Along with his wife, who adopted groups of street waifs, Riis saw an opportunity in settlement work. In his "Reform by Humane Touch" (December 1899), he spoke eloquently about the power of personal influence and asked every citizen to help: "The slum is not limited by the rookeries of Mulberry or Ludlow street. It has long roots that feed on the selfishness and dullness of Fifth Avenue quite as greedily as on the squalor of the Sixth Ward. The two are not nearly so far apart as they look. . . . When we have learned to smile and weep with the poor, we shall have mastered our problem."[22] He planned his message of time and toil well; it appeared in the Christmas issue, with the new millennium a few days away.

Riis's contributions introduced *Atlantic* readers to people and points of view they might easily have ignored. His focus on the daily suffering of individual people rather than on broad social issues altered the discussion about America's immigrant minorities. Avoiding the formulaic title "The Problem of [this or that immigrant group]," which forestalled those who would hold victims accountable for their circumstances, Riis helped to make the crises in public health, housing, and education more of a shared concern. His style—immediate, anecdotal, and persuasive—particularly suited a literary magazine with a social conscience. Although the *Atlantic* did not have a monopoly on Riis's exposés, their appearance in the magazine indicated a local and a broader public support for reform.

As the *Atlantic* approached the twentieth century, readers might have thought it had returned to its radical roots with Riis's investigative reporting and the publication of Peter Kropotkin's "The Autobiography of a Revolutionist," which took advantage of his recent tour of the United States. Known as the Anarchist Prince, Kropotkin (1842–1921) shared similarities with Clarence King. After leading an expedition to survey northern Manchuria, he spent a number of years exploring eastern Siberia before discovering glacial deposits in Finland and Sweden. Arrested in Russia for speaking against the evils of the current regime and imprisoned for two years, he escaped to England to begin the life of a vagabond propagandist, lecturing and writing for the anarchist press. From England he moved to Switzerland, which expelled him for supporting the assassination of Tsar Alexander II; then to France, where he was arrested, tried, and imprisoned for inciting workers. Pardoned after three years, he returned to England. The serialization of Kropotkin's autobiography came at a particular moment in American society when revolutionaries were accepted as folk heroes. In his introduction to the serial, the peace activist Robert Erskine Ely called Kropotkin a defender of "the most exalted of moral ideals."[23]

But whatever Kropotkin's faults or virtues—and he had both—he was a signpost for the *Atlantic*. Walter Hines Page, with his credo—suffrage for men, regardless of race, tolerance toward newcomers, and the general well-being of all Americans—had moved the magazine farther left of center than it had been for decades. Though Page's editorship had been brief, none could deny that he had made the magazine financially healthier. When its editors assessed the previous forty years of the *Atlantic*, they acknowledged that their magazine had changed with the times. Not only had its circulation risen from ten thousand to seventeen thousand between 1895 and 1899; it had also restored the political and social responsibilities of the early years and found a new energy that it, its readers, and the Western world would need.

Those who had disliked Page or worried that he might steer the *Atlantic* off course welcomed his replacement, Bliss Perry, a prolific writer, fly fisherman, and baseball fan, as their captain (1899–1909). Perry exuded a quiet confidence that people associated with ample food, a fire in the library, and friends. A professor at Williams, Princeton, and Harvard who cared deeply about the humanities, he described himself as an idealist in a nation of idealists. He defended immigration, for example, as the grist of democracy: "Far better these immigrants," he wrote, "as raw material for Democracy's wholesome take than the exhausted strain of Puritan stock which lives querulously in the cities or grows vile in the hill towns."[24] An advocate of social responsibility, though less aggressively than Page, he believed in unfettered discussion. Perry gently braked but did not want to stop the *Atlantic*'s headlong dash into the next century. If Page saw little benefit in the study of classical languages, for example, Perry thought such knowledge central to the writing of English. He too believed in "progress," but progress grounded in traditions that harked back four decades; he saw his task as making those traditions central to American life.

23

From Sea to Shining Sea

Few in these hot, dim, frictiony times are quite sane or free; choked with care like clocks full of dust, laboriously doing so much good and making so much money,—or so little,—they are no longer good themselves.

JOHN MUIR, "The Wild Parks and Forest Reservations of the West," *Atlantic*, January 1898

WHEN JOHN MUIR first met Ralph Waldo Emerson, he thought him "as serene as a sequoia." Emerson had come to Yosemite in 1871, at Muir's invitation, to experience the noble trees and mountains. Overlooking his guest's health, Muir proposed a camping expedition into the heart of the mountains. "Up there lies a new heaven and a new earth," Muir promised; "let us go to the show." Emerson's friends demurred for him. "Full of indoor philosophy," they laughed at the wild proposal, insisting that Emerson stick to the hotels and known trails. Muir swore that "there was not a single cough or sneeze in all the Sierra." He asked them to imagine how a "big climate-changing, inspiring fire" would transfigure the evening's purple light. "Come," he urged, "and make an immortal Emerson night of it. But the house habit was not to be overcome, nor the strange dread of pure night air, though it is only cooled day air with a little pure dew in it. So the carpet dust and unknowable reeks were preferred. And to think of this being a Boston choice! Sad commentary on culture and the glorious transcendentalism."

Muir missed his night with Emerson watching the sequoias' shadows dance like druids around the glow of their campfire, yet he had his memory of escorting Emerson and his party on horseback to the sequoias at the Mariposa Grove. See these commanding trees, he pleaded, these preachers stretching forth their arms in benediction. Gazing with "devout admiration" at the scene, Emerson said little, but before the party led Emerson away, he had a chance to stroll among the massive trunks: "There were giants in those days," he quoted from *Genesis*. Then a doff of his hat, a wave good-bye, a switch of the reins, and Emerson was gone. That night in the Sierras, Muir felt lonely for the first time. He mourned Emerson as he might one of the Mariposa Grove's venerable giants felled without an understanding of its nature. Sitting before the blazing fire that he had wanted to share with Emerson, he reminded himself that only Emerson had gone to Boston, not the trees nor the birds, nor in truth the spirit of his new friend. Seventeen years after Emerson waved good-bye to Muir at the south fork of the Merced River, Muir visited Emerson's grave "under a pine tree on the hill above Sleepy Hollow." "He had gone to higher Sierras," Muir wrote in his *Atlantic* essay "The Forests of the Yosemite Park" (April 1900), "and, as I fancied, was again waving his hand in friendly recognition."[1]

By 1900, the United States had five national parks, among them Yosemite (1890), in large part at Muir's urging. A photograph of Muir and Theodore Roosevelt from 1900 shows them standing high above the tree line in Yosemite. Roosevelt's legacy would include, apart from the five national parks, 150 national forests, fifty-five animal preserves, and the creation of the U.S. Forest Service. Muir's essays for the *Atlantic*, collected in *Our National Parks* (1901), form part of the magazine's continuing debate about the use, preservation, and ownership of western lands. Mary Austin, born in Illinois and transplanted to California, wrote about the problems between settlers, Indians, water rights, and sheep-raising in the "high deserts" of California and New Mexico; Gertrude Simmons Bonnin, whom readers knew as Zitkala-Sa, entered the debates from an American Indian's point of view; and John Burroughs—a contributor to the *Atlantic* since 1860—had never left the discussion. Each of these writers represented different constituencies and raised different questions. What was the West, and how should it be used and governed? Should the wilderness be managed or left untouched? Did its resources benefit the common people or only those rich enough to enjoy its wonders? What should be done with the Indians, who in those years could be slain on sight? How might private wealth and the government work together in the cause of preservation? As writers for the *Atlantic* knew, answers would determine environmental policies for decades to come. Muir felt divinely driven in his battle against Congress, and against the miners, settlers, prospectors, and the shepherds who grazed "hoofed locusts," as Muir called sheep, on God's ground. To make his point, Muir quoted Emerson's line that things refuse to be mismanaged long. Austin, by contrast, defended the grazing rights of the shepherds who drove their flocks to the High Sierra, while Zitkala-Sa questioned the government's claims to tribal lands. John Burroughs largely agreed with the policies of his friend and the nation's president, Theodore Roosevelt.

Each of these writers embodied paradoxes inherent to environmental disagreements. Muir campaigned to reserve millions of acres of western wilderness yet, in an 1897 *Atlantic* article titled "The American Forests," assured readers that the United States had room for everyone. Let immigrants come "to the woods as well as to the prairies and plains," he wrote: "Let them be as free to pick gold and gems from the hills, to cut and hew, dig and plant, for homes and bread, as the birds are to pick berries from the wild bushes, and moss and leaves for nests. . . . Mere destroyers, however, tree-killers, spreading death and confusion in the fairest groves and gardens ever planted, let the government hasten to cast them out and make an end of them."[2] The same man who wrote, "I suppose we need not go mourning the buffaloes," founded the Sierra Club in 1892 and accompanied Roosevelt and Burroughs on an 1899 expedition to Alaska, funded by the railroad magnate (and presumably "tree-killer") Edward H. Harriman.[3] In a 1906 *Atlantic* article, Burroughs would argue that "a man as big and active as Roosevelt" needed nothing less than the entire West for his laboratory: "It is to such men as he that the big game legitimately belongs . . . and as for his killing of the 'varmints,'—bears, cougars, and bobcats,—the fewer the better of these there are, the better for the useful and beautiful game."[4] Burroughs expected readers to believe that Roosevelt's instincts as a naturalist prompted his hunting, and that hunting made him a better naturalist.

Burroughs differed from Muir in relying on science for his moral authority. In "Real and Sham Natural History" (March 1903), he targeted the popular nature writers Thomas Seton and William J. Long for their sloppy methodology and sentimentalizing of animals. Long, he complained, attributed human thoughts and emotions to animals, while Seton, the man remembered for tracking Lobo the wolf, asserted in his book *Wild Animals I Have Known* that animals could reason. Burroughs's criticism of personifying animals, which included Jack London's portrait of Buck in *The Call of the Wild* (1903), raises issues of scientific objectivity. An artist, he explained, has always had the privilege of making a heroine or a landscape more beautiful for effect. "But when he paints a portrait, or an actual scene, or event, we expect him to be true to the facts of the case. Again, he may add all the charm his style can impart to the subject, and we are not deceived; the picture is true, perhaps all the more true for the style."[5] While it seems odd that one metaphoric truth may be more true in the interests of fiction than in the interests of science, there could be no denying the popularity of Long's and Seton's books. After Roosevelt publicly sided with Burroughs, Mark Twain sputtered in his journal that the president should mind the country instead of firing at a pathetic target like the Rev. William Long. "Wild creatures often do extraordinary things," Twain wrote. "Look at Mr. Roosevelt's own performances."[6] At the time Burroughs's piece appeared, the *Atlantic* had a policy of not printing controversial replies, and its editor, Bliss Perry, denied Long and Seton a chance to defend themselves. He later regretted his decision, calling it shortsighted and "pontifical."[7]

Burroughs's attack on Long and Seton reveals the tension between science and art when the authority of science was rising and writers like Burroughs felt their influence waning. Burroughs and Muir had a rival in Mary Austin, a woman whom Carey McWilliams, the California lawyer and historian who went on to edit the *Nation*, described as having "the emotional background and experience of an American housewife, the stout mental courage of a Huxley, and a streak of ineradicable mysticism."[8] Austin had little patience for nature writers like John Muir and Burroughs, who suffered, in her opinion, from enormous egos—a fault usually attributed to herself. "All the public expects of practicing Naturists," she stated in her autobiography, "is the appearance, the habits, the incidents of the wild"; and when such a creature writes about his communing with nature, "it is mistaken for poetizing."[9] Unlike Muir, Austin wanted the land to be worked, protectively, by locals, miners, and shepherds. At times she and Muir sound alike, except that she would always give priority to the native inhabitants.

Bliss Perry thought he might be making a mistake to accept Austin's "A Shepherd of the Sierras" (1900)—it seemed so unlike any other story he had read. It begins: "The two ends of this story belong, one to Pierre

Jullien, and the other to the lame coyote in the pack of the Ceriso. Pierre will have it that the Virgin is at the bottom of the whole affair. However that may be, it is known that Pierre Jullien has not lost so much as a lamb of the flocks since the burning of Black Mountain."[10] Austin's voice, both oracular and down to earth, ushers readers into the world of her story, with its unusual trinity of man, beast, and Virgin. The plot has elements of fable, since the safety of Pierre's flock results from his having nursed a coyote burned in a wildfire. Austin's wilderness, which is psychological as well as physical, houses a logic all its own. "The land," she would warn in *The Land of Little Rain* (1903), "will not be lived in except in its own fashion."[11] The writer-illustrator Mary Hallock Foote (Wallace Stegner's model for the heroine of *Angle of Repose*) described Austin's style as "pure woman," reserved yet powerfully immediate. Foote noted the unique texture of Austin's speech: "nervous," "rich," "sensual," and "straight at the mark."[12] It is also an artful blending of fiction, myth, history, and hearsay.

Austin followed "A Shepherd of the Sierras" with "The Last Antelope" (July 1903) and "The Little Town of the Grape Vines" (June 1903). *The Land of Little Rain* offered one of the first studies of the high deserts of Southern California. E. Boyd Smith, who had spent time in the West sketching native people and herders, illustrated the first edition. Forty-seven years after its initial publication, another artist, Ansel Adams, brought out an edition of *The Land of Little Rain* containing his photographs. "Many books and articles have probed the factual aspects of this amazing land," he wrote, "but no writing to my knowledge conveys so much of the spirit of earth and sky, of plants and people, of storm and the desolation of majestic wastes, of tender, intimate beauty, as does *The Land of Little Rain*."[13] Bliss Perry, who had worried that Austin would cost Houghton Mifflin money, recommended that they publish her next book of "fanciful tales for children," *The Basket Woman*. His own twelve-year-old daughter had loved them.

Editors like Perry began to pay more for what Austin called her "Indian" stories. The *Atlantic* published both "Mahala Joe" (July 1904) and "The Walking Woman" (August 1907), perhaps her most anthologized story. Austin claimed to have learned her craft sitting for hours with tribal elders, who exhibited "an almost Chinese indefatigability of pursuit of the last scrap of meaning."[14] Bridging seemingly antagonistic traditions—

oral and literary, or Anglo-European and American Indian—her writing filled a void for contemporaries disillusioned with the soulless materialism of their age. In "The Walking Woman," for instance, her protagonist literally walks off "all sense of society-made values": "It was the naked thing the Walking Woman grasped, not dressed and tricked out, for instance, by prejudices in favor of certain occupations" or even love. "To work and to love and to bear children," Austin writes, "*That* sounds easy enough. But the way we live establishes so many things of much more importance."[15]

Austin was not alone in finding a model for contemporary life in native cultures. Franz Boas and Alfred Kroeber followed pioneering anthropologists like Alice Fletcher, who tried to preserve tribal life and customs. Charles Lummis, the man who insisted he had named "the Southwest" and never tired of singing the praises of its native peoples, mentored Austin during the writing of *The Land of Little Rain*. She dedicated the book to his wife, Eve. The *Atlantic* helped to make Austin's reputation as an expert on the arts, customs, rights, and religious practices of American Indians—a development Lummis and other authorities came to resent. In 1911, her play *The Arrow-Maker* opened on Broadway to generally poor reviews, which questioned its authenticity. Boas dismissed out of hand her claim in *American Rhythm* (1923) that American poetry originated from Native American rhythms. And Carl Van Vechten satirized her in *Spider Boy* as Marna Frost (1928), a woman known "from coast to coast in the homes of representatives and senators . . . as the Little Mother of the Indian. Usually a profanely abusive epithet preceded the diminutive adjective."[16] Yet notwithstanding the fun people had at Austin's expense, few could deny her efforts to stop the Bursum Bill, which ceded Indian land and water rights to Anglo settlers; her work to preserve New Mexico's Spanish heritage; her broad knowledge of the Southwest; or her achievement in books such as *The Land of Little Rain* and *The Basket Woman*.

The topic of "the Indian" at the turn of the twentieth century formed part of the *Atlantic*'s larger discussion about assimilation. In 1896, the U.S. Supreme Court ruled that Indian courts were not bound by constitutional provisions, which made tribes independent of the federal government. The idea of nations within a nation tapped into utopian fears and fantasies. The anthropologist and naturalist George Bird Grinnell, who had lived with the Plains Indians, tried to correct misleading images of native peoples: "The wild Indian," he explained in the *Atlantic*'s January 1899 issue, "exists no longer. The game on which he lived has been destroyed; the country over which he roamed has been taken up; and his tribes, one by one, have been compelled to abandon the old nomadic life, and to settle down within the narrow confines of reservations."[17]

Known both by the Pawnee name "White Wolf" and the Cheyenne name for bird, *wikis*, Grinnell edited the natural history magazine *Forest and Stream*. He almost single-handedly preserved Glacier National Park for the nation. Grinnell asked *Atlantic* readers to forget what they thought they knew about Indians and focus on what needed correction. To his mind, the prejudice leveled at Indians matched the contempt many Americans had for obviously different peoples such as Chinese and African Americans. Grinnell repeated the advice that a widowed Indian mother gave her son: "You must always trust in God," she told him, "Be brave and face whatever danger may meet you. . . . Think about the hard times we have been through. Take pity on people who are poor, because we have been poor, and people have taken pity on us. . . . Love your friend and never desert him." According to Grinnell, the same "precepts of industry, courage, singleness of purpose, charity, and devotion to friends might worthily have been spoken by any woman of the highest civilization."[18]

The *Atlantic* also published the counterview of H. L. Dawes, who had in 1887 sponsored the General Allotment Act, which redistributed commonly held land to individual members of the tribe. According to Dawes, who claimed his act would speed assimilation, Indians would be absorbed into "civilization" when "desire and hope for a better life . . . prevail[s] over savage instincts."[19] As a result of the redistribution, the act made it possible for tribal land to pass to white settlers and hence destroy community ownership. To the question of "Have We Failed the Indian?" (August 1899), Dawes cited what he considered the triumph of Indian boarding schools and answered a resounding no. But for all their differences, neither Grinnell nor Dawes could speak for native peoples who lived with the consequences of government policies. It took Zitkala-Sa to fill that gap.

The daughter of a Sioux mother and a white father, Zitkala-Sa grew up on the Yankton Sioux Reservation in South Dakota before attending Indian boarding schools and teaching at the Carlisle Industrial Indian

School. In 1900, the *Atlantic* published three chapters of her autobiography: "Impressions of an Indian Childhood" (January 1900), "School Days of an Indian Girl" (February 1900), and "An Indian Teacher among Indians" (March 1900). Zitkala-Sa's assimilation into white society began when the stewards of the school cut off her thick braids—an indignity reserved in her culture for cowards—and she was forced to speak English rather than her native language. As she tells readers, nature no longer seemed to have a place for her: "I was neither a wee girl nor a tall one; neither a wild Indian nor a tame one."[20]

When Zitkala-Sa returned to the reservation after a three-year absence, she found her mother living in fear of local robbers and encroaching white settlers. Zitkala-Sa decided to return to school and complete her education. It too had changed with absence, or Zitkala-Sa saw it through the eyes of her mother, who had warned her to be "beware of the paleface. . . . He is the hypocrite who reads with one eye, 'Thou shalt not kill,' and with the other gloats upon the sufferings of the Indian race."[21] She now perceived that "Indian schools had a larger missionary creed . . . which included self-preservation quite as much as Indian education." The school supported the dregs of white society, a secret opium eater and a drunk doctor who rushed patients to "untimely graves." It was hard, she said, "to count that white man a teacher who tortured an ambitious Indian youth by frequently reminding the brave changeling that he was nothing but a 'government pauper.'" She remembered with bitterness the "many specimens of civilized peoples" who "visited the Indian school" to boast of their charity. How few "paused to question whether real life or long-lasting death lies beneath this semblance of civilization."[22]

Zitkala-Sa made *Atlantic* readers see themselves as they appeared to her and her people. Like many writers of autobiography, her authority came from being both an insider and an outsider. The *Atlantic* followed *Impressions of an Indian Girlhood* with the last of Zitkala-Sa's essays, defiantly titled "Why I Am a Pagan" (December 1902). Speaking eloquently of the interrelatedness of all life and nature, she offered an olive branch of sorts: "The racial lines, which once were bitterly real, now serve nothing more than marking out a living mosaic of human beings. And even here [on the reservation] men of the same color are like the ivory keys of one instrument where each resembles all the rest, yet varies from them in pitch and quality of voice."[23]

Despite her experiences, Zitkala-Sa became a strong campaigner for citizenship and assimilation. In her 1901 collection, *Old Indian Legends*, she wrote: "I have tried to transplant the native spirit of these tales—root and all—into the English language, since America in the last few centuries has acquired a new tongue. The old legends of America belong quite as much to the blue-eyed little patriot as to the black-haired aborigine. And when they are grown tall like the wise grown-ups may they not lack interest in a further study of Indian folklore."[24] To Zitkala-Sa the process of "assimilation" modified the identity of all Americans.

Zitkala-Sa went on to edit *American Indian Magazine*, and in 1930 she founded the National Council of American Indians. She worked to improve health care and education, to codify laws and redress land settlements, and to preserve native culture and history. A tribute to her husband's service in World War I and also to her own service, which resulted in the passage of the 1924 Indian Citizenship Bill, Zitkala-Sa lies in Arlington Cemetery.

The *Atlantic*'s inclusion of writers such as John Muir, Mary Austin, and Zitkala-Sa spoke to the country's changing vision of the West. Captured with richness and complexity in these writers' very dissimilar works, the West had become central to Americans' story of themselves. In "Contributions of the West to American Democracy" (January 1903), Frederick Jackson Turner argued that since the beginning of the nation the West had exerted a democratizing influence. He described his own time as having experienced the equivalent of a revolution with political divisions over socialism, the rise of industrial capitalism and immigration, and the country's political and economic expansion abroad.

Turner presented the West as a source of regeneration, which gave "the world such types as the farmer Thomas Jefferson, with his Declaration of Independence, his statute for religious toleration, and his purchase of Louisiana. She gave us Andrew Jackson, that fierce Tennessee spirit who broke down the traditions of conservative rule. . . . She gave us Abraham Lincoln," and in the process enriched our new democracy with vast mineral wealth and land, which makes our country the equal if not the superior of any on earth. "Best of all," he ended,

> the West gave, not only to the American, but to the unhappy and oppressed of all lands, a vision of hope, an assurance that the world

> held a place where were to be found high faith in man and the will and power to furnish him the opportunity to grow to the full measure of his own capacity. . . . Let us see to it that the ideals of the pioneer in his log cabin shall enlarge into the spiritual life of a democracy where civic power shall dominate and utilize individual achievement for the common good.[25]

Turner saw the West contributing to an evolutionary progression measured by the social and industrial conditions of Europe and the eastern United States.

In 1903, the *Atlantic* recognized that contribution by publishing a special issue devoted to Western writers. Though Bliss Perry said he might easily have chosen a dozen other states for the experiment, he settled on California. Praising the magazine for long "enlisting the services of writers living west of the Rocky Mountains," he thought readers—eager to track "the literary development of the various sections" of the United States—avid for things western.[26] Representing the *Atlantic*, he welcomed writers from the West and Far West, just as Emerson had welcomed Whitman.

24

A State of Uncertainty

I cannot tell you how much praise I think you deserve for maintaining the tradition of what a good magazine should be in the face of our howling mob of critics and readers. And I hope that the *Atlantic* will long continue to nurse its little flame of sweetness and light in the chaotic darkness of American "literary conditions."

EDITH WHARTON
to Bliss Perry,
undated letter

ALTHOUGH *SCRIBNER'S* was her usual outlet, Edith Wharton's history with the *Atlantic* went back to 1878, the time when her mother sent a handful of her poems to Henry Wadsworth Longfellow, who showed them to his editor, William Dean Howells. The father of a gifted daughter with literary aspirations, Howells printed one of the poems. In 1880, the last year of his editorship, he published five more. Twenty years after her earliest poems appeared in the *Atlantic*, and fresh from the success of her first novel, *The Valley of Decision* (1902), Wharton approached Bliss Perry: "Why have you never asked me for a story for the *Atlantic*?" she wanted to know. "I am tired of waiting."[1] True, she usually commanded five hundred dollars from the illustrated magazines for a story; she would, however, be satisfied with the *Atlantic*'s going rate, "first because I have always thought it an honor to appear in the *Atlantic* and second because I believe it is always advantageous to a writer to get a fresh audience."[2] Perry responded by taking "The House of the Dead Hand" (August 1904), a Gothic tale with hints of incest set in Siena. The story's title comes from a marble hand mounted above the house's doorway: "The hand was a woman's—a dead drooping hand, which hung there convulsed and helpless, as though it had been thrust forth in denunciation of some evil mystery within the house, and had sunk struggling into death."[3]

Wharton continued to publish with the *At-*

lantic, serializing her travel book, *A Motor-Flight through France*, and scoring a hit with her story "The Long Run" (February 1912). The issue sold out in two days. A story about adultery, it indicates what the editor of the best of the better magazines could now tolerate in fiction. Wharton's story speaks not only to contemporary changes in manners, morals, and marriage, but to a world and beliefs in the process of disappearing. Its narrator finds himself in New York after a twelve-year absence, where he becomes reacquainted with an old Harvard friend named Merrick. Merrick tells him the story of his relationship with the former Mrs. Trant, now Reardon, who years before had left her husband at his urging. But when she came with a single suitcase to Merrick's house, she saw his panic. "You'll take a night and not a life?" she challenged him. "One way of finding out whether a risk is worth taking," she says, "is *not* to take it, and then to see what one becomes in the long run, and draw one's inferences." Merrick balks and rues his decision for the rest of his life:

> The long run—well, we've run it, she and I. I know what I've become, but that's nothing to the misery of knowing what she's become. . . . The worst of it is that now she and I meet as friends. We dine at the same houses, we talk about the same people, we play bridge together, and I lend her books. And sometimes Reardon slaps me on the back and says: "Come in and dine with us, old man! What you want is to be cheered up!" And I go and dine with them, and he tells me how jolly comfortable she makes him, and what an ass I am not to marry; and she presses on me a second helping of *poulet Maryland*, and I smoke one of Reardon's cigars, and at half-past ten I get into my overcoat, and walk back alone to my rooms.[4]

"The Long Run" flew off the shelf largely because its endorsement of individual fulfillment undermined notions of honor, women's nature, and the sacredness of marriage, which Wharton suggests may be more immoral than infidelity.

If Wharton's fiction has an abiding theme, it might be the conflict between an individual's desire for fulfillment and society's need to preserve the status quo. She knew of what she wrote. Seeking the company of artists and intellectuals, she rented the George Vanderbilts' apartment in Paris in 1907 and began entertaining members of the French Academy. That same year, she met the charming journalist William Morton

Fullerton, with whom she would soon begin an affair. In 1913, her marriage to Teddy Wharton formally ended by decree. Wharton moved to France partly because she wanted to live in a culture that treated women as grownups. She would write in *French Ways and Their Meaning* that men and women complete one another intellectually as well as physically.

The questions that engaged Wharton engaged dissimilar kinds of *Atlantic* writers, who saw both the world and women becoming more cosmopolitan. Those who feared the consequences of female suffrage worried that voting women might affect "the nature and structure of society,—the home, the church, the industrial organism, the state, the social fabric."[5] In "Why American Marriages Fail" (September 1907), an *Atlantic* contributor named Anna K. Rogers addressed a problem that many observers considered an American social contagion: in 1907, France granted seventy-nine divorces, England one, and the United States more than three thousand.[6]

According to Rogers, the idolatry of women in the United States created a disease known as "feminine megalomania," which results in the unnatural subordination (meaning "emasculation") of men. "The rock upon which most of the flower-bedecked marriage barges go to pieces," she explained, "is the latter-day cult of individualism; [and] the worship of the brazen calf of Self." To satisfy their recently discovered selves, women demand more love, more admiration, more time, and above all more money.[7] Rogers's analysis is cruder but not substantially different from Henry James's in a series of essays on the speech and manners of American women that *Harper's Bazaar* began running in November 1906. He too noted the failure of men to assert themselves, which left culture in the untrained hands of women.[8] Discussions about marriage and motherhood formed part of the *Atlantic*'s larger conversation about the direction of American society. Charles W. Eliot, for example, presented a six-point plan for instilling empathy in the young by encouraging the magazine's standby, the habit of reading (November 1903).

As contributors struggled to come to terms with social changes, some looked to other countries, a trend that would become more conspicuous as the First World War approached. Those who, like Wharton, turned to France were attracted to the country's "more precisely ordered social fabric," which posed an alternative to confusion that passed for freedoms. In France, women seemed to find a socially useful outlet for their energies and talents by becoming versed in their husbands' commercial interests.[9] The ability of the French to live with paradox, in Wharton's view, helped to explain the apparent—and appealing—stability of their society. "No people are more capable of improvising greatness, yet more afraid of the least initiative in ordinary matters. No people are more skeptical and more religious, more realistic and more romantic, more irritable and nervous, yet more capable of a long patience and a dauntless calm."[10] *A Motor-Flight through France* might be described as a lyrical rant against the infelicities of modern life and the discarding of traditions. "Here in northern France," she wrote, "where agriculture has mated with poetry instead of banishing it, one understands the higher beauty of land developed, humanised, brought into relation to life and history, as compared with the raw material with which the greater part of our own hemisphere is still clothed. In France everything speaks of long familiar intercourse between the earth and its inhabitants; every field has a name, a history, a distinct place of its own in the village polity."[11]

Wharton found fellow Francophiles in Annie Fields and Sarah Orne Jewett, who suggested that Perry reprint twenty-five to thirty pages each month from the *Revue des deux mondes*. He declined, but expanded international coverage with reports of the year in France, Germany, and England, which gave the *Atlantic* a more cosmopolitan air. Perry also solicited articles on a host of foreign countries—Mexico, India, New Zealand, and Norway—along with reviews of Continental artists and thinkers such Anatole France, Stéphane Mallarmé, Gerhart Hauptmann, and the critic Ferdinand Brunetière.

The *Atlantic*'s increased focus on specific countries grew partly from anxieties about the fluidity of national borders and immigration at a time of rising nationalist movements across Europe and the United States. Wharton, who lived in the Faubourg, the stronghold of the ancien régime, witnessed the rise of French nationalism and the growth of organizations like Action Française, which hoped to restore the monarchy to power. In 1907, the *Atlantic* published an essay on the conservative novelist Maurice Barrès, who considered Alfred Dreyfus a traitor simply because he was a Jew. According to the author, the idea of upholding France for the French may be "a noble idea, but it leads to fanatical outbreaks and the Rousseau-like cry, 'Back to the soil!'"[12] *Atlantic* articles such as "The Lesson of the French Revolution" (April 1907); "The Social Disability of the

Jew" (April 1908), which largely blames Jews for the intolerance shown them; "Justice to the Corporations" (January 1908); and "Coddling the Criminal" (January 1911) reflect an advance of social conservatism from the turn of the century, when Abraham Cahan had criticized the federal government for attempts to restrict Jewish immigration ("The Russian Jew in America," July 1898).

Bending to political realities, the *Atlantic* paid increased attention to two foreign fronts that would soon play important parts in world politics: Germany and Japan. As Japan consolidated its position in Asia, the magazine published posthumous contributions from Lafcadio Hearn and the historian Arthur M. Knapp. Knapp argued that the Japanese are "a people who, if not wholly of our blood, can trace back their ancestry to as lofty a plane of ancient civilization as that upon which we are so complacently priding ourselves."[13] Germany, by contrast, offered a model for modern technology and production.

Thoughts of war and its consequences seemed endemic to the new century, perhaps because nationalism both encouraged and responded to aggression. To quote Wharton about the French, "when a national danger threatens, they instantly become what they proudly and justly call themselves—'a warlike nation'—and apply to the business in hand the ardour, the imagination, the perseverance that have made them for centuries the great creative force of civilization."[14] John J. Bigelow Jr., the son of the U.S. minister to France during the Civil War (and the first editor of Benjamin Franklin's autobiography), voiced what many wondered with the title of his June 1911 article, "If the United States Should Go to War." A major in the armed services at the time of his article, Bigelow saw the country as unprepared for war.

Atlantic contributors began to take sides in a war not yet declared. Havelock Ellis, a pacifist psychologist and one of the founders of the Fabian Society, contributed "The War against War" (June 1911). Arguing that war amounted to nothing more than willful self-murder, he enumerated factors that would lead to a permanent international peace. His dismissal of the Church's efforts toward peace—he called their effect nil—excited protests in the religious press. Another writer thought that further bloodshed could be averted by the adoption of a common world language, Esperanto. In 1912, Eugene Debs, the antiwar Socialist Party candidate for president of the United States, surpassed expectations by receiving 6 percent of the vote, or nine hundred thousand votes. In Oklahoma and Nevada more than 16 percent of voters preferred him. Americans continued to fear the spread of socialism at home. Kelly Miller, an African American sociologist, prophesied in the *Atlantic* that the inevitable social upheaval would end only with the appreciation "that God has made" every nation "upon the face of the earth" one blood (April 1909).[15] Convinced that the country had to act, the labor economist H. R. Mussey provocatively titled an *Atlantic* essay "Democracy or Dynamite" (April 1912).

In a world at odds, the *Atlantic* needed an editor who had broad horizons and a capacity for balancing a plethora of confounding opinions. As that editor, Perry felt pulled in two directions. On the one hand, he believed that "those periodicals which are obtaining the widest reading are those which present the most various, hopeful, and full-blooded pictures of the men and the vital forces that are daily creating for us a new world."[16] On the other, he and his magazine retained a "stubborn affection for the simple ways of the older American life."[17] Without wanting to go back to the days of New England's stranglehold on literature, Perry worried that its relaxation fed a general decline in magazine writing, and to some extent the magazine offered a refuge for contributors concerned about the need for standards in everything from speech and spelling to education.

Perry edited the *Atlantic* a little like he went fishing—with a worm. As he wrote in "Fishing with a Worm" (May 1904), "Angling's honest prose, as represented by the lowly worms, also has its exalted moments." The point is to have something "tangible in your basket" at the end of the day. The philosophy of worm-fishing "is a plea for Compromise, for cutting the coat according to the cloth, for taking the world as it actually is." According to Perry, a worm-fisherman "watches the Foe of Compromise men go stumbling forward and superbly falling, while he, with less inflexible courage, manages to keep his feet."[18] In his hands, the *Atlantic* continued its commitment to publishing contemporary writers, including the Scotsman John Buchan and Kate Douglas Wiggin, author of *Rebecca of Sunnybrook Farm*. He also contracted with the poets Edwin Arlington Robinson and William Vaughn Moody. Unlike Page, he rejected work from Kate Chopin, Theodore Dreiser, and Jack London—who he thought would do better to call himself "John" and temper his pessimism. Perry dismissed London's essay "Revolution" as something the Hearst papers would publish. Its first sentence claimed that there were nearly a million people in the United States who signed their letters "Yours for the Revolution."[19] Dreiser presented a different case. Perry discovered that Dreiser had lifted portions of an article on the mills at Fall River, Massachusetts, from the *Forum*.

In standing "somewhat apart from the insane whirl which is miscalled 'progress,'" the *Atlantic* risked appearing to be the province of "gentlemen and scholars and men of letters."[20] With half the magazine's circulation now west of the Mississippi, Perry explained to Henry James, "I confess that I am not very certain about the temper of this audience." One thing he did know: it differed "markedly from the old *Atlantic* circle of readers."[21] With the goal of broadening the magazine's subscription base, he added a series on sports and another on popular culture that included an essay on racist stereotyping in comics.

Acknowledging that readers might not care to learn more about Cervantes and Voltaire, Johnson and Carlyle, Perry sent James Parton on assignment, as Walter Hines Page had sent correspondents to the Midwest and Far West, to report on topics of the time. He wrote that though a literary magazine aspires to be "a true mirror of life," it should "reflect something deeper than the patented, nickel-plated conveniences and triumphs of a material civilization. It should also serve as a mirror for the ardors and loyalties, the patriotism and the growing world-consciousness, of the American people." To him, the *Atlantic*'s main purpose was to discuss from "month to month" and by "many minds" the issues that affected "the destiny of us all."[22] The magazine's subscription base seemed broad enough for Perry to claim with satisfaction, in 1905, that "a subscription to the *Atlantic* is apparently no longer as it once was said to be in certain newly settled communities—a sufficient evidence of one's social standing . . . a badge of respectability."[23] Instead it represented, as the title of his essay announced, "a readable proposition."

Perry's uncertainty about the temper of his audience reflected a general uncertainty about the direction of the country, which the historian Brooks Adams predicted would rise or fall on its efforts at domestic reform in the direction of a "centralized, collective state." Approving Theodore Roosevelt's emphasis on another "new nationalism," he greeted his friend as the leader of a great power who would dominate not only Wall Street and Asian markets, railroad tycoons and labor, but the world.[24] In

1907, on a bitterly cold February morning, those working at the *Atlantic*'s office on Park Street had their chance to greet the president when Roosevelt paid a visit to his publisher, George Mifflin. For a moment, the question of where power, if not culture, resided seemed moot. They just had to look out toward the Boston Commons and Saint-Gaudens's memorial to Robert Shaw and his black regiment, or note the crowd that gathered outside their building hoping to glimpse the visitor. Mifflin tried to convince Roosevelt to sneak out the French window opening toward the Old Granary Burying Ground, but Roosevelt marched straight into the cheering crowd before Secret Service men whisked him into a waiting carriage. It was, for the magazine's young employees who lined the front steps to greet the president, the stuff of literary history, and the *Atlantic* was its faithful repository: "No magazine that has the Shaw Memorial before its windows can be quite indifferent to human liberty, or be persuaded that commercial supremacy is the noblest ideal of an American citizen." The *Atlantic*, having "made a place for itself before the days of "commercial invasions" and "world records" and "Anglo-Saxon domination," would, in Perry's judgment, "continue to prosper."[25]

25

Ellery Sedgwick

POLITICS AND POETS

Two roads diverged in
a yellow wood,
And sorry I could not
travel both
And be one traveler,
long I stood
And looked down one
as far as I could
To where it bent in the
undergrowth.

ROBERT FROST,
"The Road Not
Taken," 1915

ELLERY SEDGWICK did not look as one might expect the editor of the *Atlantic* to look, except perhaps for the glasses hanging on a cord around his neck. The historian Frederick Lewis Allen thought his loud shirts and "garishly checked suits" more appropriate for the boardwalk at Atlantic City than a Boston boardroom. A naturally grave man with exuberant tastes, he spoke with fastidious deliberation. He could reduce a new secretary to tears for having misplaced a manuscript that lay within the stack of papers on his desk. Allen thought he had the mind of a born journalist, but his skills also included those of a born businessman and great editor. He aimed for an audience who would subscribe in advance and "be loyal as long as the magazine satisfied them."[1]

Before editing the *Atlantic*, Sedgwick had worked for *Leslie's Monthly Magazine* (1900–1905) and *American Magazine* (1906–1907). From his time at *Leslie's*, he learned, as its founder Frank Leslie liked to say, never to shoot over the reader's head. He stayed barely a year at *American Magazine*, which became the standard bearer of progressive muckrakers such as Lincoln Steffens and Ida Tarbell, whose exposé of John D. Rockefeller led to the 1911 breakup of Standard Oil. Sedgwick sympathized with the goals of social progressives, and under him, the *Atlantic* stood for "intelligent American opinion." The magazine allowed Sedgwick, who cut

Bliss Perry's section on recent books, to give "full rein to an intense political interest born at the age of ten." According to his own admission, he looked "about for a hero" and found one in Woodrow Wilson. After hearing Wilson speak in 1905, Sedgwick had rushed up the steps of his house, thrown open the door, and shouted to his wife, "I have been listening to a great man. I know it! I know it! Wilson will be famous."[2] Less understandable in retrospect, he would support the dictator Francisco Franco during Spain's Civil War.[3]

From as far back as his undergraduate days at Harvard, Sedgwick decided that "by hook or crook" he would someday own and edit the *Atlantic.* He felt sure that the magazine suffered for being "a very small fifth wheel" in the "cumbersome coach" of its parent company, Houghton, Mifflin, and thought its cure lay in becoming the main occupation of a smaller, more compact organization.[4] With this goal in sight, he furthered the interests of previous editors Walter Hines Page, whose progressive program he shared, and Horace Scudder, whom he admired but thought hopelessly old-fashioned. He saw his chance to buy the magazine on Bliss Perry's retirement, and did so for fifteen thousand dollars. Houghton Mifflin retained another fifteen thousand in stock.

Sedgwick felt the magazine was "long on tradition . . . [but] short on realization."[5] The magazine wanted energy, he thought, and in the spirit of Page, he relentlessly pursued stories and authors. Sedgwick tracked Gideon Welles, Lincoln's secretary of the navy, hoping to acquire his diary, which, given the diarist's "cantankerous nature," promised to be full of wonderful "proofs of human perversity." The fourth time Sedgwick approached Welles, he was permitted to see the padlocked "solid iron box" that held the manuscript. Though Sedgwick appealed to family pride and history, Welles held back. Friends with Lincoln's son, Robert, since boyhood, and best man at his wedding, he bowed to what Sedgwick surmised was Robert's decision against publication.[6] Undeterred, Sedgwick befriended Welles's son Edgar on the assumption that the diary would likely pass to him. It did, though Sedgwick got the diary over Edgar's better judgment. In 1909, Edgar Welles wrote, "I authorize the publication with hesitation, and do so only under pressure; and my father's inflexible view of right and duty, and his absolute integrity and regard for truth and honesty, must be borne in mind when some of his severe strictures are read."[7] It had taken Sedgwick more than a year to secure the diary. He publicized his coup by allowing the *New York Times* to publish and gloss excerpts from the diary during the fall of 1862, when the Army of the Potomac had suffered defeats at Bull Run before achieving its "first real victory" at Antietam. According to the *Times*, Welles's "frank disclosures show the difficulties" with which Lincoln had to contend to build "this mighty and united Nation."[8]

For advice about the magazine, Sedgwick turned away from the insiders to confer with Harvard's Charles Eliot and, perhaps for courtesy's sake, with Annie Fields, now in her midseventies. He also spoke with his friend Felix Frankfurter, a future Supreme Court justice. He felt more comfortable with politics than with literature, though during his long tenure as editor, 1909–1938, the magazine published a mix of English and American authors that included W. B. Yeats, Walter de la Mare, Robert Frost, E. M. Forster, John Steinbeck, Ernest Hemingway, and Leslie Stephen's daughter, Virginia Woolf. He solicited work from the reformer Jane Addams and courted the Russian immigrant writer Mary Antin, who described the arc of her life from Polotsk, a shtetl in the Russian Jewish Pale of Settlement, to Boston. "May I say," he wrote Antin, "quite without any attempt to place false emphasis upon The Atlantic, that the serial publication of your book in our pages will probably attract more intelligent attention than could well be aroused by its appearance in any other form?" Reading the manuscript of her disguised autobiography, *The Promised Land*, he was convinced it had "many of the qualities which should go to make up an American epic—strength, sincerity, faith—and if *The Atlantic* aims to be the exponent of American ideals, there is matter here which it behooves us to print."[9]

Entirely won over, Antin supplied five installments, for which she received seven hundred dollars. Sedgwick personally made sure that news of her book reached the editors of Jewish periodicals, whom he allowed to republish up to a third of each *Atlantic* chapter. Theodore Roosevelt would cite Antin as one of the remarkable women who made him a supporter of women's suffrage. Annie Winslow Allen acknowledged that her career, like Antin's, might never have materialized without Sedgwick's help. Everyone knew him to be "the creator of the recreated *Atlantic*," she wrote, "but not . . . of its writers."[10]

Sedgwick's *Atlantic* appealed to the same audience of educated readers who might subscribe to the *New York Review of Books* today. From the beginning, he understood that the *Atlantic*'s mission to promote a democratic ideal had always made it greater than a "news" magazine. The magazine's criticism of the verdict in the Sacco-Vanzetti case, for instance, turned attention to weaknesses in the judicial system. Writers like Jane Addams wrote to argue a point, whether about the failings of charity or the needs of women weary from years of poverty.

When Al Smith, the Catholic Democrat, ran for president, Sedgwick found yet another hero. But however much he enjoyed the political fray, literature remained "the staff of the *Atlantic*'s life": "In fact," he wrote, "it is precisely because the magazine's tastes are quiet and literary that its occasional political forays have created sound and fury." In prose, he wanted "an unpremeditated record of interesting happenings" told by an interesting person.[11] Caring little for grammar, he cared much about personality, which led him to publish Elinore Rupert's accounts of homesteading in Wyoming, Hilda Rose's experiences in the wilds of northwestern Canada, and Eleanor Risley's walk across Alabama. He severely curtailed the number of articles on literary criticism, which Perry had written and promoted. In poetry, he put his hopes in Amy Lowell and published well over a dozen of her poems.

To Sedgwick, Lowell was "a literary spinster . . . of impossible manners and a golden heart," with a penchant for "Olympian cigars" and a genius for talk. She had a gift "for exploiting her own idiosyncrasies."[12] An unusually stout woman, "with a shrewd, 'clever,' kindly face," she had a manner that varied "from the assurance of the cultivated woman of the world to that of the 'hearty' wife of a small town hotel keeper."[13] Admiring the appeal of her Imagist verse to the eye rather than the ear, Sedgwick once dreamed that he attended a meeting where the audience stood and recited Miss Lowell's latest verse about a frog: "Plop—plop—plop."[14] He woke with the words repeating in his head. As usual objecting to Lowell's experiments with verse, he wrote: "You revolutionists have dropped your rhythm, now you are fast dropping your accent. You can no longer hope to define poetry, and I tell you that as poetry loses its definition, it will gradually lose its appeal."[15] Lowell responded that she didn't give a fiddle-dee-dee whether her verse was poetry or not. She wanted her words to be vivid, compelling, occasionally even charming. Making it clear that she thought the *Atlantic* in danger of ossifying, she queried him about an essay on a new writer he'd probably think too outspoken. His name was D. H. Lawrence, and Sedgwick, who disliked excessively morbid, sexual, or psychological fare, rejected the essay out of hand. Lowell captured the tone of her relationship with Sedgwick in an *Atlantic* poem titled "Fireworks":

> You hate me and I hate you
> And we are so polite, we two!
>
> But whenever I see you, I burst apart
> And scatter the sky with my blazing heart.[16]

Sedgwick's resistance to Lowell's self-styled "polyphonic" verse—and equally to the verse of Gertrude Stein—exemplify his prejudices no less than his acute sense of audience. After publishing Lowell's "Dried Marjoram" (May 1919), he received a number of complaints from readers who feared that more monstrosities like this would "ruin the dear, old *Atlantic Monthly*."[17] Lowell added to his problems with her 1925 poem "Fool o' the Moon":

> The silver-slippered moon treads the blue tiles of the sky
> And I
> See her dressed in golden roses,
> With a single breast uncovered,
> The carnation tip of it
> Urgent for a lover's lip.

The last line read: "I have lain with Mistress Moon." Readers complained about the magazine's breach of taste and potential corruption of young people.[18] Amy Lowell philosophically ascribed her aesthetic differences with Sedgwick to taste. "You do not value what I care for," she told him, "and I really do not like what you think beautiful." That said, she could not deny the value of publishing in the *Atlantic*, nor Sedgwick her fearless independence.[19] In 1926, a year after Lowell offended *Atlantic* readers, she won a Pulitzer Prize in poetry for *What's a Clock* (1925).

Whatever his doubts about Lowell's poetry, Sedgwick could thank her for introducing him to the poetry of Robert Frost. Lowell had discovered Frost on a trip to London to court practitioners of the new Imagism. Every bookstore she passed had a display of Frost's *A Boy's Will*, which contains the sonnet "Mowing," in its front window. At the party she gave for Ezra Pound, no one talked of anything else. Pound, with his usual generosity, reviewed the volume for *Poetry* (May 1913), and Frost secured an American publisher in Henry Holt.[20] When *North of Boston* (1914), Frost's next volume, appeared, Lowell reviewed it favorably for the *New Republic*. Frost was, she wrote, "as New England as Burns is Scotch, Synge Irish, or Mistral Provençal." Her review focused on Frost's continuation of a tradition, which included John Greenleaf Whittier and her first cousin James Russell Lowell. She noted that Frost's vision differed from theirs in being neither humorous nor kindly. Instead, he captured with photographic precision "a fleeting epoch," in which one civilization gives "place to another and very different one": "Heavy thunderstorms drench the lonely roads and spatter on the walls of farm-houses rotting in abandonment; and the modern New England town, with narrow frame houses, visited by drummers alone, is painted in all its ugliness."[21]

Amy Lowell effectively reintroduced Frost to America. Having failed as a farmer, cobbler, and teacher, he had packed a few belongings in 1912 and moved with his wife and four children to a suburb outside London. With the wolf not far from the door, he hoped that the sale of his farm would support them for two years. This last attempt to "stand on his legs as a poet" led to his first success.[22] In London, he met poets such as Alice Meynell, John Drinkwater, Rupert Brooke, and W. B. Yeats and got his first book of poems published. He returned at the outbreak of World War I "when empty and facile verse" abounded, instead of "the stuff that life is made of."[23]

Frost's reputation preceded him. Invited to read at Tufts University in May 1915, he chose three unpublished poems: "Birches," "The Road Not Taken," and "The Sound of Trees." The next day he paid a visit to the *Atlantic*'s Park Street office. Ezra Pound complained more than once to readers of *Poetry* that the great American publishers would not give Frost the time of day.[24] This had certainly been true of Sedgwick, who sent back Frost's verses with a rejection meant to discourage further submissions: "We are sorry," he wrote, "that we have no place in *The Atlantic Monthly* for your vigorous verse."[25]

When Frost entered Sedgwick's office overlooking Boston Gardens, he expected to meet an "ancient enemy," but in Frost's version of their encounter, Sedgwick begged for poems—any poems—sight unseen.[26] Frost, who just happened to have the poems he had read at Tufts, held them tantalizingly beyond his reach. "Are you sure that you want to buy these poems?" he asked. Sedgwick stretched out his hand to take them; Frost drew his back. The back-and-forth continued with Sedgwick jabbing and Frost feinting until Frost asked again, "Are you sure that you want to buy these poems?" Sedgwick insisted that he did. "Then they're yours," Frost said. "Take them."[27]

Given Frost's love of a good story, it probably comes as no surprise that Sedgwick left a different record of their meeting. He wrote a friend that he found Frost

> quite delightful—as unspoiled as when he left his Vermont. . . . I took him home with me to dine and we had much talk about his theories of poetry which seem to me intelligent and genuinely instinctive. They concern themselves especially with his attempt to reproduce in his lines the very tones of the voice. The magnificent rotundities which have created our English tradition of poetry have, he thinks, served their great purpose. He . . . holds with justice that the piping modern voices we have so long heard about us are simply thin echoes of sounds once great.[28]

For his part, Frost seems to have liked the challenge of winning Sedgwick over. In 1915, he wrote disarmingly, "I shouldn't want you to be entirely incredulous of me. . . . I can stand almost anything but being taxed with free verse along with Masters and my dear friend Miss Lowell."[29]

Sedgwick had put aside any doubts about Frost after he received a letter from the English critic Edward Garnett, who announced that "since Whitman's death, no American poet has appeared, of so unique a quality, as Mr. Frost."[30] Sedgwick took anything Garnett said seriously. He had made equally astute statements about Joseph Conrad, Ford Madox Ford, Stephen Crane, and John Galsworthy before others recognized their talent. "Birches," "The Road Not Taken," and "The Sound of Trees" appeared in the August 1915 issue of the *Atlantic* preceded by Garnett's essay titled "A New American Poet."

Garnett was drawn to Frost's poetry because it did not seem the stuff of "New Poetry," which he associated with Harriet Monroe and *Poetry* magazine. Like Lowell, he saw Frost in a tradition of New England writers, foremost among them Nathaniel Hawthorne, Henry David Thoreau, and Sarah Orne Jewett. Praising Frost's magical style—"a style that obeys its own laws of grace and beauty and inner harmony"—Garnett quoted the opening lines of "Mending Wall," which begins:

> Something there is that doesn't love a wall,
> That sends the frozen-ground-swell under it,
> And spills the upper boulders in the sun;

Garnett's *Atlantic* essay explored the early dramatic poems ("The Death of the Hired Man," "A Hundred Collars," and "Home Burial"), which he thought both modern and "native." He singled out three characteristics: Frost's mastery of blank verse, the intensity of his poetic realism (rivaling, in his opinion, that of Jewett), and his originality. Borrowing Frost's own metaphor from "The Road Not Taken," he wrote that Frost "has found a way for himself. . . . Of poetical poets we have so many! of literary poets so many! of drawing-room poets so many!—of academic and dilettanti poets so many! of imitative poets so many! but of original poets how few!"[31]

Frost could not have been happier with his *Atlantic* debut, having expected "some single-bed she professor with a known preference for the beautiful in poetry" to review his work. Garnett's habit of long quotation communicated the spirit of Frost's poems to a large audience. Keeping his promise to be good to Frost, Sedgwick had written "a beautiful letter" and sent "fifty-five beautiful dollars for poetry."[32] Despite a testy start, Frost and Sedgwick achieved a measure of friendship based on mutual respect. "I don't want any of my poetry left out of The Atlantic that can be possibly got in," Frost told him.[33]

"The Road Not Taken" remains one of the most quoted poems in American literature and a staple of school curricula. "You have to be careful of that one," Frost once warned. "It's a tricky poem—very tricky."[34] It seemed ironic that a poem written with a specific person in mind—the English poet Edward Thomas, who always regretted turning left instead of right and vice versa—should resonate so profoundly with readers. Explaining his tone in the poem as "fooling my way along," Frost told another poet, Louis Untemeyer, that he'd bet "not half a dozen people can tell you who was hit and where he was hit in my Road Not Taken."[35]

When viewed in the context of articles such as Bertrand Russell's "War and Non Resistance" and Mildred Aldrich's "The Coming of the English: Adventures in the Little House on the Marne," "The Road Not Taken" might be seen speaking to the choice Americans faced in 1915. It ends plaintively:

> I shall be telling this with a sigh
> Somewhere ages and ages hence:
> Two roads diverged in a wood, and I,
> I took the one less traveled by,
> And that has made all the difference.[36]

In the year "The Road Not Taken" appeared in the *Atlantic*, Frost's friend Thomas enlisted in the Artists' Rifles, and Rupert Brooke went to the Dardanelles, where the expected lifetime for soldiers was eleven days. "It does not matter why / Men act," Conrad Aiken wrote in an *Atlantic* tribute to Brooke: "what matters most is what men do" (July 1915).[37]

In 1923, Robert Frost received his first Pulitzer Prize for *New Hampshire* (1923). His second came in 1931, to be followed in six-year intervals by a third (1937) and fourth (1943). In March 1935, Elinor Frost wrote Sedgwick asking for a favor. Their daughter, Marjorie, had died the year before from childbed fever, and on her deathbed she had asked if her poetry might ever find readers. Elinor said it would give her the greatest happiness if Sedgwick would consider publishing one of Marjorie's poems on the anniversary of her death.[38] The Frosts later chose to have the Spiral Press privately print a book of their daughter's poems.

The years surrounding the First World War produced many talented poets whose names remain absent from the *Atlantic*. Apart from Frost, Conrad Aiken, Archibald MacLeish, and Edwin Arlington Robinson, most have been forgotten. For every poet, there seemed to be more readers who thought war made poetry beside the point. In "Art and the War," John Galsworthy predicted that when the war ended, "the world will find that the thing which has changed least is art. . . . The utility of art, which in these days of blood and agony is mocked at, will be rising again into the view even of the mockers, almost before the thunder of the last shell has died away."[39] On one point, Galsworthy could not have been more wrong. A new poetry would come out of the war, written by men such as Siegfried Sassoon, Wilfred Owen, Isaac Rosenberg, T. E. Hulme, and Herbert Read. But for the moment, the world as seen through the eyes of *Atlantic* contributors had largely lost its taste for poetry.

26

Literary history and all history is a record of the power of minorities, and of minorities of one.

RALPH WALDO EMERSON, "Aspects of Culture," *Atlantic*, January 1868

A Window on the War

ATLANTIC WRITERS AND WORLD WAR I

AT TIMES OF NATIONAL CRISIS, the *Atlantic* had a clear sense of its calling to fight despotism and defend liberty. The Civil War had presented such a crisis, but though the parallels between that war and the one threatening the sovereignty of Belgium and France seemed obvious to someone like Theodore Roosevelt, it did not to many *Atlantic* contributors, who either respected Germany's achievements in the arts and sciences or considered a war in Europe to be none of America's business.

The growing conflagration in Europe demanded that the *Atlantic* increase the offerings of foreign contributors and its analysis of foreign politics. Having earlier become, as William Dean Howells said, more "southern, midwestern, and far-western" in its sympathies, the magazine now focused on three interrelated fronts, which might broadly be characterized as domestic, European, and Pan-Pacific.[1] The Japanese journalist Kiyoshi K. Kawakami, for example, who studied at the Universities of Iowa and Wisconsin, argued as early as November 1914 that the destiny of the Pacific lay in the hands of Great Britain, Japan, and the United States. Peace in the Far East, he warned in "Japan and the European War" (November 1914), could not be "maintained without preserving the territorial integrity of China."[2] Considered an apologist for Japanese abuses in China and Manchuria, Kawakami did not differ from many *Atlantic* writers who opposed the war but supported imperialism when it advanced the interests of their home country.

As the guns of August announced the beginning of the war, Germany, having planned its route through Belgium decades before, broke into northern France, smashing Belgian, English, and French armies, while soldiers began to dig new borders with trenches that would reach from the North Sea to Switzerland. Neither the offenders nor the defenders, nor writers wanting to understand the principles at stake, saw anything but brutal chaos. Trying to piece together the full picture proved especially challenging when allies seemed more foreign than foes, or foes happened to be the relatives of neighbors.

By the end of 1914, half of the *Atlantic*'s contents were related directly to the war, its coverage, analysis, and consequences. As if it were not hard enough for contributors to separate fact from feeling, arguments about specifics had a way of bleeding into larger discussions about slippery topics such as "culture," "nationalism," and "colonialism." This had happened during the Dreyfus and Zola trials, when, as John T. Morse noted, the issue for French nationals had been "the Jew," not treason (May 1898).[3] During the First World War, measures had a way of transforming. To give just two examples: Belgium, recently condemned for its policies of forced labor and systematic terror in the Congo, became a model nation compared to Germany. And the French author Paul Hervieu credited Germans, who had been previously lauded for scientific expertise, with a special talent for killing: "If these unholy innovations were to blaze the way for the future, we should find the war-makers of to-morrow causing the wheat-fields to bear a poisoned harvest and forcing the very clouds in heaven to rain down pestilences whose germs are known to us now, or would in time be brought to birth in the alembics of German laboratories."[4] John Dewey cautioned *Atlantic* readers about thinking they could understand "the German mind," because it "still entertains a type of moral conception which has well-nigh evaporated in the cultures of other modern nationalities" (February 1916).[5] According to Dewey, language has embedded in it the history and thought of a people, which makes cross-cultural translation difficult.

Events abroad helped to feed domestic fears and intolerance. With the spread of socialism, the distrust of German Americans, and widespread labor unrest, the country seemed to lose its bearings. Ford Motor Company had to raise wages from $2.40 for nine hours to $5 for eight hours, with profit-sharing. Writing in the *Atlantic,* John D. Rockefeller Jr. made protest seem unpatriotic. "In the development of this partnership [between labor and capital]," he said, "the greatest social service is rendered by that man who so coöperates in the organization of industry as to afford to the largest number of men the greatest opportunity for self-development, and the enjoyment by every man of those benefits which his own work adds to the wealth of civilization" (January 1916).[6] From another perspective, the economist Carleton H. Parker argued, in an article titled "The I. W. W." (November 1917), that the oppressed had little reason to sacrifice themselves for love of country.[7]

Commentary about the limits—and hope—of American democracy centered on parallel concerns: the movement for world peace (which would eventually be symbolized by the formation of the League of Nations in 1919) and the failure of the United States to assimilate its many different peoples, which led to the rise of the so-called "Americanization movement." The movement fell into two camps: one concerned with educating immigrants about their adopted country and improving their command of English; the other intent on social containment, which culminated after the war in the Red Scare of 1919–1920. The tart Philadelphian essayist Agnes Repplier warned *Atlantic* readers against the extremism of Americanism: "The civilization of the world," she wrote, "is the business of all who live in the world."[8] Repplier, who began contributing to the magazine in 1886, would publish her last *Atlantic* essay in 1940, the year after the war raged once again in Europe. In short, the tension between the rights of individuals and national purpose, however fractured, defined the *Atlantic*'s arguments about the war.

Although by 1916, the year of the Battle of the Somme, the *Atlantic* urged intervention in Europe, it clung to the appearance of impartiality. In 1914, for instance, Sedgwick, wanting to place contemporary history in context, had published a series of articles by the historian Kuno Francke on German culture, character, education, and government. Sedgwick must have wondered about his own judgment when Francke asked why Germany should be punished for her efforts at self-improvement. "If this desperate situation has been brought about by the very best there is in German character," Francke argued, "then it must be accepted as part of the tragedy of human greatness." Despite the "incontrovertible strength" of his arguments, the editors felt it necessary to reassert the magazine's neutrality.[9] Francke's support for the sale of American weapons to the Allies made him a pariah among some German Americans, and his comparison of Wilhelm II to Richard Wagner's Parsifal and Nietzsche's Superman disillusioned those who saw him as a moderate.

The *Atlantic*, then, like the nation itself, reflected polarities of opinion. T. Lothrop Stoddard, the author of *The Rising Tide of Color against White World Supremacy*, found legitimacy in its pages for his theories about the superiority of the Nordic races (March 1915). Filtering into contemporary consciousness in ways as profound and indelible as the process of osmosis, assumptions about race and nationality became so embedded in the discourse of the time that people no longer considered them hypotheses. The same reasoning that justified Germany's invasion of Belgium fed nationalist movements in countries like France. The *Atlantic* contributor Maurice Barrès, who belonged to Action Française, sought to reinstate Catholicism as the state religion. (A 1905 law had instituted secularism.) A. C. Benson, a poet, essayist, and biographer, whose father had been Archbishop of Canterbury, spoke for Germany's enemies when he stated that the idea of one nation imposing an ideal on another threatened everything that made the English English or the French French (July 1916).

To W. E. B. Du Bois, arguments used to rationalize the imposition of German *Kultur* and institutions on less "civilized" nations differed little from those of Belgium, which equated the plunder of Africa with "progress." In Africa, he wrote, "are hidden the roots, not simply of war today but of the menace of wars to-morrow. . . . Lying treaties, rivers of rum, murder, assassination, mutilation, rape, and torture have marked the progress of Englishman, German, Frenchman, and Belgian on the dark continent."[10] To Du Bois, the First World War differed in degree rather than kind from other wars "of the Empire, by the Empire, for the Empire."[11] In an *Atlantic* article titled "The African Roots of the War" (May 1915), he tallied the profits to Europe from tons of palm oil ($60 million annually), pounds of cocoa ($89 million), and bales of cotton ($50,000). Outlining the radical shifts in labor, land ownership, education, economic power, and government that would eliminate the real causes of strife on the continent, he argued for independence. "Our duty is clear," he wrote. "Racial slander must go. Racial prejudice will follow. . . . The domination of one people by another without the other's consent, be the subject people black or white, must stop." Du Bois ended by extending the thinnest of olive branches: "What shall the end be? The world-old and fearful things, War and Wealth, Murder and Luxury? Or shall it be a new thing—a new peace and new democracy of all races: a great humanity of equal men?"[12]

Few understood better than Du Bois how "facts" of history could be turned into propaganda. Indeed, he would argue in "Criteria of Negro Art" (1926) that all art is propaganda in a fight for civil rights. Looking back at the conquest of German East Africa, he would write that "thousands of black men from East, West and South Africa, from Nigeria and the Valley of the Nile, and from the West Indies still struggled, fought and died. For four years they fought and won and lost German East Africa; and all you hear about it is that England and Belgium conquered German Africa for the allies!"[13]

Three months before the assassination of Archduke Franz Ferdinand on 28 June 1914, H. L. Mencken addressed criticism of the press in a controversial *Atlantic* piece titled "Newspaper Morals" (March 1914). If Americans knew Mark Twain for his trademark white suit, they knew Henry Louis Mencken for his ever-present cigar. *Atlantic* readers identified Mencken with the *Smart Set*, a self-proclaimed "magazine of cleverness," which would provide a model for the *New Yorker*. Of his prose, no less a master than Joseph Conrad wrote: "Mencken's vigor is astonishing. It is like an electric current. In all he writes there is a crackle of blue sparks like those one sees in a dynamo house amongst revolving masses of metal that gives you a sense of enormous power. For that is what he has. Dynamic power."[14] Cynical, amusing, maddening, Mencken summed up his personal credo: it was better to tell the truth than lie, better to be free than enslaved, and better to know than not know. He hated prohibition, reformers, censors, boobies, and quacks.[15] He liked Twain's humor and the music of Brahms, Beethoven, and Bach. During the First World War, his unpopular defense of German culture tested the *Atlantic*'s limits of free speech.

"Newspaper Morals" gave Mencken a platform to assert that though newspapers thrived on sensation and reduced complex problems to "popular theory and emotion," they did more good than harm: reporters have unequivocally "libeled and lynched the police—but the police are the better for it. . . . They have lifted the plain people to frenzies of senseless terror over drinking-cups and neighbors with coughs—but the death-rate from tuberculosis declines. They have railroaded men to prison, denying them all common rights—but fewer malefactors escape today than yesterday. The way of ethical progress is not straight. . . . Each time, perhaps, we slip back, but each time we stop at a higher level."[16] The *Atlantic* followed Mencken's essay with a rejoinder from Ralph Pulitzer, editor of the *New York World* and son of the journalism magnate Joseph Pulitzer. Not above sarcasm himself, Pulitzer wrote that newspapers had a duty "to stir all good citizens . . . not merely engross social philosophers and political theorists," who have little understanding of the average American's life.[17] According to Pulitzer, newspapers deserved praise for what they actually did get right.

Atlantic editors supported Mencken's right to speak his mind, though he, too, tested the extent to which the magazine allowed dissenters a voice. In "The Mailed Fist and Its Prophet" (November 1914), Mencken argued that Friedrich Nietzsche's *Thus Spake Zarathustra* lent philosophical "coherence and significance" to a Germany contemptuous of weakness and convinced that a good war sanctifies every cause. Is Germany "barbarous? Ruthless? Unchristian? No doubt. But so is life. So is all progress worthy of the name. Here at least is honesty to match the barbarity, and, what is more, courage, the willingness to face great hazards, the acceptance of defeat as well as victory. . . . Let us not assume his downfall too lightly," he warned: "it will take staggering blows to break him. And let us not be alarmed by his possible triumph."[18] A second essay on Germany, which grew out of his reporting from the Eastern Front, exalted the German general Erich Ludendorff, while a third, titled "After Germany's Conquest of the United States," never appeared and seems to have been expunged from his papers. Admitting that he found Mencken's "reprehensible paper . . . damnably effective," Ellery Sedgwick declined to publish it. He harbored, he informed Mencken, "no desire to foment treason."[19] Sedgwick's response no doubt helped to shape Mencken's view of the *Atlantic*, which he described in *The American Language* (1919) as the home of the country's "refined" essay, "perhaps gently jocose but never rough."[20]

Mencken spoke out at a time when, as Sedgwick implied, the circumstances required courage. Within a few months of the federal legislature's passage of the Espionage Act (June 1917), approximately nine hundred people were imprisoned—among them Eugene Debs, who, having protested the law, would campaign for president from Atlanta Prison. Many German Americans found themselves the objects of fear and suspicion. The political climate might be gauged by the usually open-minded William Dean Howells's comment to his sister that German Americans would have to "quiet down or else declare their loyalty. They are worse than the home-Germans," he wrote, "for those cannot help being what they are. But here there is no despotism to make Germans slaves or friends of their national slavery."[21]

Two months after the passage of the Espionage Act, the *Atlantic* published an article by Frank Perry Olds that stopped just short of accusing German-language newspapers of treason. The article marked a turning point in the *Atlantic*'s coverage of the war, but also in its policy of neutrality, which—if more fiction than fact—maintained the editors' integrity. Instead of letting the article stand on its own, the editors added a bracketed coda, in which they deplored the tolerance shown to newspapers written in "the enemy language" and encouraging "sedition with a vengeance":

> The remedy is a sane war-time censorship upon enemy propaganda and a substantial war-time tax on the printed use of the enemy language. Statements which would not be tolerated in American newspapers must not find immunity in the thin guise of German type, and the publication of newspapers in the German language is a privilege which should be paid for. We have singled out the German press as the subject for Mr. Olds's article and for these remarks, because here, as in Europe, it is German thinking which is the chief offender, and fortunately because it is with Germany alone that we are at war.[22]

Despite such statements, war boosters in the "cold-roast sections of the Back Bay" thought the *Atlantic* erred on the side of fairness. They pointed to the magazine's publishing Bertrand Russell and other pacifists, who described war as a permanent institution, "just as Parliament is one of our permanent institutions in spite of the fact that it is not always sitting" (May 1916).[23] The *Atlantic* editors masked their less overt editorializing in charitable appeals for victims of the war. At the end of an article titled "Bitter Experience of Lorraine" (November 1915), they assured readers that their donations would provide urgent necessities "for a population which . . . has endured with extraordinary fortitude peculiar intensity of suffering, and with the French genius for self-help has already made marked progress in rebuilding a civilization laid flat."[24]

On the eve of the November 1916 election, Charles W. Eliot assessed the Wilson presidency in an *Atlantic* article titled "The Achievements of the Democratic Party and Its Leader since March 4, 1913." Although he acknowledged mistakes that came about from Wilson's caution, he feared more those that might be made from impetuosity and impatience. Wilson, who campaigned on the platform that "he kept us out of war," narrowly won the election against the Republican candidate, Charles Evans Hughes. The vote was so close that the country held its breath for days awaiting the result. As the war in Europe progressed, the *Atlantic* refrained from overtly criticizing Wilson by including disparate points of view. The British novelist and feminist Rebecca West spoke for the "common people" who struggle "in a changed and unkindly universe like rabbits in a blown-out burrow" (January 1916). Who, she asked, can write a happy ending for a widow whose son has died at Ypres? West noted that because history is the story of "exceptional men," the rest of humanity gets crowded out, and "that is why we forget from generation to generation what war is."[25]

Ellery Sedgwick would dub 1917 "Annus Terribilis."[26] Pulling every string at his command, he temporarily got himself assigned to the Secret Service to hear the *Atlantic*'s former contributor, Woodrow Wilson, address the U.S. Congress on 2 April. When the president entered the great chamber, Sedgwick elbowed his way forward, until he stood within six feet of his friend. Wilson acknowledged, "It is a fearful thing to lead this great, peaceful people into war, into the most terrible and disastrous of all wars, civilization itself seeming to be in the balance. But the right is more precious than peace, and . . . America is privileged to spend her blood and her might for the principles that gave her birth and happiness and the peace which she has treasured. God helping her, she can do no other."[27]

Unlike newspapers, which can respond to events almost as they happen, the *Atlantic* let two months pass before commenting on the events following Wilson's speech. "It is Good Friday, April 6, 1917," Margaret Prescott Montague wrote in the June 1917 issue:

Flags are flying all up and down the streets; they are streaming from every big building, and fluttering on automobiles. The President's great war message to Congress is being scattered by aviators inside the German lines. The newspapers blare out the headlines, "Britain Proud of America's Decision" . . . "Italy Profoundly Impressed"— "Poincaré Cables Wilson." Our President has spoken for us. Our solemn and glorious hour has come. We are at war with Germany. And now what are *you* going to do about it?[28]

27

America's War

There are other towns somewhere in France besides those from which come the horrible tales of the trenches—the trenches, those long open graves in which the men stand waiting for red and screaming death by machines.

VERNON KELLOGG, "The Belgian Wilderness," *Atlantic*, March 1916

THE WAR SOLD MAGAZINES, and Ellery Sedgwick saw subscriptions rise as the *Atlantic* devoted more of its contents to the conflict. The increase in readers was dramatic, escalating from 7,000 in 1897 to 20,000 in 1908, and 38,000 in 1915, before skyrocketing in 1918 to 100,000.[1] Part of the reason had to do with the magazine's first-person accounts of the war, which revealed, in the words of one *Atlantic* critic, "those finalities which even the shadow of death cannot eclipse."[2] Readers thought that literature expressed not only the heart of their respective nations, but also the strivings of humanity. In "Literature and Cosmopolitanism" (February 1915), Sedgwick's brother, Henry Dwight Sedgwick, wrote that though "the spirit of literature finds its home in its native place . . . every nation has need of the literature of all other nations . . . to step beyond our narrow chamber in a brave world."[3]

Journalists borrowed techniques from fiction just as novelists borrowed from journalism to find words that could not be found to touch the horror of the First Battle of the Marne or the slaughter at Gallipoli, or young nurses caring for maimed soldiers, or even the starved refugees lying in Paris railway stations. The line between reportage and fiction blurred; first-person accounts of the front were sometimes narrated in the form of journals or letters. In December 1916, the *Atlantic* published excerpts from the journal of a Canadian officer, titled "The

Trench-Raiders." The purposes of trench-raiding were multiple. Apart from terrorizing the enemy at night, gathering intelligence, and capturing equipment, they were designed to hone the troops as killing machines. The anonymous author of these entries took readers from "Grenade School," across no-man's-land at midnight, through barbed wire fences, and into a German trench ten feet deep and forty feet long, where he and his men—equipped with bayonets, brass knuckles, knives, clubs, grenades, and submarine guns—killed between forty and fifty soldiers in six minutes. This was the "first recorded instance in the war where a successful attack had been made without artillery preparation to cut the wire," he wrote, and the survivors were cheered as though they had won "a hockey match."[4]

In October 1918, the month before the war ended, the *Atlantic*'s lead article consisted of letters from an American lieutenant named Briggs Adams, who joined the Royal Flying Corps (RFC). Educated at Harvard, Adams trained at various camps in England and Scotland before volunteering for active service in France, where he joined the Bombing Group of the Eighteenth Squadron, RFC. Adams found it particularly fitting to make war on war: "Instead of aiming to kill, as in fighting on the ground or even in scout-fighting," he told his parents, "we aim to destroy war manufactories, material things made to kill me. Thus we are striking at the very base of war." He wanted his mother to know that he felt "no bitterness against the Huns as individuals. It is war that I hate, and war that I am willing to give all to end as permanently as possible: for it isn't the men that war kills, it is the mother's heart which it destroys, that makes it hateful to me."[5] Adams's letters, published under the title "The American Spirit," captured a huge audience for the magazine. Written with boyish charm, they included descriptions of throwing his plane to and fro, dropping it sideways, and crisscrossing or abandoning the controls before straightening out in a simple nose-glide.[6] To risk death seemed to him "like a great final examination in college for a degree in *summa vita in mortem*," which challenged the best in him and spurred him on to test "every last reserve of energy, strength, and thought."[7] Intent on becoming the best pilot in his squadron, Adams worried that he was "taking too much good out of such a rotten thing of war."[8] If he didn't come back, he wanted his mother to know that "we can't hope to gain such wonderful ends without paying big prices, and it is not right to shirk payment."[9] On 24 October 1917, he wrote his mother:

> "Death is the greatest event in life," and it is seldom anything is made of it. What a privilege then to be able to meet it in a manner suitable to its greatness! Once in your life to have met a crisis which required the use of every last latent capacity! It is like being able to exercise a muscle which has been in a sling for a long time. So for me the examination is comparatively easy to pass. But for you it is so much harder and the degree conferred so much more obscure.[10]

Five months later, he died in his plane while serving on the Western Front.

Adams could have been anyone's son or brother, and, oddly enough, his letters brought a kind of spiritual comfort to many readers, who believed he had died for a just cause doing what he loved best, and doing it with panache. Arthur Stanwood Pier, a writer of boys' stories and editor of the *Youth's Companion*, claimed that Adams's letters were the most immediate letters to come out of the war: "They are not only gallant and beautiful in their feeling, but singularly elevated in their style, as though his new experience had lifted him into new levels of expression and given to his language something of the clearness and freshness of the upper air."[11] One enthused *Atlantic* contributor predicted that the sacrifice and fraternity men like Adams embodied would imbue postwar life with the spirit of Christ (January 1919). A glance at poems written by soldiers hit by shrapnel or seeing friends dying in the mud tells a different story, for airborne or "going over" into no-man's-land usually ended with injury or death. This is perhaps what the critic Wilson Follett meant when he hoped that the war would make fiction more realistic by subjecting institutions to rigorous analysis ("War as Critic," May 1917).

The Swedish feminist Ellen Key ("War and the Sexes," June 1916) predicted that after the war, the Atlantic Ocean would become a highway rather than a barrier, with the new internationalized world enveloping America. The closer to the front, however, the less that such thinking seemed possible. Vera Brittain, for example, who served as a nurse at the front and lost her brother, her fiancé, and too many friends in the war, felt condemned to live with its consequences of disillusion, cynicism, and lack of faith. Like Siegried Sassoon drawing on his experiences in the trenches, however, Brittain later wrote powerful memoirs, books with the combination of autobiography, scathing history, and passages to match any well-written fiction.

Edith Wharton, who spent the war serving others, whether at the front or working to help Belgian homeless in Paris, saw her future writing as unlike any fiction she had written before. In the wake of the Great War, she said, all fiction would have to be historical: the present could no longer be assumed, because the war cleaved time in two. Novelists would have to set even fictional events before or after its declaration.

Other writers argued that the war created different kinds of readers, whose perception of "time," "reality," and "self" demanded new fictional forms of expression. Ernest Hemingway seemed to test this idea with *In Our Time* (1925), a series of related fragments and short stories based on his experience as a reporter in the Greco-Turkish theater of war. The novelist John Dos Passos, historicizing fiction and fictionalizing history in his *U.S.A.* trilogy, constructed a collage of newspaper clippings, song lyrics, fictional narratives, and biographies of public figures such as Henry Ford and Woodrow Wilson, which together communicated the competing voices or, put otherwise, the chaos of his era.

With America's entry into the war, the *Atlantic* turned to the lessons of biography and history as if they offered escape or maybe reassurance. Instead of looking forward, the magazine published portraits of Confederate generals like Jefferson Davis's vice president, Alexander H. Stephens, as well as contemporary generals like General Joffre, commander in chief of the French army. The connection between the Civil War and the First World War might seem tenuous, but to American contemporaries their legacies of suffering made for strong links within the country and across the Atlantic. The timing of the *Atlantic*'s portraits is suggestive. The South's desire to preserve the character of Southern life, coupled with its desire to preserve each sovereign state as a separate political unit, mirrored, for the historian Nathaniel Wright Stephenson (June 1919), the emotions animating Bohemia, Montenegro, and Belgium. Randolph S. Bourne, envisioning a "trans-national America" (July 1916) composed of the descendants of the foreign born, urged his compatriots to give up the idea of a distinctly American culture, since the United States was, in fact, stronger for being a "federation of cultures."[12]

At the outset of the war, the *Atlantic* had positioned itself to become a preeminent voice in America by announcing the beginning of "a new era in *The Atlantic*'s history." In the last months of the war, one writer had this to say: "Now that the barriers of nations and of continents have broken down, the old magazine has striven to do its full share in interpreting the world to America, and America to the world. The steady confidence of the public and the enlarging influence of the magazine in this time of change and great anxiety make the *Atlantic* proud and keep it humble."[13]

In May 1917, when food was short at home and people across Europe were starving, Woodrow Wilson tapped Herbert Hoover to run the Food Administration. Hoover's administrative powers included setting retail prices for food and determining what crops farmers could grow. To combat the war's disruption of production and shipment, he encouraged Americans to grow their own vegetables and to drink fewer, less sweetened beverages. A 1917 movie script for Universal Studios, written by Mary Austin and titled *The Potato Patriot*, shows Hoover exhorting his compatriots to sow "the seeds of Victory" as the camera pans to devastated farmlands in Europe. Women proved essential to the success of "Hooverization," the aim of which was to reduce domestic consumption by at least 10 percent. "Meatless Mondays" and "Wheatless Wednesdays" became commonplace, and the country exceeded Hoover's goal by 5 percent. An administrative genius, if sometimes a stubborn taskmaster, Hoover provided a lifeline to 350 million people in twenty-one countries.

Hoover, a self-made millionaire from Iowa, had risen through the ranks from clerk to gold miner to engineer and then partner in the international mining conglomerate of Bewick, Moreing. His company had international interests, and Hoover and his wife, Lou, the first woman graduate in geology from Stanford, traveled to Canada, New Zealand, Germany, Egypt, Burma, France, South Africa, Australia—and China, where they witnessed the Boxer Rebellion in 1900. After retiring from Bewick, Moreing in 1908, Hoover founded his own consulting business, which specialized in saving failing companies. Later in life, he published a number of books, including *Fishing for Fun* and one—begun at age eighty—on his mentor, titled *The Ordeal of Woodrow Wilson.*

To many Americans, Hoover came to stand for American drive and knowhow, which his friend and former teacher at Stanford, Vernon Kellogg, emphasized in his March 1918 *Atlantic* article "Herbert Hoover, as Individual and Type." In California, Kellogg had been the one academic accepted by a bohemian group of artists, drawn to Carmel for cheap living and beautiful scenery. They included at various times the poet George Sterling, Sinclair Lewis, and Jack London. Kellogg's field was entomology and genetics. In a 1913 essay titled "Eugenics and Militarism," he argued that war had few advantages, since it depleted the race of its fittest young men. But Belgium had no choice, and Kellogg spearheaded efforts to relieve its people. Like Hoover, he loved Europe, where he and his wife Clara, an accomplished actor, chose to marry on the outskirts of Florence. Kellogg wrote *The Food Problem* (1917) with Alonzo E. Taylor, based on his and Charlotte's war years. Both Kelloggs reported on the war for the *Atlantic.*

Intentionally or not, Kellogg's article on Hoover set the stage for a future presidential bid. Kellogg portrayed his friend laboring "not for salary or named position, but for the satisfaction of doing something for country and humanity." This was the same argument Jacob Riis had advanced for *his* friend, Teddy Roosevelt. Kellogg traced Hoover's roots back to Iowa, where an uncle raised the orphaned Quaker boy, who worked ten hours a day for two dollars, before bringing readers to a room in Belgium, filled with half-starved boys and girls waiting for ladles of potato stew and rice pudding: "It seems hard to reconcile our carefully cultivated ideas of 'big business' with our ideas of public service," Kellogg wrote. "But we have before our eyes the material evidence that some big-business men can be willing and generous and honest public servants."[14] After heading the European recovery program, Hoover went on to serve as secretary of commerce under Presidents Harding and Coolidge. With their support he became the thirty-first president of the United States in 1929.

At Wilson's request, Hoover attended the conference resulting in the notorious Treaty of Versailles. Along with *Atlantic* writers, he tried to anticipate a new set of political realities. How would the Allies reconfigure the world? What nations deserved sovereignty? Which could the United States count as friends—or foes? Many worried that the treaty, signed on 28 June 1919, would lead to a new world order or another war—as of course it did. In 1919 alone, the magazine published eight pieces on the rise of Bolshevism, not counting those on related issues such as socialism, immigration, militant minorities, labor agitators, and continued unrest abroad. Contributors singled out Ireland and Palestine as potential powder kegs. A future founder of the *Saturday Review of Literature*, Henry Seidel Canby, praised the patriotism of the Sinn Feiners, working for "the right to live and think and act in the Irish way."[15] And H. Sacher, a Jewish historian of Zionism, wanted readers to understand that Jewish identity could not be separated from the idea of a Jewish homeland, with Jerusalem "the mother-city" of all lands.[16]

The war had changed the expectations of returning soldiers as well as the expectations of women. One *Atlantic* writer asked the country to remember those patriots returning home to city slums. Recounting his service with African American soldiers ("Some Experiences with Colored Soldiers," August 1919), John Richards drew a picture of black and white bodies lying side by side in the fields of Europe. As with the Civil War and Spanish-American War, there were those who questioned the cost not only in lives but also in abuses of liberty. Contributors addressed the economic, medical, and psychological problems of returning soldiers.

The *Atlantic* supported the full enfranchisement of women, if not their continued employment after the war. The argument for enfranchisement rested on their war service. Nearly thirteen thousand women served in the navy and the Marine Corps; many came under fire. Others provided what would now be called physical and occupational therapy for wounded soldiers, worked the night shift in munitions factories, took the census in Rhode Island, or packed crates of cherries in the South. Referring to these contributions, President Wilson asked legislators to consider what the war had made apparent: "Are we alone to ask and take the utmost that our women can give, service and sacrifice of every kind, and still say we do not see what title that gives them to stand by our sides in the guidance of the affairs of their nations and ours?"[17] Wilson pleaded to the Senate on 30 September 1918. On 4 June 1919, Congress sent the proposed Nineteenth Amendment to the states for ratification. Women won the right to vote in 1920, when a young Congressman from Tennessee named Harry Burns listened to his mother and cast the deciding vote. The *Atlantic* responded by expanding its American portrait series to include notable women such as Mary Lyon, the founder of Mount Holyoke College, John Adams's wife Abigail, Emily Dickinson, and Frances Elizabeth Willard, who, in the words of one contributor, had more success fighting the use of "demon rum" than being published in the *Atlantic*, which now focused on women's altered perceptions of marriage, work, and motherhood.[18]

Atlantic editors could not ignore the changed tone of the women—or the young. In "Good-Bye, Dear Mr. Grundy" (November 1920), a debutante listed her teachers as "motors, movies, jazz-music, freedom of action, liberty of thought, [and] the rights of individuals." She took umbrage with elders who urge the study of religion and asserted that her generation, which could talk about the body as well as the spirit, would never be, like theirs, a slave of creeds.[19] The year 1920 ended with another of the *Atlantic*'s self-proclaimed "wild young" telling his parents' generation where to go. Ushering in the era that would become known as the Roaring Twenties and speaking as if for the generation F. Scott Fitzgerald would immortalize in *The Great Gatsby* (1925), a "Yalee" named John F. Carter Jr. wrote: "I suppose that it's too bad that we aren't humble, starry-eyed, shy, respectful innocents. . . . But we aren't, and the best thing the oldsters can do about it is to go into their respective backyards and dig for worms, great big pink ones."[20] In the 1920s, the *Atlantic* would fight to remain a touchstone for all that was at the center, if not always the forefront, of American thought and art. At best, its balancing of competing tastes and interests maintained what engineers call an "angle of repose"—the maximum angle at which unconsolidated material can bear the stress.

28

The Turbulent Twenties, I

The band began its music, and I saw
A hundred people in the cabaret
Stand up in couples meekly to obey
The arbitrary and remorseless law
Of custom.

THEODORE MAYNARD, "Jazz," *Atlantic*, January 1922

IMAGES OF FLAPPERS tossing back bootlegged gin seem to capture the spirit of the 1920s, but the decade that began after the infamously named "Red Summer" of racial violence, and a world mourning war deaths in the millions, also witnessed the Fifteenth Regiment, nicknamed Harlem's Hell Fighters, marching through the heart of Manhattan to the beat of drum major Bill ("Bojangles") Robinson. F. Scott Fitzgerald would have been the first to admit that no book, even his own *Great Gatsby*, could wholly communicate the mercurial spirit of a decade that conformed to stereotypes no more than our own does.

The Dow Jones Industrial Average reached one hundred points in 1920, and in the same year the Volstead Act outlawed the sale of alcohol and police arrested the anarchists Sacco and Vanzetti for murder. Although the influenza pandemic of 1918–1919 had decreased the lifespan of an average American by ten years, men in 1920 could expect to live about fifty-three years and women slightly longer. The average family might afford an automobile, with a Ford costing slightly less than three hundred dollars, or about a third of a teacher's annual salary. But notwithstanding peace and prosperity, the editors of the *Atlantic* recognized a crisis, in which the historic socioeconomic divide along class and racial lines now extended to the generations. If the magazine were to survive, it needed to appeal to flappers, college students, and returning veterans.[1]

Still edited by Ellery Sedgwick, the *Atlantic* developed what might be called a split personality as it tried to bridge the distance between defiant youth and bewildered maturity. The generational gap was nowhere more apparent than in a chatty new feature called The Contributors' Column, which the editors placed immediately after the long-running Contributor's Club. Although the juxtaposition of the two features, filling seven to twelve pages of any given issue, blurred their boundaries, there were differences. The Club tended toward amusing anecdotes with liberal social messages, while the Column focused on the magazine itself. The Column underscored the magazine's tendency toward self-mythologizing, realized in "The Atlantic's Bookshelf"—announcing books from the Atlantic Monthly Press, directed by Sedgwick—and "Atlantic Shop-Talk," a potpourri of information that might include circulation figures or references to the magazine in other periodicals. The March 1922 issue noted the use of newspapers as texts and credited a contributor. Unlike the Club, which featured the work of contributors, the Column—simulating the day when readers mingled with authors in the Tremont Street office—offered the opinions of subscribers and an anonymous but more personal entity called "the editors."

Oliver Wendell Holmes once observed that the *Atlantic* was a notion, a vague idea or impression that relied on the vanity and loyalty of its readers. For many of its aging subscribers, it was also a family tradition that made them part of a self-identified American meritocracy. A Civil War veteran recalled for readers of the Column the day he fled his burning camp near Nashville with some hardtack and a copy of the *Atlantic*. People in their late seventies joked about young relatives referring to bound volumes of the magazine as "novels." A woman living on a dairy farm wrote to say that she used to think the magazine too highbrow. Now, having inherited a cache of back issues, she credited the magazine with making her, a middle-aged mother of four boys, feel "an essential part of life" (April 1922).[2] Her testimony must have provided cold comfort in a decade when the *Saturday Evening Post*'s circulation exploded from 2,000 in 1899 to 1 million in 1903, and a landmark 3 million in 1936. Ellery Sedgwick nevertheless prided himself on having increased circulation from a mere 6,000 in 1898 to 84,000 in the early 1920s.[3] By 1924, a *Time* article (21 July 1924) on Sedgwick placed circulation at 117,352.[4]

On the principle that controversy sold magazines, the editors of the

Atlantic emphasized changes in American manners and mores. Verbal battles between the generations figured predominantly in the easygoing Column, with its casual standard of argumentation. The Column favored the adoption of pseudonyms, often pointing to a class of individuals, such as "A Last Year's Debutante" or "A Wild Young Person." Older subscribers expressed their concerns in essays like "Flapper Americana Novissima" (June 1922), which satirized the Zelda Fitzgeralds with painted faces and bobbed hair. The "product of the movies, automobiles, suffrage, and especially of the war," women became a symbol of society's misdirection.[5] According to a correspondent signing himself "The Old Grouch," "the Barbarian must be told plainly that the older generation is running this world; she must not make any mistake about this.... Her boarding-school 'education' does not amount to a hill of beans. It is not what she is but what she is to be that justifies her."[6] When a male contributor asked whether he should divorce his unfaithful wife (August 1924), readers responded by recounting the effect of divorce on their lives. Many found the husband's airing of dirty laundry offensive. "Were the article a creation of fiction," one subscriber wrote, "we should say the author showed bad taste in . . . pillorying his wife as an adulteress in court, while, for a stipend, pillorying her to the extent of seven and one-half pages in a magazine of international circulation."[7]

Contributors seem to have had few doubts that the balance of power between men and women had shifted, or that marriage found itself under attack. By 1923, divorce had become, in the words of the *Atlantic* editors, "the most threatening social question of our time." Women lobbied that divorcing partners should be treated equally regardless of gender. Women should not, in other words, be held to a higher standard of moral probity than men—a belief that Great Britain made law in the same year. States like Nevada with relaxed divorce laws prospered from what was seen as a national and international epidemic. In 1924, the *Atlantic* asked, "Is it all in the newspapers and on the surface of an over-jazzed existence, or has there actually been a change in the way Americans regard relations between men and women, and the institution by which those relations are surrounded?"[8] A reader had only to thumb through the pages of the magazine to learn that the spinsters of old had been replaced by female "bachelors" claiming the same freedoms as men.

In January 1924, the *Atlantic* published *My Dear Cornelia*, Stuart P.

Sherman's humorous look at changing mores. A literary critic and professor, Sherman modeled his narrator after a liberal, middle-aged gentleman rather like himself. *My Dear Cornelia* recounts the narrator's ongoing conversations with Cornelia, a Victorian-minded mother of Jazz Age children. Their talk ranges from conventions in courtship and marriage to fiction, the subject of the first installment, "My Conversation with Cornelia." They end with the narrator's tongue-in-cheek revelation that, in her day, Cornelia had more than matched her flapper-daughter.

The values Sherman ascribes to his narrator, who hopes that radical departures in American society might be more cosmetic than fundamental, also signal the *Atlantic*'s preferences for literature. Cornelia believes that books should guide instead of reflect character. The narrator mediates between the generations, explaining that while contemporary novelists challenge middle-class notions of chastity, he cannot condemn James Joyce, Willa Cather, Sinclair Lewis, or Sherwood Anderson any more than he would Joseph Fielding or William Shakespeare. To his mind, people who think D. H. Lawrence glorifies sex should be required to read *Women in Love* from cover to cover. He wonders if Cornelia realizes that F. Scott Fitzgerald's *The Beautiful and Damned* is a disguised temperance tract. For all his leanings toward the modern, however, he wishes that contemporary writers like Lawrence would help youth to value grandeurs that seemed in dangerously short supply: "beauty," "wit," "kindness," and "fortitude" (January 1924).[9]

It might be said that the *Atlantic Monthly*, devoted to literary and larger cultural issues, found itself coping with World War I long into the 1920s. Struggling to make sense of a political landscape shifting no less dramatically than that of art, the majority of contributors continued to think about the United States as a work in progress with ever more groups to be drawn into the fold of what an earlier writer had called American "trans-nationalism" (July 1916).

A backlash against immigration caused a worrisome rise in Ku Klux Klan membership after the war and redirected the attention of contributors to the travails of African Americans. In July 1922, the *Atlantic* published a critique of the Ku Klux Klan by a former U.S. senator from Greenville, Mississippi, named Leroy Percy. Percy had come to national attention when he mounted the steps of his city's courthouse and urged voters to tell the Klan to leave Greenville. They heeded his call, banning the Klan from their county. It was a pivotal moment in the South, where trials of Klan members by juries of their peers generally ended with acquittals. Over four hundred African Americans were murdered between 1918 and 1927. Returning veterans were lynched wearing their uniforms.

In his *Atlantic* piece, Percy compared the practices of the Klan to those of Russian Bolshevists and the Catholic Inquisition and wondered what, save religious intolerance and class resentment, would lead someone to join an organization that "violates every principle of Christianity." He speculated that the Klan's success depended on its secrecy and on collusion with government officials and the judiciary. Percy's recommended turning the "light of publicity" on pogroms that undermine the values Americans had just sacrificed a generation to preserve.[10] The year Percy's *Atlantic* article appeared, "Imperial Wizard" Hiram Evans and other Klan members kidnapped a bellhop named Alex Johnson and used acid to etch the letters "KKK" on his forehead. Evans gained national notoriety when *Time* placed him on its 23 June 1924 cover. The next year forty thousand members and supporters of the Klan—whose motto, according to Evans, could be boiled down to "native, white, Protestant supremacy"—marched down Pennsylvania Avenue protesting the infusion of "alien" elements into American society.[11]

Postwar contributors to the *Atlantic* wanted to believe that racism aimed at minorities resulted from competition for jobs and social status or prejudices that education could ameliorate. Reformers escalated calls for "fair wages, fair hours, fair working conditions, pay in proportion to accomplishment, profit-sharing, ownership of stock, sick-benefits, annuities, insurance, hospitals, safety, sanitation, amusement, recreation, exercise, schools, libraries, good cheap food, clothes, household goods, [and] home" (February 1922).[12]

Ellery Sedgwick prided himself on the *Atlantic*'s inoculating "the few who influence the many."[13] Woodrow Wilson, Wendell Wilkie, and Al Smith, the Catholic activist whom the Democrats proposed for president in 1928, chose the magazine for a platform. Smith would tell reporters that Sedgwick, a "High Hat from Boston," had nominated him for president.[14] He exaggerated only slightly. After Charles Marshall questioned the patriotism of Catholic politicians in an open letter to the *Atlantic* (April 1927), Sedgwick alerted every major news agency in the country to Smith's response. Going against his dictum of having others land punches for him, Sedgwick prefaced Smith's essay with an italicized mini-essay of his own. "Is the principle of religious tolerance, universal and complete, which every schoolboy has repeated for one hundred and fifty years, mere platitudinous vaporing?" he demanded. "Can men worshiping God in their differing ways believe without reservation of conscience in a common political ideal? Is the United States of America based on a delusion?" (May 1927).[15] Denied a chance to defend himself, Marshall fired off a furious letter to Sedgwick: "What you did do was to convert my letter and the answer into campaign material and throw it into the political arena." He was especially incensed that some people thought his letter had been "collusively written to give [Smith] a chance to reply."[16]

Sedgwick's defense of Smith was in keeping with the *Atlantic*'s defense of racial and religious freedom. In "The Jew and the Club" (October 1924), an anonymous writer referred to as "X" described "the gentlemen's agreement" that excluded Jews and frequently Catholics from clubs and boardrooms. The writer pointed out the undemocratic cleavage between so-called white "nationals," those of Anglo-European descent, and the country's minorities, which included, quite apart from 4 million Jews, 11 million people of African and Caribbean descent. The writer's analysis differed from that of an earlier, non-Jewish contributor, who saw "Jew-baiting in America"—the title of his May 1921 article—as a temporary stain on the country's escutcheon, which would fade as more people understood this minority's commitment to family, education, and the United States. Instead, he felt that Americans underestimated the social aspects of political equality.

Throughout the 1920s, *Atlantic* writers tackled issues that sound disturbingly familiar today: the mistreatment of prisoners ("Prison Cruelty," April 1920); the dwindling availability of fuel and its effect on global politics ("Civilization and Oil," February 1923); and the consequences of American foreign policy in Afghanistan, Cuba, Costa Rica, Nicaragua, and Mexico ("Imperialistic America," July 1924). Although many *Atlantic* writers echoed the British philosopher L. P. Jacks in looking forward to a day when "political civilization, founded on warring nationalism" and ethnicity would give way to a model founded on "cultural points of union" (February 1923), the Japanese presented a special concern.[17] In an article titled "The False Pride of Japan" (March 1921), California senator James Phelan stated his view that the Japanese were neither culturally nor temperamentally open to assimilation. The son of an Irish immigrant, Phelan made his fortune in banking and served three terms as mayor of San Francisco (1897–1902) before being elected to the U.S. Senate in 1915. His pledge to keep California "white" contributed to the loss of his Senate seat. Framing "the Japanese question" as a question of labor in the *Atlantic*, Phelan claimed that Japanese immigrants competed with unionized businesses in working-class districts, where they did nothing to support local churches and schools. Arguing that the continued allegiance of Japanese immigrants to Japan, not racism, led to their maltreatment, Phelan warned that Japanese voters would soon outnumber "real" Americans. Should the United States go to war with Japan, he assumed that many Japanese would work as active provocateurs. Phelan built to an impassioned climax about the conflict between free immigration and the achievement of both racial homogeneity and remunerative employment. Imitate America, he advised, "duplicate it on your own soil, O Asia, but do not spoil it. It is our sacred obligation to save it. Perhaps it is even of some value to you" (March 1921).[18] In 1924, Phelan testified before Congress on the Exclusion Act and predicted that the United States would eventually have to fight the Japanese. His arguments contributed to the internment of Japanese citizens living along the Pacific coast in 1942.

Phelan's essay pushed the limits of the magazine's tolerance. Soon after, the Stanford professor Payson Treat, author of *Japan and the United States, 1853–1921*, responded to Phelan with "California and the Japanese" (April 1921). Treat emphasized an international economy in which U.S. interests were tied to those of Japan (April 1921). He extended Rudyard Kipling's observation that "transportation is civilization" to argue that the "whole course of civilization has moved toward the breaking-down of barriers, at first between clans and rivals, then between nations, and finally between the great racial groups."[19] Home to over seventy thousand Japanese, California had a duty, in Treat's view, to correct false opinion like Phelan's.

Less than two decades later, when Europe engaged in a second world war, George Orwell would observe that his was neither a peaceful nor a critical age because propaganda had subsumed literature. Though he looked rather wistfully back to the 1920s as a time when writers cared more about technique than about proselytizing, he might have found in that decade the first obscuring—as the title of his 1941 essay put it—of "the frontier between art and propaganda." Speaking for the *Atlantic*, Sedgwick voiced a similar concern about the manipulation of language and blurring of genres. "It is words," he wrote, "and against the misuse of words every editorial prejudice should be fixed in concrete. . . . Politicians have attuned their long ears to the sound of words. Straight words, honest words, words that call up an accurate picture of any cause they advocate they consistently eschew, but instead twist to some alien meaning sweet and pleasant words which have hither to borne an utterly different connotation."[20]

However ready to criticize politicians' abuse of terms such as "liberal" and "radical," Sedgwick conveniently overlooked similar abuses of language by advertisers. Put bluntly, though neither he nor previous editors could keep the magazine running on subscriptions alone, the *Atlantic* had always treated advertising like an embarrassing relative who can't be disowned. For a short time after its founding, the magazine's lack of advertisement distinguished it from more "vulgar" monthlies. But soon after James T. Fields took over the editorship, the magazine added eighteen or more pages of advertisement (December 1860), not counting the back cover, and colored inserts hawking new Ticknor and Fields novels. Readers had their choice of cough remedies, sewing machines, pianos, upholstery goods, cooking ranges, mourning clothes, life insurance, pistols, and compounds like Burnett's Cocoaine (*sic*), guaranteed to prevent hair loss (May 1861). Unlike the editors, advertisers who could afford it embraced colored illustration. The *Atlantic*'s November 1870 issue contains an advertisement for the Mason & Hamlin Organ Co. that sports a rainbow of yellow, blue, brown, green, and red print. The magazine began to feature an "*Atlantic Monthly* Advertiser" which, in Christmas issues, swelled to a hundred pages.

If nothing else, the story of Listerine proved the power of advertising. Thanks apparently to a campaign featuring a young woman named Edna, whose bad breath drove men away, sales of Listerine mouthwash soared in six years, from $100,000 to more than $4 million. As the fortunes of Listerine indicate, advertising had become big business in the 1920s. An *Atlantic* article, which set the figure at $1 billion a year, estimated that newspapers helped make up that sum by bringing in $600 million; magazines and weeklies, $150 million; farm papers, $27 million; window displays, $20 million; streetcars, $11 million; and motion pictures, $5 million.[21] Ezra Pound would lay the failure of better magazines to "maintain intellectual life" at the feet of editors who made decisions based on "which given trend in art will 'git ads' from the leading corset companies."[22] For its part, the *Atlantic* bombarded readers with products such as Underwood Pure Deviled Ham, Bakelite pipes, Oshkosh wardrobe trunks, Standard Plumbing Fixtures, Cadillac cars, and children's electronically recorded books.

When Sedgwick acquired the magazine in 1908, he relied on the *Atlantic*'s name, rather than its circulation figures, to attract advertisers. He took comfort in the thought that only "a poorly educated American in those days . . . had not heard of the *Atlantic*."[23] As editor of a highbrow magazine, who considered advertisement a necessary evil or insurance against hard times, he thought neither about its profound effect on contemporary life or of its being an art in itself. It took his friend Edward W. Bok, the editor of *Ladies' Home Journal*, to do both for *Atlantic* readers.

Sedgwick and Bok became friends during the First World War, when they traveled to England together to meet with editors and journalists interested in building transatlantic relationships. Sedgwick described Bok as "first, last, and all the time . . . an individualist." Unlike many, he found it amusing that Bok spoke of himself in the third person. Originally christened Eduard Willem Gerard Cesar Hidde Bok, he had emigrated with his family from the Netherlands to Brooklyn in 1870. Only in America, some might say, would an office boy at Western Union, with no formal education beyond age thirteen, have the opportunity to gain the attention of powerful mentors such as Russell Sage, Jay Gould, and Henry Ward Beecher and amass an estate worth $23 million.

In the *Atlantic*'s October 1923 issue, Bok explained that the war "had proved a great friend of the advertisement": the government, for example, had advertised for people to join the army and navy, and banks for people to buy Liberty Bonds. Many magazines now staggered "under the weight of a greater number of pages devoted to advertisements [rather] than to reading matter." Few people understood the power and potential of advertising as well as Bok. Deciding to offer a $100,000 prize for the best proposal to further world peace, he "advertised" it in the *Atlantic* (January 1924). Bok differed from other commentators in his understanding of advertisement's embrace of both art and science. In his *Atlantic* article titled "The Day of the Advertisement," he wrote, "We ask of a poem, a novel, a play, or a newspaper editorial that it shall have certain structural qualities, and by these standards we measure them. Why not the advertisement . . . ?"[24]

Bok's argument found unexpected supporters. With Sedgwick acting as a go-between, the president of Harvard, Abbott Lawrence Lowell (Percival Lowell's brother), announced a new award that encouraged advertisers to use correct English, practice brevity, and present plans for producing and distributing products. The Pulitzer Prize committee discussed offering a prize to improve the general quality of advertisements. Never one to think small, Bok proposed a school dedicated to the formal study of advertising. When William Dean Howells predicted that literature would eventually be in the hands of the adman, he had to some extent been describing current practice. Now publishers competed with ad agencies such as J. Walter Thompson and Benton & Bowles for artists, designers, typographers, printers, copy writers, and editors.

The reliance on advertising signaled more profound changes in the conduct of public and private life, not all of them welcome. For those struggling with the aftermath of war and the perceived chaos of contemporary life, the *Atlantic* offered "Lessons in Patience, Service, and Hope" (December 1924). The anonymous author of "Lessons in Patience" noted that at eighty years of age, she had lived through an era of unimaginable catastrophes: the Irish famine of 1848, the European revolutions of 1848, the rise and fall of Prussia, the Mexican War, the Crimean War, the Italian War for Independence, the Indian Mutiny, the American Civil War, the Russo-Japanese War, Prussian wars against Austria and France, the Russo-Turkish War, and the First World War. Yet she had also seen the emancipation of Russia's serfs, the end of slavery in the United States, and the passing of legislation to improve the lives of workers, city dwellers, children, and animals. Her list of social and political advantages, which included more liberal attitudes toward divorce and illegitimacy, the education of women, and the conservation of natural resources, also applauded conveniences such as motorcars and railway travel, the airplane and Atlantic cable. Her grandchildren would live longer and healthier lives because of X-rays, penicillin, and anesthetics. The world might be bigger and people no more honest or altruistic than ever, she wrote, but if the years have taught her anything, it is to be sparing of mind and heart. Who can tell? she ended. It might actually change the world.[25]

29

The Turbulent Twenties, II

> In business, in the merchandising of stable commodities such as coal, iron, grain, wool, and the like, there are fixed and arbitrary standards which can be recognized, duplicated, and graded accurately after preliminary training. Not so in literature, that elusive, intangible, delicately beautiful product.
>
> "Fewer and Better Books," *Atlantic*, January 1925

TO VAN WYCK BROOKS, there had never been a time in America's history as favorable to the growth of its writers as the 1920s. In 1925 alone, Sinclair Lewis published *Arrowsmith*; Theodore Dreiser, *An American Tragedy*; John Dos Passos, *Manhattan Transfer*; F. Scott Fitzgerald, *The Great Gatsby*; Ellen Glasgow, *Barren Ground*; Willa Cather, *The Professor's House*; Edith Wharton, *The Mother's Recompense*; Sherwood Anderson, *Dark Laughter*; Ernest Hemingway, *In Our Time*; DuBose Heyward, *Porgy*; and Alain Locke, *The New Negro* anthology. A period of spectacular energy in the arts, the 1920s offered myriad forms of entertainment. "The Phantom of the Opera" thrilled moviegoers, while a tuxedoed Basil Sidney played Hamlet to filled houses. On the radio, Frankie and Johnnie were sweethearts, and more conventional lovers dreamed of "Just a Small Cottage by a Waterfall." Couples danced the Charleston and the Black Bottom. At West Fifty-fifth Street the novelist, music critic, and photographer Carl Van Vechten served limitless martinis to George Gershwin, Bessie Smith, Paul Robeson, and the Peruvian diva Marguerite D'Alvarez. Artists such as John Sloan and Reginald Marsh painted a grittier world, its heavenly foil suggested by the comforting obituary portraits of James Van Der Zee, Harlem's foremost photographer. Not only artists but the whole country seemed on the move to Harlem, Greenwich Village, Santa Fe, and Paris.

Atlantic contributors assumed that recent events had a direct impact on fiction and poetry. In "The Literature of Disillusion" (August 1923), Helen McFee insisted that the war had given the younger generation "a right to be morbid." Singling out Edna St. Vincent Millay's verse for both its rawness and lyricism, she attributed the closing lines of "Here Is a Wound" to "moods left by the war":

> That April should be shattered by a gust,
> That August should be leveled by a rain,
> I can endure, and that the lifted dust
> Of man should settle to the earth again;
> But that a dream can die, will be a thrust
> Between my ribs forever of hot pain.[1]

Her clumsy last line notwithstanding, Millay offered an alternative to those readers and critics bewildered by the extremes of modernism. Defining the new poetry for *Atlantic* readers, Carl Sandburg parsed the word thirty-seven times. Among his effusions, he called poetry "a mystic, sensuous mathematics of fire, smokestacks, waffles, pansies, people, and purple sunsets" (March 1923).[2] Not, in other words, those "ribs forever of hot pain."

Editors of the *Atlantic* had traditionally assumed art to be "one of the great instruments of popular education." By art, they meant the "right" kind of art, not, for example, "a holiday book for the center table of the uneducated rich," which corrupts "art at its source" and degrades popular taste.[3] Perhaps for the first time in American or European history, the distinctions between high and low art would be leaving even the critics in a daze. Samuel McChord Crothers, in "Keeping Up with the Smart Set" (1924), poked fun at contemporary poets and critics by asking readers to decipher Ezra Pound's lines from the fifth section of "Homage to Sextus Propertius":

> My muse is eager to instruct me in a new gamut
> Or gambetto.
> Up, up, my soul, from your lowly cantillation,
> put on a timely vigor.

Pound's poem had to be good, Crothers explained, because no one could understand it. Only a critic could find significance in the following lines, which might be "a little too rough" for *Atlantic* readers:

I grasped the greasy subway strap
And I read the lurid advertisements,
I chewed my gum voraciously.[4]

For his part, Pound preferred the "little" magazines that promoted everything from Imagism to anarchism. He condemned mainstream magazines like the *Atlantic* for putting profits above quality.[5] To him, they participated in a capitalistic economy that resulted in the First World War—and, later on, the Second.

The so-called "new" magazines, which set themselves apart from the "old" magazines by demanding experimentation, made the *Atlantic* appear more conservative than it was. Edith Wharton didn't help the magazine's image by insisting on English spellings, which compelled Sedgwick to add a footnote explaining the author's preference. However staid the *Atlantic* might seem in comparison to a magazine like the *Reviewer*—founded by a group of Richmonders in 1924—they nonetheless shared contributors in Agnes Repplier, Carl Van Vechten, Allen Tate, and Julia Peterkin, winner of the 1929 Pulitzer Prize for fiction. Amy Lowell complained that the *Reviewer* had not asked her for a poem. Though Sedgwick published Lowell's poems, he drew the line at Stein 'til 1933. It didn't matter that the *New York Times* called Stein "one of the most original writers of all time."[6] In an era of competing aesthetics, the *Atlantic*'s editors did their best to acknowledge changing tastes and forms without, as Pound grumbled, driving away advertisers and readers.

Readers always enjoyed a good story, and Sedgwick saw the magazine's sales rise the day a young woman named Opal Whiteley walked into his office. It was not every day that an alluring, charismatic, twenty-two-year-old woman asked him to be her Svengali. But it happened when Whiteley—who claimed to be the illegitimate daughter of Prince Henri D'Orleans raised by an Oregon logging family—tried to sell him a nature book. Whiteley charmed Sedgwick with anecdotes about her early life in the lumber camps. Learning that she had kept a diary that was now stored in California, he arranged to have it shipped to Boston. Whiteley spent the next nine months constructing the original document, which, she said, her sister had torn into hundreds of pieces during one of their girlhood spats. *The Story of Opal* (March–August 1920) lived up to Sedgwick's wildest hopes and became an international best-seller. Even the

Duchess de Chartres recognized Whiteley's claim. After hobnobbing with royalty across several continents, however, Whiteley disappeared as suddenly as she had surfaced. In 1948, she was discovered living at the Napsbury Mental Hospital.

Though *The Story of Opal* helped to boost the *Atlantic*'s circulation, it presented an ethical problem for Sedgwick, who left a scrupulous record of all correspondence surrounding the manuscript and contributed to the indigent Whiteley's support at Napsbury. While never disowning Whiteley's claims, he stated in his introduction to the 1920 edition that "the authorship does not matter, nor the life from which it came. There the book is."[7] A book lives or dies on the author's ability, as Joseph Conrad, wrote, to create a world in which readers can believe. Sedgwick would have agreed. He summed up his feelings about the case in a 1935 letter to a doubter: "I shall die in the absolute personal certainty that the story so far as it is printed in the *Atlantic* expressed Opal's personal convictions. I do not think that it was true, but I know she believed it to be true and I also know that her life was the strangest medley of fact and fiction that I have even come across."[8]

For Sedgwick, his personal and professional investment in Whitely made financial sense, at least. By 1924, his magazine competed with thirty-four hundred monthlies in the United States alone. Readers like those whom the founders had wanted to educate had a choice of magazines dedicated to decorating, fashion, fishing, outdoor life, and housekeeping—indeed, to almost any topic. The 2 million readers of *True Story*, addicted to confessions of illicit romance, supported the old publishing adage that scandal sold.[9] At another point on the spectrum, radical publications like the *Liberator*, an illustrated monthly designed to advance the interests of socialism, also competed with "capitalist" endeavors like the *Atlantic*. While other magazines embraced a host of -isms—Cubism, Impressionism, Imagism—the *Atlantic* continued to define "culture" only slightly more broadly than in earlier decades.

For those at the *Atlantic* who saw themselves upholding a tradition of Anglo-European culture, the 1920s marked a critical period in the arts, as divisions between "high" and "low" art collapsed and the Harlem Renaissance captured the country's imagination. The editors nodded to contemporary culture with critical essays on popular forms of entertainment such as jazz and the movies as they waited to see what the future might bring. Jazz, of course, was everywhere, and the composer Carl Engel explained the happy marriage of "seemingly incompatible" elements melding into something unique that made plain jazz "good jazz": "The saxophone bleats a turgid song; the clarinets turn capers of their own; the violins come forward with an *obbligato*; a saucy flute darts up and done the scale . . . [and] the trombone lumberingly slides off on a tangent—producing music that is 'unequivocally American'" (August 1922).[10] As chief of the Music Division of the Library of Congress, Engel worked to preserve recordings of contemporary jazz for future generations. Despite Engel's primer on jazz, the magazine tended to confuse the form with the blues, which led one amateur musicologist to explain, in The Contributors' Column, that the blues came from Memphis, the home of the self-proclaimed "Father of the Blues," W. C. Handy.

In fact, the magazine walked a tightrope between new and old, which Sedgwick balanced with difficulty. His custodial mission continued by featuring the work of writers like James M. Cain, a bespectacled journalist who later shot to fame with such hard-boiled hits such as *The Postman Always Rings Twice* (1934) and *Double Indemnity* (1936). His essay for the *Atlantic* in 1922, "The Battle Ground of Coal" (October), complemented Charles Rumford Walker's serialized "Chapters on Steel." Cain knew how to dramatize his subjects, as he did the battle between the United Mine Workers of America and nonunion coal-operators in West Virginia:

> If you get off the train at Williamson, county seat of Mingo, you will be at the fighting front. People there will tell you that this struggle has been going on for three years. They will tell you of the bloody day at Matewan, May 19, 1920, when ten men, including the mayor of the town, fell in a pistol battle that lasted less than a minute. They will tell you of guerrilla warfare that went on for months; how Federal troops had to be called in twice. They will tell you of the "three days battle," which resulted, in May, 1921, in the declaration of martial law. . . . The atrocity list and quantity of propaganda give this war quite an orthodox flavor. It is very hard to sift out the truth.[11]

Among the new directions in art, *Atlantic* writers balked most at film, perhaps because it promised, as Katherine F. Gerould speculated in "Movies" (July 1921), to eclipse the book. Admitting her prejudice against film, Gerould worried that a form that thrived on vulgarity and sentimentality would lead to a cheapening of ideals in the culture at large. To her, its influence raised questions not only about the survival of the novel but also about "legitimate" theater. Gerould noted the popularity of film—mainly its influence on the young—yet praised slapstick because its divorce from language aided the assimilation of non-English speakers. In 1921, *The Four Horsemen of the Apocalypse*, starring Rudolph Valentino, ranked number one at the box office, with *The Kid*, featuring Charlie Chaplin, second, and *The Three Musketeers*, third. Other hits included *The Sheik*, *Little Lord Fauntleroy*, *Every Woman's Problem*, *White and Unmarried*, and *The Idle Class*. Given that a movie ticket cost about twenty-seven cents and *The Four Horsemen of the Apocalypse* grossed $4.5 million during its first run, the number of people who saw the movie would have exceeded 16 million.[12]

The communal, voyeuristic ritual of film viewing did not concern Gerould. Nor did she speculate, as Oliver Wendell Holmes had in "The Stereoscope and the Stereograph" (1859), about the new technology's impact on people's understanding of time, reality, or self. Instead, she approached film through the lens of literature. Intrigued by film's ability to create a narrative through nonlinear plotting and shifting scenes, she foresaw a future in which novelists like John Dos Passos and Ernest Hemingway would apply the cinematic techniques of storytelling to their own genre.[13]

Just as it missed opportunities with film and music, the *Atlantic* failed to track new directions in art. In 1913, it had all but ignored one of the most influential exhibitions of modern art, held in New York City's 69th Regiment Armory. The Armory Show, as it came to be called, introduced Americans to many of the European Impressionists as well as to neo- or post-Impressionists such as Georges Seurat, Paul Gauguin, and Marcel Duchamp. One critic punned that Royal Cortissoz, the *Atlantic*'s conservative art historian, thought the Armory Show "a royal disaster." His tastes did not change in the 1920s. Making some exceptions for American artists like Georgia O'Keeffe, he blamed immigrants for the influence of modern art on American artists and dismissed artists such as Picasso, Matisse, and the earlier Van Gogh.

The *Atlantic*'s struggles with new art, new literature, and new audiences matched those of two very different magazines, one established, the other new and ready to reply to the *Atlantic* in February 1925. For the last fifteen years, as editor of the *Crisis*, the NAACP's monthly magazine, if not the voice of the NAACP itself, W. E. B. Du Bois had cajoled, scolded, and challenged his country to honor the principles of its Constitution. In the *Crisis*'s January 1925 issue, he tallied both gains and losses for Americans of color during the past twelve months. Debit: Segregation in the nation's capital. Credit: Tuskegee Hospital. Debit: the U.S. occupation of Haiti. Credit: Dyer's Anti-Lynching Bill. The credits, which in Du Bois's abacus outweighed the debits three to one, also included international efforts like the third Pan-African Congress and the achievements of individual men and women succeeding against staggering odds. As a magazine committed to economic cooperation, political empowerment, education, and the arts, the *Crisis* engaged in a frank, sometimes contentious debate with mainstream America.

From the window of his Fifth Avenue office, W. E. B. Du Bois could look at the streaming, jumbled life below. This was where he hoped to revive the spirit of Lincoln by interpreting the aspirations and struggles of African Americans to the world. Subtitled "A Record of the Darker Races," the *Crisis* had created a new national narrative by placing the United States within a global network of nations and emphasizing the contributions of people of color. Every issue included book notices, biographies of worthy men and women, letters from subscribers eager to set the editor straight, and art glorifying the verse from *Song of Solomon*, "I am black but comely." If the *Crisis* worked to correct misconceptions about race from social, anthropological, and historical perspectives, it did so to instill in readers a sense of pride and self-respect.

Du Bois pointed his staff to the success of *McClure's* and *Ladies' Home Journal*, though his emphasis on art, politics, and education recall the goals of the *Atlantic*. Like the editor of *Ladies' Home Journal*, Edward Bok, he understood the media's role in creating and shaping public sentiment. He routinely sent unsolicited copies of the magazine to other influential editors, planted press notices, and wrote tracts that Pullman porters disseminated. In 1912, Du Bois estimated his "white" audience at 20 percent. Sherwood Anderson, Gertrude Stein, Carl Van Vechten, Franz Boas, and the eccentric Philadelphian art collector Dr. Albert C. Barnes all published in the *Crisis*. Circulation of the magazine peaked at one hundred thousand readers during Du Bois's stewardship (1910–

1934)—testimony to the growth of the black middle class and the magazine's appeal to white liberals.

Few magazines bridge high and low culture; fewer still see themselves in the role of cultural ambassador or architect. Although their approaches differed, the *Crisis* and the *Atlantic Monthly* both began with a dream of educating, even perhaps remaking America. Apart from offering discounts to teachers and offering a forum to Harvard's president, Charles Eliot, the *Atlantic* had a mission to raise the general level of American education. The *Crisis* shared this goal; its back pages abounded with advertisements for African American colleges. Putting theory into practice, the *Crisis* offered prizes for the best plays dealing with a phase of African American history and experience: seventy-five dollars for first place, forty for second, and ten for third. The editor advised contestants to consider three things: audience, actors, and plot. They should, he said, think of the audience as white Americans used to going to the theater, and at the same time they should write for those who might never have attended a play. The story should not be too simple, aimless, or illogical; the actors should speak as people really speak; and playgoers must leave knowing what the play meant. He urged contestants not to confine the action to lynchings, sorrow, poverty, misfortune, and despair: "There are also sunshine and kindness and ambition and hope."[14] Like the *Atlantic*'s editors, Du Bois believed in the social and political influence of the arts.

The *Crisis* differed from the *Atlantic* in its acceptance of art as propaganda, while avoiding the *Atlantic*'s mask of neutrality. Its discussion of art never strayed far from discussions of race, whereas in the *Atlantic* race and art remained largely separate topics. A reviewer of the *Atlantic* who singled out Paul Green, a white playwright, for the authenticity of his characters' black dialect did not think it necessary to explore the concept of "authenticity" or what constituted "Negro art"—a question that the *Crisis* posed repeatedly.

In 1925, Jessie Fauset, the magazine's literary editor from 1919 to 1926, initiated a discussion about whether American Negroes should write as Americans or as Negroes and whether they should form their own publishing houses. The question deeply concerned Fauset. A novelist herself, she considered two *Atlantic* writers, the English novelist John Galsworthy and the expatriate Edith Wharton, among the finest prose writers. She advised young people who wanted to write to read them for models, along with Du Bois, Joseph Conrad, George Bernard Shaw, and Walter Pater. It troubled her that publishers ignored the lives of middle- and upper-class African Americans in favor of a sensationalized Harlem. Fauset's question about "Negro art" solicited responses from Countee Cullen and Sherwood Anderson. Cullen, who rebelled against any standards for art that appeared prescriptive, accused the editors of the *Crisis* of censorship. Anderson thought it wise to forget thinking about "Negro art" as a separate entity. Writers should leave such designations to the critics.[15]

More diffuse in contents and audience, the *Atlantic* had competed, not with the *Crisis*, but with the older literary magazines like *Harper's*, based in New York. In March 1924, the *Atlantic*'s editors bragged about having a chance to set New York right, but New York would surprise them. The following February a new and sophisticated magazine went on sale, proudly announcing itself as the *New Yorker*. Taking a page from the early *Atlantic*, the *New Yorker* relied on its name to sell both a place and the associations—the glamour and trends—attached to that place. For the *Atlantic*, Boston was Boston, but for the *New Yorker*, New York was Manhattan.

Initially the *New Yorker* presented little threat to the *Atlantic*—or any other magazine. According to James Thurber, the *New Yorker* became "the outstanding flop of 1925, a year of memorable successes in literature, music, and entertainment, and a flop that kept on going. . . . From an original run off of fifteen thousand copies in February, its circulation fell to a pernicious-anemia low of twenty-seven hundred copies in August."[16] After an emergency infusion of cash, the magazine recovered enough in 1926 to copyright features such as "Profiles" and "Goings On about Town."

Harold Ross, the mercurial editor of the *New Yorker*, seemed the antithesis of the *Atlantic*'s Sedgwick. A smallish man with a three-inch shock of hair rising from his forehead like an exclamation mark, he could have been mistaken for a barroom tough. Ross brilliantly defined his magazine by its lack of interest for "the old lady in Dubuque."[17] He did not have to say that she probably read the *Atlantic*. It was enough that her custom was unwelcome at the *New Yorker*. The very first issue of the *New Yorker* scoffed that "no matter how hard it tries, Boston cannot look like Paris—and it has tried hard."[18] Ross's mockery of the old lady in Dubuque and everything in Boston—in columns titled "Boston" and "Boston Again"—

defined his audience as young, urban, stylish, and eager for gossip. Instead of turning its nose up at movies, the *New Yorker* dedicated a column ("Motion Pictures") to the industry and ran profiles of Samuel Goldwyn and other celluloid pioneers (25 April 1925). It catered to readers with epicurean tastes, though not always deep pockets, who liked to think themselves at the vanguard of popular culture—a conceit reinforced by the weekly appearance of a new issue.

At a time when the *Atlantic* augmented its reviewing with a section called "The Atlantic's Bookshelf," the *New Yorker* introduced a column called "Tell Me a Book to Read." In the week of 28 February 1925, the editors recommended Margaret Kennedy's *The Constant Nymph,* Amy Lowell's biography of John Keats, Joseph Conrad's *Tales of Hearsay,* E. M. Forster's *A Passage to India,* and Hugh Walpole's *The Old Ladies,* with the quip "Can you imagine absorbing drama arising among three old ladies?"[19] Apart from its arch tone, perhaps nothing distinguished the *New Yorker* more from the *Atlantic* than its seeming appeal to readers on the go, who could quickly peruse one-column sections devoted to topics such as the photography of Alfred Stieglitz, sports, music, or the theater. Average articles in the *Atlantic* ranged from three to thirteen pages. People bound past issues of the *Atlantic* because they considered it literature of lasting value.

The *Atlantic* came into being "endeavoring always to keep in view that moral element which transcends all persons and parties" and promising to further Freedom, National Progress, and Honor; the *New Yorker,* to present "the whole truth without fear or favor."[20] The distinction may sound slight, yet it suggests different notions of purpose and allegiance, if not the relative nature of "truth." Unlike the *Atlantic,* which had been conceived as a democratizing force and continued to reach out to "middle" Americans, the *New Yorker* blatantly and brilliantly appealed to elitism. It would be hard to imagine the *New Yorker* at this early stage having anything considerable to say about the recent war, whereas the *Atlantic* by and large stuck to its analysis of the world around it.

However self-conscious and literary in its own way, the *New Yorker* escaped the *Atlantic*'s "highbrow" label, or the stigma of being dull and old. One wit described it as "the best magazine in the world for a person who can not read."[21] Ross, who priced his magazine at fifteen cents an issue, offered irreverent sophistication and modernity. He invited readers to join a virtual extension of the Algonquin Hotel's witty round table. Humorous and above all polished, the *New Yorker* had a distinctive, slightly mocking voice, which the *Atlantic*'s Contributors' Column in the early 1920s foreshadowed. Like its predecessor, the *New Yorker* counted on a stable of writers, including James Thurber and Dorothy Parker. Lawrence Thompson maintained that "if Holmes had lived today he certainly would have published his things in *The New Yorker* with pleasure."[22]

Notwithstanding the editor's assertions to the contrary, the *New Yorker* sold a metropolitan "lifestyle" reflected in ads for the theater, polo clubs, furriers, couturiers, and fancy automobiles. Sophisticated advertisements—for everything from Parisian perfumes to dental paste and cord balloon tires—seemed almost as central to the magazine as its signature cartoons. The plethora of ads undercut its mockery of that "group of publications engaged in tapping the Great Buying Power of the North American steppe region by trading mirrors and colored beads in the form of our best brands of hokum."[23] The *New Yorker* promised to keep readers "apprised of what is going on in the public and semi-public smart gathering places—the clubs, hotels, cafes, supper clubs, cabarets and other resorts."[24] Unlike the *Atlantic*, which had been conceived as a democratizing force and continued to reach out to "middle" Americans, the *New Yorker* blatantly and brilliantly appealed to elitism.

To some extent magazines tend to remain in the era that gave them birth. Founded in the years leading up to the Civil War, the *Atlantic* thrived on issues of public concern, the *New Yorker* on personality. Ross recruited New York journalists who gave the magazine its trademark breeziness and foreshadowed the news reporting of National Public Radio by going beyond hard facts and obvious storylines to personal anecdote and tangential illustration. Those who appeared in the pages of gossipy features such as "The Hour Glass" and "Of All Things" achieved minor celebrity status, though some, such as Willie Hoppe, "the boy wonder of billiards"—described as inclining toward the rotundity of King George—might have preferred anonymity. By contrast, the *Atlantic* reported on the political "buoyancy" or opportunism of England's new chancellor, Winston Churchill, whose failures at Antwerp and the Dardanelles failed to sink his career (February 1925).

In its coverage of events for nearly seven decades, the *Atlantic* found itself continuously appealing to and reporting on a different American people. What made us so? Sedgwick asked. The Civil War? The First World War? Darwinism? He traced the change in his own family: from his grandfather, who died with the conviction that heaven would welcome him; to his father, living on hope "for the miracle of eternity"; to his children, bored with the whole discussion. According to Sedgwick, sophistication had taken the place of conviction, disillusion the politics of hope. "Resolved that the *Atlantic* should face the whole of life," he declared no subject that concerned the mind and heart taboo.[25] "Don't print for eternity," he cautioned, counting the life of any monthly at thirty days. "Print for *now*."[26] His command reversed a policy of seventy years' standing.

In 1925, the *Atlantic*'s essayists included the British novelist E. M. Forster, the philosopher Alfred North Whitehead, the rhetorician I. A. Richards, and the editor of the *New Age*, A. R. Orage, who advised readers to "look to West Africa, to Tahiti, to the Mayas and Aztecs, to China and Japan," and above all to India, for sources of artistic rejuvenation.[27] Sedgwick introduced readers to the fiction of a young African American writer named Rudolph Fisher, a gesture that symbolically brought the first writer associated with the Harlem Renaissance and the New Negro movement into the house of Emerson, Lowell, and Holmes. If the magazine nodded to modernism, it was largely through the social and moral questions modernism raised. It published nothing in 1925, for example, from T. S. Eliot, James Joyce, Virginia Woolf, D. H. Lawrence, or George Bernard Shaw, who won that year's Nobel Prize for Drama.

Different as the *Atlantic* might be from the *Crisis* or the *New Yorker*, a comparison underscores the magazine's scope and achievement. Not strictly political, literary, or social, it managed to combine these perspectives to give a more telling, perhaps more accurate picture of contemporary life. Those who wrote for the *Atlantic* believed that words matter not only for what they said or did not say but because they force us to think more precisely, to articulate whatever lies at the core of our ethical being, and to take responsibility for our deeds as well as our words. Thomas Wentworth Higginson once said that anyone wanting "to trace American 'society' in its formative process," to see "the essential forces in action," should go to William Dean Howells.[28] He should have sent them to the *Atlantic*.

30

Across the Decades

We aren't in the news business, we're in the thinking business.

DAVID BRADLEY, e-mail read at the *Atlantic* farewell dinner to Boston, 2005

IN THE *Atlantic*'s November 1925 issue, the English novelist E. M. Forster wrote that "literature . . . is alive—not in a vague complementary sense, but alive tenaciously."[1] This was the principle that guided the magazine into the 1920s. The founders had merely reflected common belief when they asserted the centrality of literature to American identity. Nothing else—no credo, manifesto, or decree—could give form to the jumble of lives and history that in combination and against all logic reflected the spirit of the nation. The *Atlantic*'s pledge "to leave no province unrepresented . . . [and] to keep in view the moral elements that transcend all persons and parties" resonated through the decades because it spoke to America's better nature, to its dream of a more equitable and inclusive society.

If the magazine's ambitions seemed at times bigger than the size or will of its audience, its editors remained committed to frank dealing. They believed that the basis of a true and lasting national prosperity depended on a responsible press. This is not to say that the *Atlantic*'s early writers and their successors agreed about what constituted "national progress." No one, for example, underestimated the importance of controversy to sales. Rather, they argued their positions vehemently, mindful of the motives that drove great debaters like Abraham Lincoln. The *Atlantic*'s authority came partly from its mission to hold the nation to a higher ideal, and partly from example, which assured readers that even the most daunting problems could be resolved through meaningful dialogue. Writers such as Emerson and Stowe, Muir and Du Bois, still central to Americans' understanding of their heritage, transmitted through decades what the original mission statement called "the American idea"—defined by the large abstractions of "Freedom, National Progress, and Honor." Yet what the *Atlantic* achieved that no other magazine before or after has managed to achieve—whether the *Nation*, *Scribner's*, the *New Republic*, or the *New Yorker*—was a grasp of implicitly "American" aspirations, in a format that combined high literary excellence with political, ethical, and educational imperatives.

There are few more comprehensive courses in American history and culture than those contained in the *Atlantic Monthly*. To isolate any given topic recurring across the decades is not only to read history in the making but to watch a nation wrestling with its sense of right and wrong. Race relations in the United States, Middle East politics, changing social mores—the same thorny topics engage readers today. The *Atlantic* published Justice Felix Frankfurter's sympathetic analysis titled "The Case of Sacco and Vanzetti" (March 1927) and Alfred E. Smith's defense of religious freedom, "Catholic and Patriot" (May 1927)—which John F. Kennedy reiterated in his 1960 address to the Greater Houston Ministerial Association when he upheld the absolute division of church and state in the United States. The *Atlantic* also published shrewd analyses of the Cold War, the Korean War, Nixon's Checkers speech, the Tonkin Resolution, the Watergate break-in, and the wars in Iraq and Afghanistan. One of its pivotal moments remains the publication of Martin Luther King Jr.'s "Letter from Birmingham Jail" (16 April 1963). Written in response to the criticism of fellow clergymen and published under the title "The Negro Is Your Brother" (August 1963), King's letter carried on the work of other great *Atlantic* writers such as Frederick Douglass, Booker T. Washington, and W. E. B. Du Bois:

> For years now I have heard the word "Wait!" It rings in the ear of every Negro with piercing familiarity. This "Wait" has almost always meant "Never." . . . We have waited for more than 340 years for our constitutional and God-given rights. But when you have seen vicious mobs lynch your mothers and fathers at will and drown

> your sisters and brothers at whim; . . . when you suddenly find your tongue twisted and your speech stammering as you seek to explain to your six-year-old daughter why she can't go to the public amusement park that has just been advertised on television. . . . There comes a time when the cup of endurance runs over, and men are no longer willing to be plunged into the abyss of despair.[2]

In the same month that the *Atlantic* published these memorable lines, King stood on the steps of the Lincoln Memorial (28 August 1963), looked out at the sea of more than two hundred thousand demonstrators, and spoke of his dream for the United States.

Those associated with the *Atlantic Monthly* had a dream—repeated by Sedgwick's successor, Edward Weeks—to lessen the divide between "the class man" and "the mass man" by teaching "people how to read their own language." For Weeks, this kind of reading required an understanding of the uses of language and its traditions. To his mind, the magazine provided a haven from the contemporary onslaught of undigested information and garbled English. Sounding a bit like Henry James or James Russell Lowell, Weeks, in a 1958 interview with Mike Wallace, noted that "value judgments imply discrimination. . . . It's to build that bridge stronger that I work and live and dedicate myself to the *Atlantic*."[3]

As William Dean Howells noted over a century ago, publishing is a business. Though early editors felt pressures of the marketplace and teetered on the edge of bankruptcy, they had the support of the parent publishing houses, whose owners refused to set a price on the magazine's reputation for integrity. Recent publishers have felt less sanguine about a bargain that brought in half a million dollars one year to lose it the next. Notwithstanding the march of *Atlantic* authors—beginning with Emerson and extending through Wallace Stevens, Eudora Welty, John Steinbeck, and William Faulkner to James Dickey, W. H. Auden, John Updike, Bernard Malamud, and Joyce Carol Oates—the magazine continued its move, begun in the 1920s away from literature in favor of direct political and social commentary. The sale of the magazine to the real estate developer Mortimer B. Zuckerman in 1980, then to the media mogul David Bradley nineteen years later, underscored for many observers a seismic shift in publishing from the days on Tremont Street when James T. Fields offered contributors tea and sympathy. Maybe nothing characterized a different dispensation more than the announcement of the acquisition by Bradley being made over the office speakerphone, and the installation of Michael Kelly, the former editor of the *New Republic*. Kelly had mentored Stephen Glass, the reporter whose fabrication of sources provided the plot of the 2003 movie titled "Shattered Glass."

Characterized by Eric Alterman of the *Nation* as "a reporter and editor with no literary background, a volcanic temperament and history of colossal bad judgment," Kelly bore little resemblance to previous *Atlantic* editors. More disturbing to many readers, his appointment signaled the movement of a traditionally liberal magazine toward the political right. Alterman hoped that the magazine, which had survived "countless panics, depressions, world wars and even Mort Zuckerman," would manage to survive Kelly: "But those of us who retain an affection for the magazine and its role in American history might be forgiven for feeling afraid—very, very afraid."[4] Kelly stepped aside after two years (2000–2002) to cover the Second Iraq War. Embedded with the Third Infantry Division of the U.S. Army, he died on 3 April 2003. Kelly had been planning a three-part series for the *Atlantic*.

Today we live in a world where, as Cullen Murphy, the *Atlantic*'s thirteenth editor, observed, communication threatens to "re-engrave the template by which we make sense of virtually every aspect of national reality."[5] Those of us who are addicted to the weight and feel of books, who like our magazines thick and dense, and who think fiction no less true than nonfiction might feel a little like Cornelia, the Victorian mother trying to talk to her flapper children across divides not only of age but also of fundamental understanding of the self. For its part, the *Atlantic* has responded to an audience comfortable with new media by embracing online videos, blogs, podcasts, Twitter, and Facebook. The magazine that once resisted illustrations has gone online and become a "deca-monthly," dedicating only a single issue each year to fiction.[6] In December 2010, a reporter for the *New York Times* asked, "How did a 153-year-old magazine . . . reinvent itself for the 21st century?" The answer lay not in quality or price but in no longer "thinking of itself as a printed product." A column like "The Atlantic Wire" reaches approximately a million readers a month, and the magazine draws over $6 million from digital advertising. But it retains a printed circulation of 470,000. And since 2006 the *Atlantic* and the Aspen Institute have cohosted the Aspen Ideas Festival, which, in fostering leadership, open-minded discussion, and humanism, continues the magazine's original mission.[7]

Oliver Wendell Holmes's description of the *Atlantic* as "a notion" was tested in 2005 when the magazine made its farewell to Boston and moved to the nation's capital—and to the infamous Watergate Office Building. Meant to consolidate resources, the move signaled a change in the magazine's content and character. Yet Holmes may have been right to see its strength as independent of place or even time. The world has always been so big that—as a recent editor observed—there are few places "where members of the military, the clergy, and academe, where Republicans and Democrats, blacks and whites, the believer and the unbeliever, can regularly hear one another speak."[8] To generations of readers the *Atlantic Monthly* provided that service. A way of writing, living, politicking, and thinking, this magazine of presidents, soldiers, scientists, and poets lived richly and provocatively through formative years of America's history.

ACKNOWLEDGMENTS

I owe an incalculable debt to the many fine literary historians and critics mentioned in my notes, but especially to Ellen Ballou and Ellery Sedgwick for their landmark studies on American publishing and the *Atlantic Monthly*. I have benefited from the expertise of librarians at Harvard's Houghton Library, the Massachusetts Historical Society, and the University of Delaware's Morris Library. Ben Healy kindly gave me a tour of the *Atlantic*'s Washington office and Ellie Smith graciously provided facts. An NEH senior fellowship and a University of Delaware Faculty Research Enrichment allowed me time and funding for writing. I wish to thank Stan Holwitz and Jonah Straus for their belief in the project; Robert Hirst for information about Mark Twain; Jerry Loving and Ed Folsom for their long support; and Jackson Bryer for his scrupulous reading. I am doubly indebted to Stephen P. Hull for improvements both to the manuscript and to its title. Above all, I am grateful to my husband, Carl Dawson, without whom I would not have completed this book.

NOTES

Contributions to the *Atlantic* are noted by month and year (in parentheses) unless otherwise stated.

Preface

1. Prospectus of the *Atlantic Monthly*, December 1860, back cover.

2. Edmund Kirke, "A Suppressed Chapter of History," *Atlantic Monthly* 59 (April 1887): 447–448.

1. Beginnings

1. Mark A. De Wolfe Howe, *The Atlantic Monthly and Its Makers* (Boston: Atlantic Monthly Press, 1919), 14–15.

2. Frank Luther Mott, *A History of American Magazines, 1741–1850* (Cambridge: Harvard University Press, 1930), 1:341.

3. John Winthrop, "A Model'l of Christian Charity," Collections of the Massachusetts Historical Society, 3rd series (Boston, 1838), 7:47.

4. Oliver Wendell Holmes, *The Works of Oliver Wendell Holmes* (Boston: Houghton, Mifflin, Co., 1892), 2:217.

5. Quoted in Ferris Greenslet, *James Russell Lowell, His Life and Work* (Boston: Houghton, Mifflin, Co., 1905), 150.

6. Ralph Waldo Emerson, "Compensation," *The Complete Works of Ralph Waldo Emerson*, ed. Joseph Slater (Cambridge: Belknap Press of Harvard University Press, 1979), 2:64.

7. James R. Lowell to C. F. Briggs, December 1848, *Works of James Russell Lowell* (Boston: Houghton Mifflin, 1899), 14:201.

8. *Atlantic Monthly* 1 (November 1857), back cover. Also see Ellery Sedgwick, *The Atlantic Monthly, 1857–1909, Yankee Humanism at High Tide and Ebb* (Amherst: University of Massachusetts Press, 1994), 35.

9. Ralph Waldo Emerson, "Concord Hymn," in *The Complete Works of Ralph Waldo Emerson*, ed. Edward Waldo Emerson (Boston: Houghton Mifflin Co., 1932), 9:158–159.

10. See Oliver Wendell Holmes, *Ralph Waldo Emerson* (Boston: Houghton, Mifflin and Co., 1884), 115. I am playing with Holmes's description of Emerson's Phi Beta Kappa Address (1853) as an "intellectual Declaration of Independence."

11. Henry Adams, *The Education of Henry Adams*, ed. Ernest Samuels (Boston: Houghton Mifflin, 1973), 25.

12. Edgar Allan Poe, review of *The Biglow Papers* (First Series), *Southern Messenger* 15 (March 1859): 190. For the reception of this work, see *The Biglow Papers, a Critical Edition*, ed. Thomas Wortham (DeKalb: Northern Illinois University Press, 1977), xxviii–xxxi.

2. Forging Traditions

1. *Memories of a Hostess; A Chronicle of Eminent Friendships, Drawn Chiefly from the Diaries of Mrs. James T. Fields*, ed. Mark De Wolfe Howe (Boston: Atlantic Monthly Press, 1922), 109.

2. William Dean Howells, "My First Trip to New England," in *Literary Friends and Acquaintance: A Personal Retrospect of American Authorship*, ed. David F. Hiatt and Edwin H. Cady (Bloomington: Indiana University Press, 1968), 26–27.

3. John Galsworthy's tribute, *Commemoration of the Centenary of the Birth of James Russell Lowell* (New York: Charles Scribner's Sons, 1919), 11.

4. Robert Underwood Johnson, *Remembered Yesterdays* (Boston: Little, Brown and Co., 1923), 329.

5. Edward Wagenknecht, *James Russell Lowell: Portrait of a Many-Sided Man* (New York: Oxford University Press, 1971), 49–50. James Russell Lowell, "The Darkened Mind," in *The Writings of James Russell Lowell* (Boston: Houghton, Mifflin Co., 1895), 3:243.

6. See C. David Heyman, *American Aristocracy, the Lives and Times of James Russell, Amy, and Robert Lowell* (New York: Dodd, Mead and Co., 1980), 68–69. Heyman notes that Lowell placed himself under the care of Dr. Samuel McKenzie (117).

7. Marian Hooper to R. W. Hooper, 26 January 1879, quoted in Ernest Samuels, *Henry Adams* (Cambridge: Harvard University Press, 1989), 200.

8. Edward Everett Hale, *James Russell Lowell and His Friends* (Boston: Houghton, Mifflin and Co., 1899), 104.

9. Ibid., 114–115.

10. See Wagenknecht, *James Russell Lowell*, 8–9.

11. James Russell Lowell, "The Dead House," *The Complete Poetical Works of James Russell Lowell* (Boston: Houghton Mifflin Co., 1896), 309–310.

12. Horace Elisha Scudder, *James Russell Lowell, a Biography* (Boston: Houghton, Mifflin and Co., 1901), 1:421.

13. James R. Lowell to C. E. Norton, 31 December 1857, *Letters of James Russell Lowell*, ed. Charles Eliot Norton (New York: Harper and Brothers, 1894), 1:281.

14. Scudder, *James Russell Lowell*, 1:421.

15. Ralph Waldo Emerson, 17 January 1862, *Journals and Miscellaneous Notebooks of Ralph Waldo Emerson, 1860–1866*, ed. Linda Allardt et al. (Cambridge: Belknap Press of Harvard University Press, 1982), 15:164.

16. Barrett Wendell, "Mr. Lowell as Teacher," *Scribner's Magazine* 10 (November 1891): 646, 645.

17. Review of *Scenes of Clerical Life* by George Eliot, *Atlantic Monthly* 1 (May 1858): 890–891.

18. Horace Scudder, introduction to *The Complete Poetical Works of James Russell Lowell*, xv.

19. [R. W. Emerson], "Brahma," *Atlantic Monthly* 1 (November 1857): 48.

20. J. F. Trowbridge, "The Author of Quabbin," *Atlantic Monthly* 75 (January 1895): 113.

21. Oliver Wendell Holmes, *Ralph Waldo Emerson* (Boston: Houghton, Mifflin and Co., 1885), 397.

22. [James Russell Lowell], "The Origin of Didactic Poetry," *Atlantic Monthly* 1 (November 1857): 112.

23. M. A. De Wolfe Howe, ed., *New Letters of James Russell Lowell* (New York: Harper, 1932), 99.

24. [Parke Godwin], "The Financial Flurry," *Atlantic Monthly* 1 (November 1857): 115.

25. Edward L. Widmer, *Young America: The Flowering of Democracy in New York City* (New York: Oxford University Press, 1999), 62.

26. [James Russell Lowell], "The Election in November," *Atlantic Monthly* 6 (October 1860): 494.

27. [James Russell Lowell], "The Question of the Hour," *Atlantic Monthly* 7 (January 1861): 120.

28. *Atlantic Monthly* 3 (December 1859), back cover.

29. James Russell Lowell, "E Pluribus Unum," *Atlantic Monthly* 7 (February 1861): 239.

30. Leslie Stephen to Charles Eliot Norton, 11 February 1892, *Letters of James Russell Lowell*, 1:409–411.

31. "The United States and Europe," *Atlantic Monthly* 8 (July 1861): 104.

32. Noel Anan, *Leslie Stephen, the Godless Victorian* (New York: Random House, 1984), 1. Also see pages 54–57 for a description of the Lowell-Stephen friendship.

33. See Wagenknecht, *James Russell Lowell*, 8–9.

34. Leslie Stephen to Charles Eliot Norton, 11 February 1892, *Letters of James Russell Lowell*, 1:409–410.

35. James R. Lowell to C. F. Briggs, December 1848, *Works of James Russell Lowell* (Boston: Houghton Mifflin, 1899), 14:201.

36. "Conversations with Mr. Lowell," *Atlantic Monthly* 79 (January 1897): 128–129.

37. Hale, *James Russell Lowell and His Friends*, 276.

38. See Scudder, *James Russell Lowell*, 2:448.

3. John Brown's War

1. *Atlantic Monthly* 3 (December 1860), back cover.

2. William Lloyd Garrison, *Liberator*, 1 January 1831; rpt. in Wendell Phillips Garrison, *William Lloyd Garrison, 1805–1879: The Story of His Life, Told by His Children* (New York: Century Company, 1885), 1:224–226.

3. See Edward G. Bernard, "New Light on Lowell as Editor," *New England Quarterly* 10 (June 1937): 339.

4. James R. Lowell, "The Pickens-and-Stealin's Rebellion," *Atlantic Monthly* 7 (June 1861): 762.

5. See Eleanor M. Tilton, *Amiable Autocrat: A Biography of Dr. Oliver Wendell Holmes* (New York: Schuman, 1947), 227.

6. Louis Menand, *The Metaphysical Club* (New York: Farrar, Straus and Giroux, 200), 7–9.

7. Moncure D. Conway, *Life of Nathaniel Hawthorne* (1890; rpt. New York: Haskell House, 1968), 206. Also see Randall Stewart, "Hawthorne and the Civil War," *Studies in Philology* 34 (January 1937): 91–106.

8. Nathaniel Hawthorne, "Chiefly about War Matters," in *Nathaniel Hawthorne: Miscellaneous Prose and Verse*, ed. Thomas Woodson, Claude M. Simpson, and L. Neal Smith (Columbus: Ohio State University Press, 1994), 414.

9. Nathaniel Hawthorne, "Chiefly about War Matters, by a Peaceable Man," *Atlantic Monthly* 10 (July 1862): 47. For the history of this article, see James Bense, "Nathaniel Hawthorne's Intention in 'Chiefly about War Matters,'" *American Literature* 61 (May 1989): 200–220, esp. 210. Also see "Chiefly about War Matters," in *The Complete Works of Nathaniel Hawthorne*, ed. George Parsons Lathrop (1883; rpt., Boston: Houghton Mifflin, 1891), 12:312.

10. Nathaniel Hawthorne, "Leamington Spa," *Atlantic Monthly* 10 (October 1862): 451.

11. Moncure D. Conway, *Life of Nathaniel Hawthorne* (1890; rpt., New York: Haskell House, 1968), 206.

12. Henry James, *The American Scene*, ed. Richard Howard, in *Henry James, Collected Travel Writings: Great Britain and America* (New York: Library of America, 1993), 565.

13. Rebecca Harding Davis, *Bits of Gossip* (Boston: Houghton, Mifflin and Co., 1904), iii.

14. Ibid., 165–166.

15. Ibid., 32–33.

16. Ibid., 33.

17. Mary Thatcher Higginson, *Thomas Wentworth Higginson: The Story of His Life* (Boston: Houghton Mifflin, Co., 1914), 97; and Davis, *Bits of Gossip*, 189.

18. Davis, *Bits of Gossip*, 37–38.

19. A. Bronson Alcott, *Concord Days* (Boston: Roberts Brothers, 1872), 13. See *Alcott in Her Own Time*, ed. Daniel Shealy (Iowa City: University of Iowa Press, 2005), insert between pages 152 and 153.

20. John Albee, *Remembrances of Emerson* (New York: Robert Grier Cooke, 1901), 41–42, 46–47.

21. Charles Russell Lowell Jr., "Oration at Commencement 1854," quoted in Edward Waldo Emerson, *Life and Letters of Charles Russell Lowell* (1907; rpt. Columbia: University of South Carolina Press, 2005), 11.

22. Henry David Thoreau, "A Plea for Captain John Brown," in *The Major Essays of Henry David Thoreau*, ed. Richard Dillman (Albany, NY: Whitston, 2002), 85.

23. Ralph Waldo Emerson, epigraph to *Public Life of John Brown, by James Redpath, with an Auto-Biography of His Childhood and Youth* (Boston: Thayer and Eldridge, 1860). Also see his description of Brown in "Courage," in *The Complete Works of Ralph Waldo Emerson*, ed. Edward Waldo Emerson (Boston: Houghton Mifflin Co., 1932), 7:270; and Moncure Daniel Conway, *Emerson at Home and Abroad* (London: Trübner & Co., 1883), 251.

24. Thomas Wentworth Higginson, *Cheerful Yesterdays* (Boston: Houghton, Mifflin and Co., 1898), 228.

25. David Reynolds, *John Brown, Abolitionist: The Man Who Killed Slavery, Sparked the Civil War, and Seeded Civil Rights* (New York: Alfred A. Knopf, 2005), 343.

26. Unsigned, "Public Life of Capt John Brown, by J. Redpath," *Atlantic Monthly* 5 (March 1860): 378, 380, 378.

27. R. H. Dana, "How We Met John Brown," *Atlantic Monthly* 28 (July 1871): 9.

28. See "Nat Turner's Insurrection," *Atlantic Monthly* 8 (August 1861): 173–187.

29. "John Brown and His Friends," *Atlantic Monthly* 30 (July 1872): 61.

30. [O. W. Holmes], "Bread and the Newspaper," *Atlantic* 8 (September 1861): 349.

31. See Thomas P. Slaughter, *Bloody Dawn: The Christiana Riot and Racial Violence in the Antebellum North* (New York: Oxford University Press, 1991); Roderick W. Nash, "William Parker and the Christiana Riot," *Journal of Negro History* 46 (January 1961): 24–31; and Ella Forbes, "'By My Own Right Arm': Redemptive Violence and the 1851 Christiana, Pennsylvania Resistance," *Journal of Negro History* 83 (1998): 159–167.

32. "The Mission to Richmond: A Card from 'Edmund Kirke,' Mr. Davis' Ultimatum," *New York Times* (taken from the *Boston Transcript*), 24 July 1864, p. 8.

33. William Parker, "The Freedman's Story," Part 1, ed. E. K., *Atlantic Monthly* 17 (February 1866): 152–153.

34. William Parker, "The Freedman's Story," Part 2, ed. E. K., *Atlantic Monthly* 17 (March 1866): 283. Also see Jonathan Katz, *Resistance at Christiana: The Fugitive Slave Rebellion, Christiana Pennsylvania, September 11, 1851: A Documentary Account* (New York: Crowell, 1974), 284–290.

35. Katz, *Resistance at Christiana*, 298.

4. The Battle of the Hundred Pines

1. Thomas Wentworth Higginson, "Massachusetts in Mourning," reprinted from *The Worcester Daily Spy* (Boston: James Munroe and Co., 1854), 14.

2. See Howard Schwartz, "Fugitive Slave Days in Boston," *New England Quarterly* 27 (June 1954): 191–212, esp. 204–210.

3. Thomas Wentworth Higginson, journal entry, 23 November 1862, in *The Complete Civil War Journal* and *Selected Letters of Thomas Wentworth Higginson*, ed. Christopher Looby (Chicago: University of Chicago Press, 2000), 42.

4. Thomas Wentworth Higginson, *Army Life in a Black Regiment* (1869; Boston: Beacon Press, 1970), 267.

5. Report of Col. T. W. Higginson, First South Carolina Infantry (Union), 1 February 1863, *The War of the Rebellion: A Compilation of the Official Records of the Union and Confederate Armies*, Series 1 (Washington: Government Printing Office, 1885), 14:195–198.

6. "The Federal Government and the Negro Soldier, 1861–1865," *Journal of Negro History* 11 (October 1926): 575–576.

7. Higginson, *Army Life in a Black Regiment*, 70.

8. Mary Thatcher Higginson, *Thomas Wentworth Higginson, The Story of His Life* (Boston: Houghton, Mifflin Co., 1914), 223.

9. Thomas Wentworth Higginson, "Up the St. Mary's," *Atlantic Monthly* 15 (April 1865): 428.

10. Thomas Wentworth Higginson, "A Night on the Water," *Atlantic Monthly* 14 (October 1864): 399.

11. Ibid., 398, 395.

12. Ibid., 398.

13. Frederick Douglass, "Reconstruction," *Atlantic Monthly* 18 (December 1866): 765.

14. Thomas Wentworth Higginson, "Fair Play the Best Policy," *Atlantic Monthly* 15 (May 1865): 623.

15. See T. W. Higginson, "Some War Scenes Revisited," *Atlantic Monthly* 42 (July 1878): 4.

16. S. Weir Mitchell addressed the carnage in "The Case of George Dedlow" (July 1866), an *Atlantic* story that explores the phantom sensations of an officer who lost all his limbs to amputation and gangrene.

17. *A Diary from Dixie, as Written by Mary Boykin Chesnut, Wife of James Chesnut, Jr., United States Senator from South Carolina, 1859–1861, and Afterward an Aide to Jefferson Davis and a Brigadier-General in the Confederate Army* (New York: D. Appleton and Company, 1905), 231, 404.

18. John Greenleaf Whittier, "The Grave by the Lake," *Atlantic Monthly* 15 (May 1865): 563.

19. C. C. Coffin, "Late Scenes in Richmond," *Atlantic Monthly* 15 (June 1865): 747.

20. Thomas Wentworth Higginson, "Emily Dickinson's Letters," *Atlantic Monthly* 68 (October 1891): 445–446.

21. Ibid., 445.

22. Thomas Wentworth Higginson, preface to *Poems by Emily Dickinson* (Boston: Little, Brown, and Co., 1922), iii.

23. *The Years and Hours of Emily Dickinson*, ed. Jay Leyda (New Haven: Yale University Press, 1960), 2:263.

24. "Thomas Wentworth Higginson," *New York Times*, 21 May 1911, BR314.

25. *The Magnificent Activist: The Writings of Thomas Wentworth Higginson (1823–1911)*, ed. Howard N. Meyer (New York: Da Capo Press, 2002), 354–355.

5. Dueling Visions

1. Louis Agassiz to Rose Agassiz, 2 December 1846; quoted in Edward Lurie, *Louis Agassiz, a Life in Science* (Chicago: University of Chicago Press, 1960), 257.

2. F. E. Melsheimer to Samuel H. Haldeman, 7 November 1846; quoted in ibid., 125. For Agassiz's wheeling and dealing to get to America, see ibid., 114–117, 127.

3. Lucy Allen Payton, *Elizabeth Carey Agassiz: A Biography* (Cambridge: Radcliffe College, 1919), 34.

4. *Proceedings, Agassiz Memorial Meeting, Monday Evening, December 22, 1873*, Mercantile Library Hall (San Francisco: Published by the Academy of Sciences, 1874), 3.

5. Louis Agassiz to Henri Milne Edward, 31 May 1847; quoted in Lurie, *Louis Agassiz*, 124–125.

6. W. G. Farlow, *Memoir of Asa Gray* (Washington, 1890), 763–764.

7. Elias Durand to Asa Gray, 16 April 1859; quoted in Lurie, *Louis Agassiz*, 282.

8. Cited in Adrian Desmond and James Moore, *Darwin* (New York: W. W. Norton, 1991), 456.

9. William Irvine, *Apes, Angels, and Victorians: The Story of Darwin, Huxley, and Evolution* (New York: McGraw-Hill, 1955), 7.

10. See Edward Lurie, *The Founding of the Museum of Comparative Zoölogy*

(Cambridge: Harvard University, Museum of Comparative Zoölogy, 1859), written for the museum's centennial and dated 14 November 1859.

11. "Report to the Committee of Overseers," 28 December 1859; quoted in Lurie, *Louis Agassiz*, 246.

12. Asa Gray to J. D. Hooker, 5 January 1860, *The Correspondence of Charles Darwin*, ed. Frederick Burkhardt and Sidney Smith (Cambridge: Cambridge University Press, 1985), 8:16.

13. Asa Gray, "Darwin on the Origin of Species," *Atlantic Monthly* 6 (July 1860): 109, 110, 111–112, 116.

14. Ibid. (August 1860): 236, 232.

15. Asa Gray, "Darwin and His Reviewers," *Atlantic Monthly* 6 (October 1860): 419–420, 421, 424–425.

16. See Adrian Desmond and James Moore, *Darwin* (New York: W. W. Norton, 1991), 456, 502.

17. See A. Hunter Dupree, *Asa Gray, 1810–1888* (Cambridge: Belknap Press of Harvard University Press, 1959), 299.

18. Oliver Wendell Holmes to Louis Agassiz, 20 October 1862; cited in Lurie, *Louis Agassiz*, 309.

19. Asa Gray to Charles Darwin, 23 November 1863; cited in ibid., 311.

20. L. Agassiz, *Methods of Study in Natural History* (Boston: Ticknor and Fields, 1863), iv.

21. Quoted in *American Heritage Magazine* 28 (June 1977); http://www.americanheritage.com/articles/magazine/ah/1977/4/1977_4_4.shtml.

22. Henry James to Mrs. Henry James Sr., 31 March 1865; quoted in Lurie, *Louis Agassiz*, 347.

23. *Brazil through the Eyes of William James: Diaries, Letters, and Drawings, 1865–1866*, ed. Maria Helena P. T. Machado (Cambridge: Harvard University Press, 2006), 61.

24. Professor and Mrs. Louis Agassiz, *A Journey to Brazil* (Boston: Houghton, Osgood and Co., 1879), 516–571.

6. Reconstructions

1. For a history of Oliver Wendell Holmes Jr.'s regiment, see Richard Miller, *Harvard's Civil War* (Hanover, NH: University Press of New England, 2006). Known officially as the Twentieth Massachusetts Volunteer Infantry, it first faced fire at Ball's Bluff, and after placing its flag on the Confederate works at Yorktown, it went on to stand rear guard for General McClellan's Army of the Potomac during the Seven Days' Campaign. Following the slaughter in Antietam's West Woods, its soldiers confronted Pickett at Gettysburg in July and fought in the Battle of the Wilderness.

2. Oliver Wendell Holmes, "My Hunt after 'the Captain,'" *Atlantic Monthly* 10 (December 1862): 738.

3. Ibid., 752.

4. Ibid., 761.

5. Ibid., 760.

6. Louis Menand, *The Metaphysical Club* (New York: Farrar, Straus and Giroux, 200), 40–41.

7. Oliver Wendell Holmes Jr. to Oliver Wendell Holmes, 20 December 1862; quoted in G. Edward White, *Justice Oliver Wendell Holmes: Law and the Inner Self* (New York: Oxford University Press, 1995), 60.

8. Herbert Mason to his father, 19 September 1862; quoted in Miller, *Harvard's Civil War*, 179.

9. Liva Baker, *The Justice from Beacon Hill, the Life and Times of Oliver Wendell Holmes* (New York: HarperCollins, 1991), 132.

10. Quoted in W. M. Whitehill, *Boston and the Civil War* (Boston: Boston Athenaeum, 1963), 10. Also see Carol Bundy, *The Nature of Sacrifice: A Biography of Charles Russell Lowell, 1835–64* (New York: Farrar, Straus and Giroux, 2005); Thomas K. Tate, "James Russell Lowell's Nephews," *New England Quarterly* 64 (March 1991): 127–129; and Robert D. Richardson, *William James: In the Maelstrom of American Modernism* (Boston: Houghton Mifflin, 2006), 55.

11. Oliver Wendell Homes, "My Hunt after 'the Captain,'" *Atlantic Monthly* 10 (December 1862): 749.

12. Oliver Wendell Holmes Jr. to unnamed correspondent, 26 July 1914; quoted in White, *Justice Oliver Wendell Holmes*, 10.

13. Oliver Wendell Holmes, "The Contagiousness of Puerperal Fever," *New England Quarterly Journal of Medicine* (1843), in *The Works of Oliver Wendell Holmes, Medical Essays* (Boston: Houghton Mifflin and Co., 1891), 9:140.

14. Oliver Wendell Holmes, "The Stereoscope and the Stereograph," *Atlantic Monthly* 3 (June 1859): 747.

15. Ibid., 748.

16. Oliver Wendell Holmes, *The Last Leaf* (Boston: Houghton Mifflin and Co., 1886), 8.

17. William Dean Howells, "Oliver Wendell Holmes," in *Literary Friends and Acquaintance: A Personal Retrospect of American Authorship*, ed. David F. Hiatt and Edwin H. Cady (Bloomington: Indiana University Press, 1968), 134; Weinstein, *The Imaginative Prose of Oliver Wendell Holmes* (Columbia: University of Missouri Press, 2006), 4–6, 26, 48–49.

18. William James to Henry James, 2 October 1869; quoted in Edward Digby Baltzell, *Puritan Boston and Quaker Philadelphia* (New Brunswick, NJ: Transaction, 1996), 14n2.

19. Alexander Woolcott, "The Second Hunt after the Captain," *Atlantic Monthly* 170 (December 1942): 50.

20. Oliver Wendell Holmes Jr., ["In Our Youth Our Hearts Were Touched by Fire"], in *The Collected Works of Justice Holmes: Complete Public Writings and Selected Judicial Opinions of Oliver Wendell Holmes* (Chicago: University of Chicago Press, 1993–), 3:462.

21. Oliver Wendell Holmes Jr., "The Common Law," in *The Collected Works of Justice Holmes*, 3:115.

22. Oliver Wendell Holmes Jr., "Natural Law," in *The Collected Works of Justice Holmes*, 3:446. Holmes writes that "men to a great extent believe what they want to."

23. Holmes Jr., "The Common Law," 3: 115.

24. O. W. Holmes, "The Professor at the Breakfast-Table," *Atlantic Monthly* 4 (December 1859): 757.

25. See Alexander Woolcott, "Get Down, You Fool!" *Atlantic Monthly* 161 (February 1938): 169–173. See also Baker, *The Justice from Beacon Hill*, 151–152.

26. O. W. Holmes, "Doings of the Sunbeam," *Atlantic Monthly* 12 (July 1863): 11–12.

27. Ibid.

7. James and Annie Fields

1. Elizabeth Stuart Phelps, *Chapters from a Life* (Boston: Houghton, Mifflin and Co., 1897), 147.

2. Rose Terry Cooke, "Miss Lucinda," *Atlantic Monthly* 8 (August 1861): 141.

3. Charles Alan Johanningsmeier, *Fiction and the American Literary Marketplace: The Role of Newspaper Syndicates in America, 1860–1900* (New York: Cambridge University Press, 1997), 15.

4. W. D. Howells, "The Man of Letters as a Man of Business," *Literature and Life* (New York: Harper's & Brothers, 1902), 9.

5. Ellery Sedgwick, *The Atlantic Monthly, 1857–1909, Yankee Humanism at High Tide and Ebb* (Amherst: University of Massachusetts Press, 1994), 56.

6. Warren S. Tryon, *Parnassus Corner: A Life of James T. Fields, Publisher to the Victorians* (Boston: Houghton Mifflin, 1963), 294.

7. The poet was George S. Hillard. See Jeffrey D. Groves, "Judging Literary Books by Their Covers: House Styles, Ticknor and Fields, and Literary Styles," *Essays on the Material Text and Literature in America*, ed. Michele Moylan and Lane Stiles (Amherst: University of Massachusetts Press, 1996), 87–88. Also see Groves, "Ticknor-and-Fields-ism of All Kinds": Thomas Starr King, Literary Promotion, and Canon Formation," *New England Quarterly* 68 (June 1995): 214; and Tryon, *Parnassus Corner*, 31.

8. Quoted in Tryon, *Parnassus Corner*, 378.

9. Ibid., 226.

10. Rebecca Harding Davis, *Bits of Gossip* (Boston: Houghton, Mifflin and Co., 1904), 54; Martin Green, *The Problem of Boston: Some Readings in Cultural History* (New York: Norton, 1966), 78.

11. Quoted in Anne E. Boyd, *Writing for Immortality: Women and the Emergence of High Culture in America* (Baltimore: John Hopkins University Press, 2004), 203. Also see Boyd, "What! Has She Got Into the 'Atlantic'? Women Writers, the *Atlantic Monthly*, and the Formation of the American Canon," *American Studies* 39 (Fall 1998): 5–36.

12. Tryon, *Parnassus Corner*, 85, 189.

13. William M. Riding, "Literary Life in Boston," *American Magazine* 6 (1887): 52.

14. Mark Twain to William Dean Howells, 18 May 1880, in *Mark Twain's Letters*, ed. Albert B. Paine (New York: Harper & Brothers, 1912), 379.

15. Henry James Jr., "Mr. and Mrs. Fields," *Atlantic Monthly* 116 (July 1915): 25. See also Harriet Prescott Spofford, *A Little Book of Friends* (Boston: Little Brown, 1916), 16–17.

16. Willa Cather, "148 Charles Street," in *Not under Forty* (New York: Knopf, 1936), 73.

17. Henry James, *The American Scene*, ed. Richard Howard, in *Henry James, Collected Travel Writings*, 556; Cather, "148 Charles Street," 61. The house was originally numbered as 34 Charles Street.

18. Harriet Beecher Stowe, *Life and Letters of Harriet Beecher Stowe*, ed. Annie Fields (Boston: Houghton Mifflin, 1898), 340–341.

19. Spofford, A *Little Book of Friends*, 16–17.

20. Cather, "148 Charles Street," 64.

21. Ibid., 58. See Susan K. Harris, *The Literary Work of the Late Nineteenth-Century Hostess* (New York: Palgrave, 2002). Harris focuses on Annie Fields and Mary Gladstone.

22. Helen Maria Winslow, *Literary Boston of To-Day* (Boston: L. C. Page, 1902), 60.

23. Annie Fields, 16 July 1879, in *Memories of a Hostess; A Chronicle of Eminent Friendships, Drawn Chiefly from the Diaries of Mrs. James T. Fields*, ed. Mark De Wolfe Howe (Boston: Atlantic Monthly Press, 1922), 119–120.

24. James, "Mr. and Mrs. Fields," 28.

25. Cather, "148 Charles Street," 73.

26. Spofford, *A Little Book of Friends*, 6.

8. Harriet Beecher Stowe Tests the Magazine

1. Annie Fields, *Life and Letters of Harriet Beecher Stowe* (Boston: Houghton Mifflin and Co, 1897), 376.

2. See Charles Edward Stowe, *The Life of Harriet Beecher Stowe* (New York: Harper & Brothers, 1889), 445–447.

3. Annie Fields, "Days with Mrs. Stowe," in *Authors and Friends* (Boston: Houghton Mifflin, 1895), 164–165.

4. Harriet Beecher Stowe to Annie Fields, 28 May [1860], quoted in Rita K. Gollin, *Annie Fields, Woman of Letters* (Amherst: University of Massachusetts Press, 2002), 137.

5. [Harriet Beecher Stowe], "The Minister's Wooing," *Atlantic Monthly* 2 (December 1858): 877, 878, 884. For a discussion of this novel, I am indebted to Joan D. Hedrick's excellent biography, *Harriet Beecher Stowe: A Life* (Oxford: Oxford University Press, 1993), 279–282.

6. Arthur Gilman, "Atlantic Dinners and Diners," *Atlantic Monthly* 100 (November 1907): 648.

7. Thomas Wentworth Higginson to Louisa Storrow Higginson, 10 July 1869, in *Letters and Journals of Thomas Wentworth Higginson*, ed. Mary Thatcher Higginson (Boston: Houghton Mifflin, 1921), 208–209.

8. Arthur Gilman, "Atlantic Dinners and Diners," *Atlantic Monthly* 100 (November 1907): 657.

9. [Harriet Beecher Stowe,] "House and Home Papers, I," *Atlantic Monthly* 13 (January 1864): 46; and Hedrick, *Harriet Beecher Stowe*, 314–316.

10. [Harriet Beecher Stowe], "House and Home Papers, II," *Atlantic Monthly* 13 (February 1864): 206.

11. Hedrick, *Harriet Beecher Stowe*, 318.

12. Harriet Beecher Stowe to James Fields, 3 June 1864, quoted in James C. Austin, *Fields of the Atlantic Monthly* (San Marino, CA: Huntington Library, 1953), 278.

13. Justin McCarthy, "Mrs. Stowe's Last Romance, Letter to the Editor of *The Independent*," 26 August 1869; rpt. in Elizabeth Ammons, *Critical Essays on Harriet Beecher Stowe* (Boston: G. K. Hall, 1980), 169–172.

14. Luther Mott, *History of American Magazines, 1741–1820* (Cambridge: Harvard University Press, 1930), 2:509.

15. Quoted in "Forty Years of the *Atlantic Monthly*," *Atlantic Monthly* 80 (October 1897): 572.

16. Quoted in Austin, *Fields of the Atlantic Monthly*, 290–291.

17. Harriet Beecher Stowe, "The True Story of Lady Byron's Life," *Atlantic Monthly* 143 (September 1869): 302.

18. Ibid., 296, 302.

19. Harriet Beecher Stowe to W. D. Howells, n.d. [July 1869]; quoted in Hedrick, *Harriet Beecher Stowe*, 362.

20. James Russell Lowell to Edmund Quincy, 15 September 1869, in *New Letters of James Russell Lowell*, ed. M. A. De Wolfe Howe (New York: Harper, 1932), 146.

21. William Dean Howells to William Cooper Howells, 22 September 1869, in *Selected Letters of William Dean Howells*, ed. George Arms et al. (Boston: Twayne, 1879–1983), 1:339–340.

22. William Dean Howells to James T. Fields, 24 August 1869, in ibid., 1:334.

23. McCarthy, "Mrs. Stowe's Last Romance," 169–172. Also see "The Moral of the Byron Case," *Independent*, 9 September 1869, rpt. in Ammons, *Critical Essays*, 174–176.

24. Austin, *Fields of the Atlantic Monthly*, 294.

25. W. D. Howells, "Literary Boston as I Knew It," in *Literary Friends and Acquaintance: A Personal Retrospect of American Authorship*, ed. David F. Hiatt and Edwin H. Cady (Bloomington: Indiana University Press, 1968), 120.

26. Harriet Beecher Stowe to James R. Osgood, n.d., quoted in Hedrick, *Harriet Beecher Stowe*, 366.

27. "The Stowe Garden Party—Supplement," *Atlantic Monthly* 50 (August 1882): A012–A013.

28. Charles Edward Stowe and Lyman Beecher Stowe, *Harriet Beecher Stowe, the Story of Her Life* (Boston: Houghton Mifflin Co., 1911), 275–276.

29. Stowe, "The True Story of Lady Byron's Life," 305.

30. Algernon Charles Swinburne, *Essays and Studies* (London: Chatto & Windus, 1888), 240.

31. Oliver Wendell Holmes to Harriet Beecher Stowe, 25 September 1869; Charles Edward Stowe, *The Life of Harriet Beecher Stowe* (Boston: Houghton Mifflin and Co, 1889), 456.

9. Battle of the Books

1. Harriet Prescott Spofford, "Biographical Sketch," *Gail Hamilton's Life in Letters*, ed. Augusta Dodge (Boston: Lee and Shepard, 1901), 1:ix–xiv.

2. Fanny Fern [Sara Payson Parton], "Gail Hamilton—Miss Dodge," in *Eminent Women of the Age: Being Narratives of the Lives and Deeds of the Most Prominent Women of the Present Generation*, ed. James Parton (Hartford: S. M. Betts and Company, 1869), 1:84–85.

3. Dodge, *Gail Hamilton's Life in Letters*, 1:506.

4. Fern, "Gail Hamilton—Miss Dodge," 203.

5. Harriet Prescott Spofford, *A Little Book of Friends* (Boston: Little Brown, 1916), 97.

6. Quoted in Warren S. Tryon, *Parnassus Corner: A Life of James T. Fields, Publisher to the Victorians* (Boston: Houghton Mifflin, 1963), 223.

7. Quoted in ibid., 346.

8. Mary Abigail Dodge to [Wood], 23 March 1868, in Dodge, *Gail Hamilton's Life in Letters*, 2:611–612. For a detailed account of this dispute, see Susan

Coultrap-McQuin, *Doing Literary Business: American Women Writers in the Nineteenth Century* (Chapel Hill: University of North Carolina Press, 1990), 120–135. Also see James C. Austin, *Fields of the Atlantic Monthly* (San Marino, CA: Huntington Library, 1953), 312–313; Tryon, *Parnassus Corner*, 334–349; and Rita K. Gollin, *Annie Adams Fields, Woman of Letters* (Boston: University of Massachusetts Press, 2002), 89–91.

9. Gail Hamilton, *A Battle of the Books* (Boston: H. O. Houghton, 1870), 4.

10. Quoted in Randall Stewart, "'Pestiferous Gail Hamilton,' James T. Fields, and the Hawthornes," *New England Quarterly* 17 (September 1944): 423.

11. Hamilton, *A Battle of the Books*, 119.

12. Ibid., 2, 285, 288.

13. Stewart, "'Pestiferous Gail Hamilton,' James T. Fields, and the Hawthornes," 421–423.

14. Spofford, *A Little Book of Friends*, 18. Also see Richard H. Brodhead, *Culture of Letters: Scenes of Reading and Writing in Nineteenth-Century America* (Chicago: University of Chicago Press, 1993), 154–157.

15. William Dean Howells, "Literary Boston as I Knew It," in *Literary Friends and Acquaintance: A Personal Retrospect of American Authorship*, ed. David F. Hiatt and Edwin H. Cady (Bloomington: Indiana University Press, 1968), 107.

16. Michael Winship, *American Literary Publishing in the Mid-Nineteenth Century: The Business of Ticknor and Fields* (Cambridge: Cambridge University Press, 1995), 190.

17. William Dean Howells, "The Man of Letters as a Man of Business," in *Life and Literature*, 1.

10. Henry David Thoreau, John Burroughs, and a Changing Magazine

1. H. D. Thoreau, "Walking," *Atlantic Monthly* 9 (June 1862): 665, 657.

2. [Ralph Waldo Emerson], "The Forester," *Atlantic Monthly* 9 (April 1862): 444, 443; Daniel Shealy, ed., *Alcott in Her Own Time* (Iowa City: University of Iowa Press, 2005), 16.

3. Henry David Thoreau to James Russell Lowell, 22 June 1858, in *The Correspondence of Henry David Thoreau*, ed. Walter Harding and Carl Bode (New York: New York University Press, 1959), 515–516.

4. William Dean Howells, "My First Visit to New England," in *Literary Friends and Acquaintance: A Personal Retrospect of American Authorship*, ed. David F. Hiatt and Edwin H. Cady (Bloomington: Indiana University Press, 1968), 54.

5. Austin Warren, "Lowell on Thoreau," *Studies in Philology* 27 (July 1930): 446, 452–461. Also see Ellery Sedgwick, *The Atlantic Monthly, 1857–1909, Yankee Humanism at High Tide and Ebb* (Amherst: University of Massachusetts Press, 1994), 60.

6. Henry David Thoreau to James Russell Lowell, 22 June 1858, in *The Correspondence of Henry David Thoreau*, 515–516.

7. *Writings of James Russell Lowell* (Boston: Houghton Mifflin, 1904), 2:139, 150.

8. A new edition of *A Week on the Concord and Merrimack Rivers* and *Seasons*, extracted from his journal and a 1906 manuscript edition of his works, established Thoreau's reputation into the next century. See Walter Harding, "Thoreau's Reputation," in *The Cambridge Companion to Thoreau*, ed. Joel Myerson (Cambridge: Cambridge University Press, 1995), 1–11. See also Lawrence Buell, "Henry Thoreau Enters the Literary Canon," in *New Essays on Walden*, ed. Robert Sayre (New York: Cambridge University Press, 1992), 36.

9. H. D. Thoreau, "Walking," *Atlantic Monthly* 9 (June 1862): 665, 666.

10. Ibid., 668.

11. John Burroughs, "Henry D. Thoreau," Part 1, *Century* 24 (July 1882): 369.

12. John Burroughs, "The Divine Soil," *Atlantic Monthly* 101 (April 1908): 446.

13. See "Children Give Party for John Burroughs," *New York Times*, 12 April 1912; and Stephen M. Mercier, "Ornithological Testimonies: Letters to John O'Birds," *American Transcendental Quarterly* 21 (1 December 2007): 275.

14. See Dallas Lore Sharp, *The Boys' Life of John Burroughs* (New York: Century Co., 1928; rpt. Whitefish, MT: Kessinger, 2007), 89.

15. John Burroughs, "With the Birds," *Atlantic Monthly* 15 (May 1865): 514.

16. John Burroughs, *The Writings of John Burroughs*, vol. 1: *Wake-Robin* (Boston: Houghton Mifflin Co., 1895), xv.

17. John Burroughs, "The Poet and the Modern," *Atlantic Monthly* 78 (October 1896): 566.

18. Walt Whitman, *Leaves of Grass* (Boston: Small, Maynard & Co., 1904), 78.

19. C. C. Coffin, "Communication with the Pacific," *Atlantic Monthly* 17 (March 1866): 333, 343. Also see Charles Sumner, "Prophetic Voices about America: A Monograph," *Atlantic Monthly* 20 (September 1867): 306.

20. M. Ed Brown, "A Winter Adventure on the Prairie," *Atlantic Monthly* 19 (April 1867): 501.

21. Rev. I. N. Tarbox, "Old Connecticut vs. *The Atlantic Monthly*," *New Englander* (24 April 1865): 319, 323. Tarbox took offense to F. Sheldon's "The Pleiades of Connecticut," published in the *Atlantic*'s February 1865 issue.

22. [John Weiss], "War and Literature," *Atlantic Monthly* 9 (June 1862): 683.

23. Thomas W. Higginson, "Americanism in Literature," *Atlantic Monthly* 25 (January 1870): 57. Higginson quotes the historian Jeremiah Whipple.

11. William Dean Howells

1. William Dean Howells, "My First Visit to New England," in *Literary Friends and Acquaintance: A Personal Retrospect of American Authorship*, ed. David F. Hiatt and Edwin H. Cady (Bloomington: Indiana University Press, 1968), 16.

2. Elinor M. Howells to William C. Howells, 23 January 1866, in *If Not Literature: Letters of Elinor Mead Howells*, ed. Ginette de B. Merrill and George Arms (Columbus: Published for Miami University by the Ohio State University Press), 93.

3. Howells, "My First Visit to New England," 21.

4. W. D. Howells, *Years of My Youth* (New York: Harper & Brothers, 1916), 122, 178.

5. Howells, "Literary Boston as I Knew It," in *Literary Friends and Acquaintance*, 102.

6. Ibid., 117.

7. Annie Howells to W. D. Howells, 17 October 1877, Alfred University; quoted in Susan Goodman and Carl Dawson, *William Dean Howells: A Writer's Life* (Berkeley: University of California Press, 2005), 140–141.

8. W. D. Howells to Hamlin Garland, 23 July 1917; quoted in ibid., 388.

9. See Philip F. Gura, "The View from Quabbin Hill," *New England Quarterly* 60 (March 1987): 94.

10. C. W. Eliot, "The New Education: Its Organization," *Atlantic Monthly* 23 (February 1869): 203.

11. James Russell Lowell, "Oration [Given at Harvard's 250th Anniversary]," Supplement to *Atlantic Monthly* 58 (December 1886): a016.

12. John T. Morse, *Life and Letters of Dr. Oliver Wendell Holmes* (Boston: Houghton, Mifflin and Co., 1896), 2:187.

13. Eliot, "The New Education," 367.

14. Ibid.

15. W. D. Howells to Henry James, 2 January and 6 March 1870, in *Selected Letters of William Dean Howells*, ed. and annotated by George Arms et al. (Boston: Twayne, 1879–1983), 1:354.

16. W. D. Howells, "Recollections of an *Atlantic* Editorship," *Atlantic Monthly* 100 (November 1907): 601–602.

17. Howells, "The Man of Letters as a Man of Business," in *Life and Literature*, 23.

18. W. D. Howells, *My Mark Twain: Reminiscences and Criticism* (New York: Harper's & Bros., 1910), 4. See also Howells, "Recollections of an *Atlantic* Editorship," *Atlantic Monthly* 100 (November 1907): 596.

19. Howells, *My Mark Twain*, 4.

20. Ibid. See also Howells, "Recollections of an *Atlantic* Editorship," 596.

21. Unsigned review, "Mark Twain's *The Adventures of Tom Sawyer*," *Atlantic Monthly* 37 (May 1876): 620–622.

22. Sam Clemens to W. D. Howells, 22 September 1889, *Mark Twain-Howells Letters: The Correspondence of Samuel L. Clemens and William D. Howells, 1872–1910*, ed. Henry Nash Smith and William M. Gibson (Cambridge: Harvard University Press, 1960), 2:613.

23. W. D. Howells, "Professor Barrett Wendell's Notions of American Literature," in *Selected Literary Criticism*, ed. Ulrich Halfmann, Donald Pizer, and Ronald Gottesman (Bloomington: Indiana University Press, 1993), 3:50.

24. Sam Clemens to W. D. Howells, 18 January 1876, in *Mark Twain-Howells Letters*, 1:121; Howells, *My Mark Twain*, 60.

25. W. D. Howells to Sam Clemens, 21 November 1875, *Mark Twain-Howells Letters*, 1:110–111. See Alan Gribben, "Manipulating a Genre: *Huckleberry Finn*, as Boy Book," *South Central Quarterly* 5 (Winter 1988): 15–21.

26. Mark Twain, "Sixty-Seventh Birthday," 28 November 1902, in *Mark Twain's Speeches*, intro. by William Dean Howells (New York: Harper, 1910), 187.

27. See G. MacLaren, *Morally We Roll Along* (Boston: Little, Brown and Co., 1938), 66; quoted in *The Wit and Wisdom of Mark Twain*, ed. Alex Ayres (New York: Harper & Row, 1987), 10.

28. Ellery Sedgwick, *The Atlantic Monthly, 1857–1909, Yankee Humanism at High Tide and Ebb* (Amherst: University of Massachusetts Press, 1994), 297. Also see Shirley Marchalonis, "Women Writers and the Assumption of Authority: The *Atlantic Monthly*, 1857–1898," in *In Her Own Voice: Nineteenth-Century American Women Essayists*, ed. Shirley Lee Linkon (New York: Garland, 1997), 17.

29. Harriet Waters Preston, "Latest Novels of Howells and James," *Atlantic Monthly* 91 (January 1903): 80, 77, 79.

30. A. Schade van Westrum, "Mr. Howells on Love and Literature," in *Interviews with William Dean Howells*, ed. Ulrich Halfmann, special issue of *American Literary Realism* 6 (Fall 1973): 352.

31. Samuel Clemens to W. D. Howells, 22 August [1878], *Mark Twain-Howells Letters*, 1:21.

32. W. D. Howells to Edmund C. Steadman, 12 December 1876, in *Selected Letters of William Dean Howells*, 2:141n1.

33. Robert Underwood Johnson, *Remembered Yesterdays* (Boston: Little, Brown and Co., 1923), 319; and W. D. Howells to Samuel Clemens, 10 October 1876, *Mark Twain-Howells Letters*, 1:156–157.

34. W. D. Howells, "Editorial," *Atlantic Monthly* 39 (January 1877): 100.

35. Johnson, *Remembered Yesterdays*, 319; and W. D. Howells to Samuel Clemens, 10 October 1876, in *Mark Twain-Howells Letters*, 1:156–157.

36. Philip B. Eppard and George Monteiro, *A Guide to The Atlantic Monthly Contributors' Club* (Boston: G. K. Hall, 1983), xviii–xiv.

37. "The Contributor's Club," *Atlantic Monthly* 40 (September 1877): 364.

38. See *Atlantic Monthly* 39 (January 1877): 100; and Philip B. Eppard, "Mark Twain Dissects an Overrated Book," *American Literature* 49 (November 1977): 430–440.

39. Mark Twain, "An Overrated Book," *Atlantic Monthly* 39 (June 1877): 738–741.

40. "Amusements: Bret Harte's New Drama. 'The Two Men of Sandy Bar' at Union Square Theatre," *New York Times*, 29 August 1876, section 5, p. 5.

41. *New York Sun*, 14 September 1876, section 2, p. 6; rpt. in the *Boston Transcript*, 15 September 1876, section 4, pp. 1–2. I am indebted to Gary Scharnhorst for details about this controversy. See Scharnhorst, *Bret Harte* (New York: Twayne, 1992), 52–59.

42. "The Contributors' Club," *Atlantic Monthly* 40 (October 1877): 488.

43. Howells, "The Man of Letters as a Man of Business," 2.

12. John Greenleaf Whittier's Seventieth Birthday

1. "The Whittier Dinner," *Boston Daily Advertiser*, 18 December 1877, p. 1. All descriptions come from this article unless otherwise noted. The epigraph comes from Howells's speech, reprinted in the *Boston Globe*, 18 December 1877. For reprinted speeches and newspaper accounts, see http://etext.virginia.edu/railton/onstage/whittier.html (accessed 30 March 2011).

2. *Mark Twain-Howells Letters: The Correspondence of Samuel L. Clemens and William D. Howells, 1872–1910*, ed. Henry Nash Smith and William M. Gibson (Cambridge: Harvard University Press, 1960), 1:212n1; Howells, *My Mark Twain: Reminiscences and Criticism* (New York: Harper's & Bros., 1910), 60.

3. *Boston Globe*, 18 December 1877.

4. Howells to Twain, 8 December 1974, in Smith and Gibson, *Mark Twain-Howells Letters*, 1:46.

5. "Mark Twain's Offense against Good Taste" (from the *Cincinnati Gazette*), *Boston Globe*, 26 December 1877.

6. Howells, *My Mark Twain*, 53.

7. Mark Twain, "Chapters from My Autobiography," *North American Review* 598 (7 September 1906): 488–489. For an analysis of the occasion, see Richard S. Lowery, *Littery Man: Mark Twain and Modern Authorship* (New York: Oxford University Press, 1996), 24–33.

8. Frances Elizabeth Willard, *Glimpses of Fifty Years: The Autobiography of an American Woman*, published by the Woman's Temperance Publication Association (Chicago: H. J. Smith & Co., 1889), 549–550. Also see Willard's

anonymously published "The Atlantic-Whittier Dinner—A Woman's Thoughts Thereon," *Boston Daily Advertiser*, 20 December 1877, p. 1.

9. "The Absence of Women at the Whittier Dinner," *Boston Daily Advertiser*, 18 December 1877, p. 2.

10. "Whittier, a Famous Dinner in His Honor—Women Not Invited—A Forgotten Skit about It," *New York Times*, 24 February 1900, BR3.

11. "The Holmes Breakfast," *Atlantic Monthly* 45, Supplement (February 1880): A007–A008.

12. *Mark Twain's Notebook*, ed. Albert Bigelow Paine (Harper & Brothers, 1935), 344.

13. William Dean Howells to Mark Twain, 14 February 1904, in *Selected Letters of William Dean Howells*, ed. George Arms et al. (Boston: Twayne, 1879–1983), 5:77–78.

13. Bret Harte to the Lions

1. Henry Adams, *The Education of Henry Adams*, ed. Ernest Samuels (Boston: Houghton Mifflin, 1973), 259.

2. Samuel Clemens to W. D. Howells, 27 June 1878, in *Mark Twain–Howells Letters: The Correspondence of Samuel L. Clemens and William D. Howells, 1872–1910*, ed. Henry Nash Smith and William M. Gibson (Cambridge: Harvard University Press, 1960), 1:235.

3. *Mark Twain Letters*, ed. A. B. Paine (New York: Harper & Bros., 1917), 1:182–183.

4. Samuel L. Clemens to T. B. Aldrich, 15 January [1871], in Ferris Greenslet, *The Life of Thomas Bailey Aldrich* (Boston: Houghton Mifflin Co., 1908), 95.

5. Unsigned, "Reviews and Literary Notices," *Atlantic Monthly* 25 (May 1870): 633.

6. Quoted in Axel Nissen, *Bret Harte: Prince and Pauper* (Jackson: University Press of Mississippi, 2000), xv.

7. Bret Harte to W. D. Howells, 5 August 1869, in *Selected Letters of Bret Harte*, ed. Gary Scharnhorst (Norman: University of Oklahoma Press, 1997), 29.

8. W. D. Howells, "Editor's Easy Chair," *Harper's* 108 (December 1903): 155.

9. Bret Harte to James R. Osgood, 6 March 1871, in *Selected Letters of Bret Harte*, 48–49.

10. Bret Harte, "The Poet of Sierra Flat," *Atlantic Monthly* 28 (July 1871): 116, 120. See J. David Stevens, "'She war a woman': Family Roles, Gender, and Sexuality in Bret Harte's Western Fiction," *American Literature* 69 (September 1997): 571–593.

11. Charles Warren Stoddard, "Early Recollections of Bret Harte," *Atlantic Monthly* (November 1896): 678.

12. W. D. Howells to W. C. Howells, 22 January 1871, in *Selected Letters of*

William Dean Howells, ed. George Arms et al. (Boston: Twayne, 1879–1983), 1:363–364.

13. "Bret Harte and Mark Twain in the 'Seventies,' Pages from the Diaries of Mrs. James T. Fields," ed. Mark De Wolfe Howe, *Atlantic Monthly* 122 (September 1922): 342–348.

14. See Gary Scharnhorst, *Bret Harte: Opening the American Literary West* (Norman: University of Oklahoma Press, 2000), 78; and Scharnhorst, *Bret Harte* (New York: Twayne, 1992), 45.

15. Elinor M. Howells to "Dear Girls," [17 March 1871], *If Not Literature*, 137.

16. W. D. Howells to William C. Howells, 26 February 1871; quoted in Susan Goodman and Carl Dawson, *William Dean Howells: A Writer's Life* (Berkeley: University of California Press, 2005), 136.

17. Henry James to Elizabeth Boot, [April 1871], in *The Selected Letters of Henry James*, ed. Leon Edel (New York: Farrar, Straus, and Cudahy, 1955), 40–41.

18. Bret Harte to W. D. Howells, 25 March 1872, quoted in Scharnhorst, *Bret Harte*, 44.

19. Gary Scharnhorst, "W. D. Howells and Bret Harte: The Star System in Nineteenth-Century American Literature," *Essays in Arts and Science* 25 (October 1996): 104.

20. Scharnhorst, *Bret Harte: Opening the Literary West*, 85.

21. Bret Harte, "Grandmother Tenterden," *Atlantic Monthly* 29 (January 1872): 105–106.

22. W. D. Howells to Samuel Clemens, in *Mark Twain–Howells Letters*, 1:162; W. D. Howells, "Editorial," *Atlantic Monthly* 39 (January 1877): 103.

23. W. D. Howells to Matthew Brander, 22 July 1911, in *Life in Letters of William Dean Howells*, ed. Mildred Howells (Garden City, NY: Doubleday, Doran, 1928), 2:301.

24. Oliver Wendell Holmes to John L. Motley, 16 November 1862, in *The Life and Letters of Oliver Wendell Holmes*, ed. John T. Morse Jr. (Boston: Houghton, Mifflin and Co., 1897), 195–199.

25. Ellen Ballou, *The Building of the House: Houghton Mifflin's Formative Years* (Boston: Houghton, Mifflin, 1970), 200. On 28 December 1879, another fire struck the Boston office of Houghton, Osgood & Co., with a loss amounting to $1.5 million. Before the debris had a chance to cool and axes freed the water-sodden paper from its bins, a secretary had begun notifying customers that all orders would be filled (ibid., 270).

26. See ibid., 200.

27. Bret Harte to James R. Osgood, 18 November 1872, in *Selected Letters of Bret Harte*, 73.

28. Bret Harte to Anna Harte, 19 October [1873], in *The Letters of Bret Harte*, ed. Geoffrey Bret Harte (Boston: Houghton Mifflin, 1926), 26.

29. Bret Harte to Samuel Clemens, 1 April 1872; quoted in Margaret Duckett, *Mark Twain and Bret Harte* (Norman: University of Oklahoma Press, 1964), 76.

30. Bret Harte to Clemens, 1 March 1877, in ibid., 134–137.

31. Quoted in Anthony Arthur, *Literary Feuds: A Century of Celebrated Quarrels—From Mark Twain to Tom Wolfe* (New York: Thomas Dunne Books, 2002), 15.

32. *Cincinnati Gazette*, 10 January 1878, section 5, p. 4.

33. Mark Twain to W. D. Howells, 21 June 1877, quoted in Francis Murphy, "The End of a Friendship: Two Unpublished Letters from Twain to Howells about Bret Harte," *New England Quarterly* 58 (March 1985): 89–90.

34. W. D. Howells to Rutherford B. Hayes, 27 June 1878, in *Selected Letters of William Dean Howells*, 2:235.

35. Howells, *My Mark Twain: Reminiscences and Criticism* (New York: Harper's & Bros., 1910), 8.

36. Charles Warren Stoddard, "Early Recollections of Bret Harte," *Atlantic Monthly* (November 1896): 678.

14. Straddling the Atlantic

1. Edith Wharton to Sara Norton, 5 June 1903, in *The Letters of Edith Wharton*, ed. R. W. B. Lewis and Nancy Lewis (New York: Charles Scribner's Sons, 1988), 84–85.

2. Henry James, "George Eliot's Life," *Atlantic Monthly* 55 (May 1885): 668, 678.

3. Henry James to H. G. Wells, 1915, in *Henry James Letters*, ed. Leon Edel (Cambridge: Belknap Press of Harvard University Press, 1974–1984), 4:770.

4. W. D. Howells to Edmund C. Stedman, 5 December 1866, in *Selected Letters of William Dean Howells*, ed. George Arms et al. (Boston: Twayne, 1879–1983), 1:271.

5. W. D. Howells to James Russell Lowell, 22 June 1878, in ibid., 2:231.

6. There are many lists of the hundred best books. See, for example, http://www.greatbooksguide.com/OneHundredGreatestNovels.html; http://www.randomhouse.com/modernlibrary/100bestnovels.html (accessed 30 March 2011).

7. Sharon O'Brien, *Willa Cather: The Emerging Voice* (New York: Oxford University Press, 1987), 297.

8. Henry James, "The Art of Fiction," in *Henry James: Literary Criticism*, ed. Leon Edel (New York: Library of America, 1984), 53; Willa Cather, *Willa Cather on Writing* (Lincoln: University of Nebraska Press, 1988), 37.

9. Henry James, *Notes of a Son and Brother*, in *Henry James: Autobiography*, ed. Frederick W. Dupee (New York: Criterion, 1956), 277.

10. Henry James, "Preface to *The Spoils of Poynton*," in *The Art of the Novel*, ed. R. P. Blackmur (New York: Charles Scribner's Sons, 1934), 129–130.

11. "Book Reviews: James's Partial Portraits," *Atlantic Monthly* 62 (October 1888): 566.

12. "Books Reviewed: Henry James: *Essays in London and Elsewhere*," *Atlantic Monthly* 73 (February 1894): 267.

13. Henry James, "The Novels of George Eliot," *Atlantic Monthly* 18 (October 1866): 479, 480, 492.

14. Howells, *Literature and Life* (New York: Harper's & Brothers, 1902), 202.

15. "Book Reviews: James's *Portrait of a Lady* [and] Howell's [*sic*] *Dr. Breen's Practice*," *Atlantic Monthly* 49 (January 1882): 128–129.

16. Henry James, "Miss Woolson," in *Henry James: Literary Criticism*, ed. Leon Edel (New York: Library of America, 1984), 1:640, 649.

17. William Dean Howells, "Henry James Jr.," *Century Magazine*, November 1882, in *Letters, Fictions, Lives*, 234.

18. I am borrowing from Henry James's list of all America lacks in "Hawthorne," in *Literary Criticism: Essays on Literature, American Writers, English Writers*, ed. Leon Edel (New York: Library of America, 1984), 351–352.

19. George Moore, *Confessions of a Young Man* (Montreal: McGill-Queen's University Press, 1972), 152.

20. Unsigned, "What Is an American?" *Atlantic Monthly* 35 (May 1875): 561–562.

21. Henry James, "Recent Florence," *Atlantic Monthly* 41 (May 1878): 591–592.

22. See Albert Camus, *Notebooks, 1935–1942*, trans. Philip Thody (New York: Harcourt Brace Jovanovich, 1978), 13–14.

15. Clarence King, Scholar-Adventurer

1. William H. Brewer, in Clarence King, *Clarence King Memoirs* (New York: Putnam, 1904), 54.

2. See Robert Wilson, *The Explorer King: Adventure, Science, and the Great Diamond Hoax* (New York: Scribner, 2006), 55. King attended Agassiz's lectures in 1863, after graduating from Yale's Sheffield Scientific School.

3. Clarence King, "Mountaineering in the Sierra Nevada," Part 3, *Atlantic Monthly* 28 (July 1871): 71–72.

4. Ibid., 68–69, 71–72.

5. Ibid., 76.

6. Ibid.

7. *John Muir: His Life and Letters and Other Writings*, ed. Terry Gifford (Seattle: Mountaineers Books, 1996), 194–195. Also see Donald Worster's excellent biography, *A Passion for Nature: The Life of John Muir* (New York: Oxford University Press, 2008).

8. John Hay quoting an unnamed friend, in King, *Clarence King Memoirs*, 131–132.

9. See J. D. Hague in ibid., 397; S. F. Emmons, "Clarence King," *Engineering and Mining Journal* (4 January 1902): 9; and E. B. Bronson, "A Man of East and West," *Century* 130 (July 1910): 376–382. Also see Robert Berkelman, "Clarence King: Scientific Pioneer," *American Quarterly* 5 (Winter 1953): 301–324.

10. William Dean Howells to Rutherford B. Hayes, 4 January 1879, *Life in Letters of William Dean Howells*, ed. Mildred Howells (Garden City, NY: Doubleday, Doran, 1928), 1:261–262.

11. Clarence King, "Kaweah's Run," Part 4, *Atlantic Monthly* 28 (October 1871): 402.

12. King, *Clarence King Memoirs*, 319.

13. Clarence King, "Wayside Pikes," *Atlantic Monthly* 28 (November 1871): 572.

14. Henry Adams, *The Education of Henry Adams*, ed. Ernest Samuels (Boston: Houghton Mifflin, 1973), 346.

15. King, "Kaweah's Run," 404.

16. Brewer, in King, *Clarence King Memoirs*, 54.

17. Howells, in ibid., 139.

18. Adams, *The Education of Henry Adams*, 416.

19. See Martha A. Sandweiss, *Passing Strange: A Gilded Age Tale of Love and Deception across the Color Line* (New York: Penguin, 2009), 253–255, 288–289.

20. Samuel Franklin Emmons, "Biographical Memoir of Clarence King," *Biographical Memoirs* 6 (Washington, DC: National Academy of Sciences, 1909).

21. "Mr. Beecher's Vacation Sermons," *New York Times*, 14 August 1876, p. 8.

22. Thomas Sergeant Perry, "Mountains in Literature," *Atlantic Monthly* 44 (September 1879): 311.

16. The Gilded Eighties

1. Mark Twain, "The Revised Catechism," *New York Tribune*, 27 September 1871; quoted in Arthur L Vogelback, "Mark Twain and the Tammany Ring," *PMLA* 7 (March 1955): 69.

2. Wayne Craven, *Gilded Mansions: Grand Architecture and High Society* (New York: W. W. Norton, 2009), 8. Craven dates the Gilded Age from 1865 to approximately 1918.

3. Bernard Berenson to Mary Berenson, September 1897; quoted in Ernest

Samuels, *Bernard Berenson: The Making of a Connoisseur* (Cambridge: Belknap Press of Harvard University Press, 1979), 286.

4. Isabella Stewart Gardner to Bernard Berenson, 20 January [1898], in *The Letters of Isabella Stewart Gardner and Bernard Berenson*, ed. Rollin N. van Halley (Boston: Northeastern University Press, 1987), 125.

5. Henry Adams to Isabella Gardner, 9 February 1906; quoted in Douglass Shand-Tucci, *The Art of Scandal: The Life and Times of Isabella Stewart Gardner* (New York: HarperCollins, 1997), 237.

6. Henry James, *The American Scene*, in *Henry James, Collected Travel Writings: Great Britain and America*, ed. Richard Howard (New York: Library of America, 1993), 564.

7. Bliss Perry, *The Saturday Club* (Boston: Houghton, Mifflin, 1958), 5–6; reprinted in Clara Kirk, *W. D. Howells and Art in His Time* (New Brunswick, NJ: Rutgers University Press, 1965), 314–315.

8. "Zola's Essays," *Atlantic Monthly* 47 (January 1881): 117.

9. Henry Demarest Lloyd, "Story of a Great Monopoly," *Atlantic Monthly* 47 (March 1881): 322, 333, 334.

10. Ellery Sedgwick, "Henry James and the '*Atlantic Monthly*': Editorial Perspectives on James' Friction with the Market," *Studies in Bibliography* 45 (1992): 317.

11. Arthur John, *The Best Years of the Century: Richard Watson Gilder, Scribner's Monthly, and the Century, 1870–1909* (Urbana: University of Illinois Press, 1981), 213, 236.

12. Ibid., 126–128.

13. Luther Mott, *A History of American Magazines, 1865–1885* (Cambridge: Belknap Press of Harvard University Press, 1957), 3:459. For an overview of *Scribner's* and the *Century*, see ibid., 458–480.

14. Richard Watson Gilder to G. W. Cable, 1 February 1882; quoted in John A. Tomsich, *A Genteel Endeavor: American Culture and Politics in the Gilded Age* (Palo Alto, CA: Stanford University Press, 1971), 122.

15. Richard Watson Gilder to Editor of the AM, 10 January 1906, Houghton Library, Houghton Mifflin Papers, Box 1 (40), bMS Am 1925.1.

16. See John, *The Best Years of the Century*, 119.

17. Kermit Vanderbilt, Introduction to William Dean Howells, *The Rise of Silas Lapham* (New York: Penguin, 1986), xiii–xiv.

18. Richard Watson Gilder to G. W. Cable, 1 February 1882; quoted in Tomsich, *A Genteel Endeavor*, 122.

19. Thomas Hardy to Thomas Bailey Aldrich, 13 January 1882; quoted in Carl J. Weber, "Thomas Hardy and His New England Editors," *New England Quarterly* 15 (December 1942): 685.

20. Weber, "Thomas Hardy and His New England Editors," 688–689.

21. Carl J. Weber, "More about Lowell's 'Dead Rat,'" *New England Quarterly* 9 (December 1936): 687.

22. Carl J. Weber, "Lowell's Dead Rat in the Wall," *New England Quarterly* 9 (September 1936): 471.

23. Edmund Gosse to W. D. Howells, 19 November 1886, quoted in Evan Chateris, *The Life and Letters of Sir Edmund Gosse* (New York: Harper & Brothers, 1931), 200.

24. James R. Lowell to Charles Eliot Norton, 26 October 1886, in *Letters of James Russell Lowell*, ed. Charles Eliot Norton (New York: Harper and Brothers, 1894), 2:319.

25. They included "An Adventure of Huckleberry Finn: With an Account of the Famous Grangerford-Shepherdson Feud" (December 1884), "Jim's Investments and King Sollermun" (January 1885), and "Royalty on the Mississippi" (February 1885).

26. See James, *The Art of the Novel*, ed. R. P. Blackmur (New York: Charles Scribner's Sons, 1934), 59–61.

27. Henry James, "The Princess Casamassima," *Atlantic Monthly* 57 (March 1886): 346.

28. Henry James, "The Princess Casamassima," *Atlantic Monthly* 57 (May 1886): 656.

29. Ibid., 645.

30. George Woodcock, *Anarchism: A History of Libertarian Ideas and Movements* (Peterborough, Canada: Broadview, 2004), 376–377.

31. George Frederic Parsons, "The Labor Question," *Atlantic Monthly* 58 (July 1886): 112.

17. Thomas Bailey Aldrich, Guardian at the Gate

1. Ferris Greenslet, *The Life of Thomas Bailey Aldrich* (Boston: Houghton Mifflin Co., 1908), 142.

2. Johnson, *Remembered Yesterdays*, 362.

3. Ibid., 201.

4. Greenslet, *The Life of Thomas Bailey Aldrich*, 145.

5. See Mark Twain, *Mark Twain in Eruption: Hitherto Unpublished Pages about Men and Events*, ed. Mark DeVoto (New York: Harper & Brothers, 1940), 293–295.

6. Henry James to Alice James, 29 May 1870, in *Letters/Henry James*, ed. Leon Edel (Cambridge: Belknap Press of Harvard University Press, 1974–1984), 2:235.

7. Albert B. Paine, *Mark Twain, a Biography* (New York: Harper, 1912), 1:537–538.

8. Edith Wharton to F. Scott Fitzgerald, 8 June 1925, in *The Letters of Edith*

Wharton, ed. R. W. B. Lewis and Nancy Lewis (New York: Charles Scribner's Sons, 1988), 481.

9. Thomas Bailey Aldrich, *The Poems of Thomas Bailey Aldrich: The Revised and Complete Household Edition* (Boston: Houghton Mifflin, 1897), 273–274.

10. J. P. Logan, "American Prose Style," *Atlantic Monthly* 87 (May 1901): 29.

11. For a chart of poems and their percentage, see Reinhold Schiffer, "Small Expectations: Poetry and Criticism of Poetry in the *Atlantic Monthly* between 1890 and 1905," in *American Poetry between Tradition and Modernism, 1865–1914*, ed. Roland Hagenbüchle (Regensburg: Pustet, 1984), 21–22.

12. Greenslet, *The Life of Thomas Bailey Aldrich*, 151.

13. John Jay Chapman to Annie Fields, 27 September 1891, in *John Jay Chapman and His Letters*, ed. Mark De Wolfe Howe (Boston: Houghton Mifflin, 1937), 86.

14. Thomas Bailey Aldrich to Edmund C. Stedman, 20 November 1880; quoted in Greenslet, *The Life of Thomas Bailey Aldrich*, 303. For an overview of Whitman's relationship to the magazine, see Portia Baker, "Walt Whitman and *The Atlantic Monthly*," *American Literature* 6 (November 1934): 283–301.

15. "Whitman's *Leaves of Grass*," *Atlantic Monthly* 49 (January 1882): 126.

16. Oliver Wendell Holmes, "Over the Teacups," *Atlantic Monthly* 66 (September 1890): 237–238.

17. Allen Walker Read, "The Membership in Proposed American Academies," *American Literature* 7 (May 1935): 155.

18. See Ellen Ballou, *The Building of the House: Houghton Mifflin's Formative Years* (Boston: Houghton, Mifflin, 1970), 378–379.

19. Charles Egbert Craddock, "The Prophet of the Smokey Mountains," *Atlantic Monthly* 55 (January 1885): 1.

20. Charles Chesnutt to Houghton Mifflin, summer 1891; quoted in Helen Chesnutt, *Charles Waddell Chesnutt* (Chapel Hill: University of North Carolina Press, 1953), 68–69.

21. Charles W. Chesnutt, "The Goophered Grapevine," *Atlantic Monthly* 60 (August 1887): 259–260.

22. "Plantation Tales," a review of *The Conjure Woman*, in "Literature," *Morning Times* [Washington], 9 April 1899, 20.

23. William Dean Howells, "Mr. Charles W. Chesnutt's Stories," *Atlantic Monthly* 85 (May 1900): 699–701.

24. William Dean Howells to Henry Blake Fuller, 10 November 1901, in in *Selected Letters of William Dean Howells*, ed. George Arms et al. (Boston: Twayne, 1879–1983), 4:274.

25. Thomas Bailey Aldrich, "At the Funeral of a Minor Poet," in *The Poems of Thomas Bailey Aldrich* (Boston: Houghton Mifflin Co., 1907), 2:94.

26. William Stanley Braithwaite, "On the Death of Thomas Bailey Aldrich,

II," in *The House of Falling Leaves with Other Poems* (Boston: John W. Luce and Co., 1908), 25–26.

27. *Autobiography of Mark Twain*, ed. Charles Neider (New York: Harper, [1959]), 468–469.

28. Ibid., 358.

29. *Nation* 42 (25 February 1886): 171.

18. In the Wake of Louis Agassiz

1. See G. Frederick Wright, "Agassiz and the Ice Age," *American Naturalist* 32 (March 1898): 166.

2. *Louis Agassiz, His Life and Correspondence*, ed. Elizabeth Agassiz (Boston: Houghton, Mifflin and Co., 1885), 783.

3. Oliver Wendell Holmes, "Farewell to Agassiz," in *The Poetical Works of Oliver Wendell Holmes* (Boston: Houghton, Mifflin and Co., 1892), 2:98.

4. Proceedings, Agassiz Memorial Meeting, Monday Evening, December 22, 1873, Mercantile Library Hall (San Francisco: Published by the Academy of Sciences, 1874), 10.

5. Journal of Addison E. Verrill, 26 January 1860; quoted in Edward Lurie, *Louis Agassiz, a Life in Science* (Chicago: University of Chicago Press, 1960), 240.

6. James Russell Lowell, "Agassiz," *Atlantic Monthly* 33 (May 1874): 587.

7. William James to Henry James, 12–15 September 1865, in *The Letters of William James*, ed. by his son Henry James (Boston: Atlantic Monthly Press, 1920), 1:65.

8. Unsigned review of *Louis Agassiz, His Life and Correspondence*, *Atlantic Monthly* 56 (December 1885): 848.

9. See Samuel H. Scudder, "In the Laboratory with Agassiz," *Every Saturday* 16 (4 April 1974): 369–370.

10. William James to Nathaniel S. Shaler, [1901?], in *The Letters of William James*, 153.

11. Donald Johnson, "W. E. B. DuBois, Thomas Jesse Jones and the Struggle for Social Education, 1900–1930," *Journal of Negro History* 85 (Summer 2000): 72. Also see David N. Livingstone, "Science and Society: Nathaniel S. Shaler and Racial Ideology," *Transactions of the Institute of British Geographers* 9 (1984): 181–210.

12. N. S. Shaler, "Martha's Vineyard," *Atlantic Monthly* 34 (December 1874): 734.

13. N. S. Shaler, "Natural History of Politics," *Atlantic Monthly* 43 (March 1879): 310.

14. N. S. Shaler, *The Neighbor* (Boston: Houghton Mifflin Co., 1904), 191, vii.

15. N. S. Shaler, "Race Prejudices," *Atlantic Monthly* 58 (October 1886): 518.

16. N. S. Shaler, "The Immigration Problem Historically Considered," *America* 1 (1888): 2.

17. N. S. Shaler, "The Negro Problem," *Atlantic Monthly* 54 (November 1884): 697.

18. Livingstone, "Science and Society," 181.

19. John Spencer Clark, *The Life and Letters of John Fiske* (Boston: Houghton Mifflin, 1917), 139.

20. Quoted in Ronald E. Martin, *American Literature and the Universe of Force* (Durham, NC: Duke University Press, 1981), 71.

21. Mark Twain, "Taxes and Morals," in *Mark Twain's Speeches*, intro. by William Dean Howells (New York: Harper, 1910), 112.

22. See Albert Bushnell Harte, "John Fiske's Services to History," *New York Times*, 12 October 1901, Saturday Review of Books and Art, BR11.

23. "The Doctrine of Evolution," in *A Century of Science and Other Essays* (Boston: Houghton, Mifflin, 1902), 40. Also see Martin, *American Literature and the Universe of Force*, 70–71.

24. Theodore Dreiser, *A Book about Myself* (New York: Liveright, 1929), 458.

25. *1876: A Centennial Exhibition*, ed. Robert C. Post (Washington, DC: Smithsonian Institution Press, 1976), 22.

26. W. D. Howells, "A Sennight of the Centennial," *Atlantic Monthly* 38 (July 1876): 96.

27. Henry Adams, *The Education of Henry Adams*, ed. Ernest Samuels (Boston: Houghton Mifflin, 1973), 379.

28. For one of the few discussions of "The Brazen Android," see Jerome Loving, *Walt Whitman's Champion: William Douglas O'Connor* (College Station: Texas A&M University Press, 1978), 44–47. Based on a legend about Francis Bacon, its characters include Henry III and Simon de Monfort.

19. A Magazine in Decline and Ascension

1. John Hope Franklin, "Edward Bellamy and the Nationalist Movement," *New England Quarterly* 11 (December 1938): 740, 759.

2. Thomas W. Higginson, "Edward Bellamy's Nationalism," in *The Magnificent Activist: The Writings of Thomas Wentworth Higginson (1823–1911)*, ed. Howard N. Meyer (New York: Da Capo, 2000), 388.

3. Henry Van Brunt, "The Columbian Exposition and American Civilization," *Atlantic Monthly* 71 (May 1893): 577, 579.

4. Bliss Perry, *And Gladly Teach* (Boston: Houghton Mifflin Co., 1935), 166.

5. Ellen Ballou, *The Building of the House: Houghton Mifflin's Formative Years* (Boston: Houghton, Mifflin, 1970), 437.

6. Johnson, *Remembered Yesterdays*, 392.

7. Ellery Sedgwick, *The Atlantic Monthly, 1857–1909, Yankee Humanism at High Tide and Ebb* (Amherst: University of Massachusetts Press, 1994), 201.

8. "The Scudder Family: The New Editor of the *Atlantic Monthly* and His Relatives," *New York Times*, 13 July 1890, p. 8.

9. Horace Scudder, diary, 5 July 1898; quoted in Sedgwick, *The Atlantic Monthly, 1857–1900*, 241.

10. Horace Scudder, 17 June 1890; quoted in ibid., 206.

11. In-house fighting led to a break with the publisher Charles Scribner's Sons and *Scribner's Monthly*'s reincarnation as the more conservative *Century Illustrated Monthly* (1881–1899).

12. Sedgwick, *The Atlantic Monthly, 1857–1900*, 23.

13. Oliver Wendell Holmes to James Russell Lowell, 7 October 1882, in *The Life and Letters of Oliver Wendell Holmes*, ed. John T. Morse Jr. (Boston: Houghton, Mifflin and Co., 1897), 1:221–222.

14. See Ellery Sedgwick, *The Happy Profession* (Boston: Little, Brown, 1948), 178.

15. Horace Scudder to W. P. Garrison, 30 June 1891; quoted in Ballou, *The Building of the House*, 441.

16. Edmund C. Stedman, "On a Great Man Whose Mind Is Clouding," *Atlantic Monthly* 49 (March 1882): 399.

17. Oliver Wendell Holmes, "James Russell Lowell," *Atlantic Monthly* 68 (October 1891): 553.

18. John Greenleaf Whittier, "To Oliver Wendell Holmes," *Atlantic Monthly* 70 (September 1892): 402.

19. Oliver Wendell Holmes, "In Memory of John Greenleaf Whittier," *Atlantic Monthly* 70 (November 1892): 648, 649.

20. The Editor [Horace Scudder], "Dr. Holmes," *Atlantic Monthly* 74 (December 1894): 833.

21. Horace Scudder, "Authorship in America," *Atlantic Monthly* 51 (June 1883): 817.

22. The Editor, "Dr. Holmes," 833–834.

20. From the Far East to Mars

1. Van Wyck Brooks, *Fenollosa and His Circle, with Other Essays in Biography* (New York: E. P. Dutton and Co., 1962), 59; and Curtis Prout, "William Sturgis Bigelow: Brief Life of an Idiosyncratic Brahmin, 1850–1926," *Harvard Magazine* 1 (September 1997): 50. Also available at http://harvardmagazine.com/1997/09/vita.html.

2. "Recent Books on Japan," *Atlantic Monthly* 75 (June 1892): 830, 831.

3. Lafcadio Hearn, "The Genius of Japanese Civilization," *Atlantic Monthly* 76 (October 1895): 457.

4. Lafcadio Hearn to Ellwood Kenwood, August 1895, in *The Life and Letters of Lafcadio Hearn*, ed. Elizabeth Bisland (Boston: Houghton Mifflin, 1906), 2:272.

5. Lafcadio Hearn to Elizabeth Bisland, 1890, in ibid., 2:3.

6. Quoted in ibid., 1:294. Also see *The Writings of Lafcadio Hearn* (Boston: Houghton Mifflin, 1922), 13:294. Also see Carl Dawson, *Lafcadio Hearn and the Vision of Japan* (Baltimore: Johns Hopkins University Press, 1992).

7. Quoted in Brooks, *Fenollosa and His Circle*, 26.

8. Lafcadio Hearn, "The Genius of Japanese Civilization," *Atlantic Monthly* 76 (October 1895): 451.

9. John Greenleaf Whittier, "Hymn," in *Poems of American History*, ed. Burton Egbert Stevenson (Boston: Houghton Mifflin Co., 1908), 573.

10. Lafcadio Hearn, "The Japanese Smile," *Atlantic Monthly* 71 (May 1893): 644.

11. Hearn, "The Genius of Japanese Civilization," 458.

12. Lafcadio Hearn, "Dust," *Atlantic Monthly* 78 (November 1896): 644.

13. Hearn, "The Genius of Japanese Civilization," 453.

14. James L. Huffman, *A Yankee in Meiji Japan: The Crusading Journalist Edward H. House* (Lanham, MD: Rowman and Littlefield, 2003), 30–31.

15. Quoted in Wrexie Louise Leonard, *Percival Lowell: An Afterglow* (Boston: Badger, 1921), 25. Also see Ferris Greenslet, *The Lowells and Their Seven Worlds* (Boston: Houghton Mifflin Co., 1936), 366; and A. L. Lowell, *Biography of Percival Lowell* (New York: Macmillan, 1935).

16. Greenslet, *The Lowells and Their Seven Worlds*, 355.

17. "Japanese Miracles and Trances; *Occult* Japan," *New York Times*, 30 December 1894, p. 23.

18. Percival Lowell, "Noto: An Unexplored Corner of Japan," *Atlantic Monthly* 67 (January 1891): 1.

19. Ibid., 15.

20. Percival Lowell, "Fate of a Japanese Reformer," *Atlantic Monthly* 66 (November 1890): 692.

21. Percival Lowell, "Soul of the Far East," *Atlantic Monthly* 60 (September 1887): 406.

22. Percival Lowell, "Mars," *Atlantic Monthly* 76 (August 1895): 234–235.

23. Lafcadio Hearn to Basil Hall Chamberlain, 14 January 1893, in *The Japanese Letters of Lafcadio Hearn*, ed. Elizabeth Bisland (Boston: Houghton Mifflin Co., 1910), 30.

24. W. D. Howells, "On Coming Back," *Atlantic Monthly* 78 (October 1896): 563–564.

21. Booker T. Washington and W. E. B. Du Bois

1. Booker T. Washington, *Up from Slavery* (New York: Doubleday & Co., 1963), 160.

2. Booker T. Washington, "My View of Segregation Laws," *New Republic* (September 1915): 113–114.

3. "Choate and Twain Plead for Tuskegee," *New York Times*, 23 January 1906, p. 1.

4. *Mark Twain's Autobiography*, ed. Albert B. Paine (New York: P. F. Collier, 1924), 2:3. See pp. 1–4 for description of the Carnegie Hall event.

5. Mark Twain, *The Tragedy of Pudd'nhead Wilson* (Hartford, CT: Wilson Publishing Co., 1933), 33.

6. Paine, *Mark Twain's Autobiography*, 2:2.

7. Mary Austin, *Earth Horizon*, ed. Melody Graulich (Albuquerque: University of New Mexico Press, 1991), 347.

8. Samuel Clemens to Francis Wayland, 24 December 1885, in Shelley Fisher Fishkin, *Lighting Out for the Territory: Reflections on Mark Twain and American Culture* (New York: Oxford University Press, 1998), 101.

9. "Choate and Twain Plead for Tuskegee," *New York Times*, 23 January 1906, p. 1.

10. Booker T. Washington, "The Awakenings of the Negro," *Atlantic Monthly* 78 (September 1896): 332–334.

11. Booker T. Washington, "The Case of the Negro," *Atlantic Monthly* 84 (November 1899): 584.

12. See *The Autobiography of W. E. B. Du Bois*, 159, 162, 170–71, 197, 183. Also see David Levering Lewis, *W. E. B. Du Bois: Biography of a Race, 1868–1919* (New York: Henry Holt, 1993), 134–135. I have relied on this splendid biography for the facts of Du Bois's life and his relationship to the NAACP.

13. "The Niagara Movement, Address to the Country," *Pamphlets and Leaflets by W. E. B. Du Bois*, ed. Herbert Aptheker (White Plains, NY: Kraus-Thomson, 1986), 63. The riot in Springfield took place on 14 August 1908.

14. W. E. Burghardt Du Bois, "Strivings of the Negro People," *Atlantic Monthly* 80 (August 1897): 194.

15. Ibid.

16. Ibid., 198, 197. Also see T. W. Higginson, "Negro Spirituals," *Atlantic Monthly* 19 (June 1867): 685–694.

17. W. E. Burghardt Du Bois, "A Negro Schoolmaster in the New South," *Atlantic Monthly* 83 (January 1899): 105.

18. Booker T. Washington, "The Case of the Negro," *Atlantic Monthly* 84 (November 1899): 584.

19. Bliss Perry, *And Gladly Teach* (Boston: Houghton Mifflin Co., 1935), 181.

20. W. E. B. Du Bois, "The Training of Black Men," *Atlantic Monthly* 90 (September 1902): 297.

21. "The Night President Teddy Roosevelt Invited Booker T. Washington to Dine at the White House," *Journal of Blacks in Higher Education* 35 (Spring 2002): 24–25.

22. Mark Twain, *Mark Twain in Eruption: Hitherto Unpublished Pages about Men and Events*, ed. Mark DeVoto (New York: Harper & Brothers, 1940), 30.

23. Washington, "The Case of the Negro," 586.

24. Henry James, Preface to "Lady Barbarina," in *The Art of the Novel: Critical Prefaces by Henry James*, ed. Richard P. Blackmur (New York: Charles Scribner's Sons, 1934), 203. See letter of W. E. B. Du Bois to Herbert Aptheker, 10 January 1956, in *The Correspondence of W. E. B. Du Bois*, ed. Herbert Aptheker (Amherst: University of Massachusetts Press, 1973), 3:394–396. Also see letter of Henry James to W. E. B. Du Bois, 9 August 1907, *Correspondence*, 1:134. James writes to tell Du Bois that he will call on him in London, but Aptheker notes that the two never met.

25. Frederick Douglass, "An Appeal to Congress for Impartial Suffrage," *Atlantic Monthly* 19 (January 1867): 113.

22. Progressive Politics under Walter Hines Page

1. F. N. Doubleday, *The Memoirs of a Publisher* (New York: Doubleday, 1972), 186–187.

2. Walter Hines Page to E. L. Godkin, 31 January 1899; quoted in Sedgwick, *Atlantic Monthly, 1857–1909*, 260.

3. [Walter Hines Page], "The War with Spain, and After," *Atlantic Monthly* 81 (June 1898): 727.

4. Burton J. Hendrick, *The Life and Letters of Walter Hines Page* (Garden City, NY: Doubleday, Page & Co., 1923), 1:55.

5. Walter Hines Page, *A Publisher's Confession* (Garden City, NY: Doubleday, Page & Co., 1905), 46.

6. Walter Page to Ellen Glasgow, 8 December 1897; quoted in *The Training of an American: The Early Life and Letters of Walter H. Page, 1855–1913*, ed. Burton J. Hendrick (Boston: Houghton Mifflin, 1928), 336–337.

7. Frank Norris, "Comida: An Experience in Famine," *Atlantic Monthly* 83 (March 1899): 343.

8. Walter Hines Page to John MacMaster, 6 October 1896; quoted in Sedgwick, *Atlantic Monthly, 1857–1909*, 250.

9. Manuscript report 6743; quoted in Ellen Ballou, *The Building of the House: Houghton Mifflin's Formative Years* (Boston: Houghton, Mifflin, 1970), 455–456.

10. John Burroughs, "Camping with the President," *Atlantic Monthly* 97 (May 1906): 595.

11. Woodrow Wilson, "Character of Democracy in the United States," *Atlantic Monthly* 64 (November 1889): 588.

12. Theodore Roosevelt, "The College Graduate and Public Life," *Atlantic Monthly* 74 (August 1894): 260.

13. Bliss Perry, *And Gladly Teach* (Boston: Houghton Mifflin Co., 1935), 224.

14. Brooks Adams to Ellery Sedgwick, 23 March 1912, Ellery Sedgwick Papers, Carton 2, Massachusetts Historical Society, Boston; and Mark Twain, *Mark Twain in Eruption: Hitherto Unpublished Pages about Men and Events*, ed. Mark DeVoto (New York: Harper & Brothers, 1940), 12.

15. Perry, *And Gladly Teach*, 184–185.

16. Jacob A. Riis, *The Making of an American* (New York: Macmillan, 1901), 144.

17. Theodore Roosevelt, *Outlook* 149 (6 June 1914): xvi.

18. Jacob A. Riis, "Out of the Book of Humanity," *Atlantic Monthly* 78 (November 1896): 698.

19. Jacob A. Riis, "The Tenement House Blight," *Atlantic Monthly* 84 (July 1899): 761.

20. Jacob A. Riis, "The Battle with the Slum," *Atlantic Monthly* 83 (May 1899): 631.

21. Jacob A. Riis, "The Genesis of the Gang," *Atlantic Monthly* 84 (September 1899): 302, 308.

22. Jacob A. Riis, "Reform by Humane Touch," *Atlantic Monthly* 84 (December 1899): 745, 753.

23. Robert Erskine Ely, "Prince Kropotkin," *Atlantic Monthly* 82 (September 1898): 346. Also see Alex Butterworth, *The World That Never Was: A True Story of Dreamers, Schemers, Anarchists and Secret Agents* (New York: Pantheon, 2010).

24. Bliss Perry, "Whittier," *Atlantic Monthly* 100 (December 1907): 856.

23. From Sea to Shining Sea

1. John Muir, "The Forests of Yosemite Park," *Atlantic Monthly* 85 (April 1900): 505–507.

2. John Muir, "The American Forests," *Atlantic Monthly* 80 (August 1897): 156.

3. Ibid., 146.

4. John Burroughs, "Camping with President Roosevelt," *Atlantic Monthly* 97 (May 1906): 586.

5. John Burroughs, "Real and Sham Natural History," *Atlantic Monthly* 91 (March 1903): 303.

6. Mark Twain, *Mark Twain in Eruption: Hitherto Unpublished Pages about Men and Events*, ed. Mark DeVoto (New York: Harper & Brothers, 1940), 20–21.

7. Perry, *And Gladly Teach*, 171.

8. Carey McWilliams, *Los Angeles Times*, 14 September 1934, p. A4.

9. Mary Austin, *Earth Horizon*, ed. Melody Graulich (Albuquerque: University of New Mexico Press, 1991), 188.

10. Mary Austin, "A Shepherd of the Sierra," *Atlantic Monthly* 86 (July 1900): 54.

11. Mary Austin, *The Land of Little Rain*, intro. by T. M. Pearce (Albuquerque: University of New Mexico Press, 1974), 59.

12. Mary Hallock Foote to Austin, 12 October 1902; quoted in Susan Goodman and Carl Dawson, *Mary Austin and the American West* (Berkeley: University of California Press, 2009), 62.

13. Ansel Adams, "A Note on the Land and on the Photographs," in Mary Austin, *The Land of Little Rain*, with photographs by Ansel Adams; introduction by Carl Van Doren (Boston: Houghton Mifflin, 1950), 109.

14. Austin to Alfred Vincent Kidder, [1929]; quoted in Goodman and Dawson, *Mary Austin and the American West*, 67.

15. Mary Austin, "The Walking Woman," *Atlantic Monthly* 100 (August 1907): 220, 219.

16. Carl Van Vechten, *Spider Boy* (New York: Alfred A. Knopf, 1928), 168.

17. George Bird Grinnell, "The Wild Indian," *Atlantic Monthly* 83 (January 1899): 20.

18. Ibid., 25.

19. H. L. Dawes, "Have We Failed the Indian?" *Atlantic Monthly* 83 (August 1899): 285.

20. Zitkala-Sa, "The School Days of an Indian Girl," *Atlantic Monthly* 85 (February 1900): 191.

21. Zitkala-Sa, "An Indian Teacher among Indians," *Atlantic Monthly* 85 (March 1900): 385.

22. Ibid.

23. Zitkala-Sa, "Why I Am a Pagan," *Atlantic Monthly* 90 (December 1902): 802–803.

24. Zitkala-Sa, *Old Indian Legends* (Boston: Ginn & Co., 1902), vi.

25. Frederick Jackson Turner, "Contributions of the West to American Democracy," *Atlantic Monthly* 91 (January 1903): 95–96.

26. *Atlantic Monthly* 92 (July 1903): 1.

24. A State of Uncertainty

1. Edith Wharton to Bliss Perry, 9 November 1903; in Ellery Sedgwick, *The Atlantic Monthly, 1857–1909, Yankee Humanism at High Tide and Ebb* (Amherst: University of Massachusetts Press, 1994), 289–290.

2. Ibid.

3. Edith Wharton, "The House of the Dead Hand," *Atlantic Monthly* 94 (August 1904): 146.

4. Edith Wharton, "The Long Run," *Atlantic Monthly* 109 (February 1912): 163.

5. Lyman Abbott, "Why Women Do Not Wish the Suffrage," *Atlantic Monthly* 92 (September 1903): 289.

6. "Woman's Work in the World Is Marriage; Man the Breadwinner and Provider," *New York Times*, 22 September 1907, p. SM3.

7. Anna A. Rogers, "Why American Marriages Fail," *Atlantic Monthly* 100 (September 1907): 290, 292–293. Rogers followed her *Atlantic* article on marriage with another titled "Why American Mothers Fail" (March 1908).

8. Henry James, "The Speech of American Women," Part 1, *Harper's Bazaar* 40, no. 11 (November 1906): 980. Also see *French Writers and American Women Essays*, ed. Peter Buitenhaus (Branford, CT: Compass, 1960), 33.

9. Rogers, "Why American Marriages Fail," 293.

10. Edith Wharton, *French Ways and Their Meaning* (New York: D. Appleton-Century Co., 1919), 132, 148.

11. Edith Wharton, "A Motor-Flight through France," *Atlantic Monthly* 98 (December 1906): 734.

12. James Huneker, "The Evolution of an Egoist: Maurice Barrès," *Atlantic Monthly* 100 (August 1907): 214.

13. Arthur M. Knapp, "Who Are the Japanese?" *Atlantic Monthly* 110 (September 1912): 340.

14. Edith Wharton, *Fighting France: From Dunkerque to Belfort* (New York: Charles Scribner's Sons, 1915), 234.

15. Kelly Miller, "The Ultimate Race Problem," *Atlantic Monthly* 103 (April 1909): 542.

16. Bliss Perry, *Park Street Papers* (Boston: Houghton Mifflin Co., 1908), 51.

17. Ibid., 14.

18. Bliss Perry, "Fishing with a Worm," *Atlantic Monthly* 93 (May 1904): 702, 704.

19. Jack London, *Revolution and Other Essays* (New York: Macmillan Co., 1910), 1.

20. Perry, *Park Street Papers*, 14.

21. Bliss Perry to Henry James, 31 October 1899; quoted in Sedgwick, *Atlantic Monthly, 1857–1909*, 280.

22. Perry, *Park Street Papers*, 50.

23. Bliss Perry, "A Readable Proposition," *Atlantic Monthly* 95 (January 1905): 1–2, 4.

24. See Charles Hirschfeld, "Brooks Adams and American Nationalism," *American Historical Review* 69 (January 1964): 372, 381. Also see Brooks

Adams, "A Problem with Civilization," *Atlantic Monthly* 105 (January 1910): 26–32.

25. Perry, *Park Street Papers*, 14–15.

25. Ellery Sedgwick

1. Frederick Lewis Allen, "Sedgwick and the *Atlantic*," *Outlook and Independent* 150 (26 December 1928): 1406.

2. Ellery Sedgwick, *The Happy Profession* (Boston: Little, Brown, 1948), 180.

3. Ibid., 178. See Michael E. Chapman, "Pro-Franco Anti-Communism: Ellery Sedgwick and the *Atlantic Monthly*," *Journal of Contemporary History* 41 (October 2006): 641–662.

4. Sedgwick, *The Happy Profession*, 154.

5. Ibid.

6. See Sedgwick, *The Happy Profession*, 158–159.

7. "The Diary of Gideon Welles," *Atlantic Monthly* 103 (February 1909): 154.

8. "Mr. Welles on Lincoln," *New York Times*, 1 February 1909, p. 8.

9. Ellery Sedgwick to Mary Antin, 17 July 1911, Ellery Sedgwick Papers, Carton 2, Massachusetts Historical Society, Boston.

10. Annie Winslow Allen to Ellery Sedgwick, 6 December 1919, Ellery Sedgwick Papers, Carton 2, Massachusetts Historical Society, Boston.

11. Sedgwick, *The Happy Profession*, 187, 197.

12. Elizabeth Shepley Sergeant, "Mary Austin: A Portrait," *Saturday Review of Literature* 11 (8 September 1934): 36.

13. Mary Austin to Daniel T. MacDougal, 28 January [1922]; quoted in Susan Goodman and Carl Dawson, *Mary Austin and the American West* (Berkeley: University of California Press, 2009), 208.

14. Ellery Sedgwick to Amy Lowell, 1 July 1921; in Ellery Sedgwick III, "'Fireworks': Amy Lowell and *The Atlantic Monthly*," *New England Quarterly* 51 (December 1978): 503.

15. Sedgwick, *The Happy Profession*, 175–176; Ellery Sedgwick to Amy Lowell, 8 October 1914, quoted in Ellery Sedgwick III, "'Fireworks,'" 492.

16. Amy Lowell, "Fireworks," *Atlantic Monthly* 115 (April 1915): 512.

17. Letter to the Editor, 4 May 1919; quoted in Ellery Sedgwick III, "'Fireworks,'" 502.

18. Amy Lowell, "Fool o' the Moon," *Atlantic Monthly* 136 (July 1925): 47, 49.

19. Amy Lowell to Ellery Sedgwick, 3 January 1918 and 8 February 1919, Ellery Sedgwick Papers, Carton 7, Massachusetts Historical Society, Boston.

20. For a history of Frost's relationship with Ezra Pound, see B. J. Sokol, "What Went Wrong between Robert Frost and Ezra Pound," *New England Quarterly* 49 (December 1976): 521–541.

21. Amy Lowell, review of *North of Boston, New Republic* 2 (20 February 1915): 81–82.

22. See Robert Frost to John Bartlett, in *Selected Letters of Robert Frost,* ed. Lawrance Thompson (New York: Holt, Rinehart and Winston, 1964), 98.

23. Ellery Sedgwick to Amy Lowell, 4 November 1912; quoted in Ellery Sedgwick III, "'Fireworks,'" 490.

24. *Poetry: A Magazine of Verse* 2 (May 1913): 72, and 5 (December 1914): 127–130. Also see Edward H. Cohen, "Robert Frost in England: An Unpublished Letter," *New England Quarterly* 43 (June 1970): 28.

25. Elizabeth Shipley Sergeant, *Robert Frost: The Trial by Existence* (New York: Holt, Rinehart, and Winston, 1960), 115.

26. Robert Frost to Sidney Cox, 22 March 1915, in Thompson, *Selected Letters of Robert Frost,* 162.

27. Peter Davison, "The First Three Poems and One That Got Away," *Atlantic Online,* February 1996; www.theatlantic.com/doc/199604u/frost-intro (accessed 31 March 2011).

28. Ellery Sedgwick to Edward Garnett, 26 May 1915, in Thompson, *Selected Letters of Robert Frost,* 176.

29. Robert Frost to Ellery Sedgwick, 15 September 1915, Ellery Sedgwick Papers, Carton 2, Massachusetts Historical Society, Boston.

30. See Edward Garnett to Ellery Sedgwick, 24 April 1915, in Thompson, *Selected Letters of Robert Frost,* 169–170.

31. Edward Garnett, "A New American Poet," *Atlantic Monthly* 116 (August 1915): 221.

32. Robert Frost to Edward Garnett, 12 June 1915, in Thompson, *Selected Letters of Robert Frost,* 178–179.

33. Robert Frost to Ellery Sedgwick, 20 September 1926, Ellery Sedgwick Papers, Carton 4, Massachusetts Historical Society, Boston.

34. Quoted in Thompson, *Selected Letters of Robert Frost,* xv.

35. Robert Frost to Louis Untemeyer, 9 September 1915; see William H. Pritchard, *Frost: A Literary Life Reconsidered* (New York: Oxford University Press, 1984), 128.

36. Robert Frost, "The Road Not Taken," *Atlantic Monthly* 116 (August 1915): 223.

37. Conrad Aiken, "Rupert Brooke," *Atlantic Monthly* 116 (July 1915): 98.

38. Elinor Frost to Ellery Sedgwick, 8 March [1935], Ellery Sedgwick Papers, Carton 4, Massachusetts Historical Society, Boston.

39. John Galsworthy, "Art and the War," *Atlantic Monthly* 116 (November 1915): 626.

26. A Window on the War

1. W. D. Howells, "Recollections of an *Atlantic* Editorship," *Atlantic Monthly* 100 (November 1907): 601–602.

2. Kiyoshi K. Kawakami, "Japan and the European War," *Atlantic Monthly* 114 (November 1914): 713.

3. John T. Morse Jr., "The Dreyfus and Zola Trials," *Atlantic Monthly* 81 (May 1898): 589.

4. Paul Hervieu, "Science and Conscience," in *The Book of the Homeless (Livre des Sans-Foyer)*, ed. Edith Wharton (New York: Charles Scriber's Sons, 1916), 107.

5. John Dewey, "On Understanding the Mind of Germany," *Atlantic Monthly* 117 (February 1916): 259.

6. John D. Rockefeller Jr., "Labor and Capital—Partners," *Atlantic Monthly* 117 (January 1916): 13.

7. Carleton H. Parker, "The I. W. W.," *Atlantic Monthly* 120 (November 1917): 651, 662.

8. Agnes Repplier, "Americanism," *Atlantic Monthly* 117 (March 1916): 297.

9. Kuno Francke, "The Kaiser and His People," *Atlantic Monthly* 114 (October 1914): 567, 570.

10. W. E. Burghardt Du Bois, "The African Roots of the War," *Atlantic Monthly* 115 (May 1915): 707, 708.

11. L. P. Jacks, "The Changing Mind of a Nation at War," *Atlantic Monthly* 115 (April 1915): 535.

12. W. E. Burghardt Du Bois, "The African Roots of the War," *Atlantic Monthly* 115 (May 1915): 714.

13. W. E. B. Du Bois, "Criteria of Negro Art," *Crisis* 32 (October 1926): 292–293.

14. Quoted in Terry Teachout, *The Skeptic: The Life of H. L. Mencken* (New York: HarperCollins, 2002), 17.

15. H. L. Mencken, "Addendum on Aims," in *Letters of H. L. Mencken*, ed. Guy Forgue (New York: Knopf, 1961), 189; and H. L. Mencken, "What I Believe," *Forum* 84 (September 1930): 139.

16. H. L. Mencken, "Newspaper Morals," *Atlantic Monthly* 113 (March 1914): 296, 297.

17. Ralph Pulitzer, "Newspaper Morals: A Reply," 113 (June 1914): 774–775.

18. H. L. Mencken, "The Mailed Fist and Its Prophet," *Atlantic Monthly* 114 (November 1914): 606, 607.

19. See www.theatlantic.com/unbound/flashbks/mencken.htm (accessed 31 March 2011). Sedgwick may be referring to Mencken's missing article.

20. H. L. Mencken, *The American Language* (New York: Cosimo, 2009), 361.

21. William Dean Howells to Aurelia H. Howells, 23 May 1915, in *Selected Letters of William Dean Howells*, ed. George Arms (Boston: Twayne, 1979–1983), 6:77.

22. Frank Perry Olds, "The Disloyalty of the German-American Press," *Atlantic Monthly* 120 (July 1917): 140.

23. Frederick Lewis Allen, "Sedgwick and the *Atlantic*," *Outlook and Independent* 150 (26 December 1928): 1408; and Bertrand Russell, "War as an Institution," *Atlantic Monthly* 117 (May 1916): 603.

24. Léon Mirman, "Bitter Experience of Lorraine," *Atlantic Monthly* 116 (November 1915): 711.

25. Rebecca West, "Women of England," *Atlantic Monthly* 117 (January 1916): 3, 4.

26. Ellery Sedgwick, *The Happy Profession* (Boston: Little, Brown, 1948), 181.

27. Ibid., 185–186.

28. Margaret Prescott Montague, "Good Friday, 1917," *Atlantic Monthly* 119 (June 1917): 749.

27. America's War

1. See Ellery Sedgwick III, "World War I as Failed Apocalypse: A View from the *Atlantic Monthly*," *Markham Review* 9 (Winter 1980): 21.

2. Wilson Follett, "The War as Critic," *Atlantic Monthly* 119 (May 1917): 661.

3. Henry Dwight Sedgwick, "Literature and Cosmopolitanism," *Atlantic Monthly* 115 (February 1915): 271, 220.

4. "Trench-Raiders," *Atlantic Monthly* 118 (December 1916): 827.

5. Briggs Adams, "The American Spirit," *Atlantic Monthly* 122 (October 1918): 438, 436.

6. Ibid., 434.

7. Ibid., 436.

8. Ibid., 445.

9. Briggs Adams to his mother, Grace Wilson Adams, 14 December 1917, in *The American Spirit, the Letters of Briggs Kilburn Adams* (Boston: Atlantic Monthly Press, 1917), 53.

10. Adams, "The American Spirit," *Atlantic Monthly* 122 (October 1918): 436–437.

11. Caroline Ticknor, *New England Aviators, 1914–1918: Their Portraits and Their Records* (Boston: Houghton Mifflin, 1919), 254–256.

12. Randolph S. Bourne, "Trans-National America," *Atlantic Monthly* 118 (July 1916): 91.

13. *Atlantic Monthly Almanac*, 1918, back cover.

14. Vernon Kellogg, "Herbert Hoover as Individual and Type," *Atlantic Monthly* 121 (March 1918): 385.

15. Henry Seidel Canby, "The Irish Mind," *Atlantic Monthly* 123 (January 1919): 41–42.

16. H. Sacher, "A Jewish Palestine," *Atlantic Monthly* 124 (July 1919): 116, 125. Rabbi Milton Steinberg would continue the argument for a Jewish state in "The Creed of an American Zionist" (February 1945).

17. President Woodrow Wilson: Address to the Senate on the 19th Amendment, 30 September 1918, www.public.iastate.edu/~aslagell/SpCm416/Woodrow_Wilson_suff.html (accessed 31 March 2011).

18. Thomas E. Tallmadge, "The Contributors' Column," *Atlantic Monthly* 136 (August 1925): 287.

19. "Good-Bye, Dear Mr. Grundy by a Last Year's Debutante," *Atlantic Monthly* 126 (November 1920): 643–644, 646.

20. [John F. Carter Jr.], "'These Wild Young People,'" *Atlantic Monthly* 126 (September 1920): 304.

28. The Turbulent Twenties, I

1. For facts about this decade, see kclibrary.lonestar.edu/decade20.html (accessed 31 March 2011).

2. Marguerite Knoff Perryam, "The Contributors' Column," *Atlantic Monthly* 129 (April 1922): 576.

3. Roy Elbert Hiebert and Sheila Jean Gibbons, *Exploring Mass Media for a Changing World* (Mahwah, NJ: Lawrence Erlbaum, 2000), 175. For circulation numbers of the *Saturday Evening Post*, see Jan Cohn, *Creating America: George Lorimer and the Saturday Evening Post* (Pittsburgh: Pittsburgh University Press, 1989), 20–24, 25, 44, 60–61, 63–66, 161, 165–166, 191, 307n18. Also see Ellery Sedgwick, *The Happy Profession* (Boston: Little, Brown, 1948), 296.

4. Circulation figures vary. In January 1922, the *Atlantic* announced that its circulation had reached 143,000.

5. G. Stanley Hall, "Flapper Americana Novissima," *Atlantic Monthly* 129 (June 1922): 773.

6. "The Contributors' Column," *Atlantic Monthly* 130 (July 1922): 286.

7. Roe L. Henrick, "The Contributors' Column," *Atlantic Monthly* 134 (September 1924): 576.

8. *Atlantic Monthly* 133 (January 1924): 141.

9. Stuart P. Sherman, "A Conversation with Cornelia," *Atlantic Monthly* 133 (January 1924): 19.

10. Leroy Percy, "The Modern Ku Klux Klan," *Atlantic Monthly* 130 (July 1922): 122–128, esp. 128.

11. Hiram W. Evans, "The Klan's Fight for Americanism," *North American Review* 223 (March 1926): 38–39.

12. Waddill Catchings, "Our Common Enterprise," *Atlantic Monthly* 129 (February 1922): 229.

13. Sedgwick, *The Happy Profession*, 296–297.

14. Ibid., 186.

15. Alfred E. Smith, "Catholic and Patriot: Governor Smith Replies," *Atlantic Monthly* 139 (May 1927): 721, 728.

16. Charles Marshall to Ellery Sedgwick, 3 May 1927, Ellery Sedgwick Papers, Carton 14, Massachusetts Historical Society, Boston.

17. L. P. Jacks, "The Contributors' Column," *Atlantic Monthly* 131 (February 1923): 285.

18. James D. Phelan, "The False Pride of the Japanese," *Atlantic Monthly* 127 (March 1921): 402–403.

19. Payson J. Treat, "California and the Japanese," *Atlantic Monthly* 127 (April 1921): 546.

20. Sedgwick, *The Happy Profession*, 243.

21. Edward W. Bok, "The Day of the Advertisement," *Atlantic Monthly* 132 (October 1923): 533–534.

22. Ezra Pound, "Small Magazines," *English Journal* 19 (November 1930): 690.

23. Sedgwick, *The Happy Profession*, 296.

24. Edward W. Bok, "The Day of the Advertisement," *Atlantic Monthly* 132 (October 1923): 535.

25. "A Woman's Memoirs at Eighty-One: Their Lessons in Patience, Service, and Hope," *Atlantic Monthly* 134 (December 1924): 801–803.

29. The Turbulent Twenties, II

1. Helen McFee, "The Literature of Disillusion," *Atlantic Monthly* 132 (August 1923): 234.

2. Carl Sandburg, "Poetry Reconsidered," *Atlantic Monthly* 131 (March 1923): 342–343.

3. [George Edward Woodberry], "Book Reviews: Jane's The Artist's Year," *Atlantic Monthly* 50 (December 1882): 849.

4. Samuel McChord Crothers, "Keeping Up with the Smart Set in Literature," *Atlantic Monthly* 134 (August 1924): 146, 148, 149, 153.

5. Ezra Pound, "Small Magazines," *English Journal* 19 (November 1930): 689. For an informed study of little magazines, see Mark S. Morrison, *The Public Face of Modernism: Little Magazines, Audiences, and Reception, 1905–1920* (Madison: University of Wisconsin Press, 2000).

6. "Fame Contests," *New York Times*, 24 February 1924, E6.

7. Ellery Sedgwick, Introduction to *The Story of Opal: The Journal of an Understanding Heart* (Boston: Atlantic Monthly Press, 1920), xv.

8. Ellery Sedgwick to Elbert Bede, 16 March 1935, Ellery Sedgwick Papers, Carton 16, Massachusetts Historical Society, Boston.

9. Theodore Peterson, *Magazines in the Twentieth Century* (Urbana: University of Illinois Press, 1956), 275.

10. Carl Engel, "Jazz: A Musical Discussion," *Atlantic Monthly* 130 (August 1922): 182, 186, 187.

11. James M. Cain, "The Battle Ground for Coal," *Atlantic Monthly* 130 (October 1922): 433–434.

12. See http://www.filmsite.org/20sintro.html.

13. Katherine Gerould, "The Movies," *Atlantic Monthly* 128 (July 1921): 22–30.

14. Mark Seybolt, "Play-Writing," *Crisis* 29 (February 1925): 165.

15. Sherwood Anderson to Jesse Fauset, 17 November 1925, in *The Correspondence of W. E. B. Du Bois*, ed. Herbert Aptheker (Amherst: University of Massachusetts Press, 1973), 1:329–330.

16. James Thurber, *The Years with Ross* (Boston: Little, Brown, 1959), 18–19. See George H. Douglas, *The Smart Magazines: 50 Years of Literary Revelry and High Jinks at Vanity Fair, the New Yorker, Life, Esquire, and Smart Set* (Hamden, CT: Archon Books, 1991), 129. According to Douglas, Ross printed 30,000 copies of the first issue, and claimed that 18,000 sold in New York within thirty-six hours. The third issue sold 12,000 copies and the fourth 10,500.

17. *New Yorker* 1 (February 1925): 2. Also see Douglas, *The Smart Magazines*, 130.

18. *New Yorker* 1 (28 February 1925): 31.

19. Ibid., 27.

20. Douglas, *The Smart Magazines*, 143.

21. Quoted in Ben Yogoda, *About Town: The New Yorker and the World It Made* (New York: Scribner, 2000), 65.

22. Memo to Raoul Fleischmann, Lloyd Paul Stryker, and Hawley Truax, 23 August 1943, in *Letters from the Editor: The New Yorker's Harold Ross*, ed. Thomas Kunkel (New York: Modern Library, 2000), 219.

23. *New Yorker* 1 (February 1925): 2.

24. Douglas, *The Smart Magazines*, 143. Also see Thomas Kunkel, *Genius in Disguise: Harold Ross of the New Yorker* (New York: Random House, 1995), 94.

25. Frederick Lewis Allen, "Sedgwick and the *Atlantic*," *Outlook and Independent* 150 (26 December 1928): 1407.

26. Ibid.

27. A. R. Orage, "New Standards in Art and Literature," *Atlantic Monthly* 135 (February 1925): 206.

28. Thomas Wentworth Higginson, *Short Studies of American Authors* (Boston: Lee and Shepard; New York: Charles T. Dillingham, 1888), 36–37.

30. Across the Decades

1. E. M. Forster, "Anonymity: An Inquiry," *Atlantic Monthly* 136 (November 1925): 591.

2. Martin Luther King Jr., "The Negro Is Your Brother," *Atlantic Monthly* 212 (August 1963): 78–81, 86–88.

3. Transcript, Mike Wallace interview of Edward Weeks, 24 August 1958, Harry Ransom Center, University of Texas, Austin; solstice.ischool.utexas.edu/tmwi/index.php/The_Mike_Wallace_Interview. Weeks quotes from José Ortega y Gasset's *The Revolt of the Masses* (1930).

4. Eric Alterman, "Navigating '*The Atlantic*,'" *Nation*, 25 October 1999; www.thenation.com/doc/19991025/alterman.

5. From a presentation given in 1994 by Cullen Murphy; www.theatlantic.com/about/atlhistf.htm (accessed 31 March 2011).

6. Jack Shafer, "The New Atlantic Monthly: Unsolicited Advice for James Bennet, the Magazine's Incoming Editor"; www.slate.com/id/2137687/.

7. Jeremy W. Peters, "Web Focus Helps Revitalize *The Atlantic*," *New York Times*, 13 December 2010, 1, 4.

8. Cullen Murphy; www.theatlantic.com/about/atlhistf.htm (accessed 31 March 2011).

INDEX